THIS IS THE LAST PAGE.

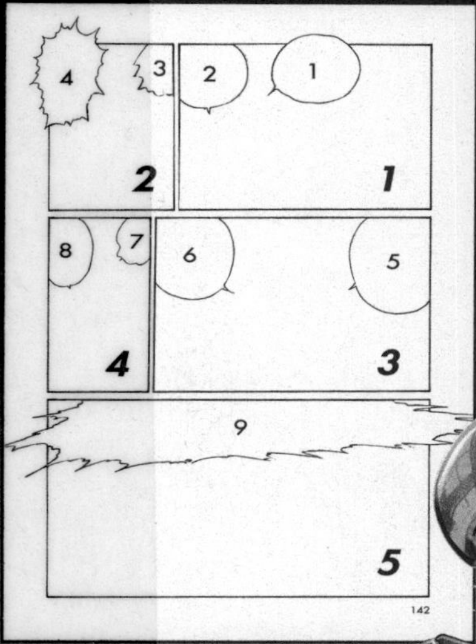
1
1
2
2
3
4
3
5
6
4
7
8
5
9
142
←Follow the action this way.

GOLDEN KAMUY has been printed in the original Japanese format in order to preserve the orientation of the original artwork.

Please turn it around and begin reading from right to left. Unlike English, Japanese is read right to left, so Japanese comics are read in reverse order from the way English comics are typically read. Have fun with it!

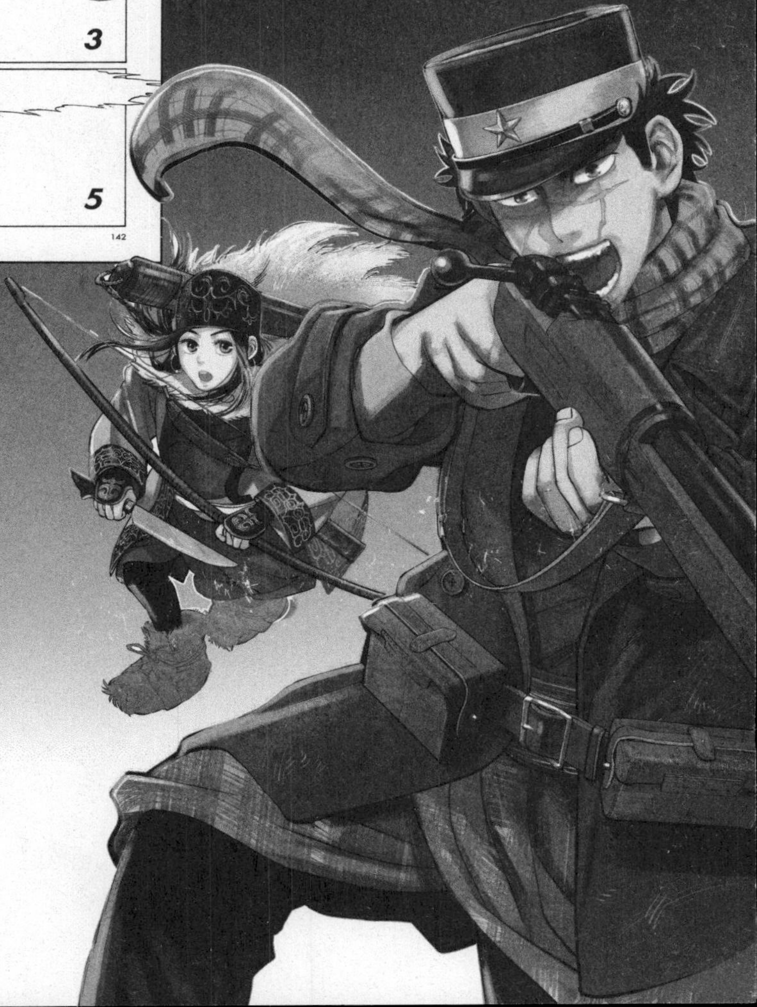

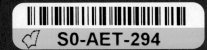

The Groups Battling Over the Hidden Gold

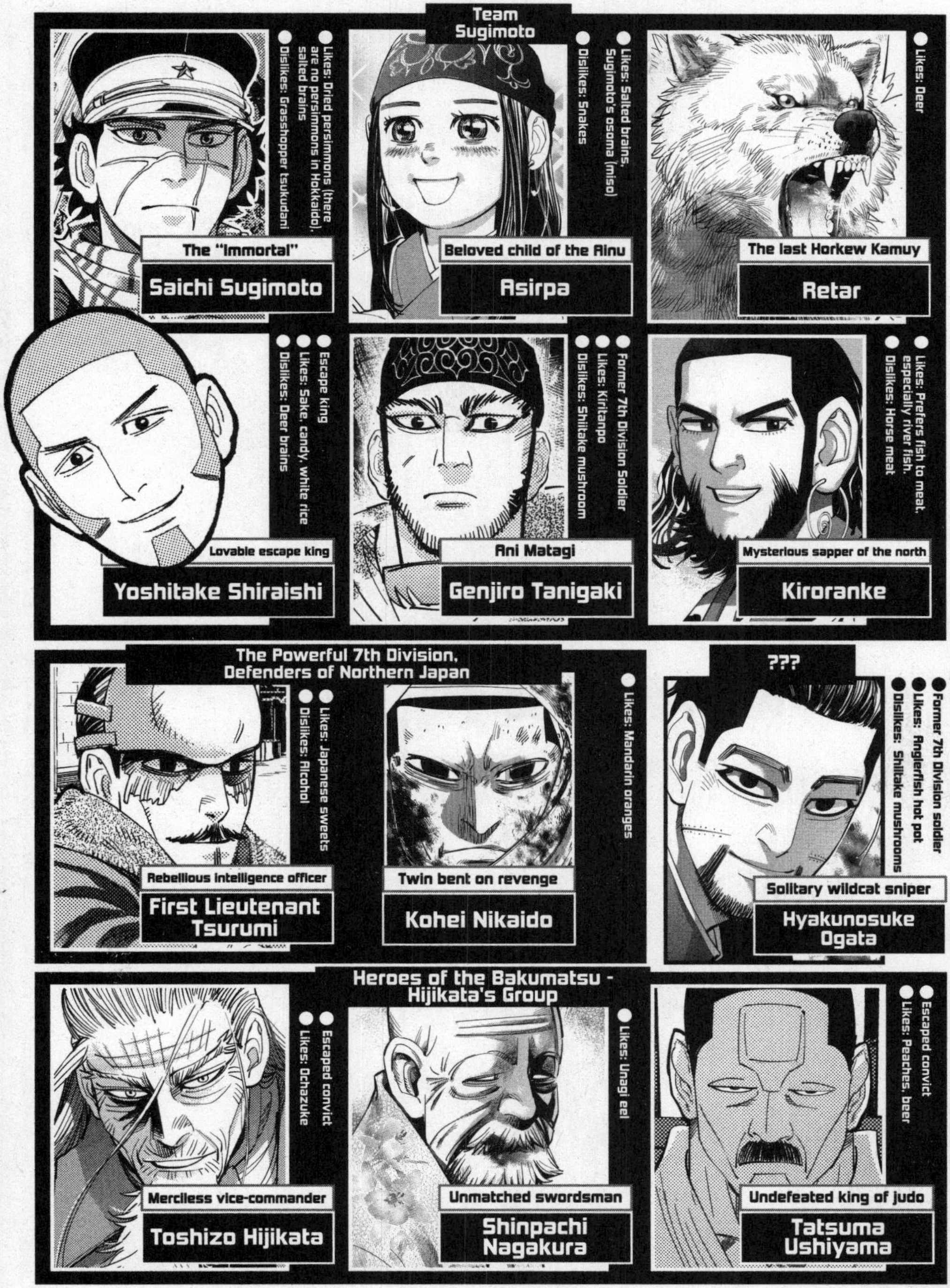
Team Sugimoto
The "Immortal"
Saichi Sugimoto
● Likes: Dried persimmons (there are no persimmons in Hokkaido), salted brains
● Dislikes: Grasshopper tsukudani
Beloved child of the Ainu
Asirpa
● Likes: Salted brains, Sugimoto's osoma (miso)
● Dislikes: Snakes
The last Horkew Kamuy
Retar
● Likes: Deer
Lovable escape king
Yoshitake Shiraishi
● Escape king
● Likes: Sake, candy, white rice
● Dislikes: Deer brains
Ani Matagi
Genjiro Tanigaki
● Former 7th Division Soldier
● Likes: Kiritanpo
● Dislikes: Shiitake mushroom
Mysterious sapper of the north
Kiroranke
● Likes: Prefers fish to meat, especially river fish.
● Dislikes: Horse meat
The Powerful 7th Division, Defenders of Northern Japan
Rebellious intelligence officer
First Lieutenant Tsurumi
● Likes: Japanese sweets
● Dislikes: Alcohol
Twin bent on revenge
Kohei Nikaido
● Likes: Mandarin oranges
???
Solitary wildcat sniper
Hyakunosuke Ogata
● Former 7th Division soldier
● Likes: Anglerfish hot pot
● Dislikes: Shiitake mushrooms
Heroes of the Bakumatsu - Hijikata's Group
Merciless vice-commander
Toshizo Hijikata
● Escaped convict
● Likes: Ochazuke
Unmatched swordsman
Shinpachi Nagakura
● Likes: Unagi eel
Undefeated king of judo
Tatsuma Ushiyama
● Escaped convict
● Likes: Peaches, beer

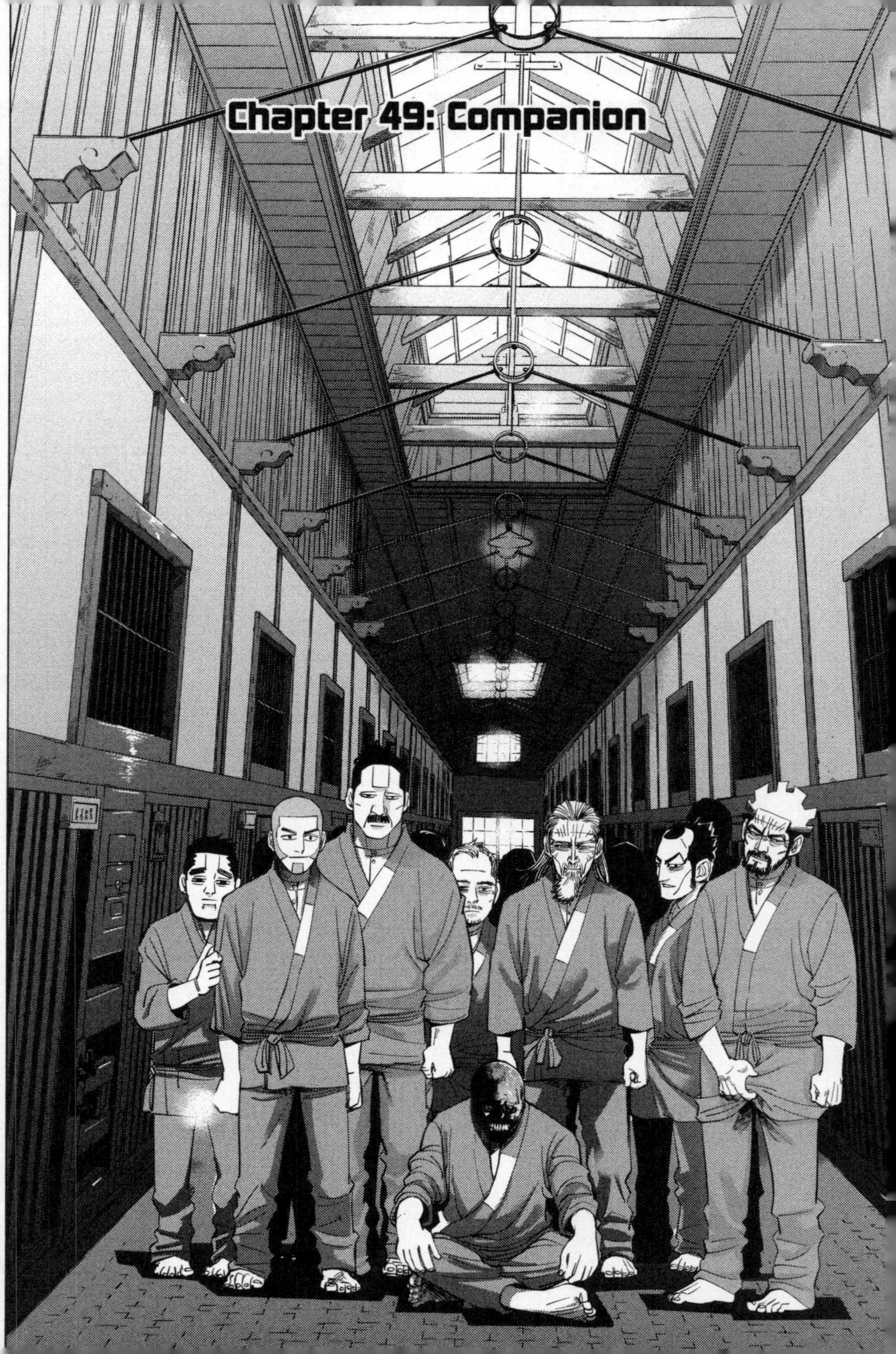
Chapter 49: Companion

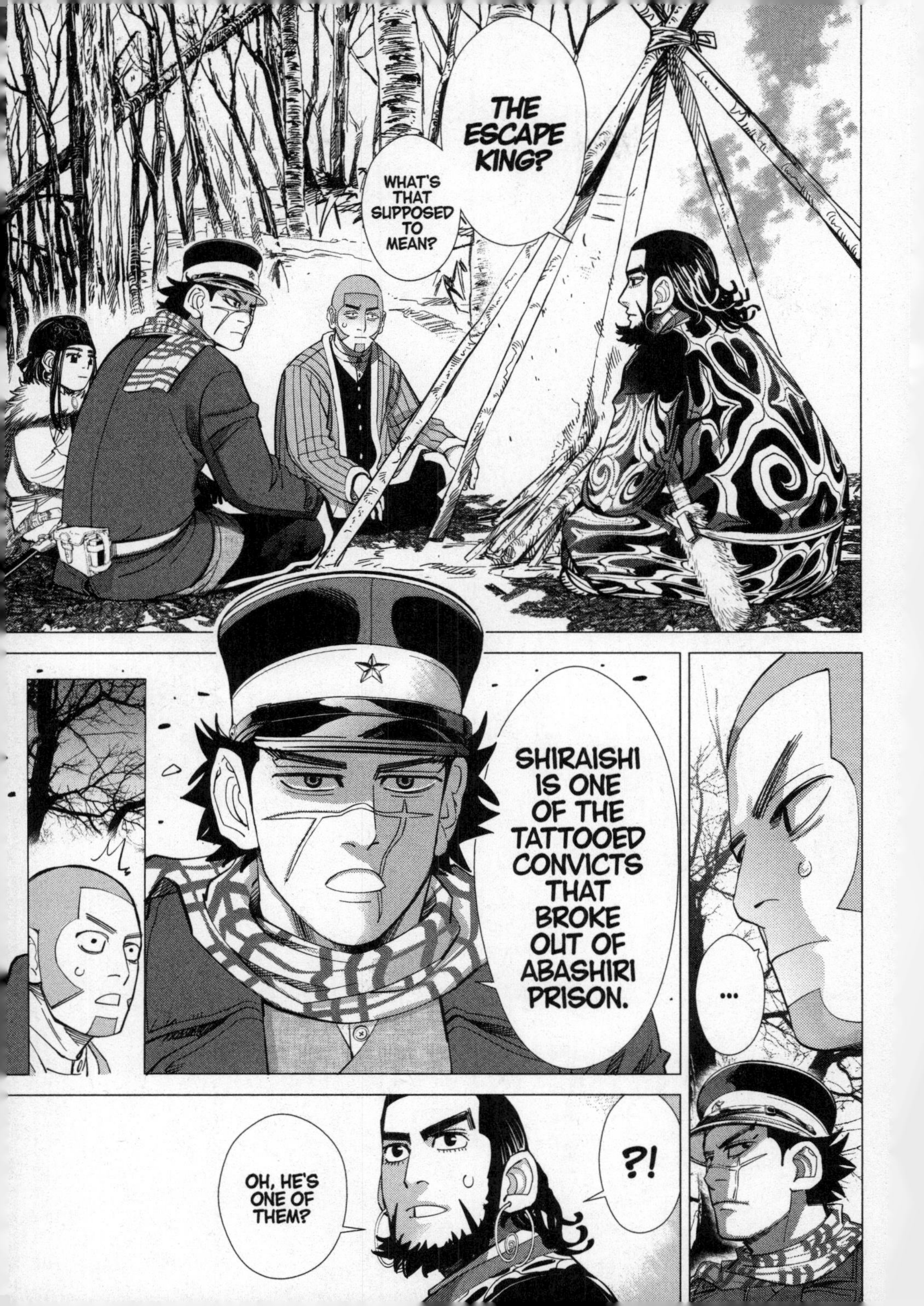
THE ESCAPE KING?
WHAT'S THAT SUPPOSED TO MEAN?
...
SHIRAISHI IS ONE OF THE TATTOOED CONVICTS THAT BROKE OUT OF ABASHIRI PRISON.
?!
OH, HE'S ONE OF THEM?

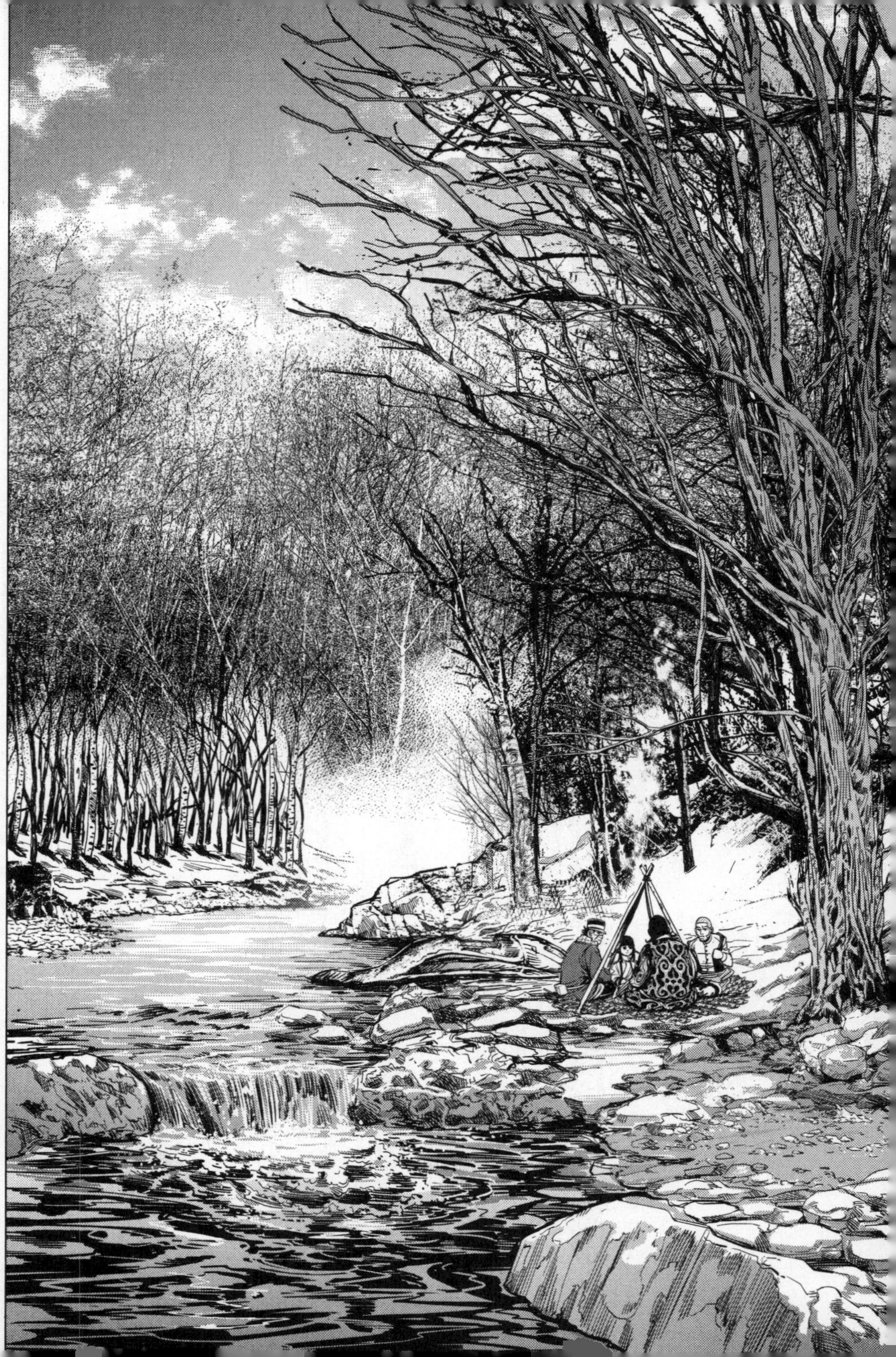

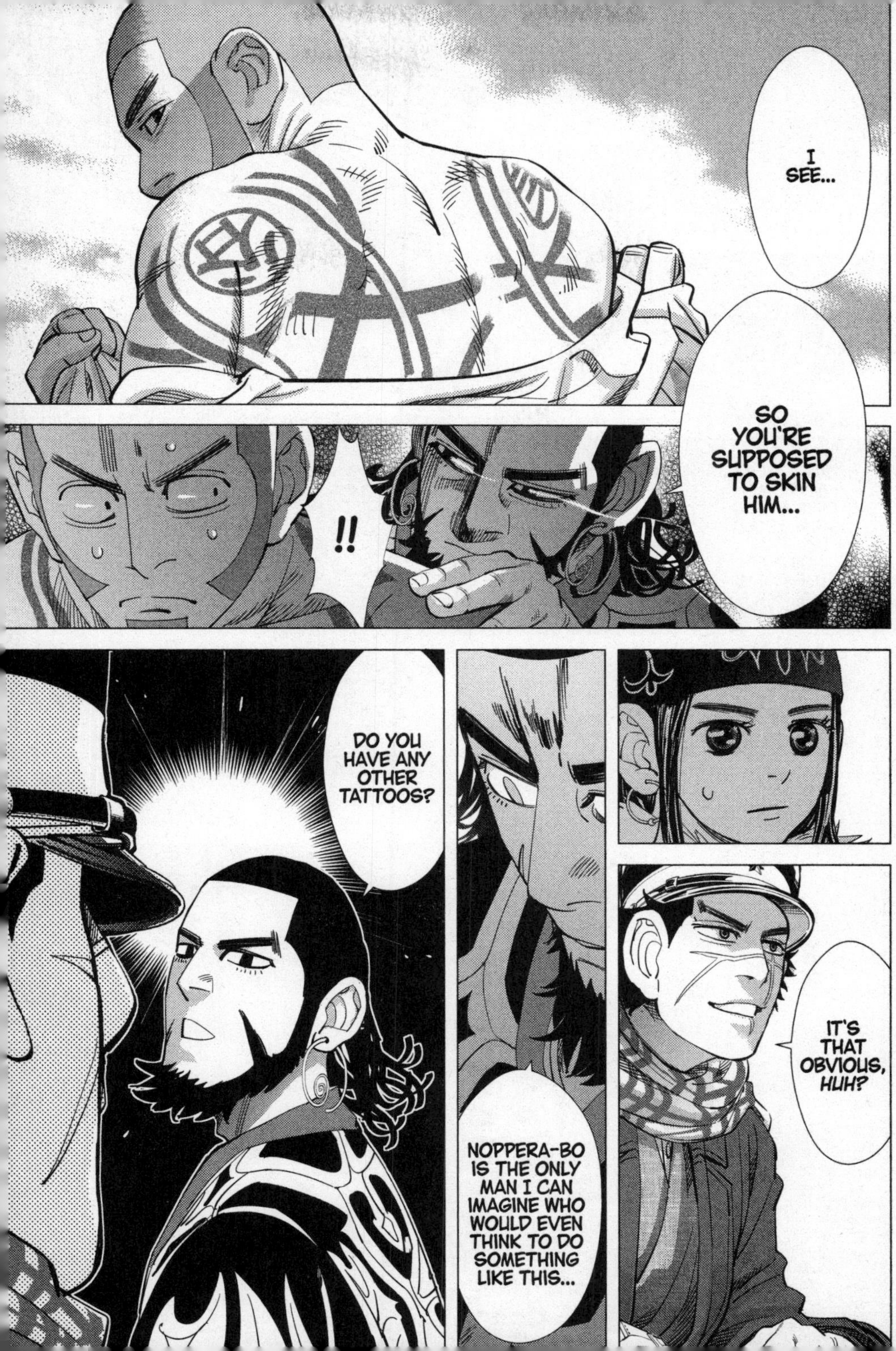
I SEE...
SO YOU'RE SUPPOSED TO SKIN HIM...
!!
DO YOU HAVE ANY OTHER TATTOOS?
IT'S THAT OBVIOUS, HUH?
NOPPERA-BO IS THE ONLY MAN I CAN IMAGINE WHO WOULD EVEN THINK TO DO SOMETHING LIKE THIS...

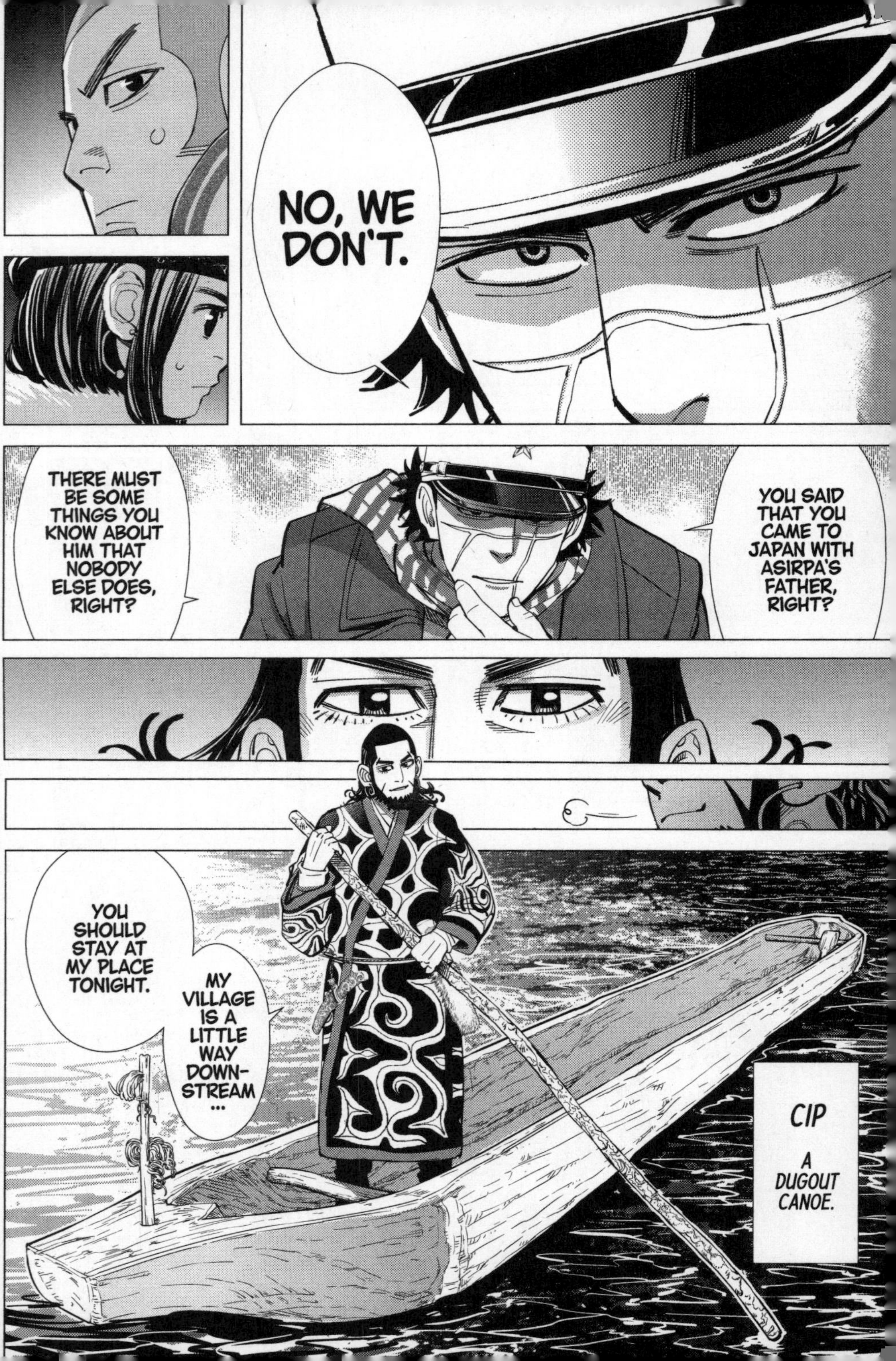
NO, WE DON'T.
YOU SAID THAT YOU CAME TO JAPAN WITH ASIRPA'S FATHER, RIGHT?
THERE MUST BE SOME THINGS YOU KNOW ABOUT HIM THAT NOBODY ELSE DOES, RIGHT?
CIP
A DUGOUT CANOE.
MY VILLAGE IS A LITTLE WAY DOWN-STREAM...
YOU SHOULD STAY AT MY PLACE TONIGHT.

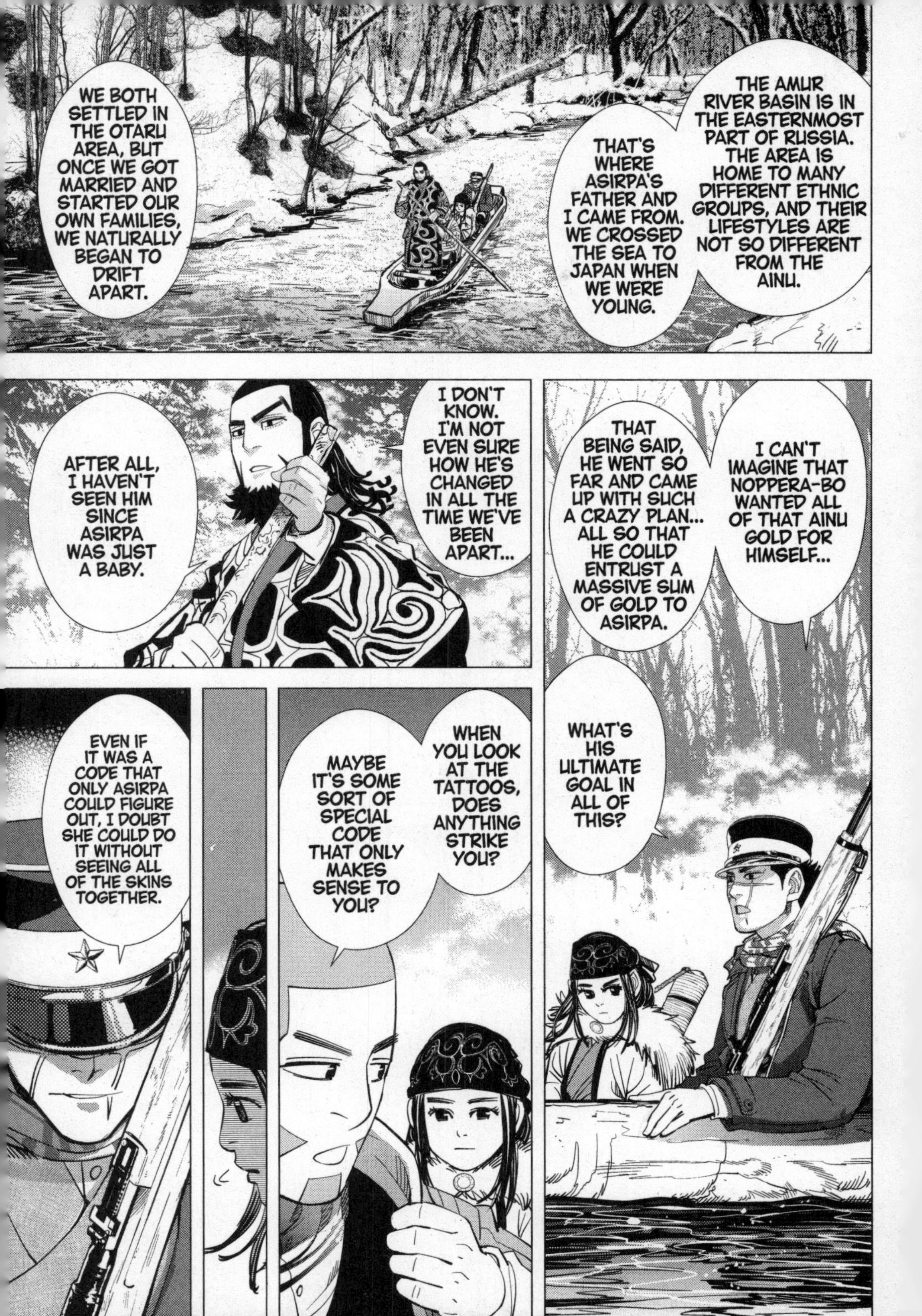
THE AMUR RIVER BASIN IS IN THE EASTERNMOST PART OF RUSSIA. THE AREA IS HOME TO MANY DIFFERENT ETHNIC GROUPS, AND THEIR LIFESTYLES ARE NOT SO DIFFERENT FROM THE AINU.
THAT'S WHERE ASIRPA'S FATHER AND I CAME FROM. WE CROSSED THE SEA TO JAPAN WHEN WE WERE YOUNG.
WE BOTH SETTLED IN THE OTARU AREA, BUT ONCE WE GOT MARRIED AND STARTED OUR OWN FAMILIES, WE NATURALLY BEGAN TO DRIFT APART.
I CAN'T IMAGINE THAT NOPPERA-BO WANTED ALL OF THAT AINU GOLD FOR HIMSELF...
THAT BEING SAID, HE WENT SO FAR AND CAME UP WITH SUCH A CRAZY PLAN... ALL SO THAT HE COULD ENTRUST A MASSIVE SUM OF GOLD TO ASIRPA.
WHAT'S HIS ULTIMATE GOAL IN ALL OF THIS?
I DON'T KNOW. I'M NOT EVEN SURE HOW HE'S CHANGED IN ALL THE TIME WE'VE BEEN APART...
AFTER ALL, I HAVEN'T SEEN HIM SINCE ASIRPA WAS JUST A BABY.
WHEN YOU LOOK AT THE TATTOOS, DOES ANYTHING STRIKE YOU?
MAYBE IT'S SOME SORT OF SPECIAL CODE THAT ONLY MAKES SENSE TO YOU?
EVEN IF IT WAS A CODE THAT ONLY ASIRPA COULD FIGURE OUT, I DOUBT SHE COULD DO IT WITHOUT SEEING ALL OF THE SKINS TOGETHER.

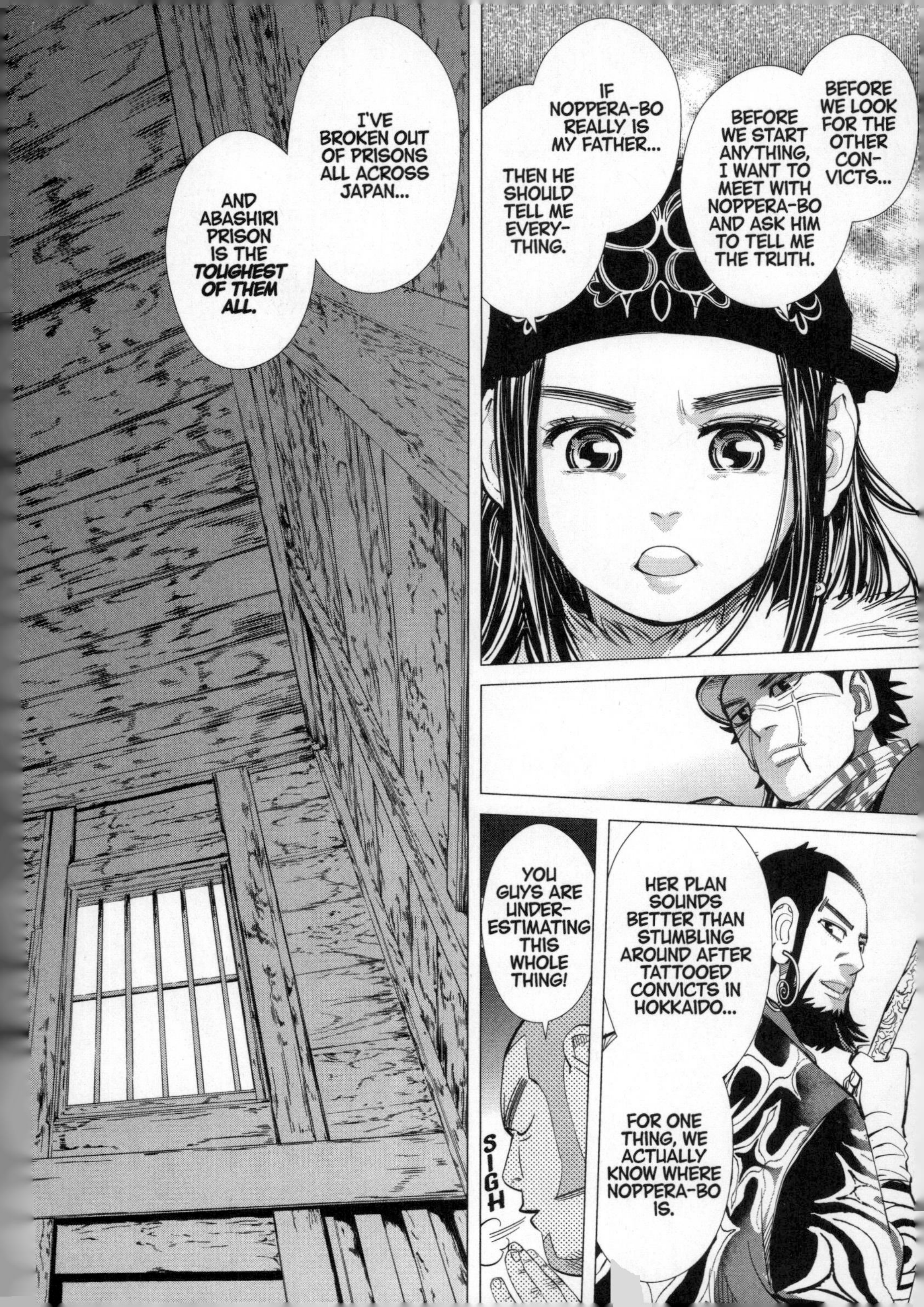
BEFORE WE LOOK FOR THE OTHER CONVICTS...
BEFORE WE START ANYTHING, I WANT TO MEET WITH NOPPERA-BO AND ASK HIM TO TELL ME THE TRUTH.
IF NOPPERA-BO REALLY IS MY FATHER...
THEN HE SHOULD TELL ME EVERYTHING.
HER PLAN SOUNDS BETTER THAN STUMBLING AROUND AFTER TATTOOED CONVICTS IN HOKKAIDO...
FOR ONE THING, WE ACTUALLY KNOW WHERE NOPPERA-BO IS.
YOU GUYS ARE UNDERESTIMATING THIS WHOLE THING!
SIGH
I'VE BROKEN OUT OF PRISONS ALL ACROSS JAPAN...
AND ABASHIRI PRISON IS THE *TOUGHEST* OF THEM ALL.

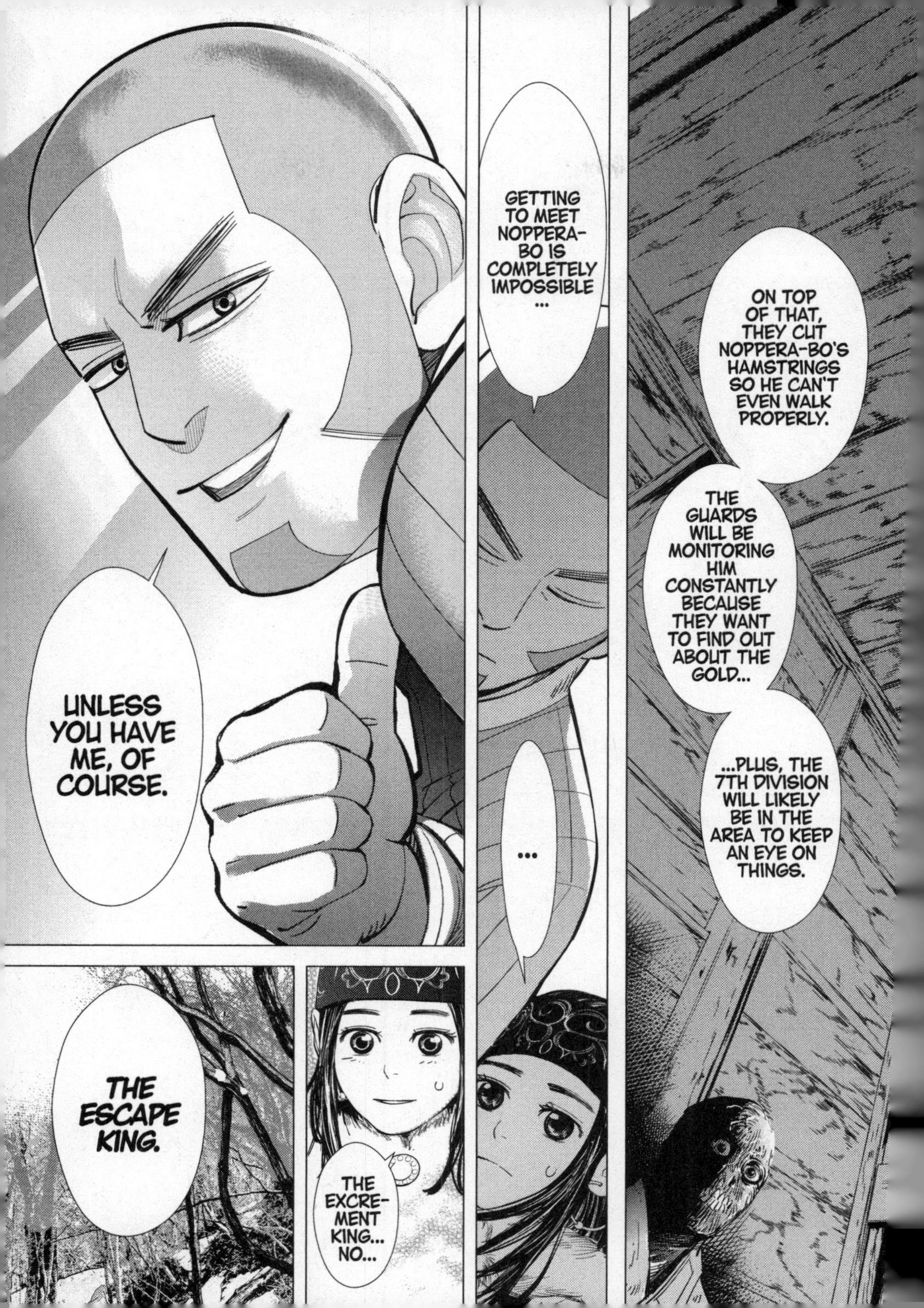
ON TOP OF THAT, THEY CUT NOPPERA-BO'S HAMSTRINGS SO HE CAN'T EVEN WALK PROPERLY.
THE GUARDS WILL BE MONITORING HIM CONSTANTLY BECAUSE THEY WANT TO FIND OUT ABOUT THE GOLD...
...PLUS, THE 7TH DIVISION WILL LIKELY BE IN THE AREA TO KEEP AN EYE ON THINGS.
GETTING TO MEET NOPPERA-BO IS COMPLETELY IMPOSSIBLE ...
...
UNLESS YOU HAVE ME, OF COURSE.
THE EXCREMENT KING... NO...
THE ESCAPE KING.

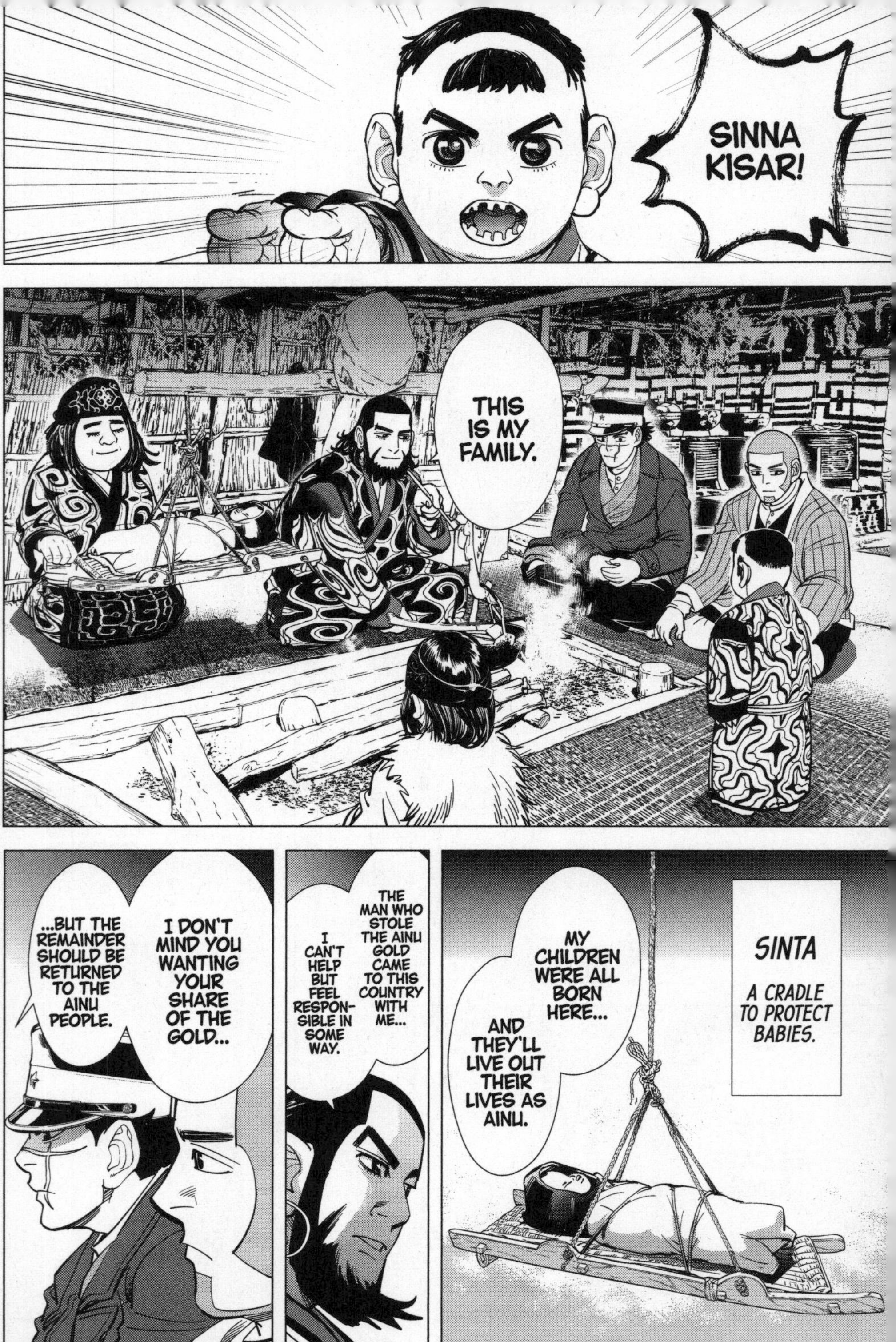
SINNA KISAR!
THIS IS MY FAMILY.
SINTA
A CRADLE TO PROTECT BABIES.
MY CHILDREN WERE ALL BORN HERE...
AND THEY'LL LIVE OUT THEIR LIVES AS AINU.
THE MAN WHO STOLE THE AINU GOLD CAME TO THIS COUNTRY WITH ME...
I CAN'T HELP BUT FEEL RESPONSIBLE IN SOME WAY.
I DON'T MIND YOU WANTING YOUR SHARE OF THE GOLD...
...BUT THE REMAINDER SHOULD BE RETURNED TO THE AINU PEOPLE.

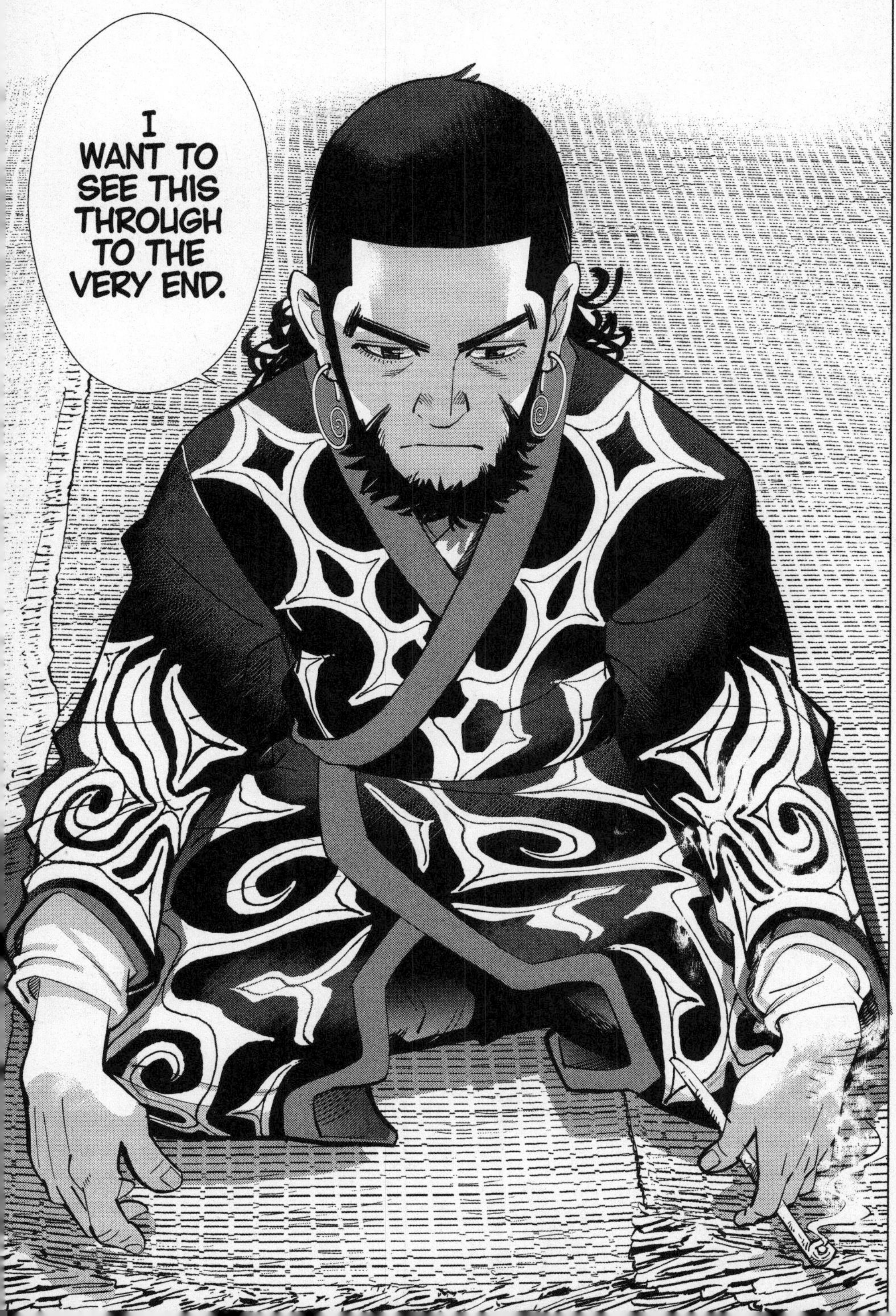
I WANT TO SEE THIS THROUGH TO THE VERY END.

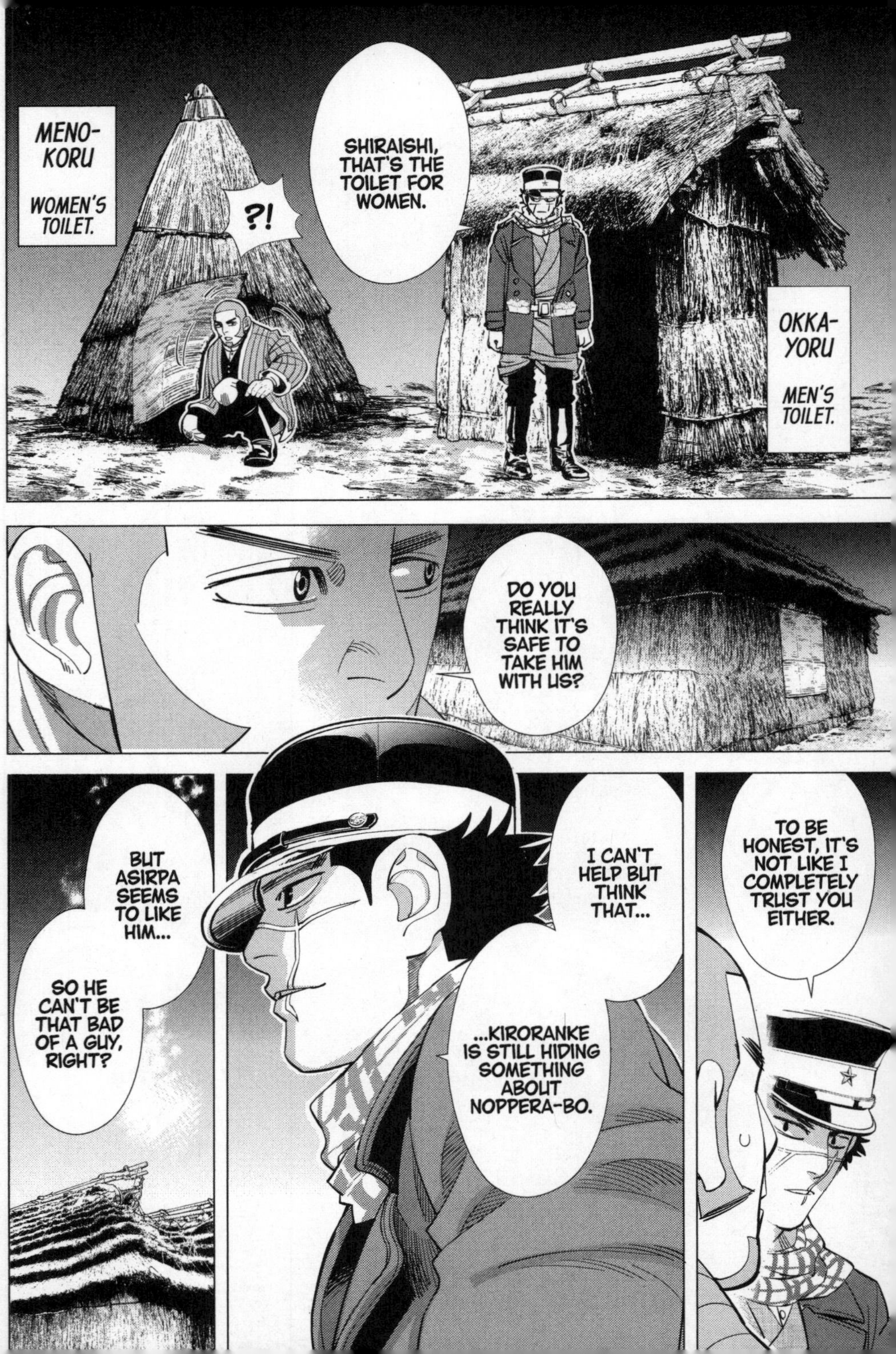
OKKA-YORU
MEN'S TOILET.
SHIRAISHI, THAT'S THE TOILET FOR WOMEN.
?!
MENO-KORU
WOMEN'S TOILET.
DO YOU REALLY THINK IT'S SAFE TO TAKE HIM WITH US?
TO BE HONEST, IT'S NOT LIKE I COMPLETELY TRUST YOU EITHER.
I CAN'T HELP BUT THINK THAT...
...KIRORANKE IS STILL HIDING SOMETHING ABOUT NOPPERA-BO.
BUT ASIRPA SEEMS TO LIKE HIM...
SO HE CAN'T BE THAT BAD OF A GUY, RIGHT?

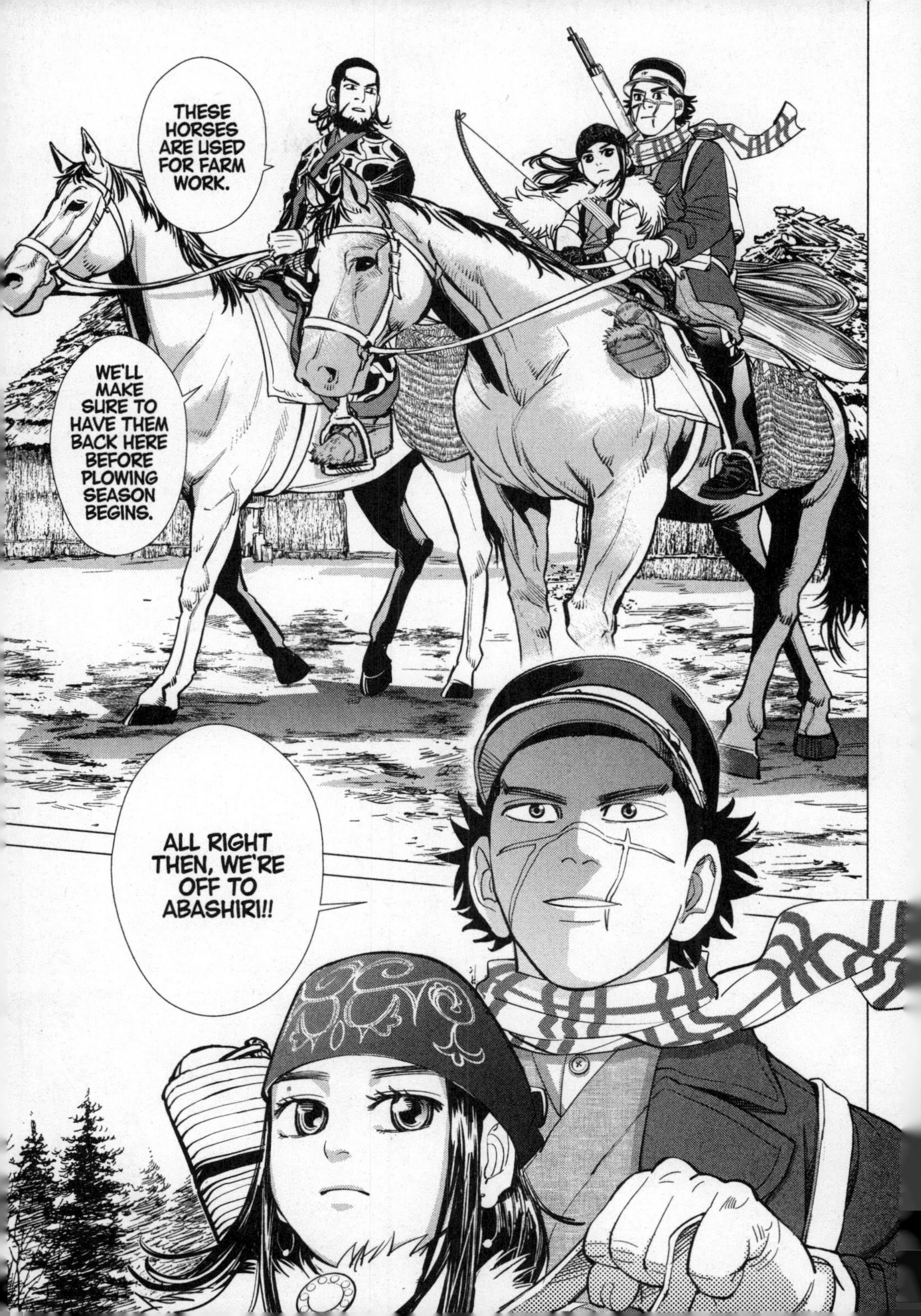
THESE HORSES ARE USED FOR FARM WORK.
WE'LL MAKE SURE TO HAVE THEM BACK HERE BEFORE PLOWING SEASON BEGINS.
ALL RIGHT THEN, WE'RE OFF TO ABASHIRI!!

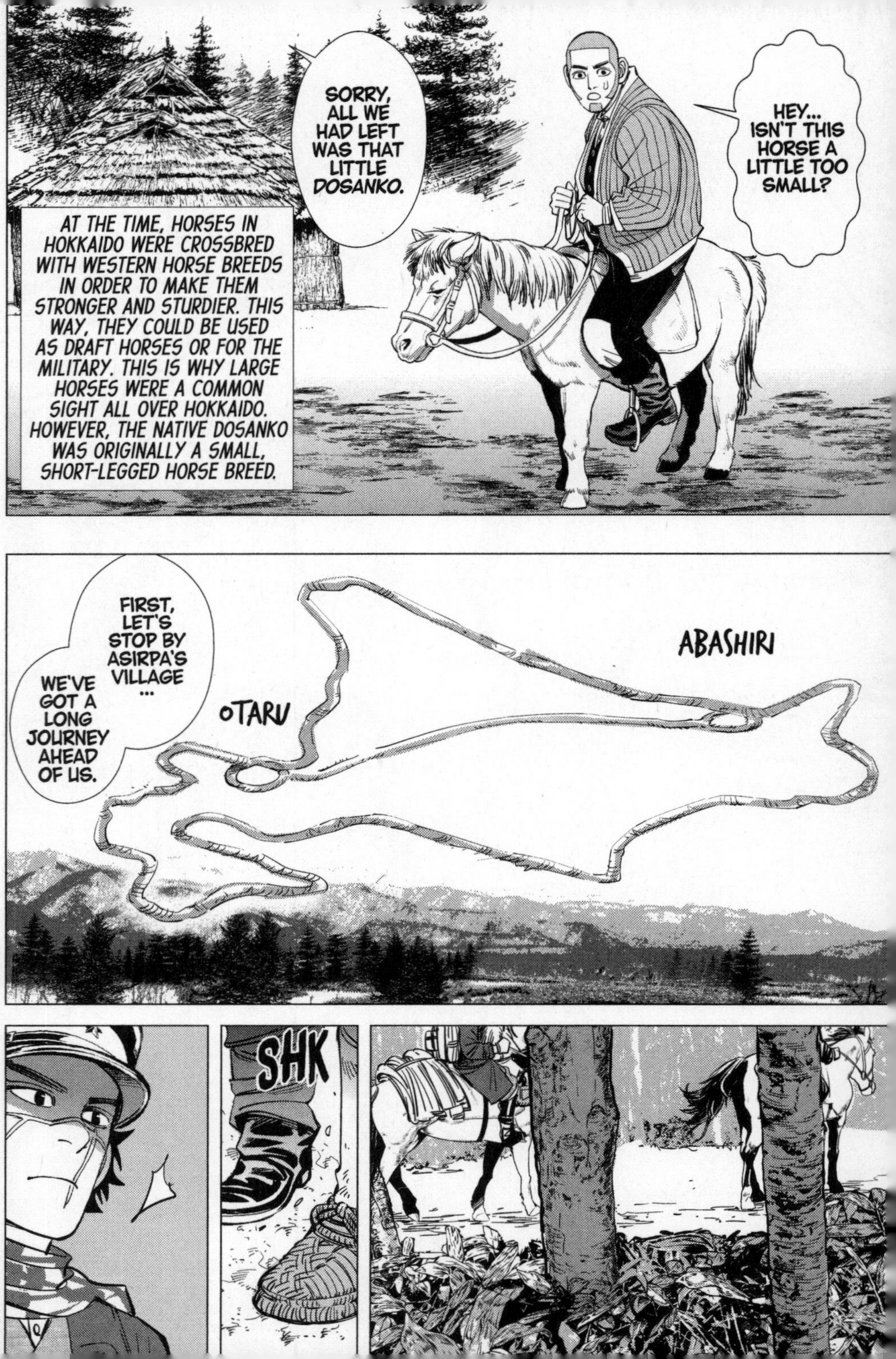
HEY... ISN'T THIS HORSE A LITTLE TOO SMALL?
SORRY, ALL WE HAD LEFT WAS THAT LITTLE DOSANKO.
AT THE TIME, HORSES IN HOKKAIDO WERE CROSSBRED WITH WESTERN HORSE BREEDS IN ORDER TO MAKE THEM STRONGER AND STURDIER. THIS WAY, THEY COULD BE USED AS DRAFT HORSES OR FOR THE MILITARY. THIS IS WHY LARGE HORSES WERE A COMMON SIGHT ALL OVER HOKKAIDO. HOWEVER, THE NATIVE DOSANKO WAS ORIGINALLY A SMALL, SHORT-LEGGED HORSE BREED.
ABASHIRI
OTARU
FIRST, LET'S STOP BY ASIRPA'S VILLAGE ...
WE'VE GOT A LONG JOURNEY AHEAD OF US.
SHK

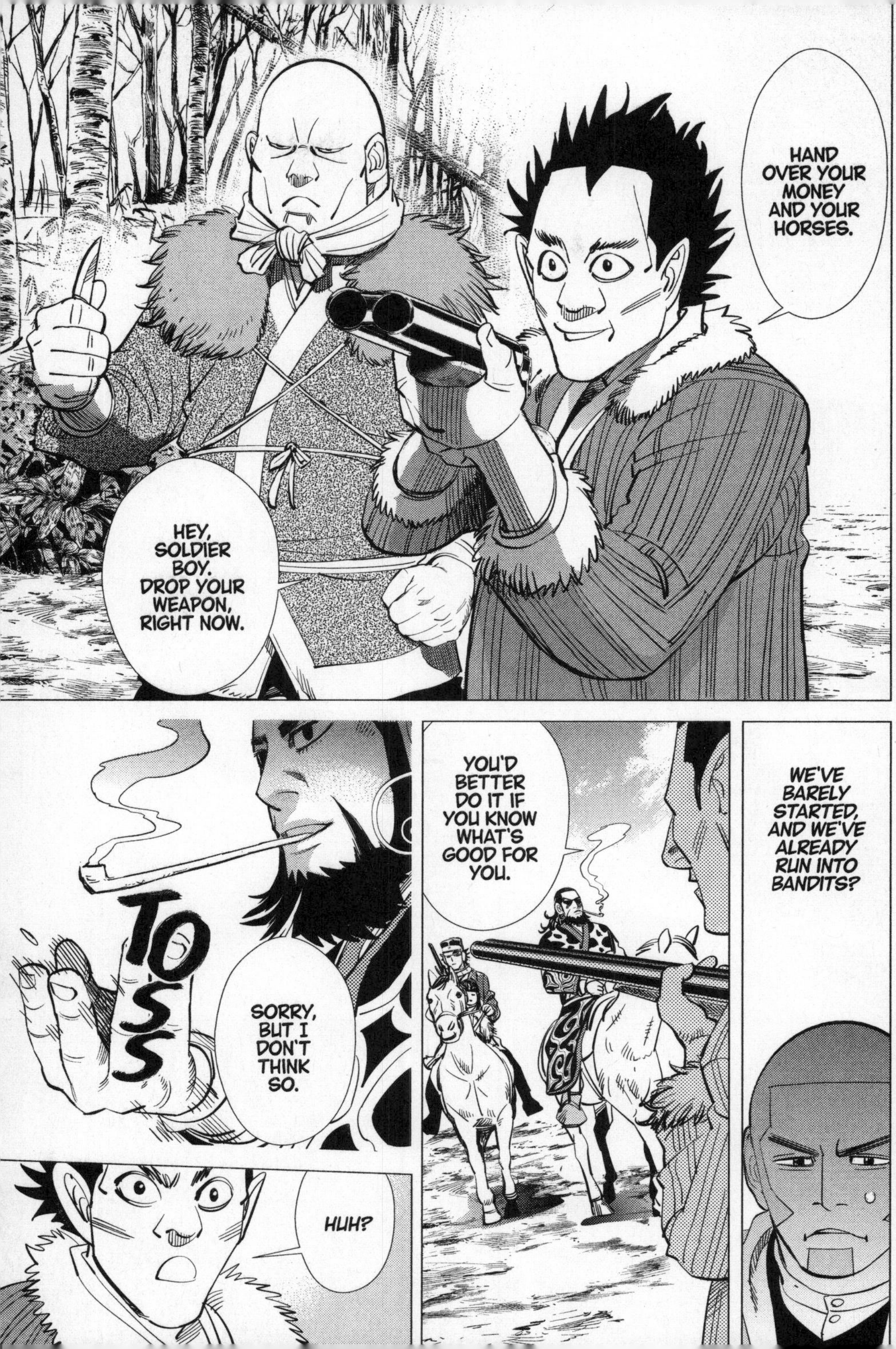
HAND OVER YOUR MONEY AND YOUR HORSES.
HEY, SOLDIER BOY. DROP YOUR WEAPON, RIGHT NOW.
WE'VE BARELY STARTED, AND WE'VE ALREADY RUN INTO BANDITS?
YOU'D BETTER DO IT IF YOU KNOW WHAT'S GOOD FOR YOU.
SORRY, BUT I DON'T THINK SO.
TOSS
HUH?

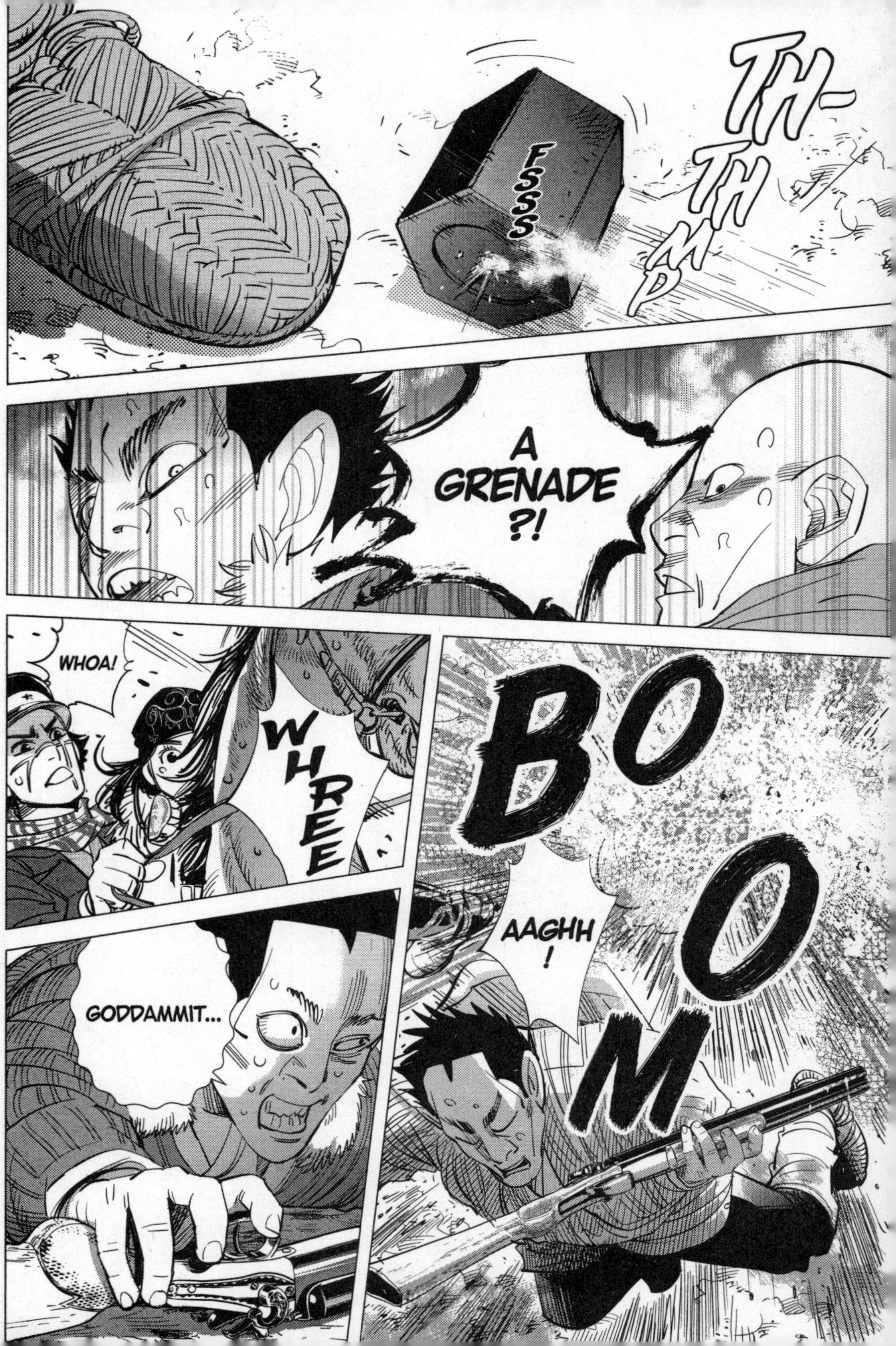
TH-TH-MP
FSSS
A GRENADE?!
BOOM
AAGHH!
WHREE
WHOA!
GODDAMMIT...

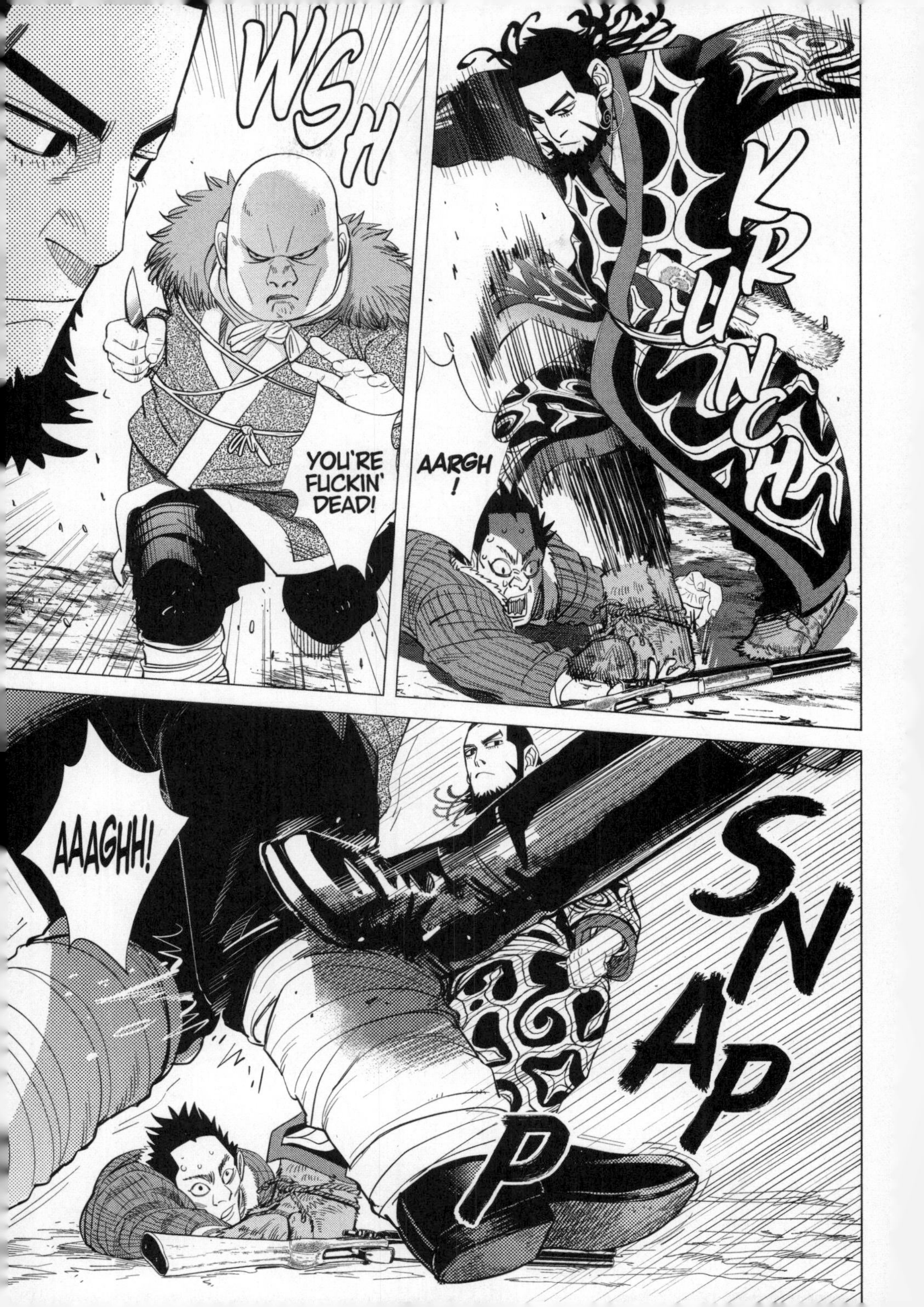
KRUNCH
AARGH!
WSH
YOU'RE FUCKIN' DEAD!
SNAP
AAAGHH!

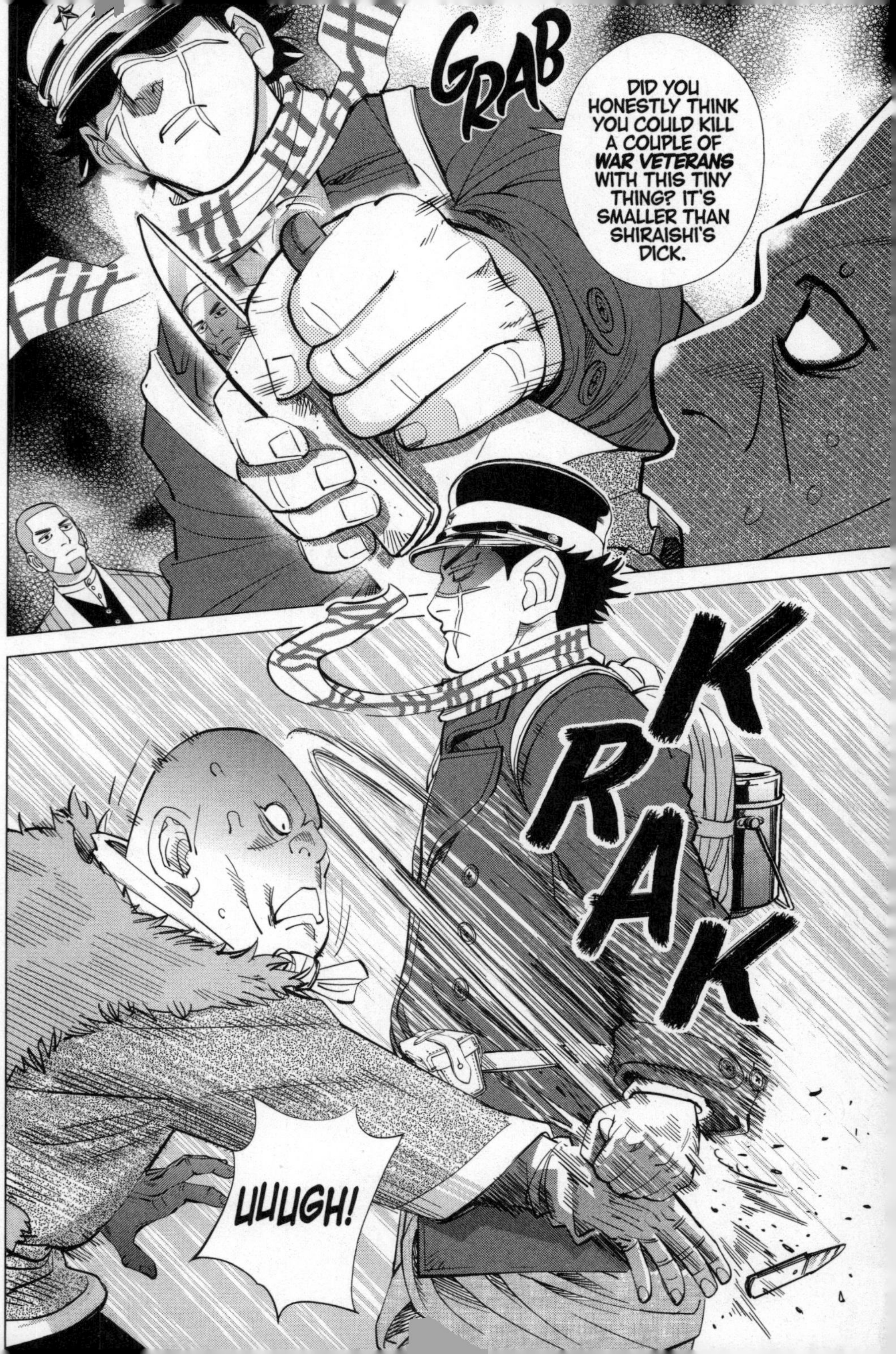

GRAB
DID YOU HONESTLY THINK YOU COULD KILL A COUPLE OF **WAR VETERANS** WITH THIS TINY THING? IT'S SMALLER THAN SHIRAISHI'S DICK.
KRAK
UUUGH!

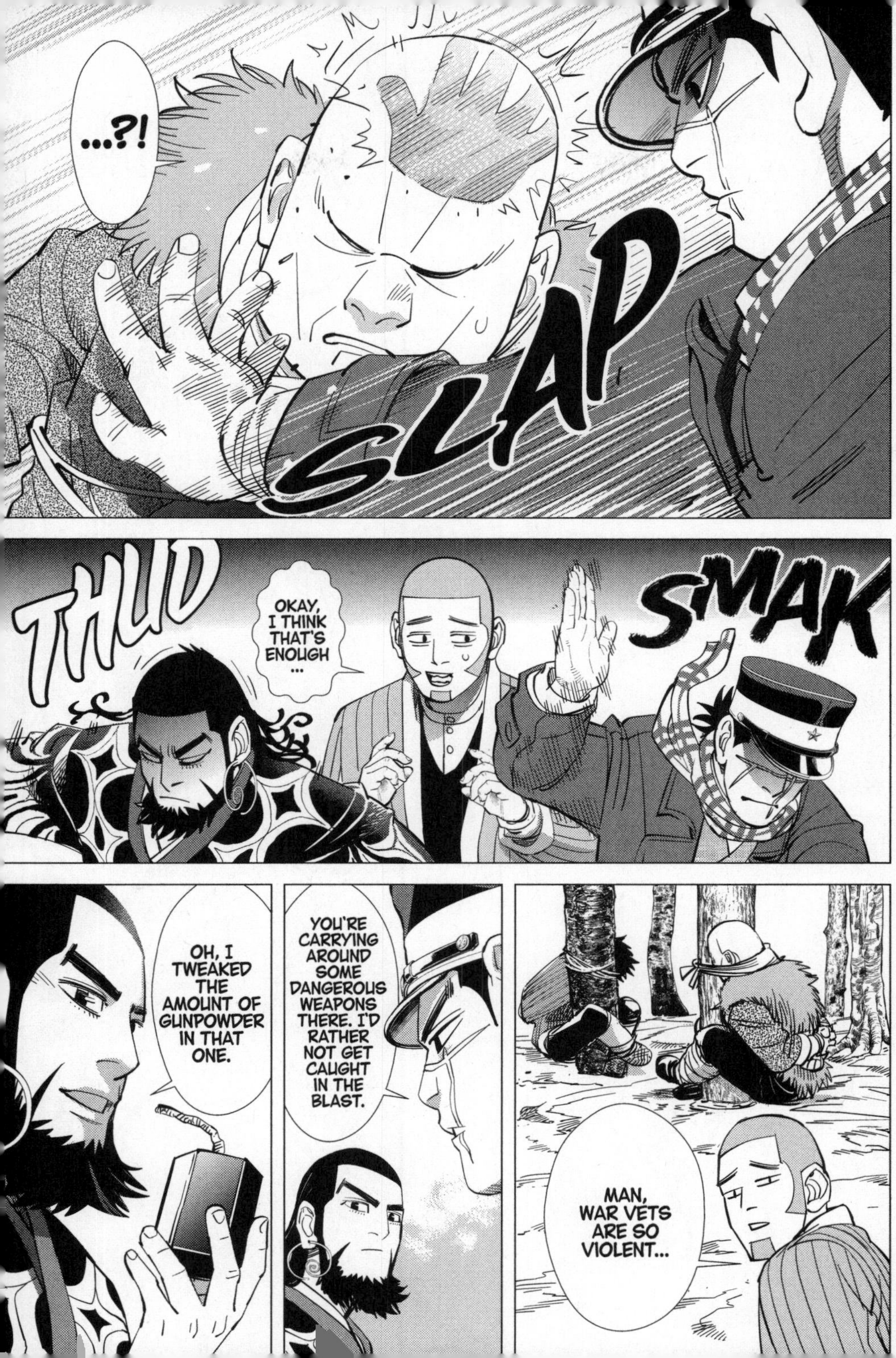
SLAP
...?!
SMAK
OKAY, I THINK THAT'S ENOUGH ...
THUD
MAN, WAR VETS ARE SO VIOLENT...
YOU'RE CARRYING AROUND SOME DANGEROUS WEAPONS THERE. I'D RATHER NOT GET CAUGHT IN THE BLAST.
OH, I TWEAKED THE AMOUNT OF GUNPOWDER IN THAT ONE.

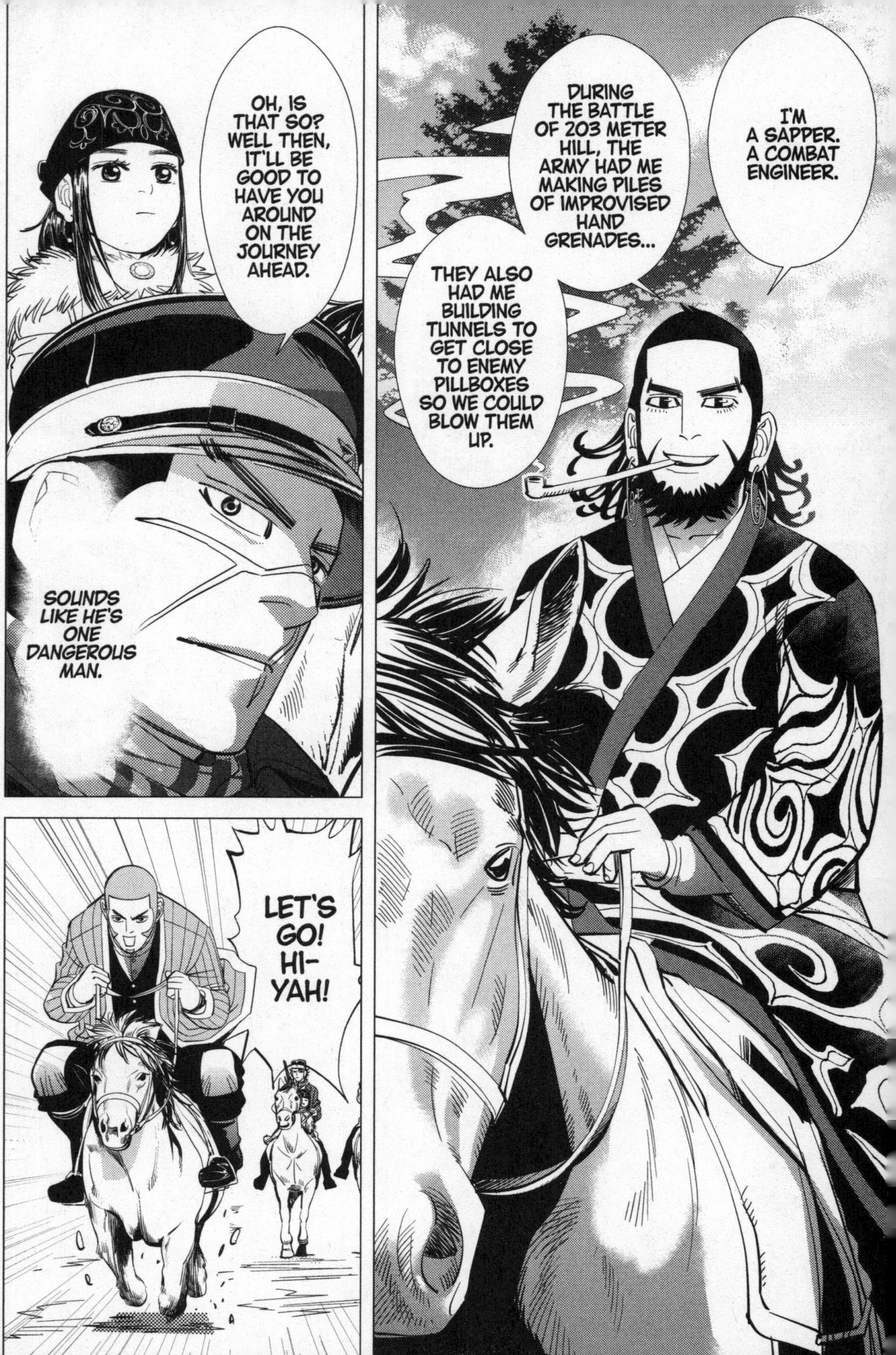
I'M A SAPPER. A COMBAT ENGINEER.
DURING THE BATTLE OF 203 METER HILL, THE ARMY HAD ME MAKING PILES OF IMPROVISED HAND GRENADES...
THEY ALSO HAD ME BUILDING TUNNELS TO GET CLOSE TO ENEMY PILLBOXES SO WE COULD BLOW THEM UP.
OH, IS THAT SO? WELL THEN, IT'LL BE GOOD TO HAVE YOU AROUND ON THE JOURNEY AHEAD.
SOUNDS LIKE HE'S ONE DANGEROUS MAN.
LET'S GO! HI-YAH!

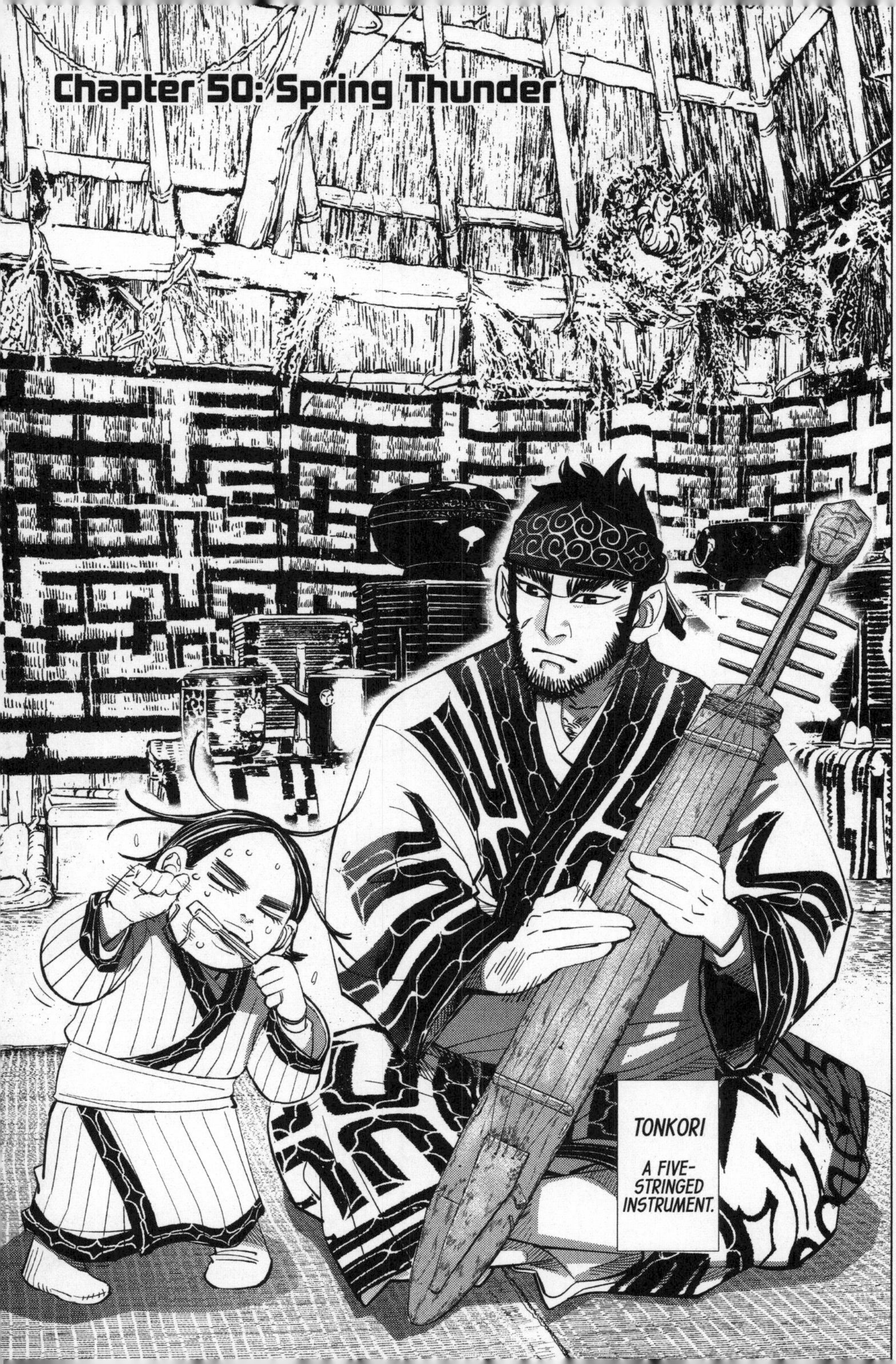
Chapter 50: Spring Thunder
TONKORI
A FIVE-STRINGED INSTRUMENT.

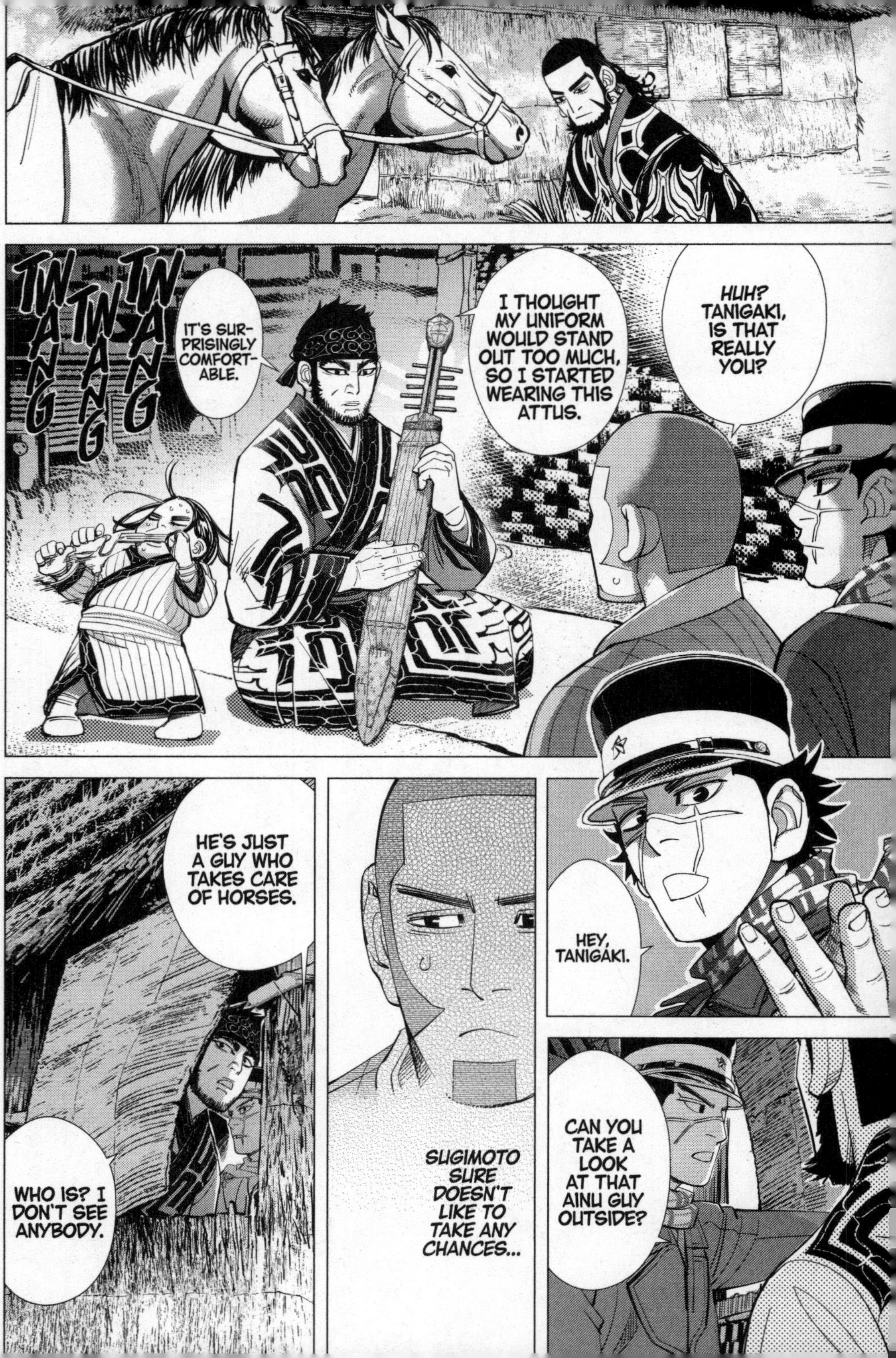
HUH? TANIGAKI, IS THAT REALLY YOU?
I THOUGHT MY UNIFORM WOULD STAND OUT TOO MUCH, SO I STARTED WEARING THIS ATTUS.
IT'S SUR-PRISINGLY COMFORT-ABLE.
TWANG
TWANG
TWANG
HEY, TANIGAKI.
CAN YOU TAKE A LOOK AT THAT AINU GUY OUTSIDE?
SUGIMOTO SURE DOESN'T LIKE TO TAKE ANY CHANCES...
HE'S JUST A GUY WHO TAKES CARE OF HORSES.
WHO IS? I DON'T SEE ANYBODY.

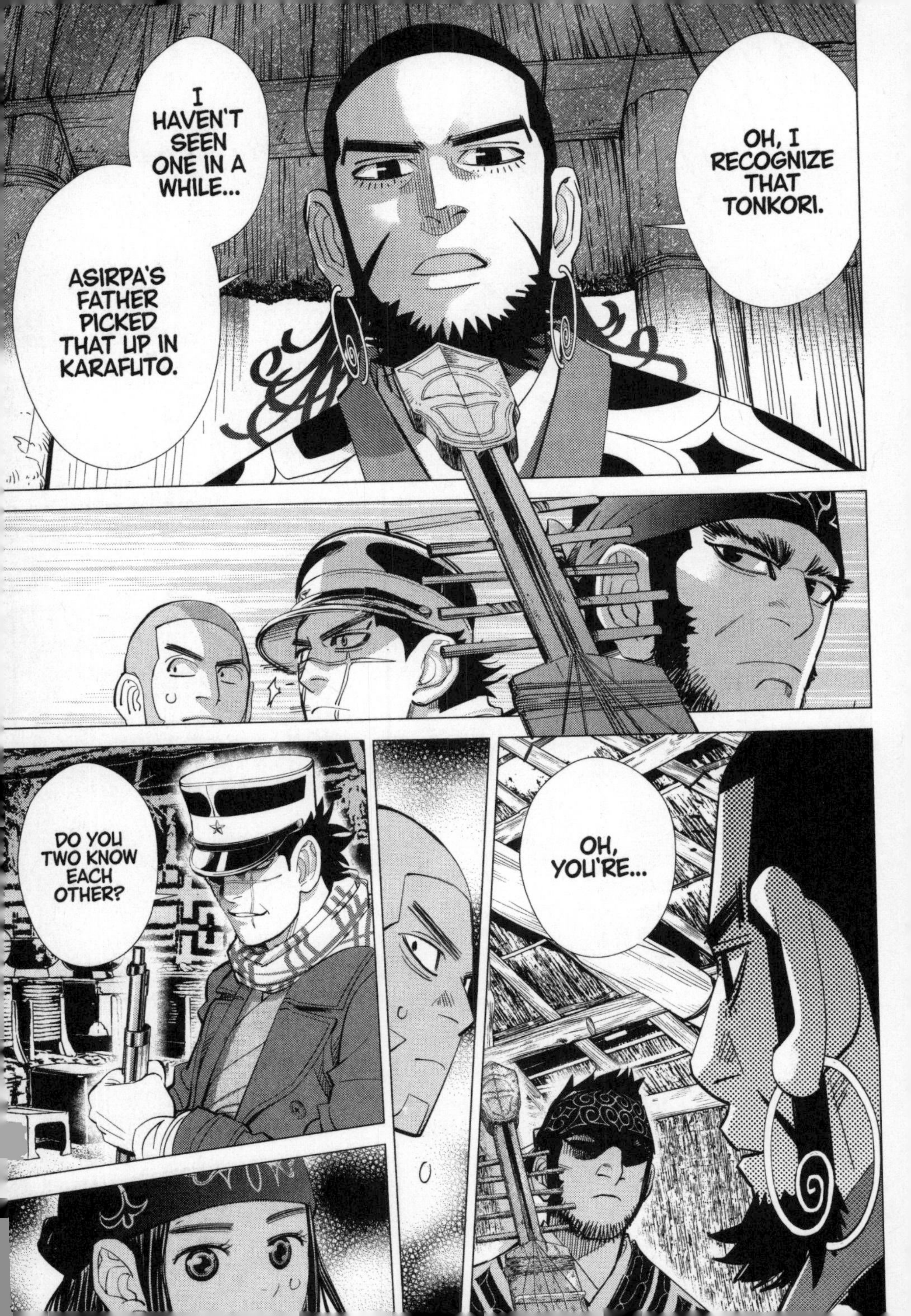
OH, I RECOGNIZE THAT TONKORI.
I HAVEN'T SEEN ONE IN A WHILE...
ASIRPA'S FATHER PICKED THAT UP IN KARAFUTO.
OH, YOU'RE...
DO YOU TWO KNOW EACH OTHER?

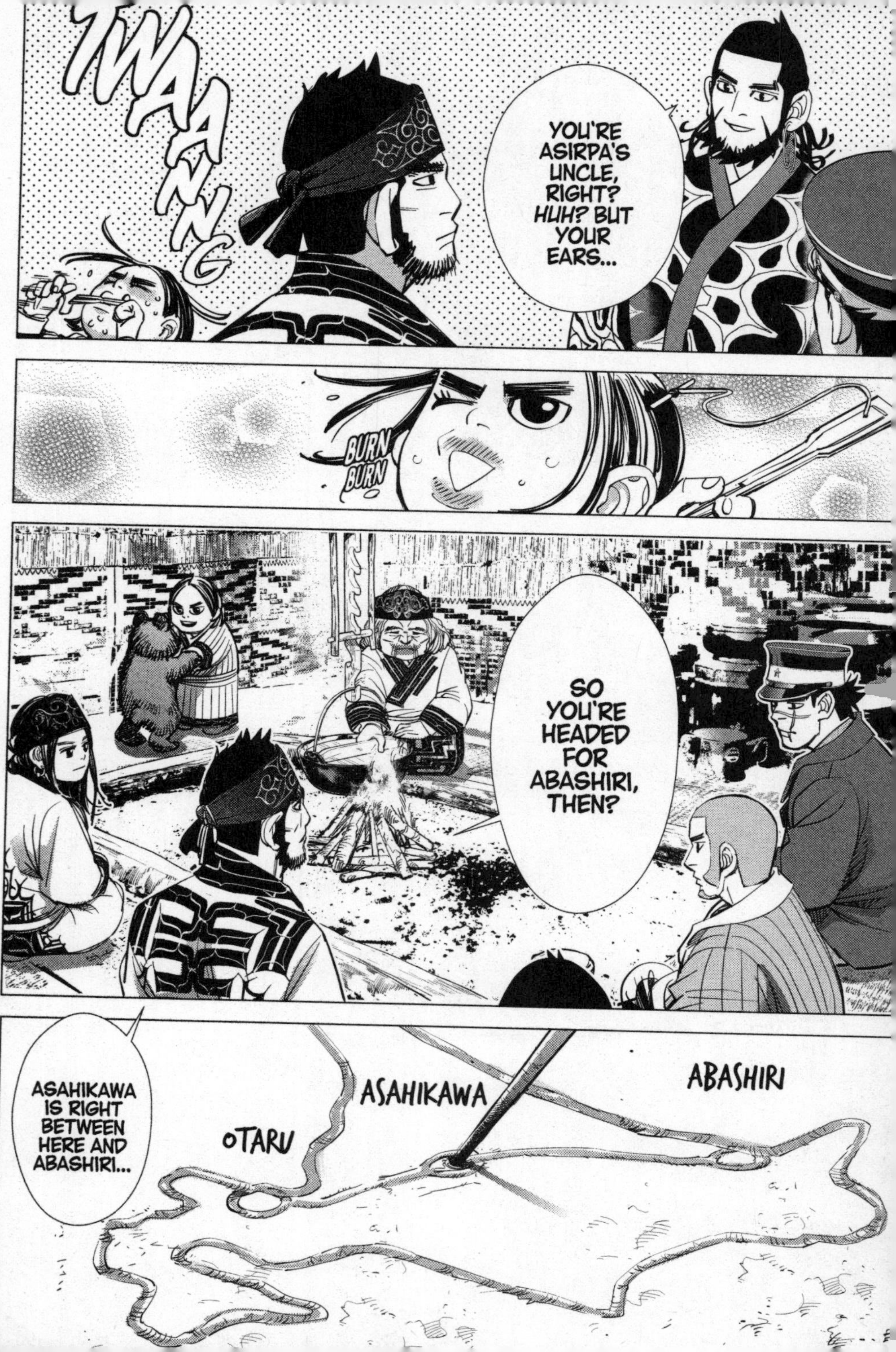
IWAAANNG
YOU'RE ASIRPA'S UNCLE, RIGHT? HUH? BUT YOUR EARS...
BURN BURN
SO YOU'RE HEADED FOR ABASHIRI, THEN?
ASAHIKAWA IS RIGHT BETWEEN HERE AND ABASHIRI...
ABASHIRI
ASAHIKAWA
OTARU

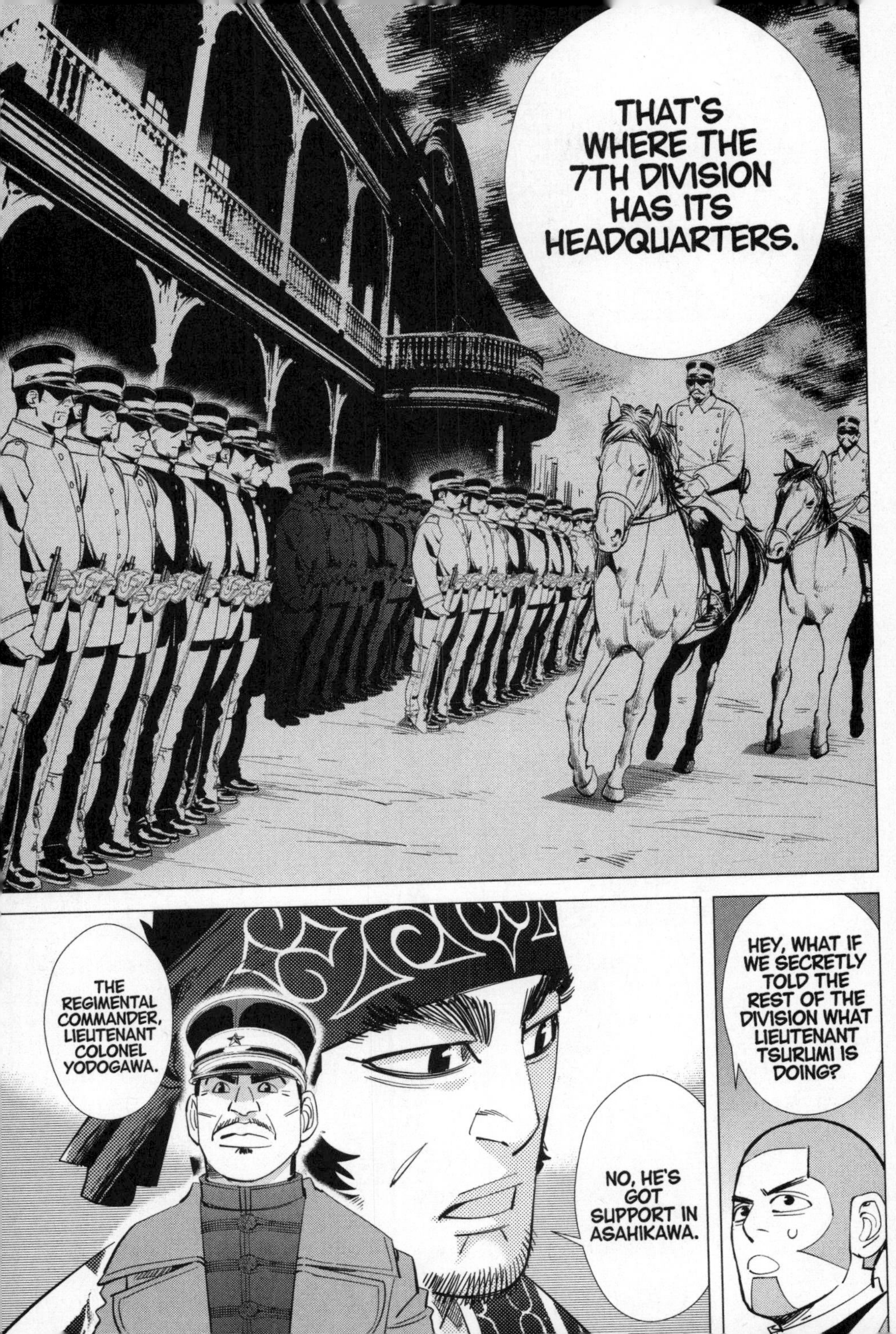
THAT'S WHERE THE 7TH DIVISION HAS ITS HEADQUARTERS.
HEY, WHAT IF WE SECRETLY TOLD THE REST OF THE DIVISION WHAT LIEUTENANT TSURUMI IS DOING?
NO, HE'S GOT SUPPORT IN ASAHIKAWA.
THE REGIMENTAL COMMANDER, LIEUTENANT COLONEL YODOGAWA.

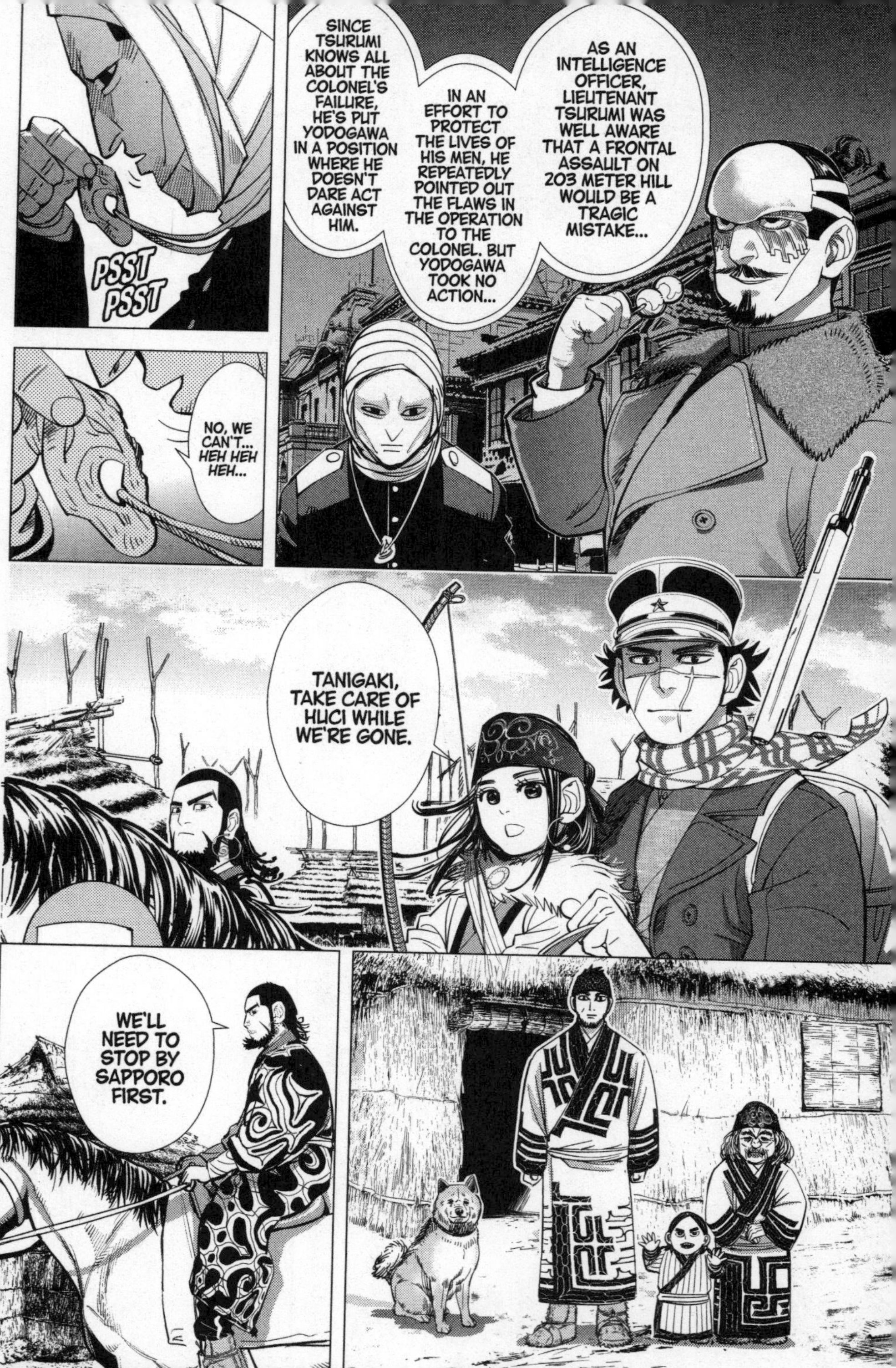
AS AN INTELLIGENCE OFFICER, LIEUTENANT TSURUMI WAS WELL AWARE THAT A FRONTAL ASSAULT ON 203 METER HILL WOULD BE A TRAGIC MISTAKE...
IN AN EFFORT TO PROTECT THE LIVES OF HIS MEN, HE REPEATEDLY POINTED OUT THE FLAWS IN THE OPERATION TO THE COLONEL. BUT YODOGAWA TOOK NO ACTION...
SINCE TSURUMI KNOWS ALL ABOUT THE COLONEL'S FAILURE, HE'S PUT YODOGAWA IN A POSITION WHERE HE DOESN'T DARE ACT AGAINST HIM.
PSST PSST
NO, WE CAN'T... HEH HEH HEH...
TANIGAKI, TAKE CARE OF HUCI WHILE WE'RE GONE.
WE'LL NEED TO STOP BY SAPPORO FIRST.

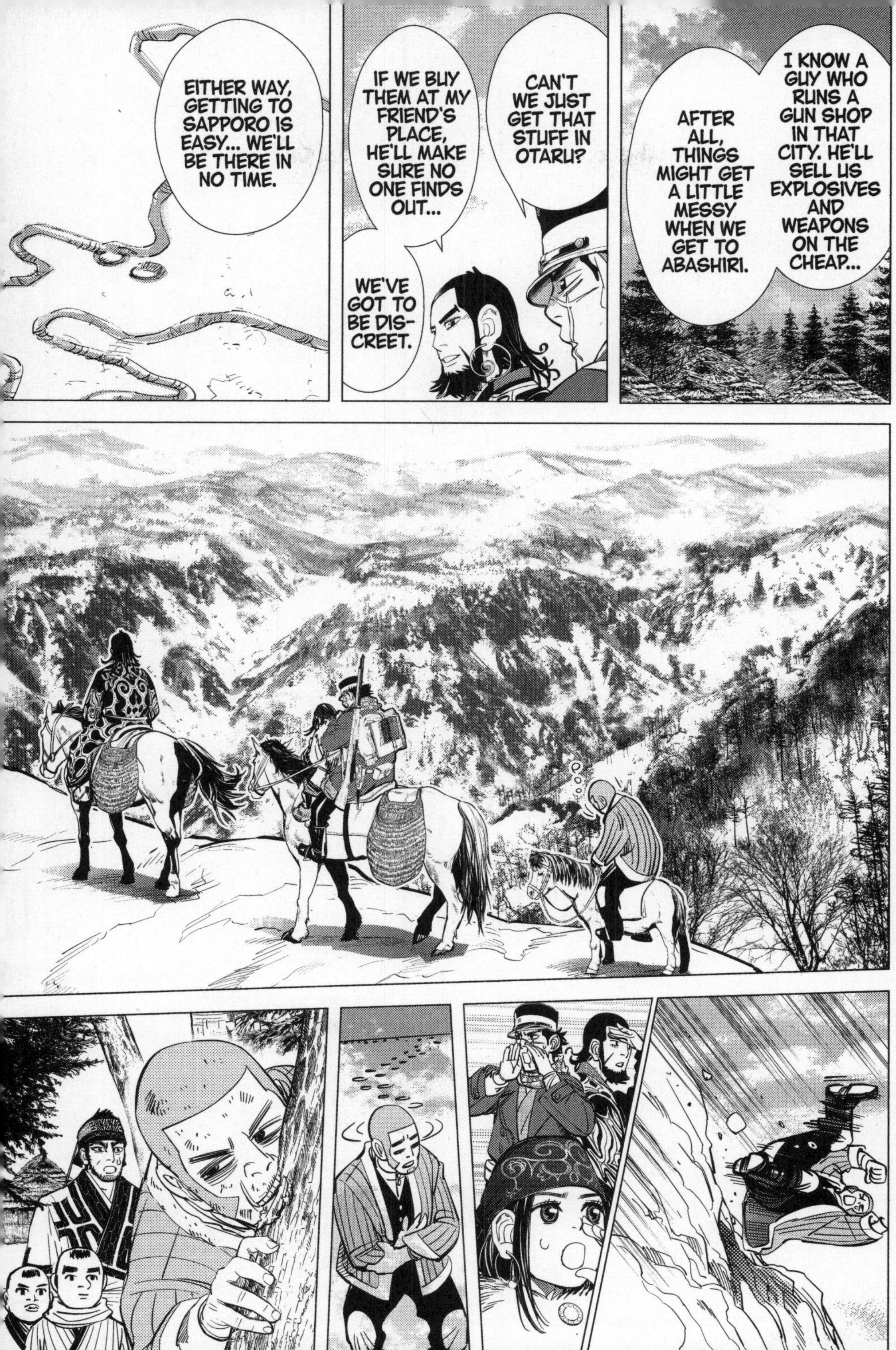
I KNOW A GUY WHO RUNS A GUN SHOP IN THAT CITY. HE'LL SELL US EXPLOSIVES AND WEAPONS ON THE CHEAP...
AFTER ALL, THINGS MIGHT GET A LITTLE MESSY WHEN WE GET TO ABASHIRI.
CAN'T WE JUST GET THAT STUFF IN OTARU?
IF WE BUY THEM AT MY FRIEND'S PLACE, HE'LL MAKE SURE NO ONE FINDS OUT...
WE'VE GOT TO BE DIS-CREET.
EITHER WAY, GETTING TO SAPPORO IS EASY... WE'LL BE THERE IN NO TIME.

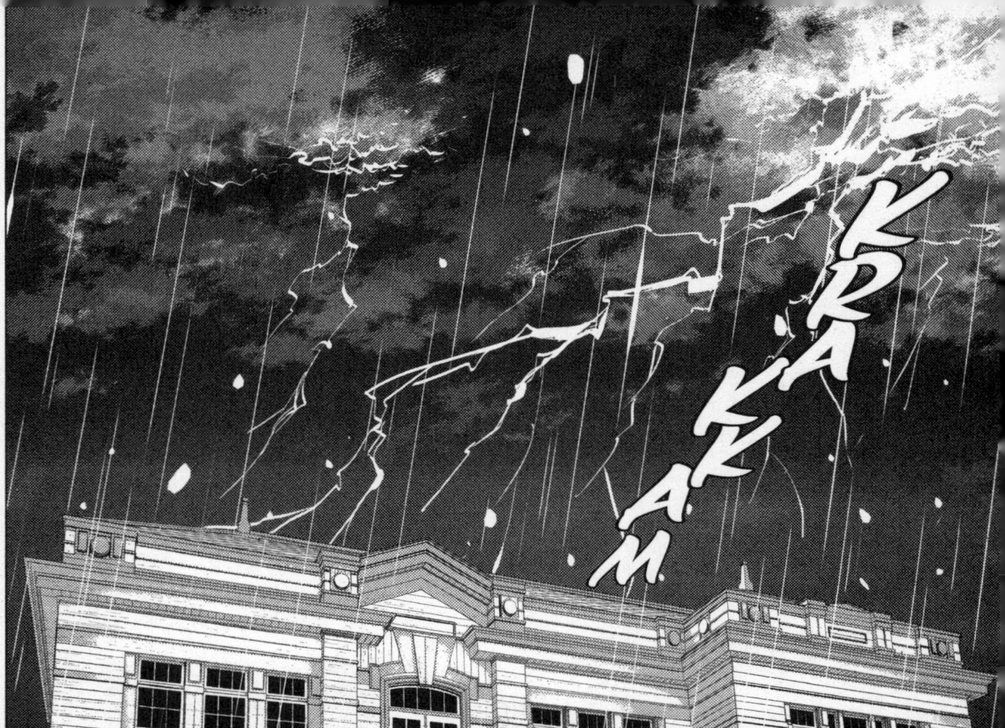
KRAKKAM
札幌世界ホテル
*SAPPORO WORLD HOTEL

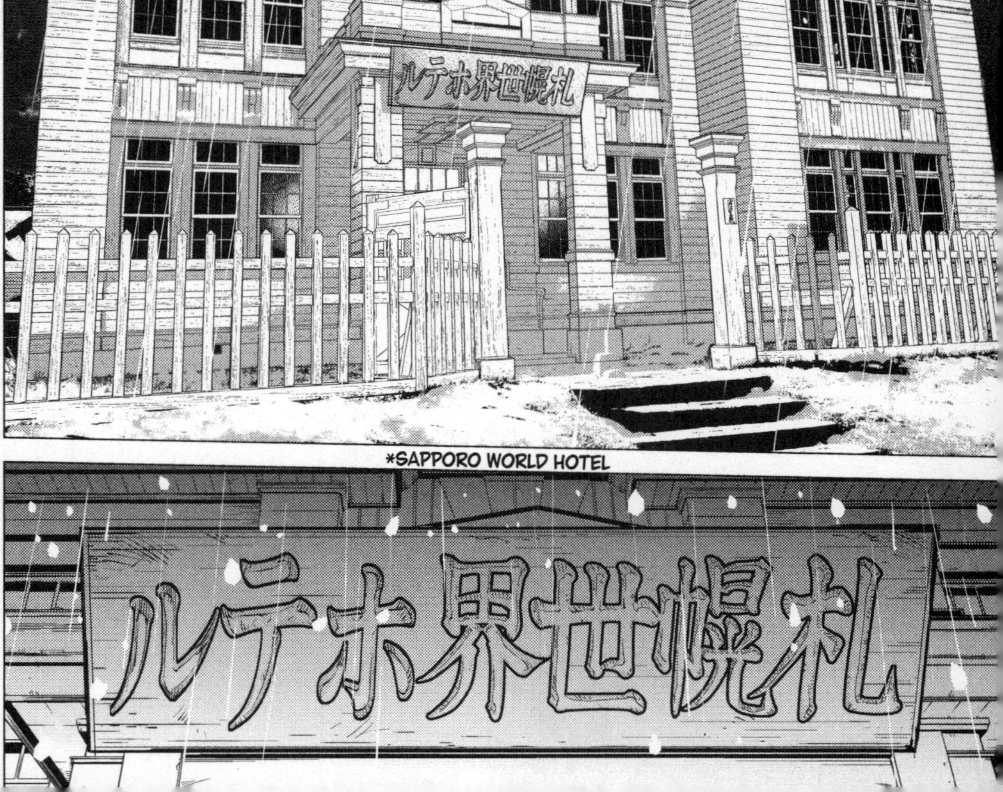
札幌世界ホテル

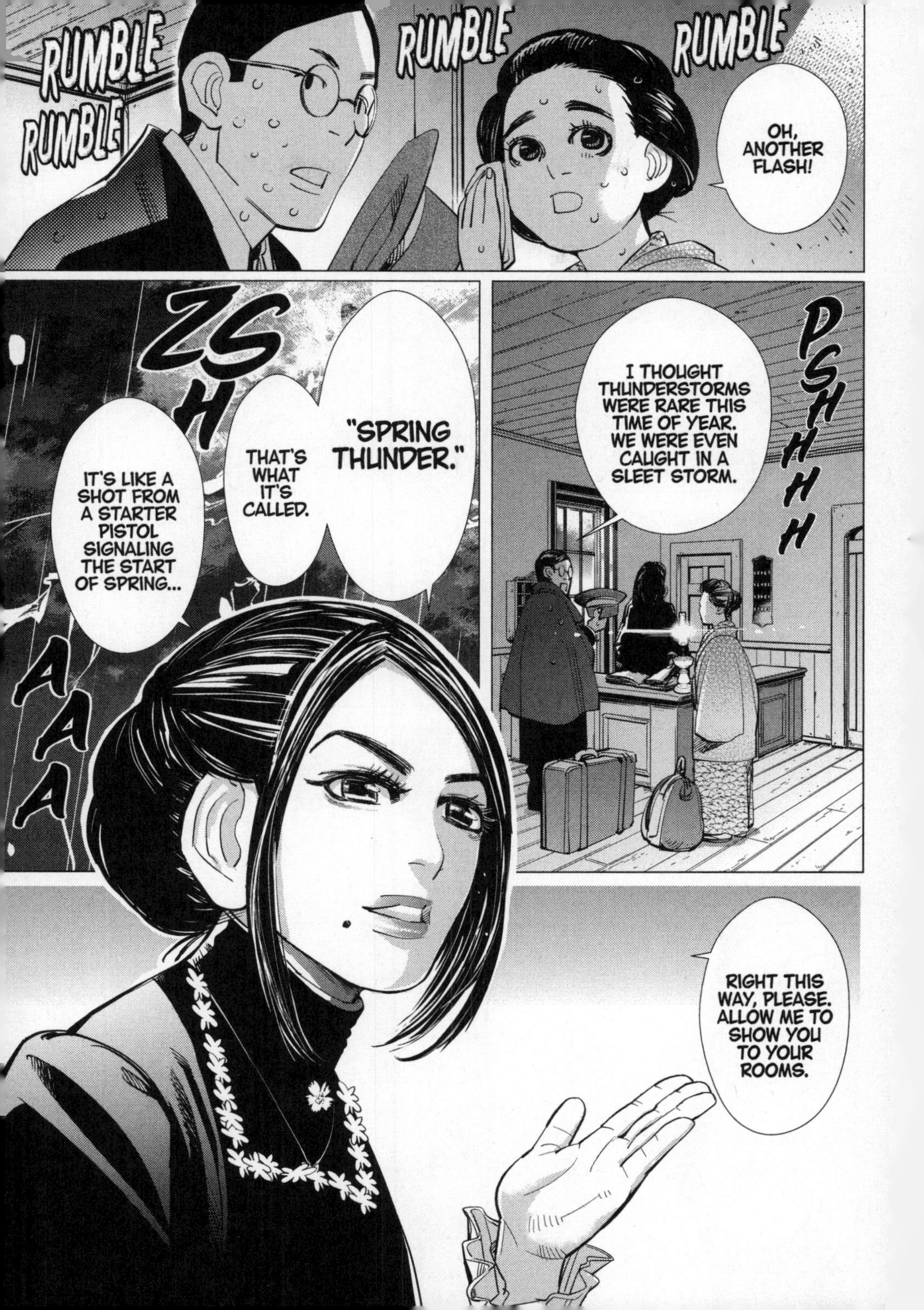
RUMBLE
OH, ANOTHER FLASH!
RUMBLE
RUMBLE
RUMBLE
PSHHHHH
I THOUGHT THUNDERSTORMS WERE RARE THIS TIME OF YEAR. WE WERE EVEN CAUGHT IN A SLEET STORM.
ZSH
"SPRING THUNDER."
THAT'S WHAT IT'S CALLED.
IT'S LIKE A SHOT FROM A STARTER PISTOL SIGNALING THE START OF SPRING...
AAAA
RIGHT THIS WAY, PLEASE. ALLOW ME TO SHOW YOU TO YOUR ROOMS.

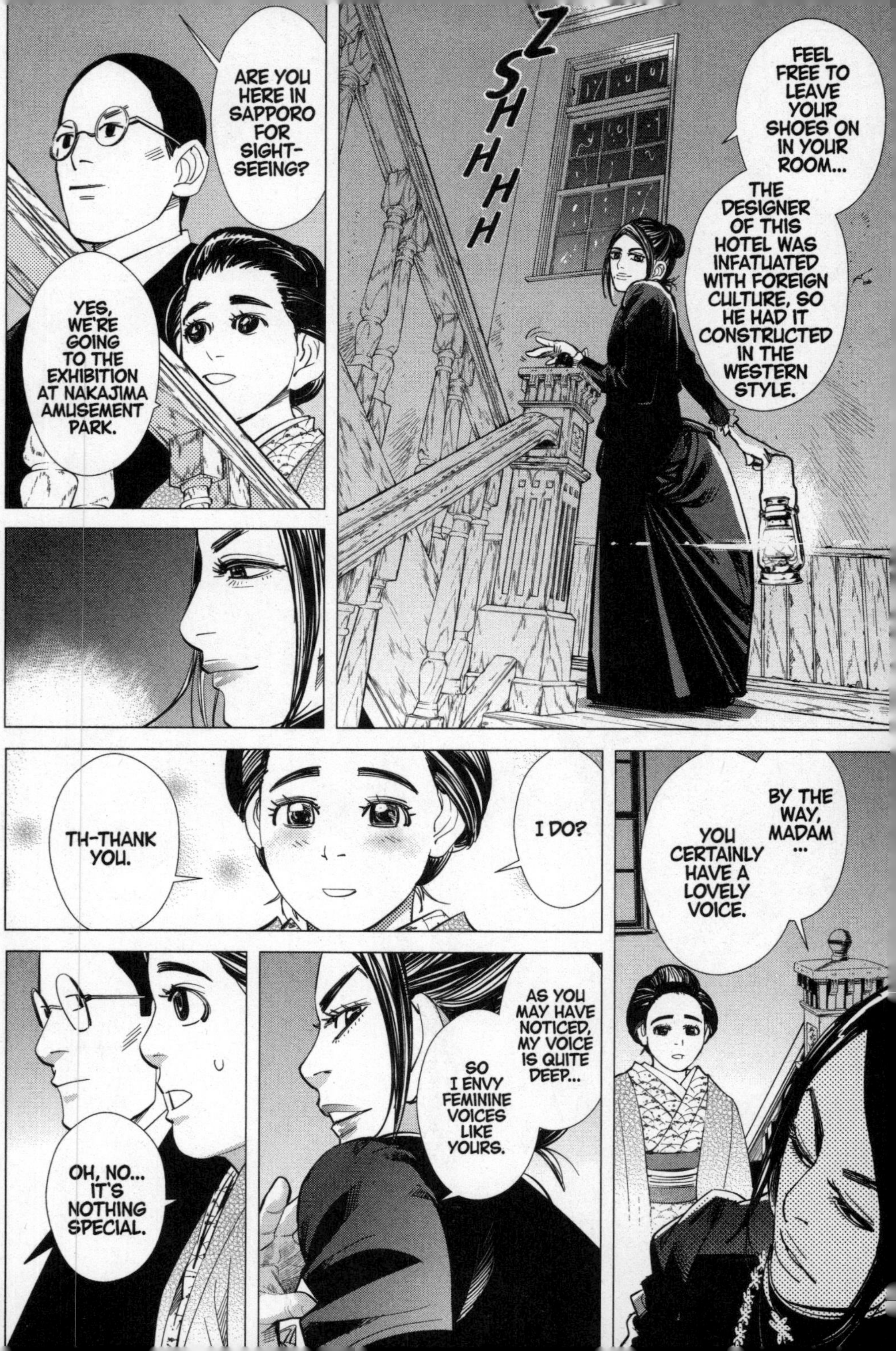
ZSHHHH
FEEL FREE TO LEAVE YOUR SHOES ON IN YOUR ROOM...
THE DESIGNER OF THIS HOTEL WAS INFATUATED WITH FOREIGN CULTURE, SO HE HAD IT CONSTRUCTED IN THE WESTERN STYLE.
ARE YOU HERE IN SAPPORO FOR SIGHT-SEEING?
YES, WE'RE GOING TO THE EXHIBITION AT NAKAJIMA AMUSEMENT PARK.
BY THE WAY, MADAM ...
YOU CERTAINLY HAVE A LOVELY VOICE.
I DO?
TH-THANK YOU.
AS YOU MAY HAVE NOTICED, MY VOICE IS QUITE DEEP...
SO I ENVY FEMININE VOICES LIKE YOURS.
OH, NO... IT'S NOTHING SPECIAL.

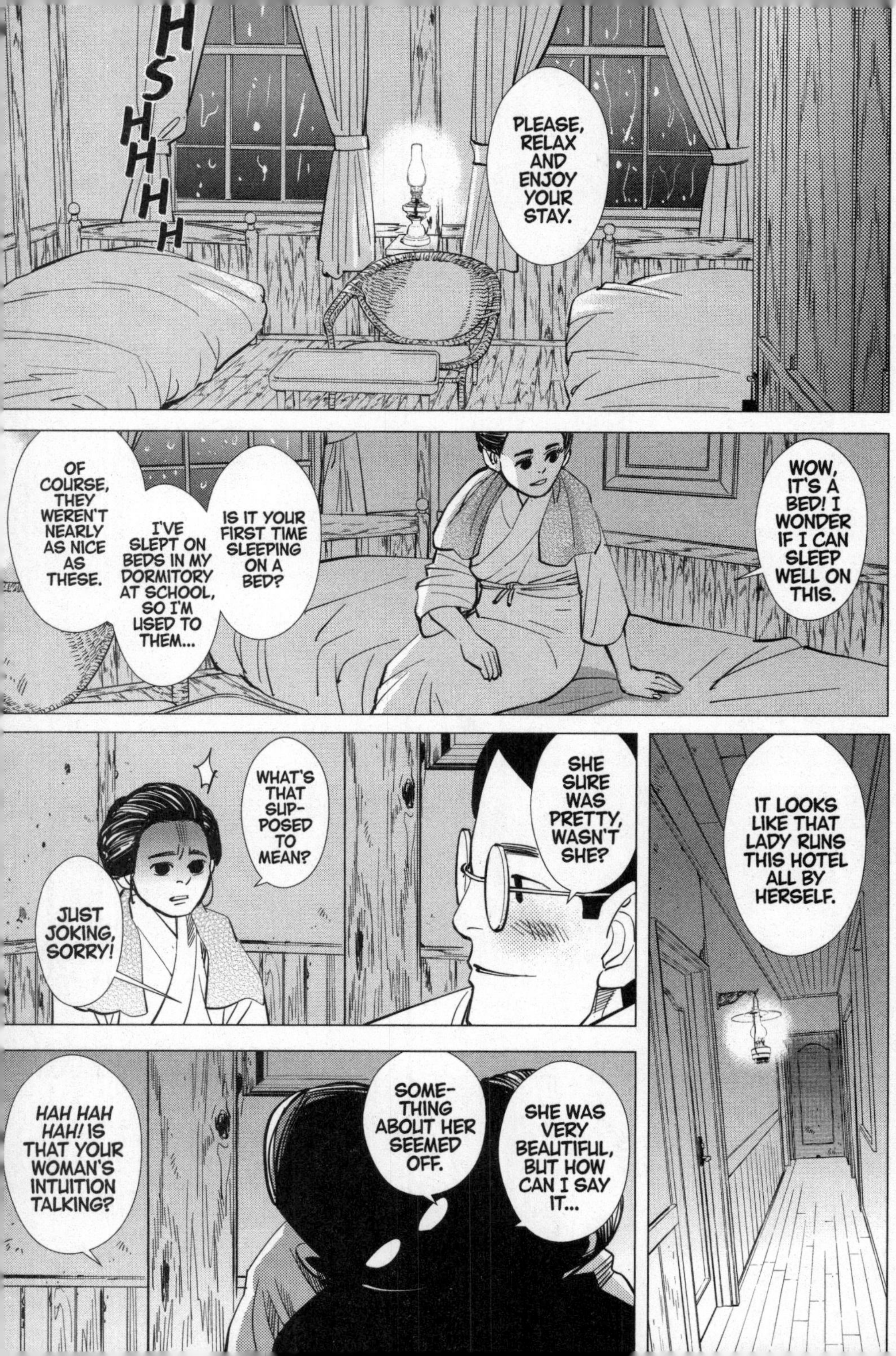
PLEASE, RELAX AND ENJOY YOUR STAY.
HSHHHH
WOW, IT'S A BED! I WONDER IF I CAN SLEEP WELL ON THIS.
IS IT YOUR FIRST TIME SLEEPING ON A BED?
I'VE SLEPT ON BEDS IN MY DORMITORY AT SCHOOL, SO I'M USED TO THEM...
OF COURSE, THEY WEREN'T NEARLY AS NICE AS THESE.
IT LOOKS LIKE THAT LADY RUNS THIS HOTEL ALL BY HERSELF.
SHE SURE WAS PRETTY, WASN'T SHE?
WHAT'S THAT SUPPOSED TO MEAN?
JUST JOKING, SORRY!
SHE WAS VERY BEAUTIFUL, BUT HOW CAN I SAY IT...
SOMETHING ABOUT HER SEEMED OFF.
HAH HAH HAH! IS THAT YOUR WOMAN'S INTUITION TALKING?

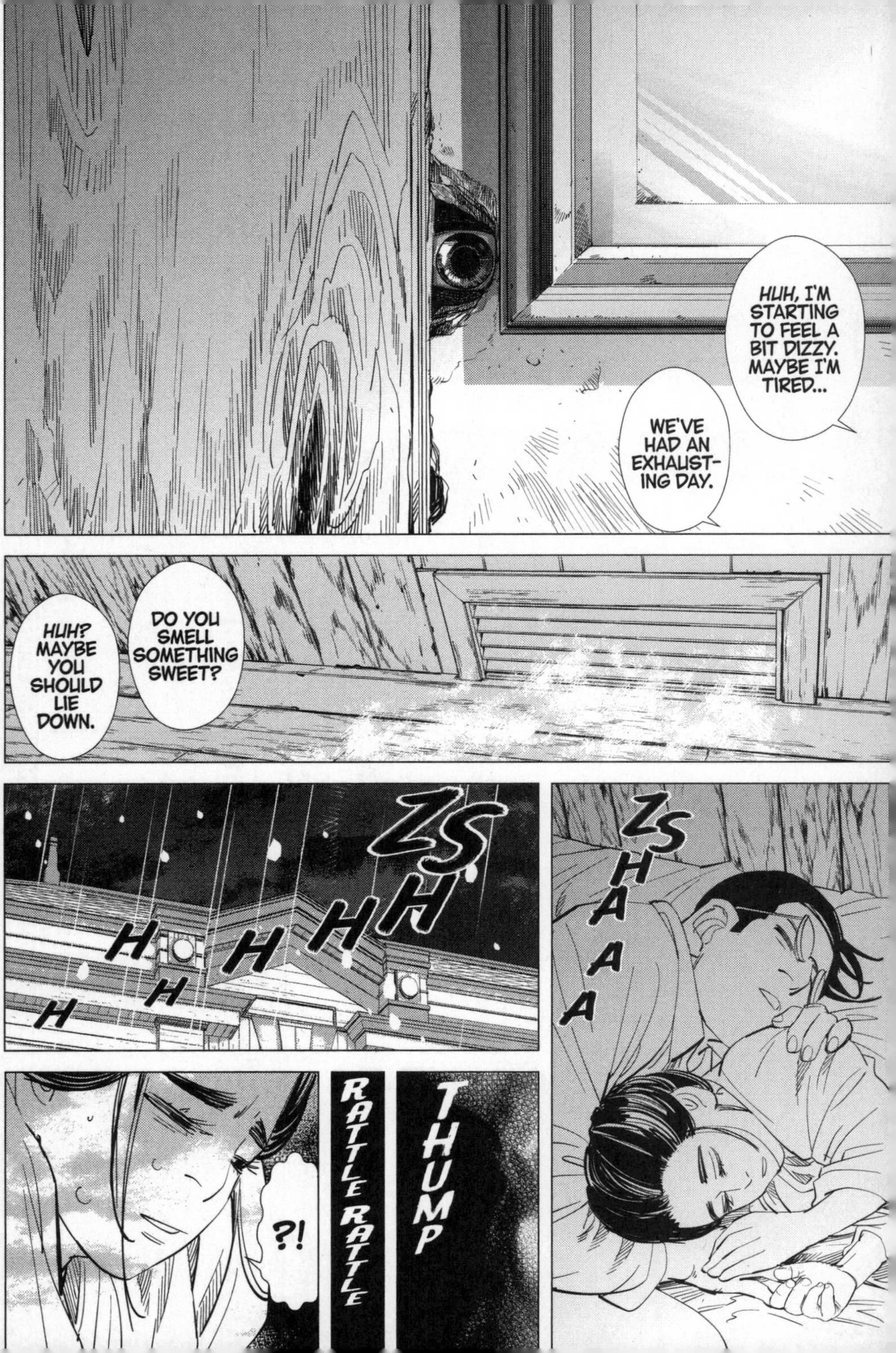
HUH, I'M STARTING TO FEEL A BIT DIZZY. MAYBE I'M TIRED...
WE'VE HAD AN EXHAUSTING DAY.
DO YOU SMELL SOMETHING SWEET?
HUH? MAYBE YOU SHOULD LIE DOWN.
ZSHAAAA
ZSHHHHHHH
THUMP
RATTLE RATTLE
?!

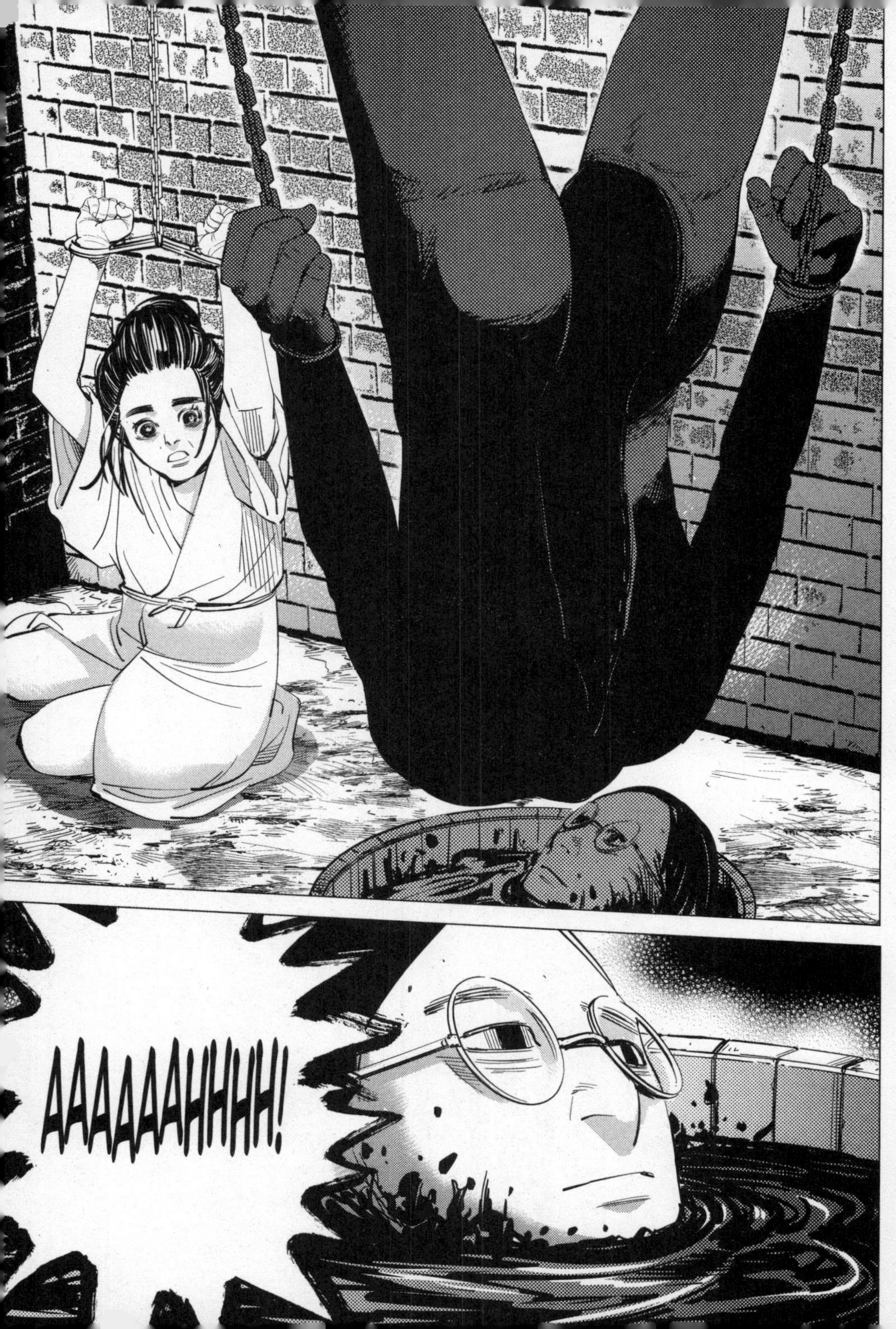
AAAAAAHHHH!

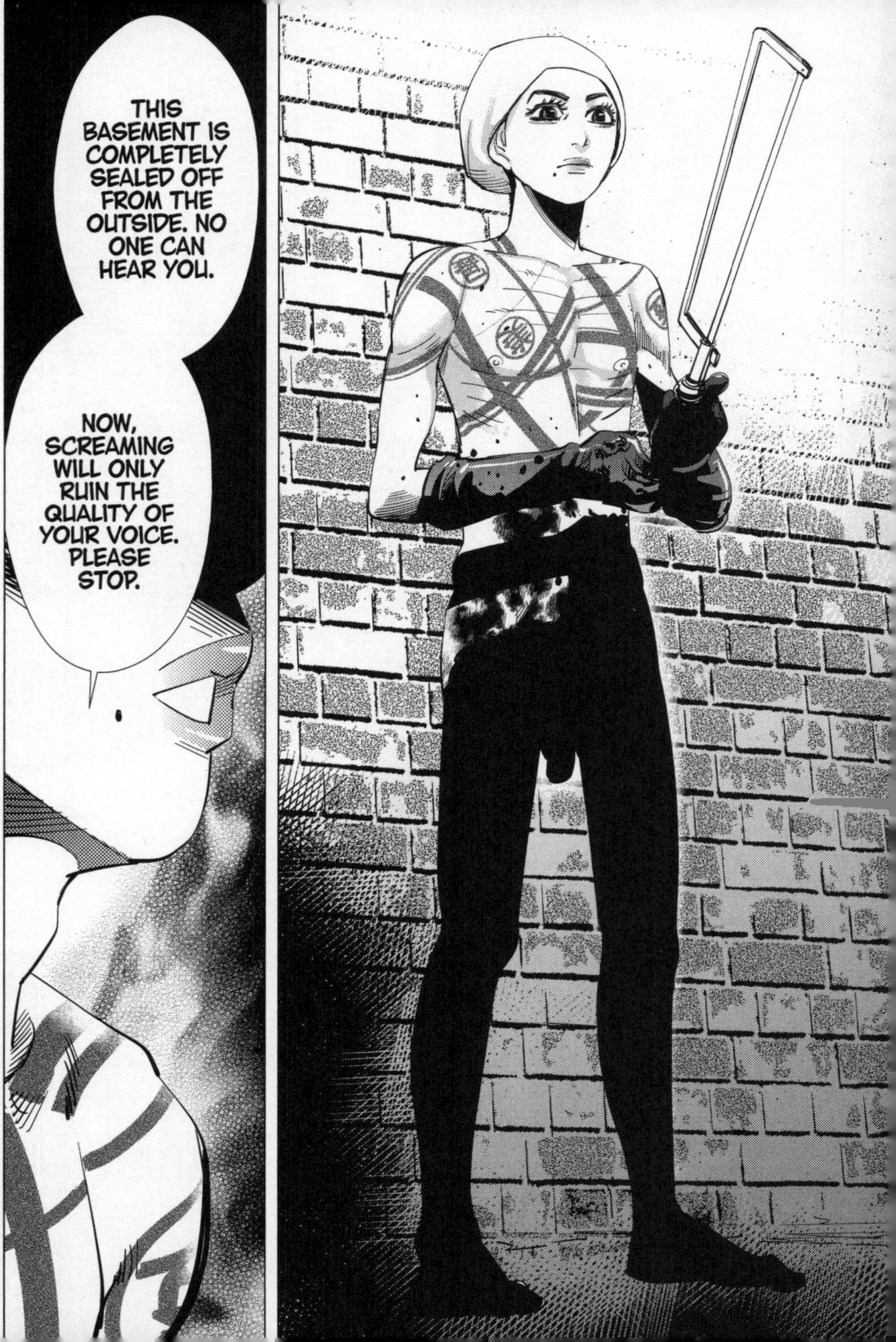
THIS BASEMENT IS COMPLETELY SEALED OFF FROM THE OUTSIDE. NO ONE CAN HEAR YOU.
NOW, SCREAMING WILL ONLY RUIN THE QUALITY OF YOUR VOICE. PLEASE STOP.

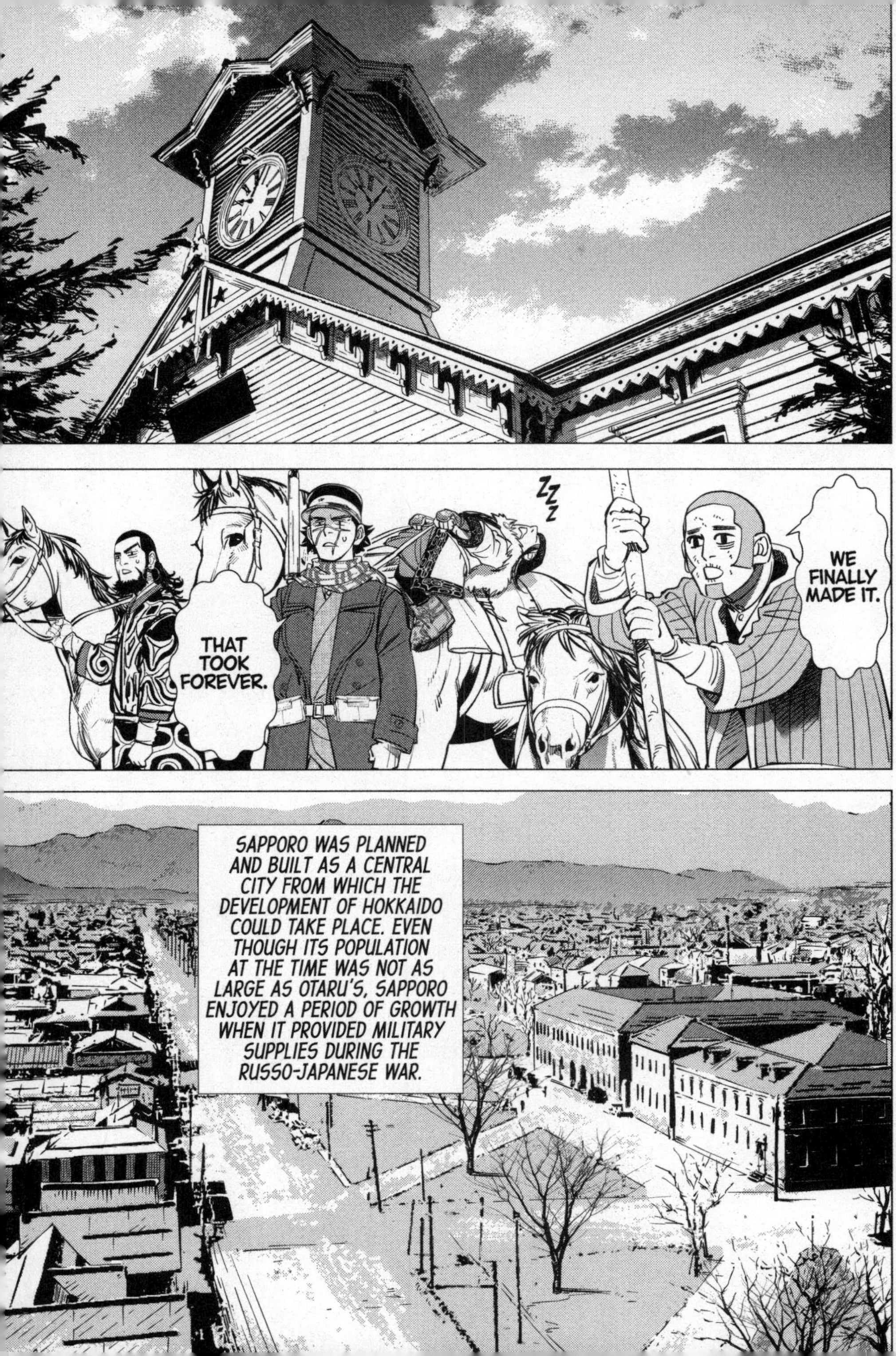
WE FINALLY MADE IT.
ZZZ
THAT TOOK FOREVER.
SAPPORO WAS PLANNED AND BUILT AS A CENTRAL CITY FROM WHICH THE DEVELOPMENT OF HOKKAIDO COULD TAKE PLACE. EVEN THOUGH ITS POPULATION AT THE TIME WAS NOT AS LARGE AS OTARU'S, SAPPORO ENJOYED A PERIOD OF GROWTH WHEN IT PROVIDED MILITARY SUPPLIES DURING THE RUSSO-JAPANESE WAR.

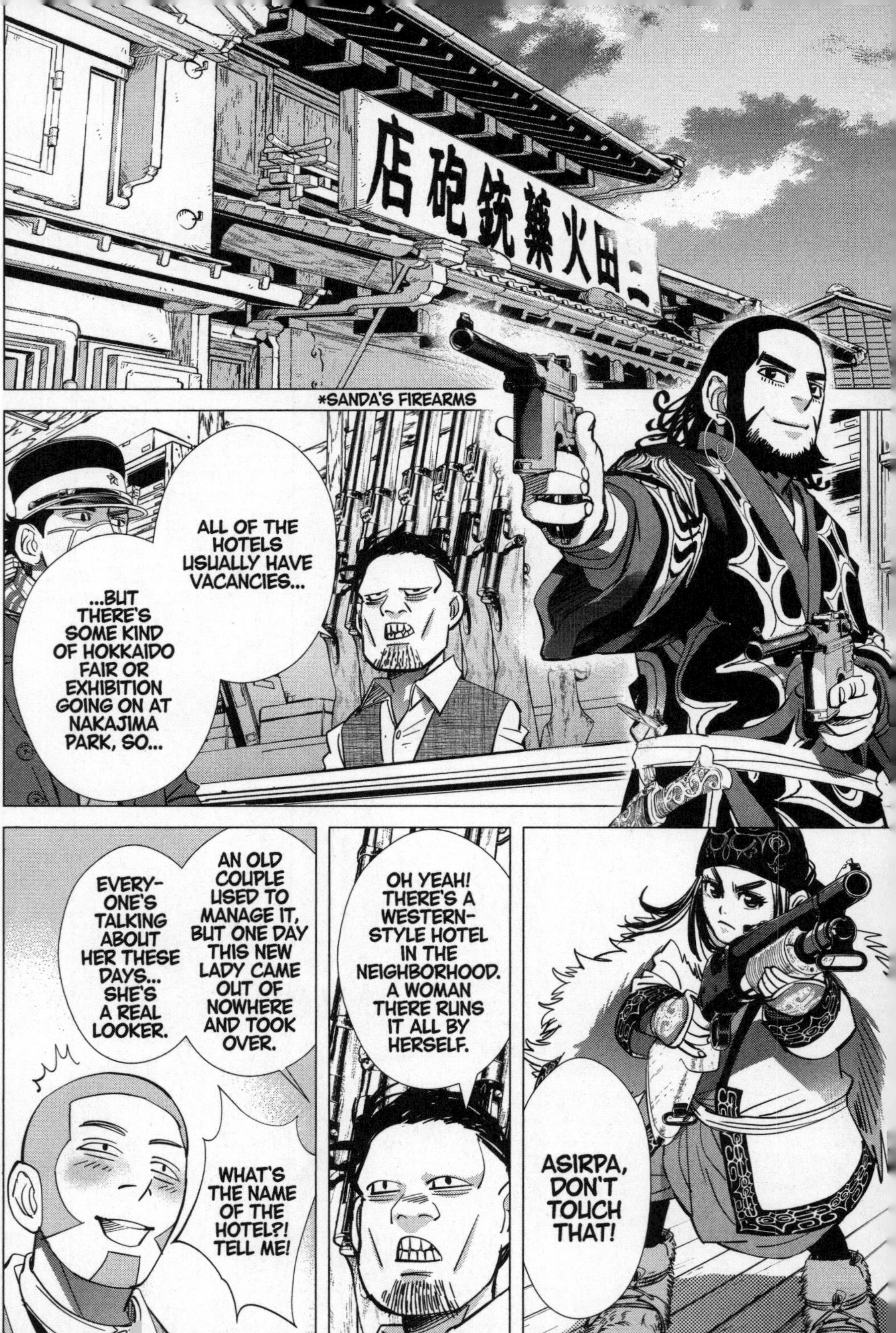
二田火藥銃砲店
*SANDA'S FIREARMS
ALL OF THE HOTELS USUALLY HAVE VACANCIES...
...BUT THERE'S SOME KIND OF HOKKAIDO FAIR OR EXHIBITION GOING ON AT NAKAJIMA PARK, SO...
ASIRPA, DON'T TOUCH THAT!
OH YEAH! THERE'S A WESTERN-STYLE HOTEL IN THE NEIGHBORHOOD. A WOMAN THERE RUNS IT ALL BY HERSELF.
AN OLD COUPLE USED TO MANAGE IT, BUT ONE DAY THIS NEW LADY CAME OUT OF NOWHERE AND TOOK OVER.
EVERY-ONE'S TALKING ABOUT HER THESE DAYS... SHE'S A REAL LOOKER.
WHAT'S THE NAME OF THE HOTEL?! TELL ME!

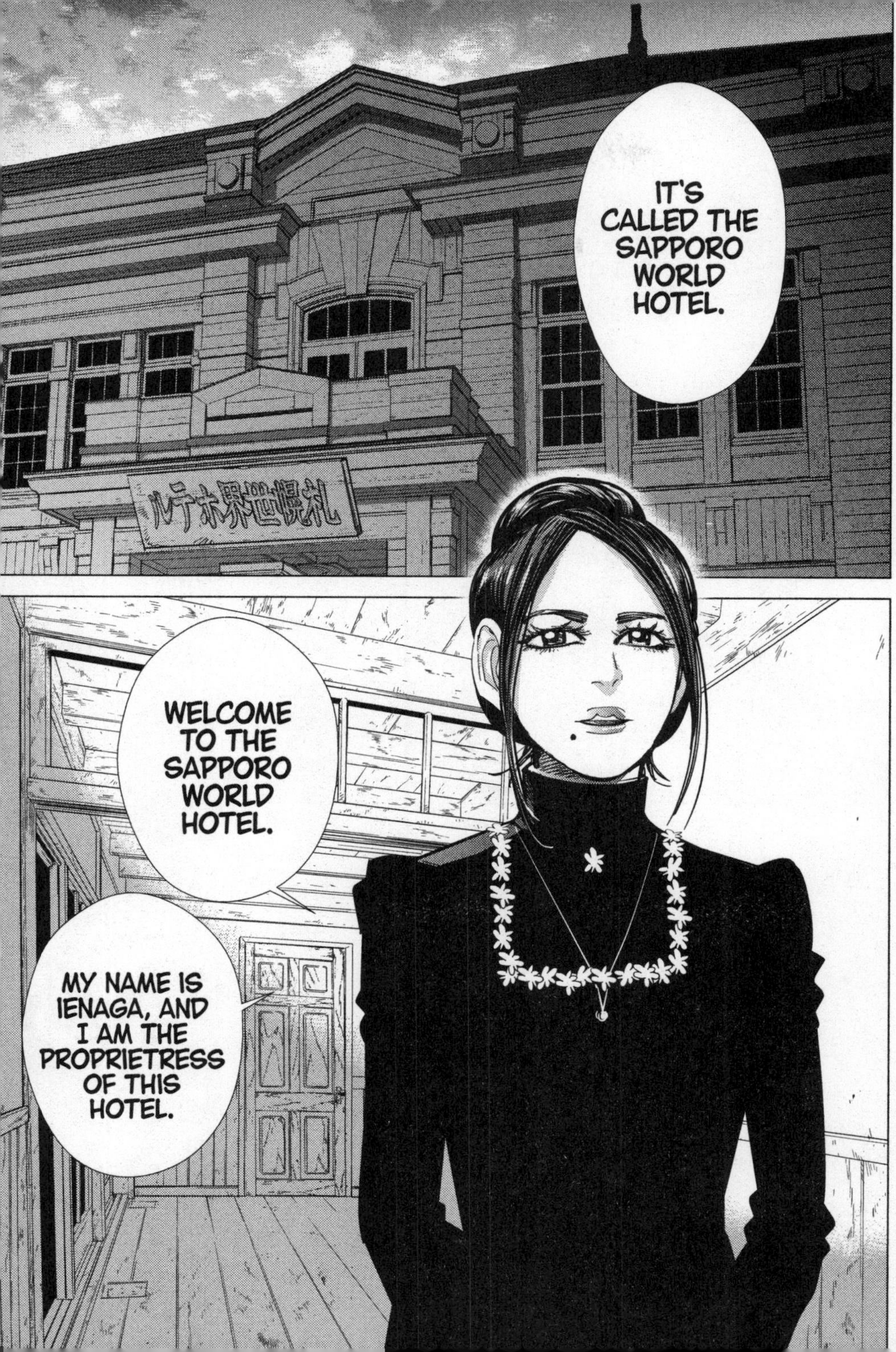
札幌世界ホテル
IT'S CALLED THE SAPPORO WORLD HOTEL.
WELCOME TO THE SAPPORO WORLD HOTEL.
MY NAME IS IENAGA, AND I AM THE PROPRIETRESS OF THIS HOTEL.

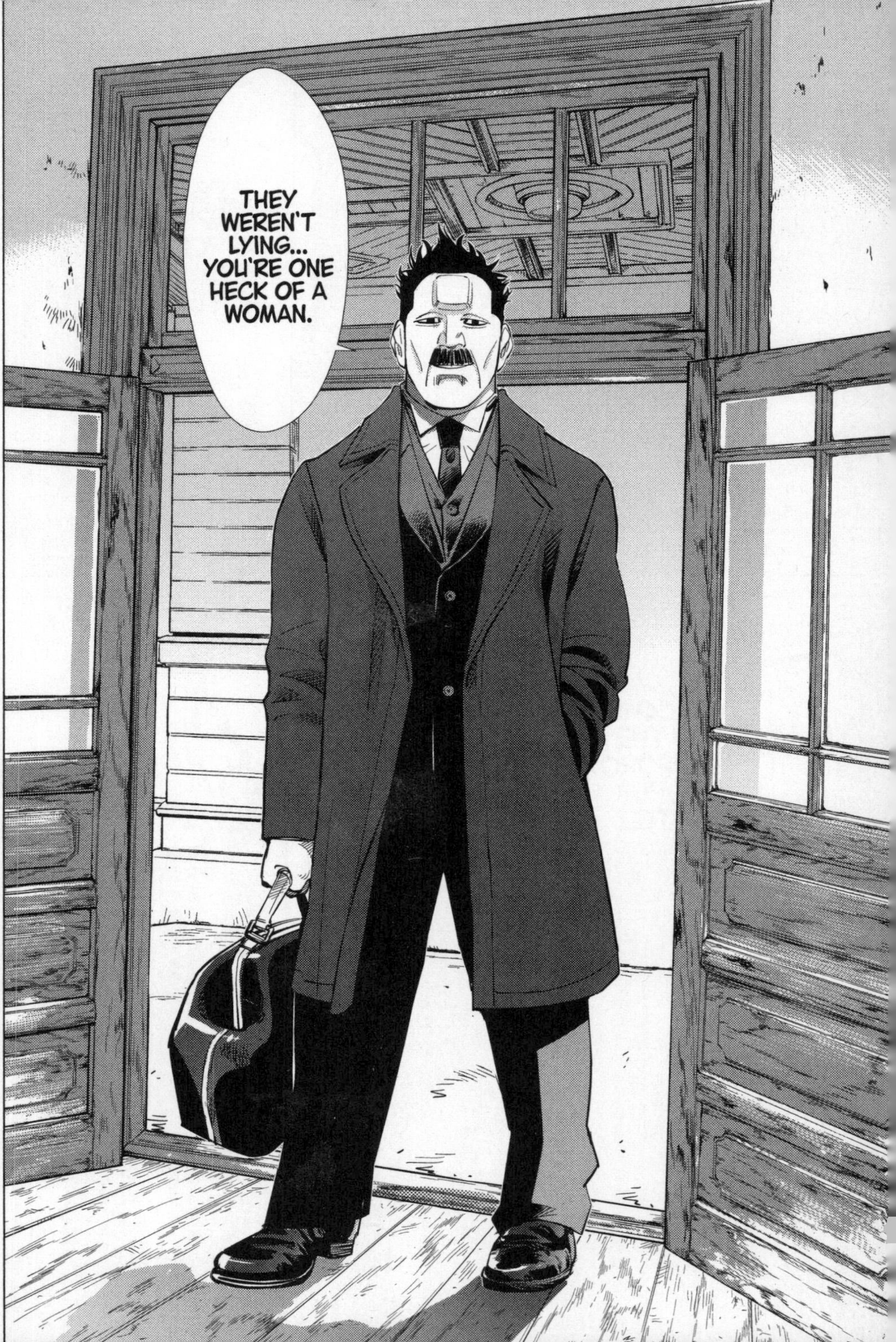
THEY WEREN'T LYING... YOU'RE ONE HECK OF A WOMAN.

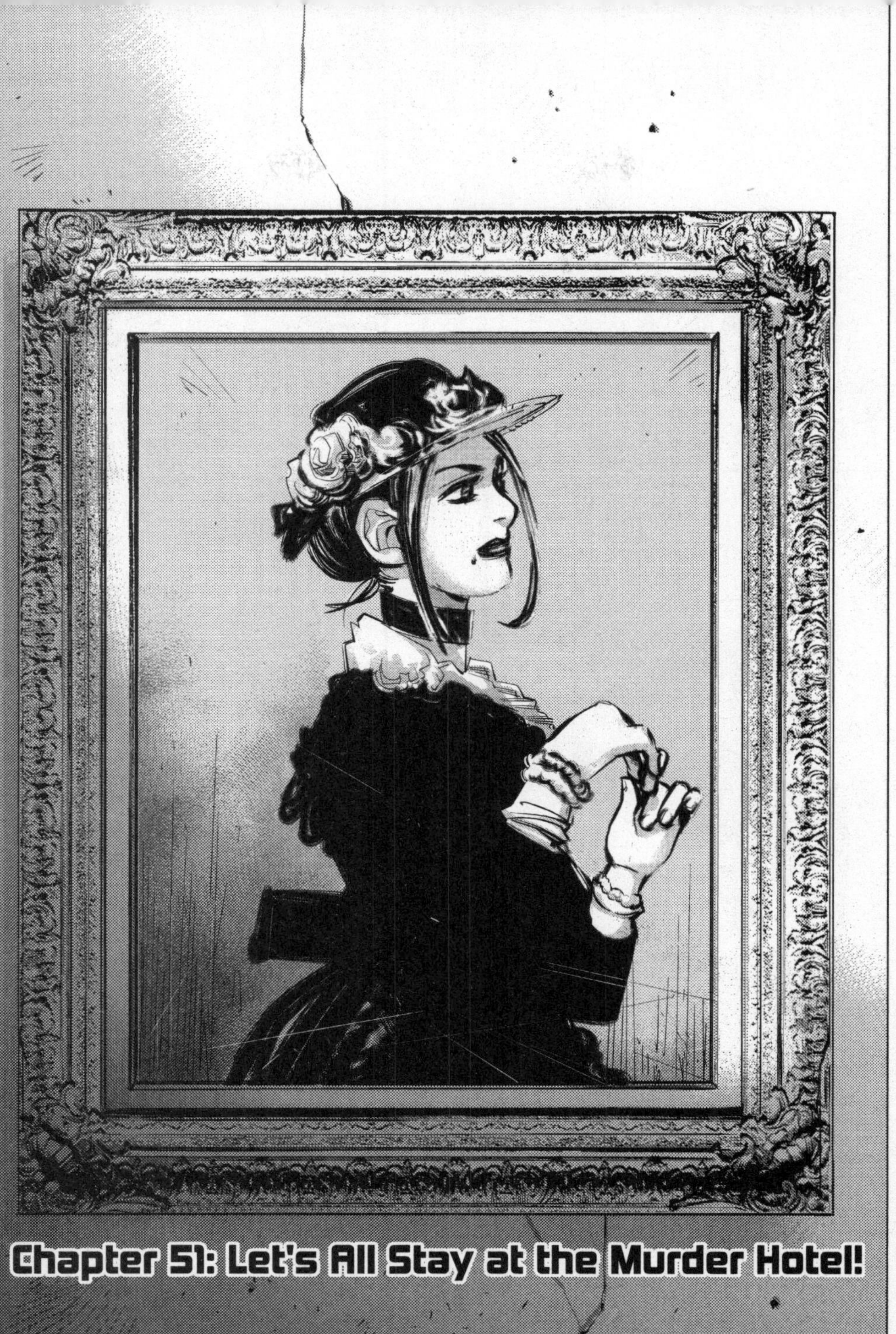

Chapter 51: Let's All Stay at the Murder Hotel!

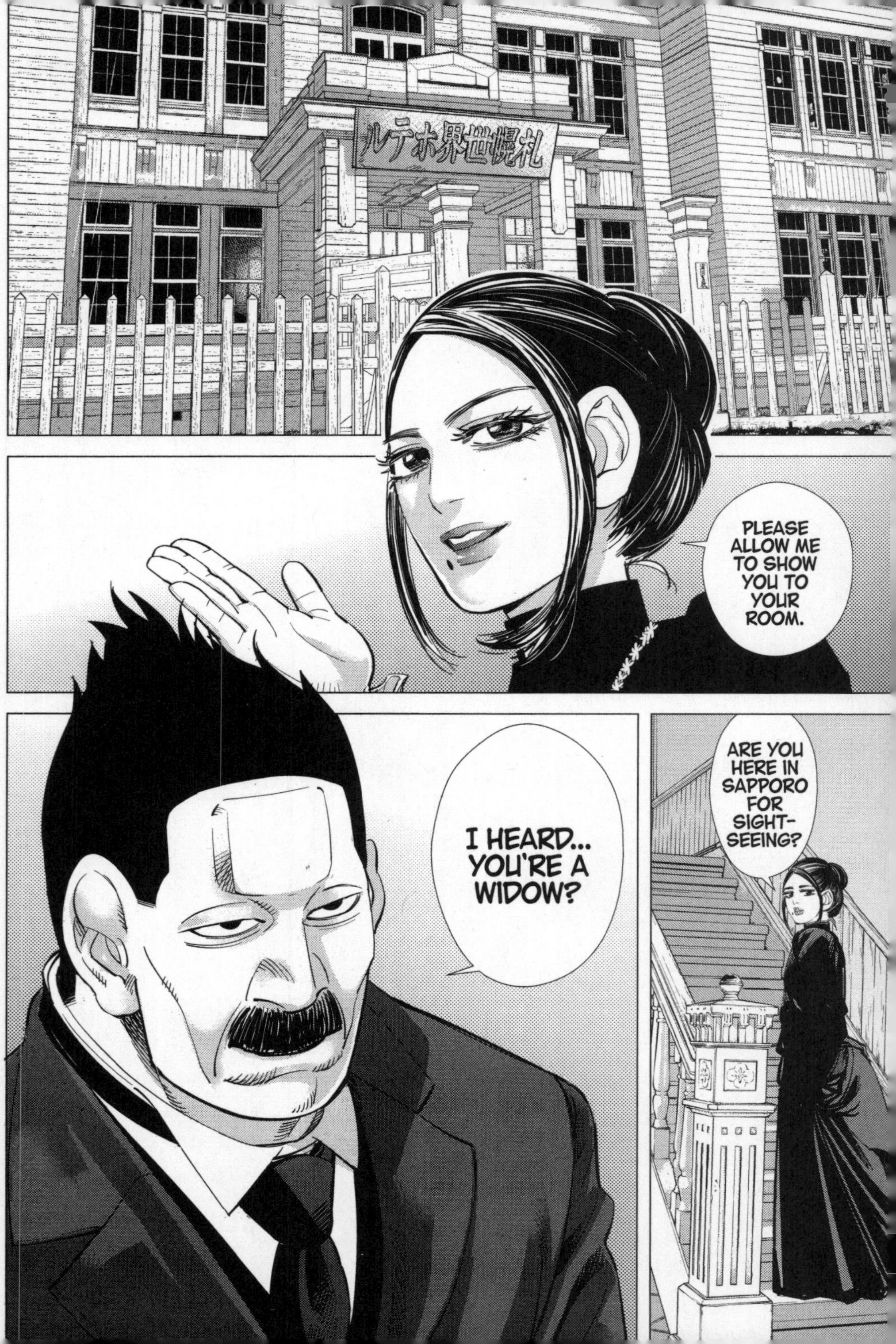
札幌世界ホテル
PLEASE ALLOW ME TO SHOW YOU TO YOUR ROOM.
ARE YOU HERE IN SAPPORO FOR SIGHT-SEEING?
I HEARD... YOU'RE A WIDOW?

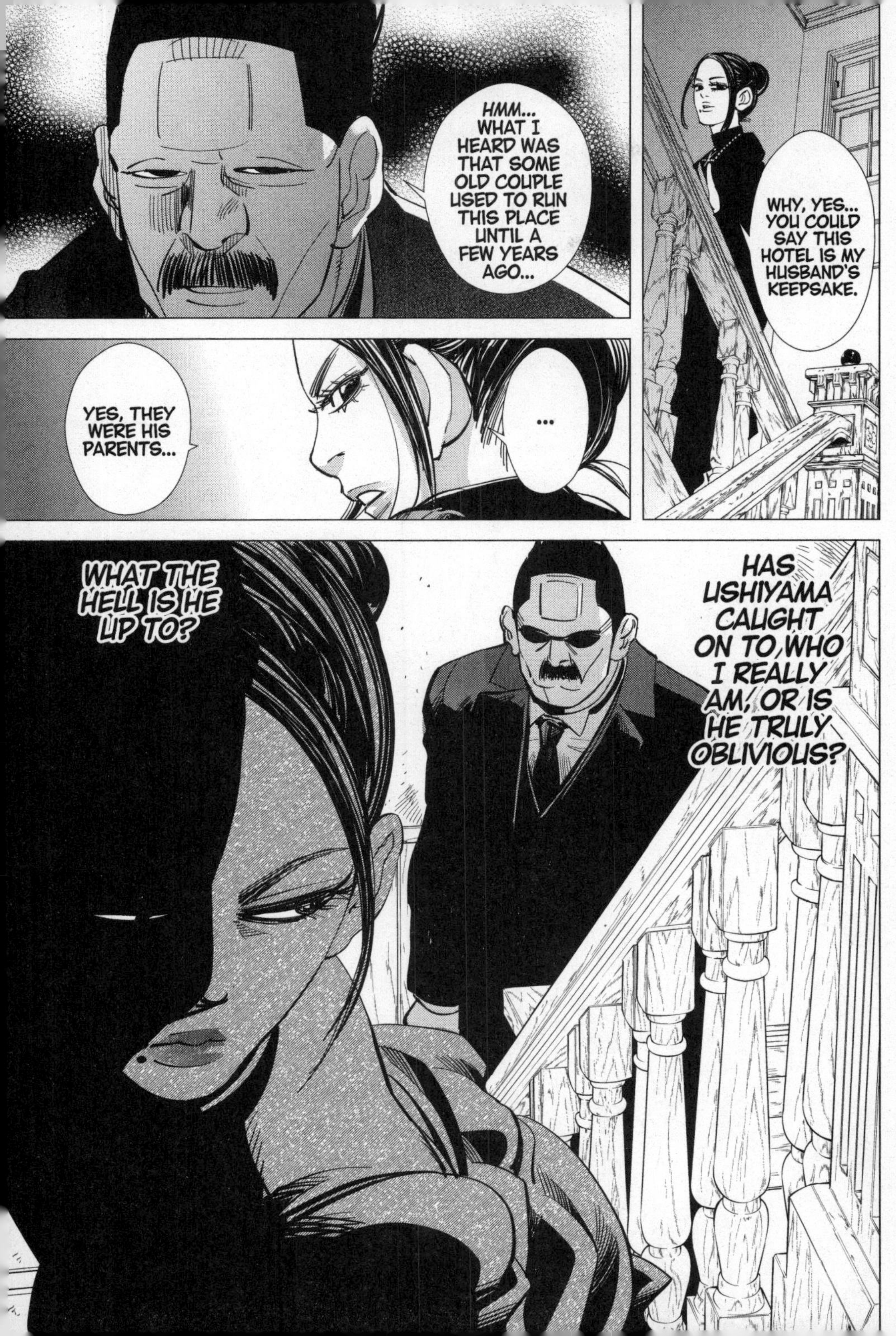
WHY, YES... YOU COULD SAY THIS HOTEL IS MY HUSBAND'S KEEPSAKE.
HMM... WHAT I HEARD WAS THAT SOME OLD COUPLE USED TO RUN THIS PLACE UNTIL A FEW YEARS AGO...
...
YES, THEY WERE HIS PARENTS...
HAS USHIYAMA CAUGHT ON TO WHO I REALLY AM, OR IS HE TRULY OBLIVIOUS?
WHAT THE HELL IS HE UP TO?

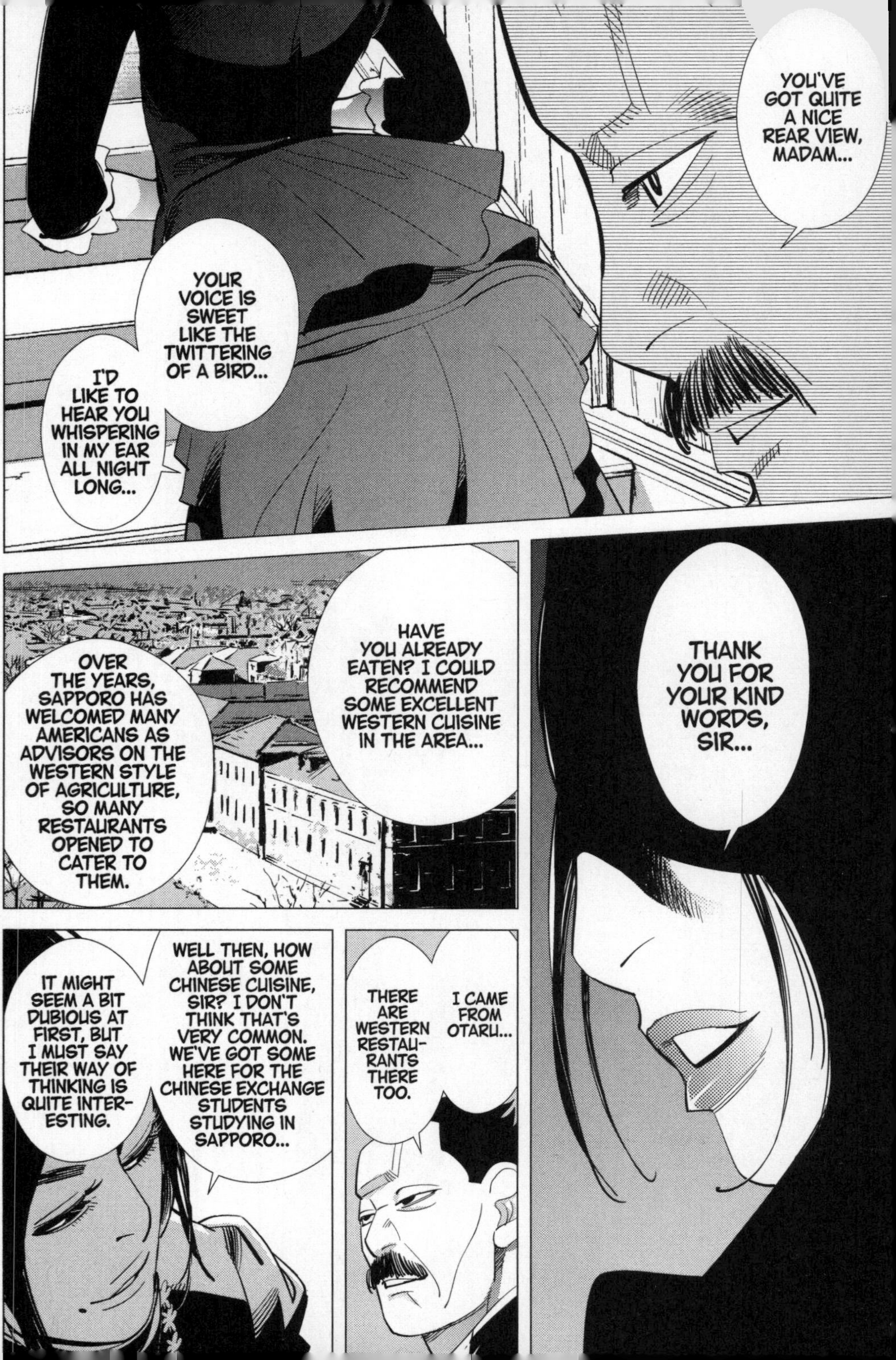
YOU'VE GOT QUITE A NICE REAR VIEW, MADAM...
YOUR VOICE IS SWEET LIKE THE TWITTERING OF A BIRD...
I'D LIKE TO HEAR YOU WHISPERING IN MY EAR ALL NIGHT LONG...
THANK YOU FOR YOUR KIND WORDS, SIR...
HAVE YOU ALREADY EATEN? I COULD RECOMMEND SOME EXCELLENT WESTERN CUISINE IN THE AREA...
OVER THE YEARS, SAPPORO HAS WELCOMED MANY AMERICANS AS ADVISORS ON THE WESTERN STYLE OF AGRICULTURE, SO MANY RESTAURANTS OPENED TO CATER TO THEM.
I CAME FROM OTARU...
THERE ARE WESTERN RESTAU-RANTS THERE TOO.
WELL THEN, HOW ABOUT SOME CHINESE CUISINE, SIR? I DON'T THINK THAT'S VERY COMMON. WE'VE GOT SOME HERE FOR THE CHINESE EXCHANGE STUDENTS STUDYING IN SAPPORO...
IT MIGHT SEEM A BIT DUBIOUS AT FIRST, BUT I MUST SAY THEIR WAY OF THINKING IS QUITE INTER-ESTING.

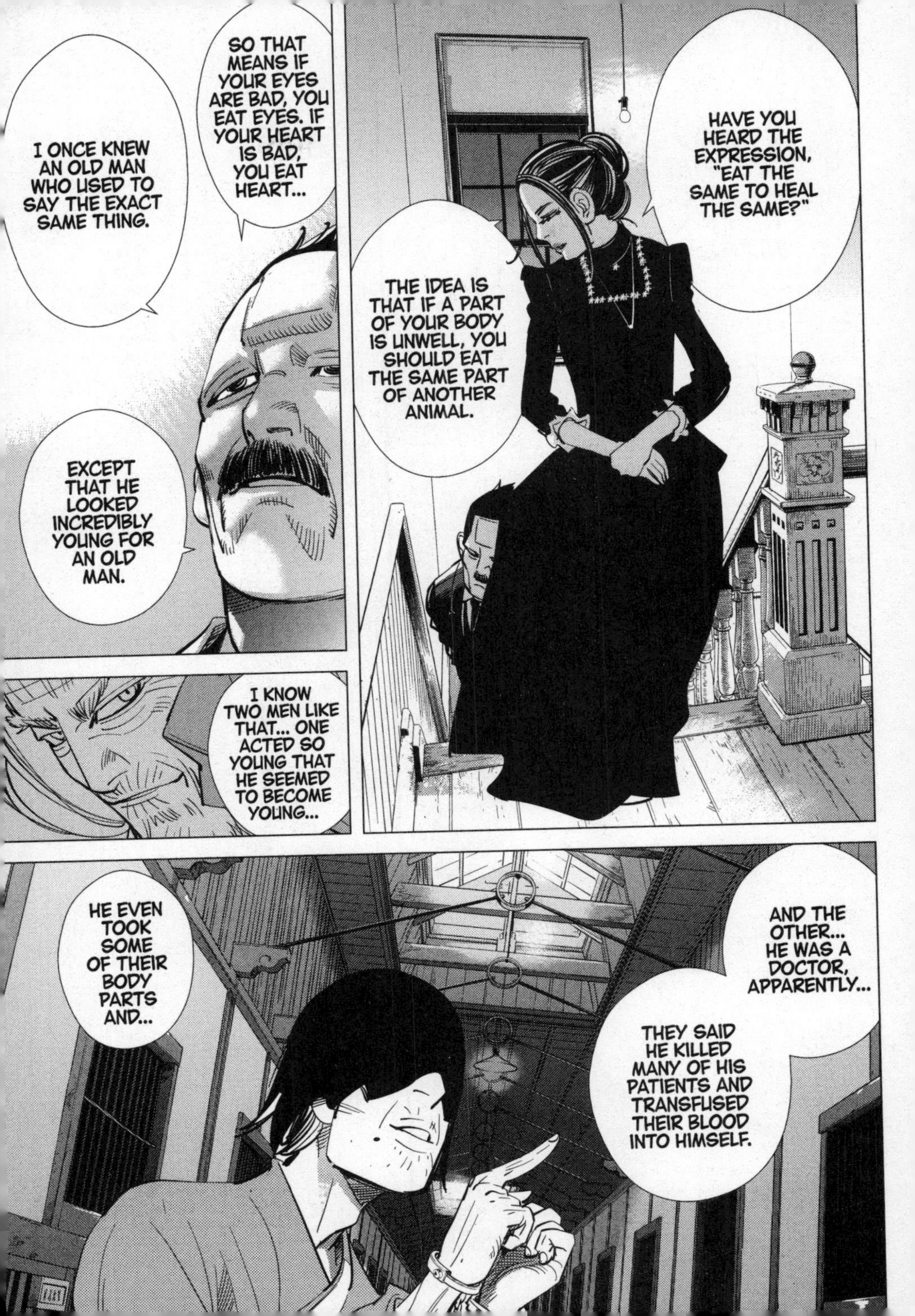
HAVE YOU HEARD THE EXPRESSION, "EAT THE SAME TO HEAL THE SAME?"
THE IDEA IS THAT IF A PART OF YOUR BODY IS UNWELL, YOU SHOULD EAT THE SAME PART OF ANOTHER ANIMAL.
SO THAT MEANS IF YOUR EYES ARE BAD, YOU EAT EYES. IF YOUR HEART IS BAD, YOU EAT HEART...
I ONCE KNEW AN OLD MAN WHO USED TO SAY THE EXACT SAME THING.
EXCEPT THAT HE LOOKED INCREDIBLY YOUNG FOR AN OLD MAN.
I KNOW TWO MEN LIKE THAT... ONE ACTED SO YOUNG THAT HE SEEMED TO BECOME YOUNG...
HE EVEN TOOK SOME OF THEIR BODY PARTS AND...
AND THE OTHER... HE WAS A DOCTOR, APPARENTLY...
THEY SAID HE KILLED MANY OF HIS PATIENTS AND TRANSFUSED THEIR BLOOD INTO HIMSELF.

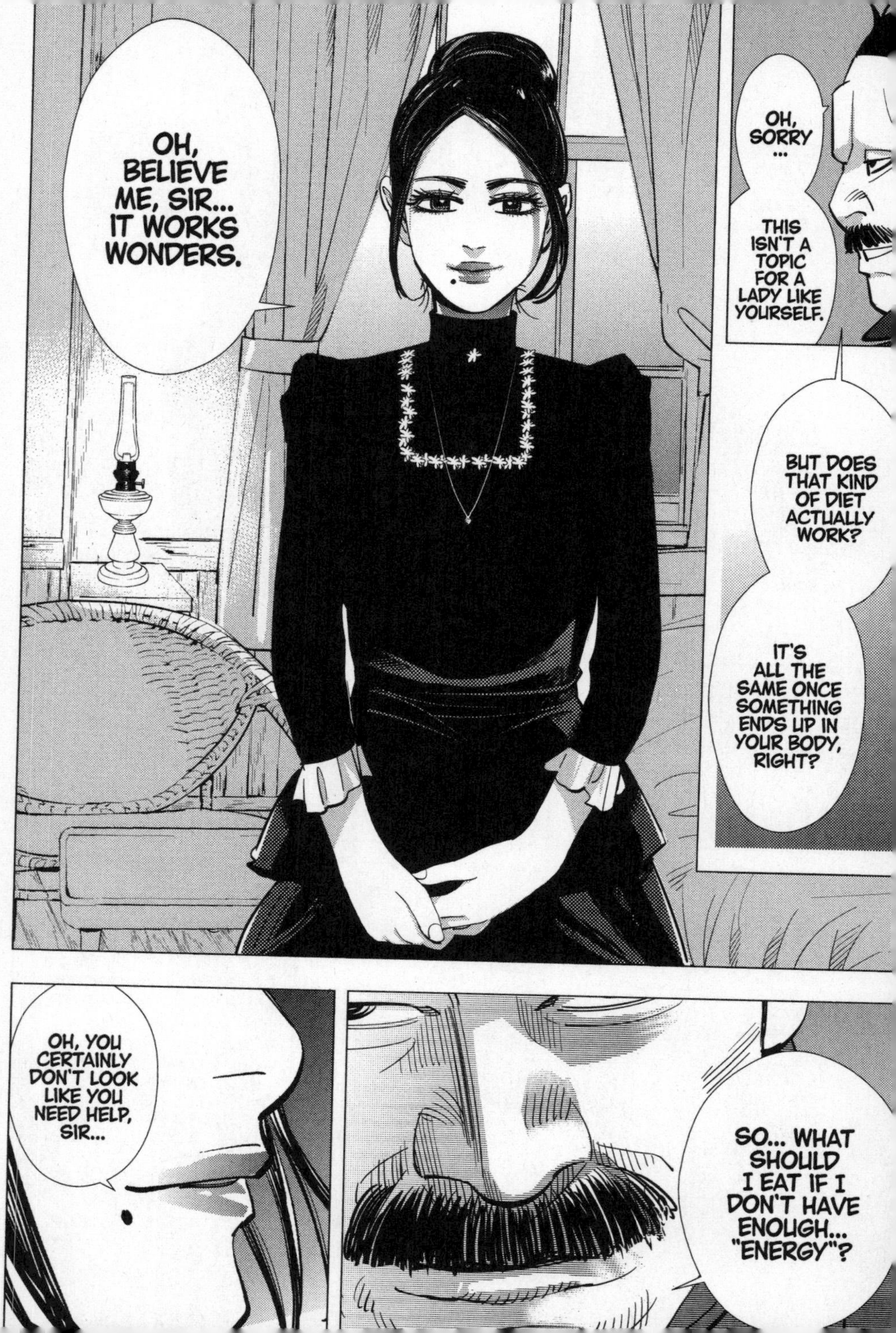
OH, SORRY...
THIS ISN'T A TOPIC FOR A LADY LIKE YOURSELF.
BUT DOES THAT KIND OF DIET ACTUALLY WORK?
IT'S ALL THE SAME ONCE SOMETHING ENDS UP IN YOUR BODY, RIGHT?
OH, BELIEVE ME, SIR... IT WORKS WONDERS.
SO... WHAT SHOULD I EAT IF I DON'T HAVE ENOUGH... "ENERGY"?
OH, YOU CERTAINLY DON'T LOOK LIKE YOU NEED HELP, SIR...

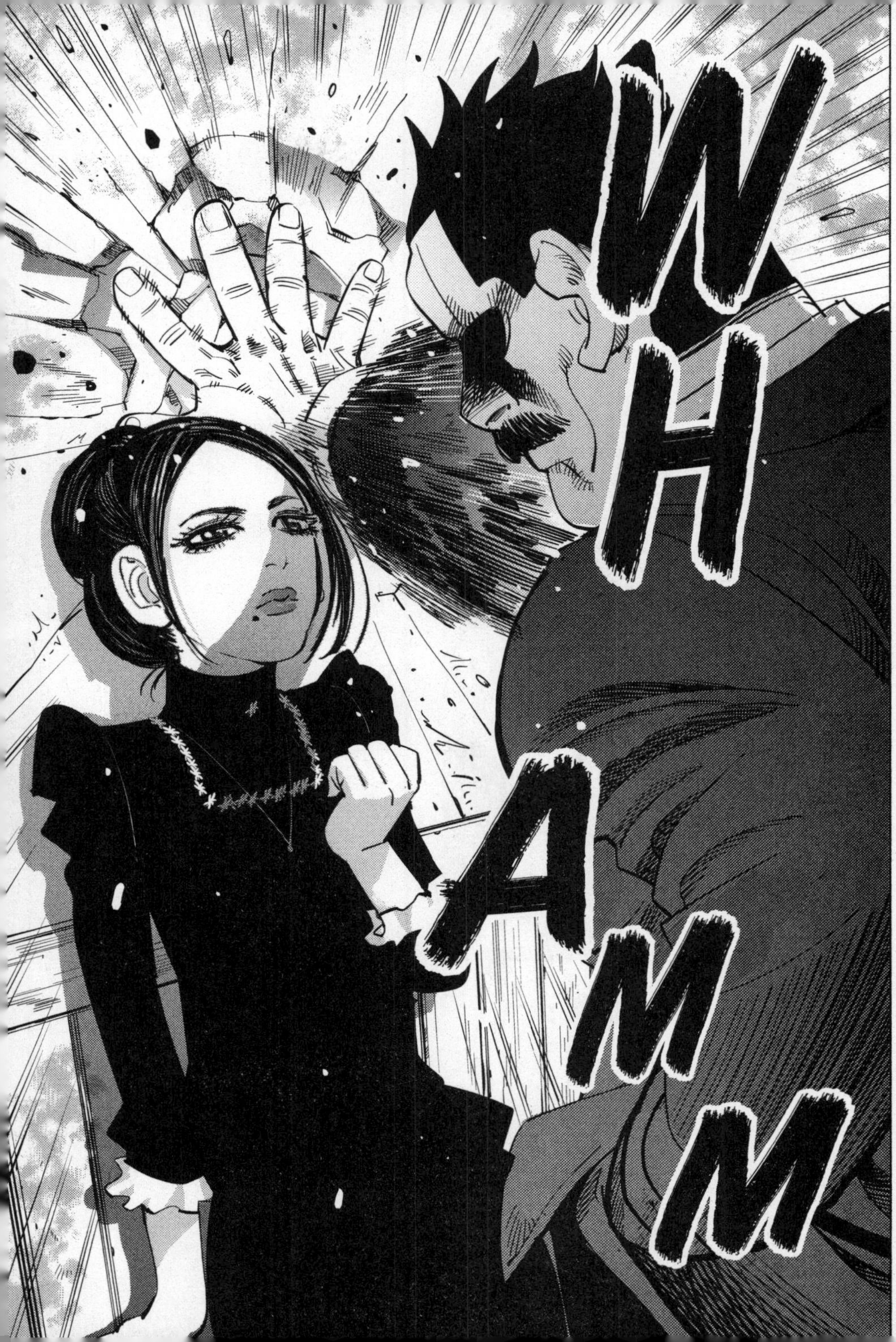
WHAMM

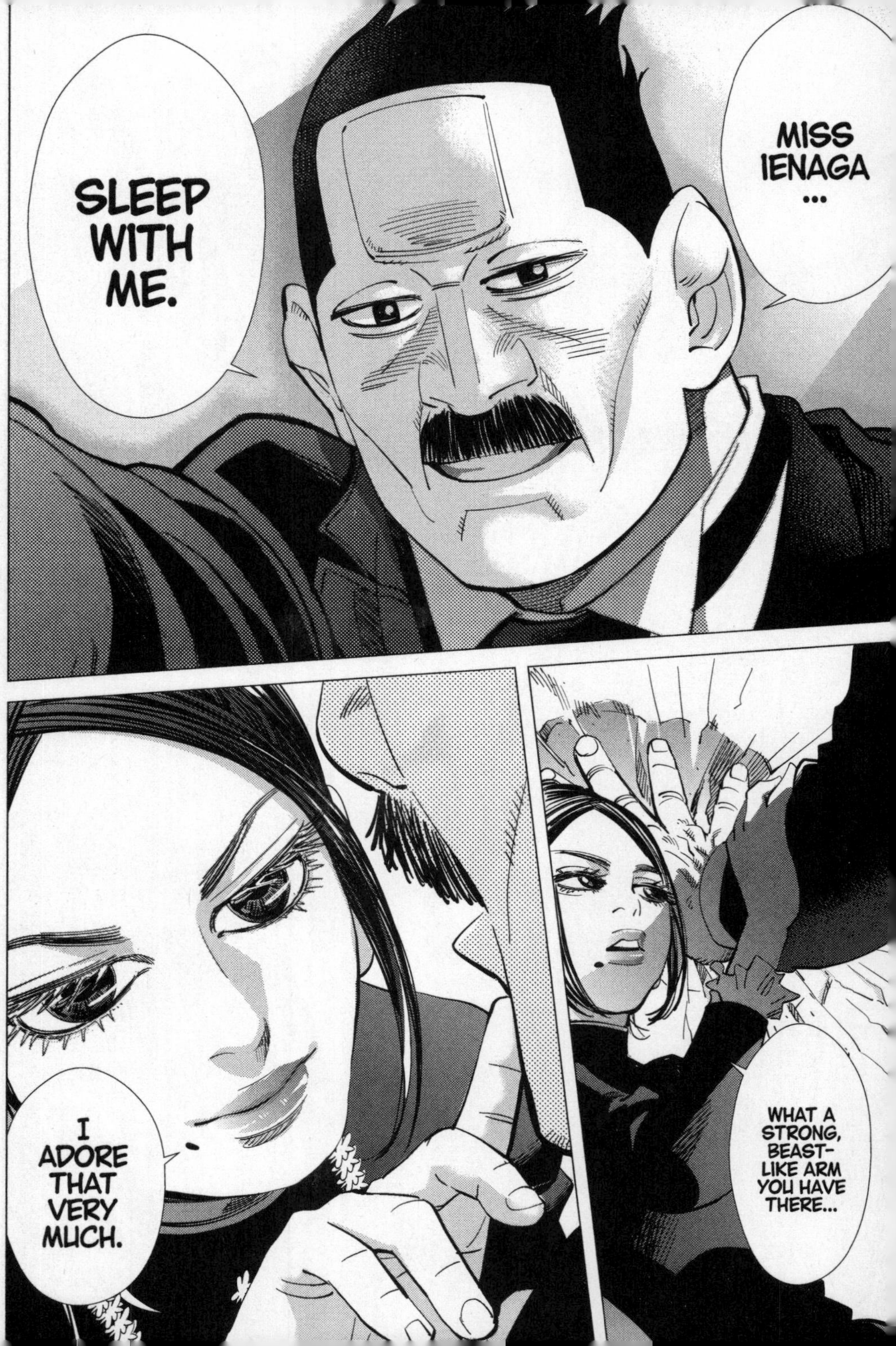
MISS IENAGA ...
SLEEP WITH ME.
WHAT A STRONG, BEAST-LIKE ARM YOU HAVE THERE...
I ADORE THAT VERY MUCH.

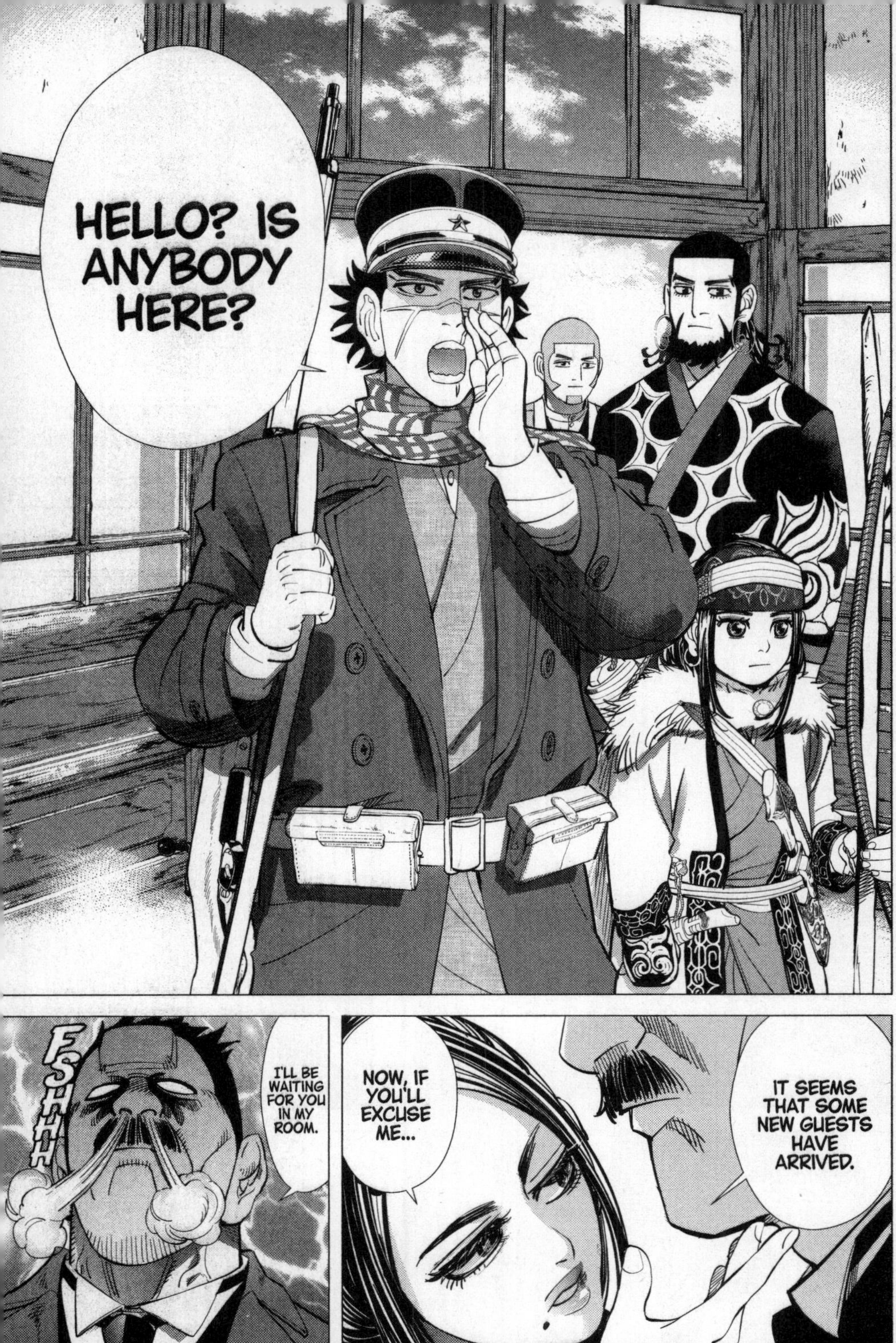
HELLO? IS ANYBODY HERE?
IT SEEMS THAT SOME NEW GUESTS HAVE ARRIVED.
NOW, IF YOU'LL EXCUSE ME...
I'LL BE WAITING FOR YOU IN MY ROOM.
FSHHH

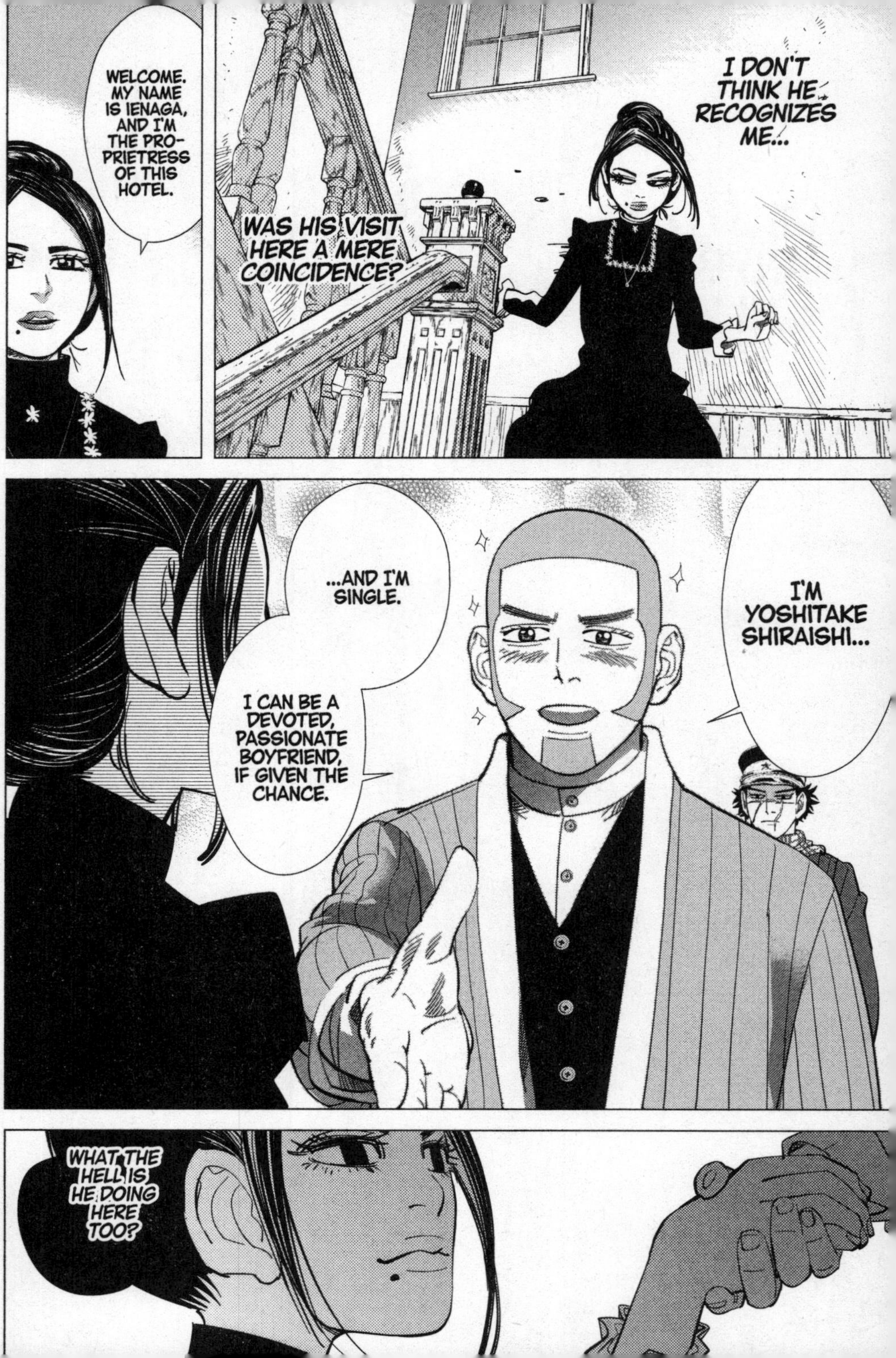
I DON'T THINK HE RECOGNIZES ME...
WAS HIS VISIT HERE A MERE COINCIDENCE?
WELCOME. MY NAME IS IENAGA, AND I'M THE PROPRIETRESS OF THIS HOTEL.
I'M YOSHITAKE SHIRAISHI...
...AND I'M SINGLE.
I CAN BE A DEVOTED, PASSIONATE BOYFRIEND, IF GIVEN THE CHANCE.
WHAT THE HELL IS HE DOING HERE TOO?

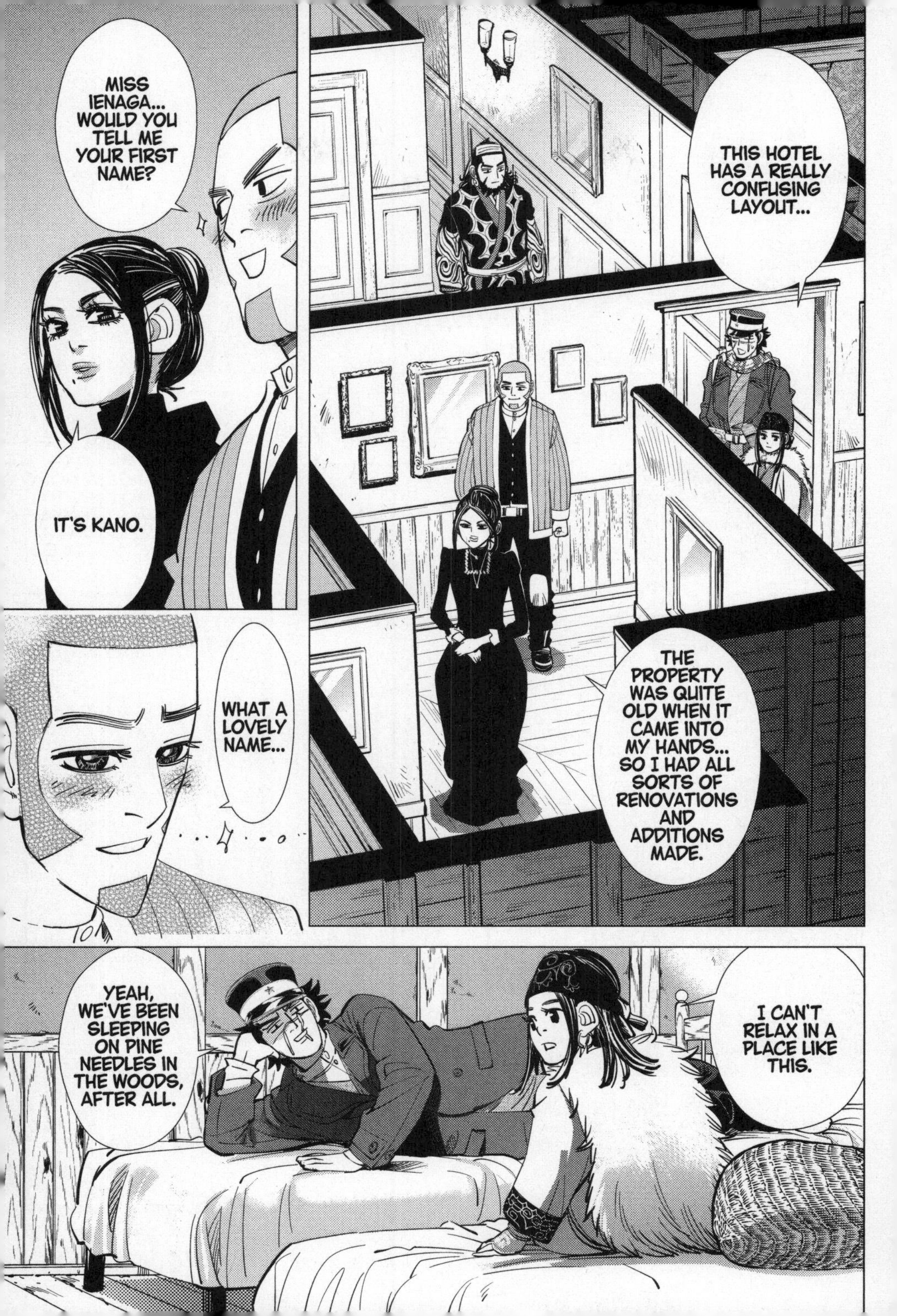
THIS HOTEL HAS A REALLY CONFUSING LAYOUT...
THE PROPERTY WAS QUITE OLD WHEN IT CAME INTO MY HANDS... SO I HAD ALL SORTS OF RENOVATIONS AND ADDITIONS MADE.
MISS IENAGA... WOULD YOU TELL ME YOUR FIRST NAME?
IT'S KANO.
WHAT A LOVELY NAME...
I CAN'T RELAX IN A PLACE LIKE THIS.
YEAH, WE'VE BEEN SLEEPING ON PINE NEEDLES IN THE WOODS, AFTER ALL.

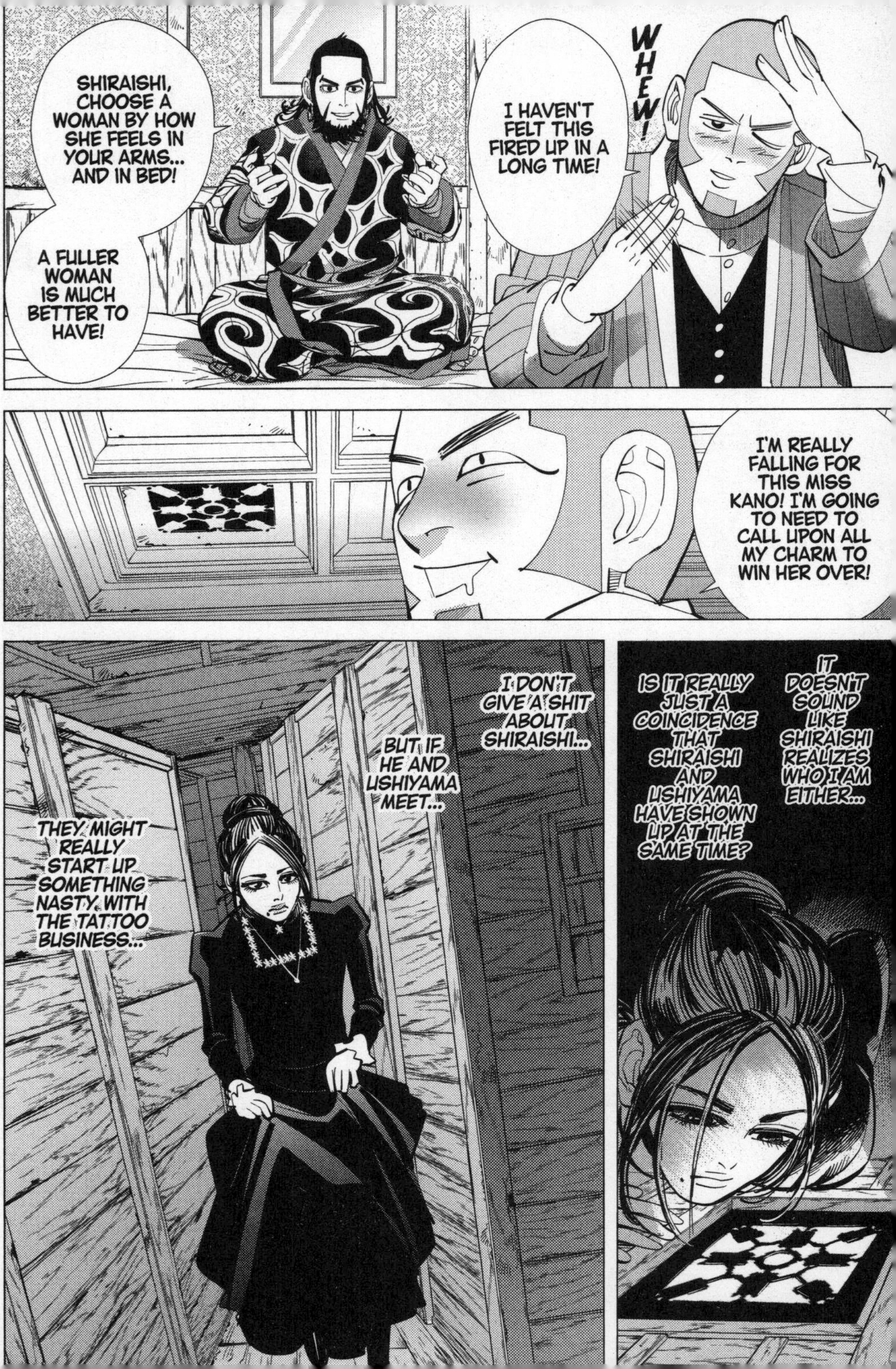
WHEW!
I HAVEN'T FELT THIS FIRED UP IN A LONG TIME!
SHIRAISHI, CHOOSE A WOMAN BY HOW SHE FEELS IN YOUR ARMS... AND IN BED!
A FULLER WOMAN IS MUCH BETTER TO HAVE!
I'M REALLY FALLING FOR THIS MISS KANO! I'M GOING TO NEED TO CALL UPON ALL MY CHARM TO WIN HER OVER!
IT DOESN'T SOUND LIKE SHIRAISHI REALIZES WHO I AM EITHER...
IS IT REALLY JUST A COINCIDENCE THAT SHIRAISHI AND USHIYAMA HAVE SHOWN UP AT THE SAME TIME?
I DON'T GIVE A SHIT ABOUT SHIRAISHI...
BUT IF HE AND USHIYAMA MEET...
THEY MIGHT REALLY START UP SOMETHING NASTY WITH THE TATTOO BUSINESS...

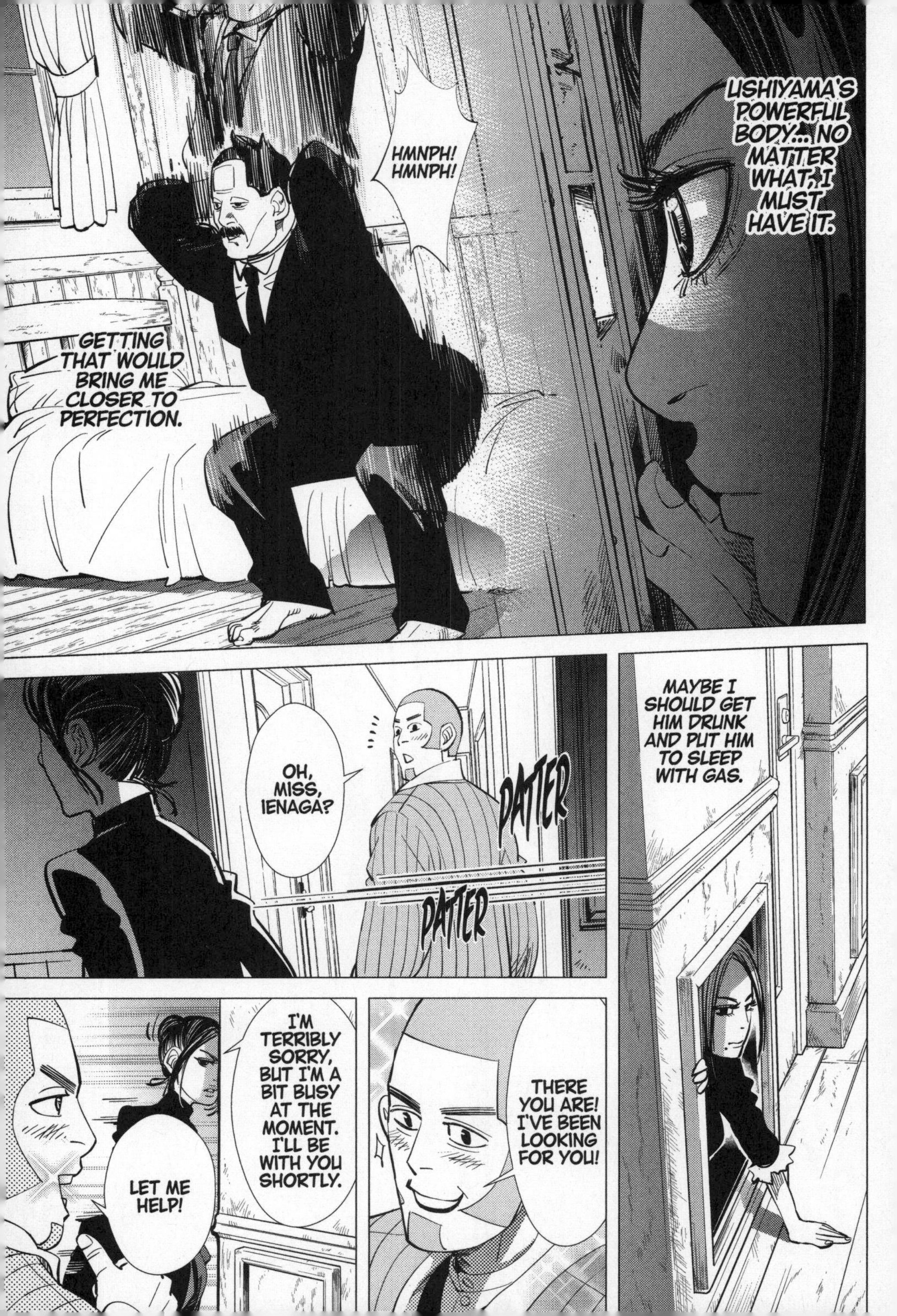

USHIYAMA'S POWERFUL BODY... NO MATTER WHAT, I MUST HAVE IT.
HMNPH! HMNPH!
GETTING THAT WOULD BRING ME CLOSER TO PERFECTION.
MAYBE I SHOULD GET HIM DRUNK AND PUT HIM TO SLEEP WITH GAS.
OH, MISS, IENAGA?
PATTER
PATTER
THERE YOU ARE! I'VE BEEN LOOKING FOR YOU!
I'M TERRIBLY SORRY, BUT I'M A BIT BUSY AT THE MOMENT. I'LL BE WITH YOU SHORTLY.
LET ME HELP!

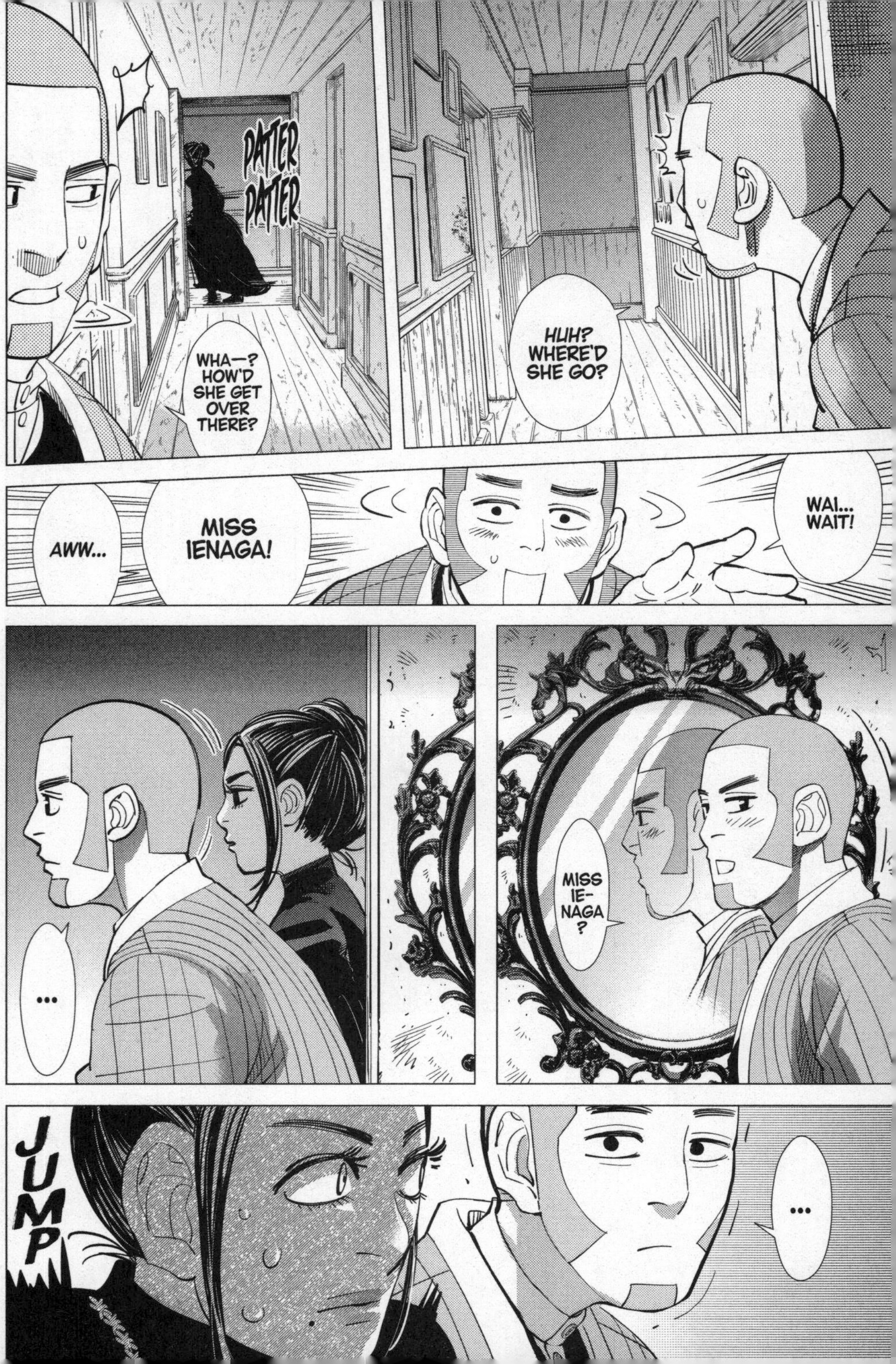
HUH? WHERE'D SHE GO?
PATTER PATTER
WHA—? HOW'D SHE GET OVER THERE?
WAI... WAIT!
MISS IENAGA!
AWW...
MISS IE-NAGA?
...
...
JUMP

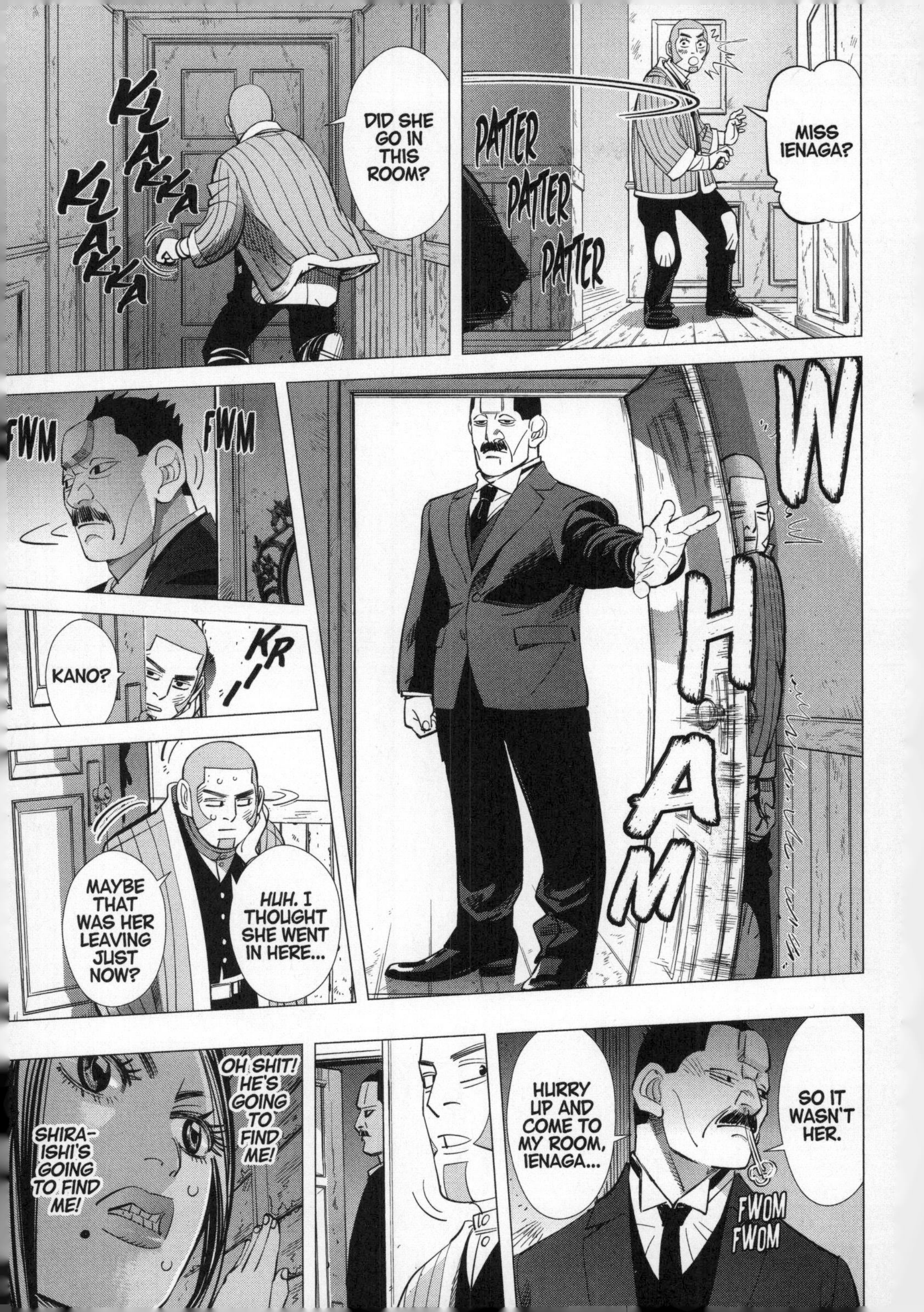
MISS IENAGA?
PATTER PATTER PATTER
DID SHE GO IN THIS ROOM?
KLAKKA KLAKKA
WHAM
FWM FWM
KANO?
KR-I-I
HUH. I THOUGHT SHE WENT IN HERE...
MAYBE THAT WAS HER LEAVING JUST NOW?
SO IT WASN'T HER.
FWOM FWOM
HURRY UP AND COME TO MY ROOM, IENAGA...
OH SHIT! HE'S GOING TO FIND ME!
SHIRA-ISHI'S GOING TO FIND ME!

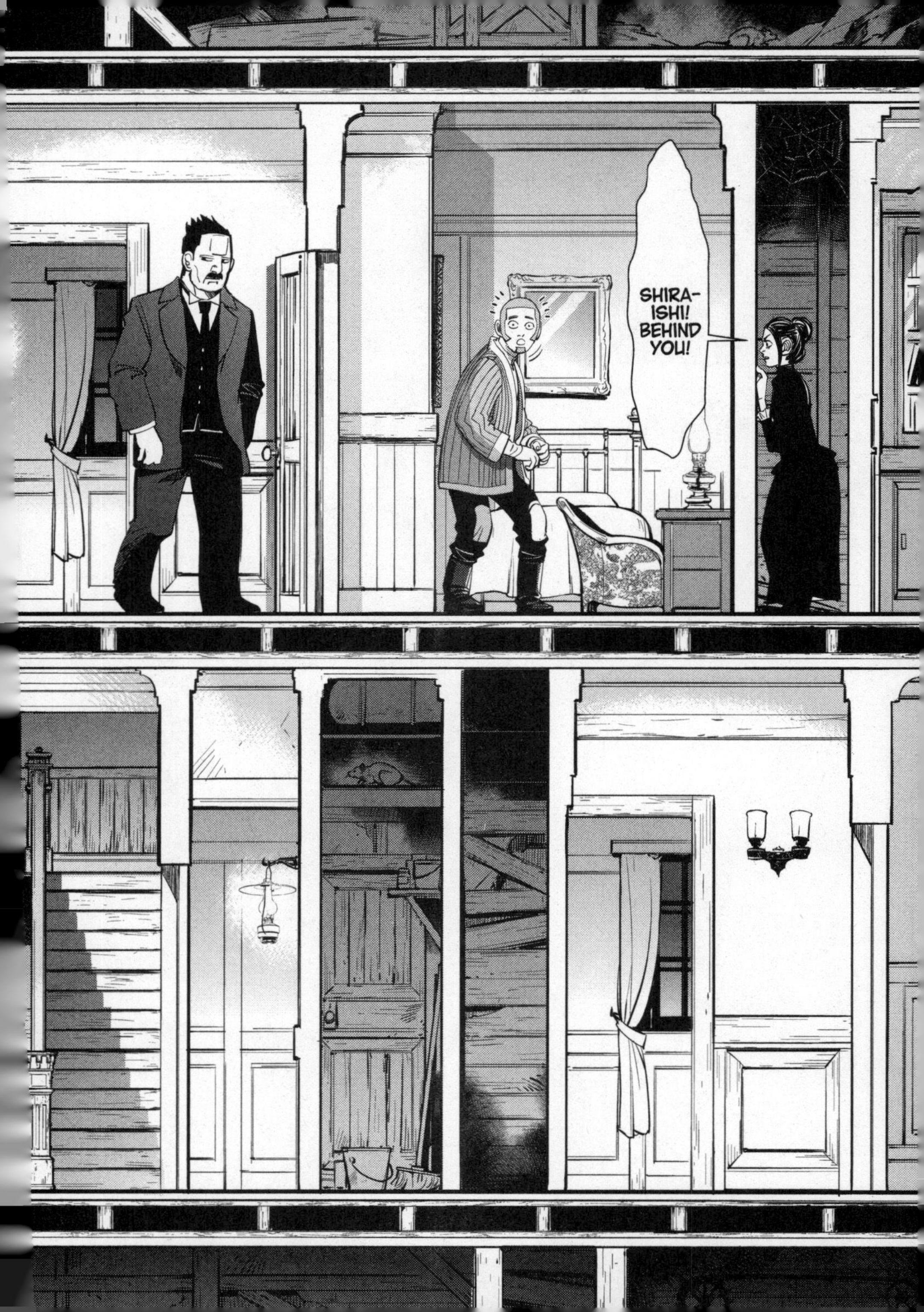
SHIRA-ISHI! BEHIND YOU!

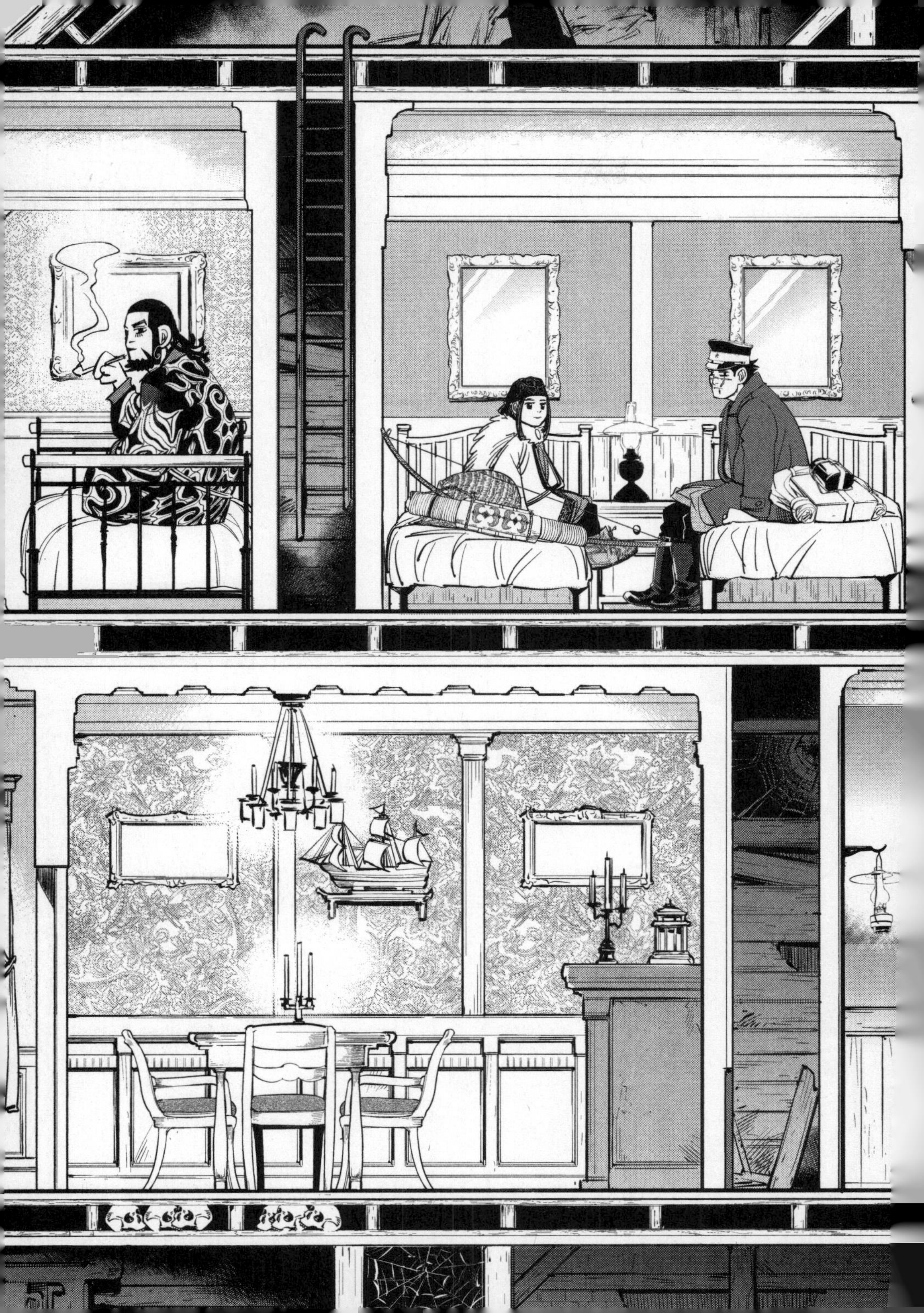

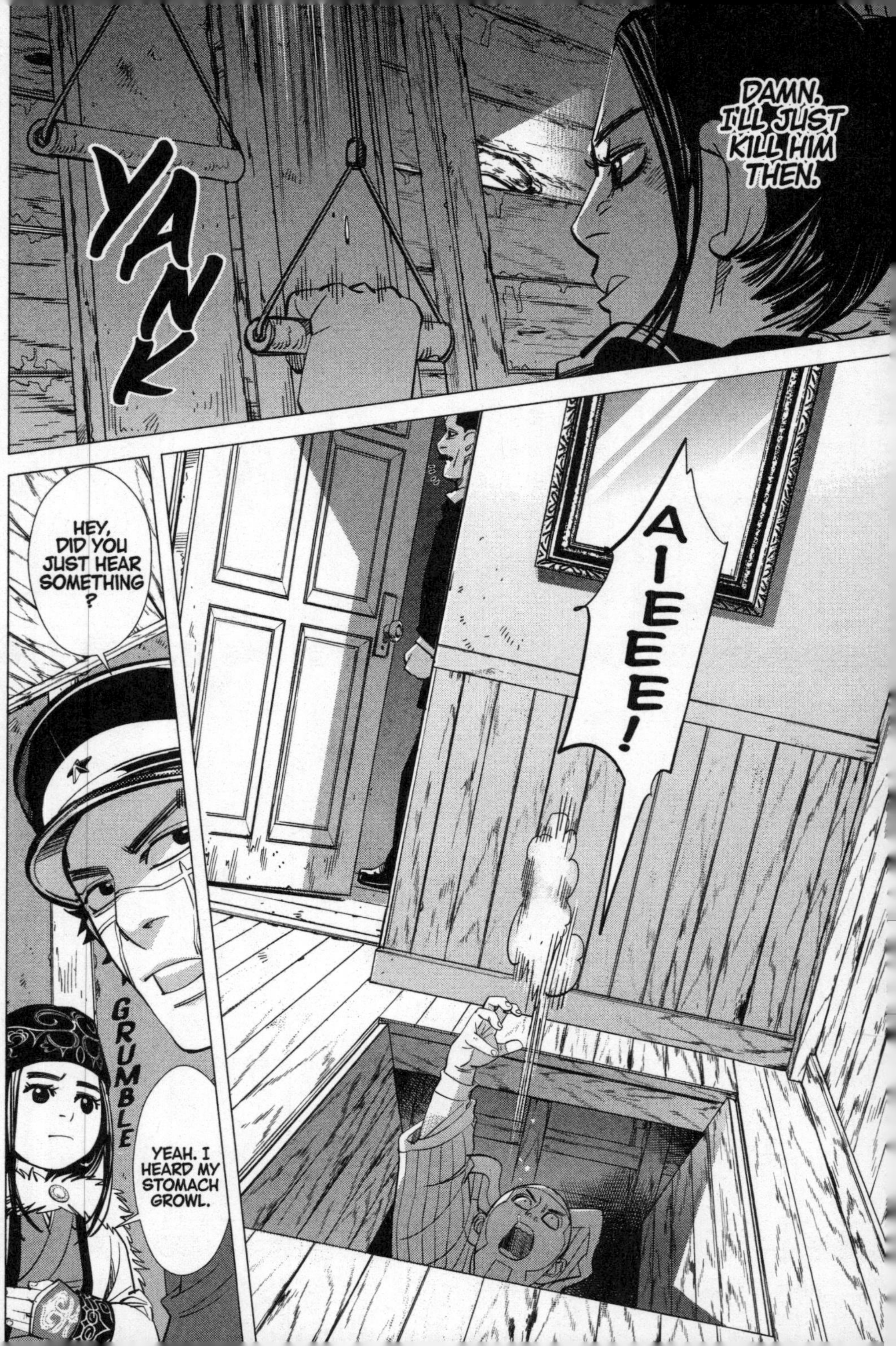
DAMN. I'LL JUST KILL HIM THEN.
YANK
AIEEE!
HEY, DID YOU JUST HEAR SOMETHING?
GRUMBLE
YEAH. I HEARD MY STOMACH GROWL.

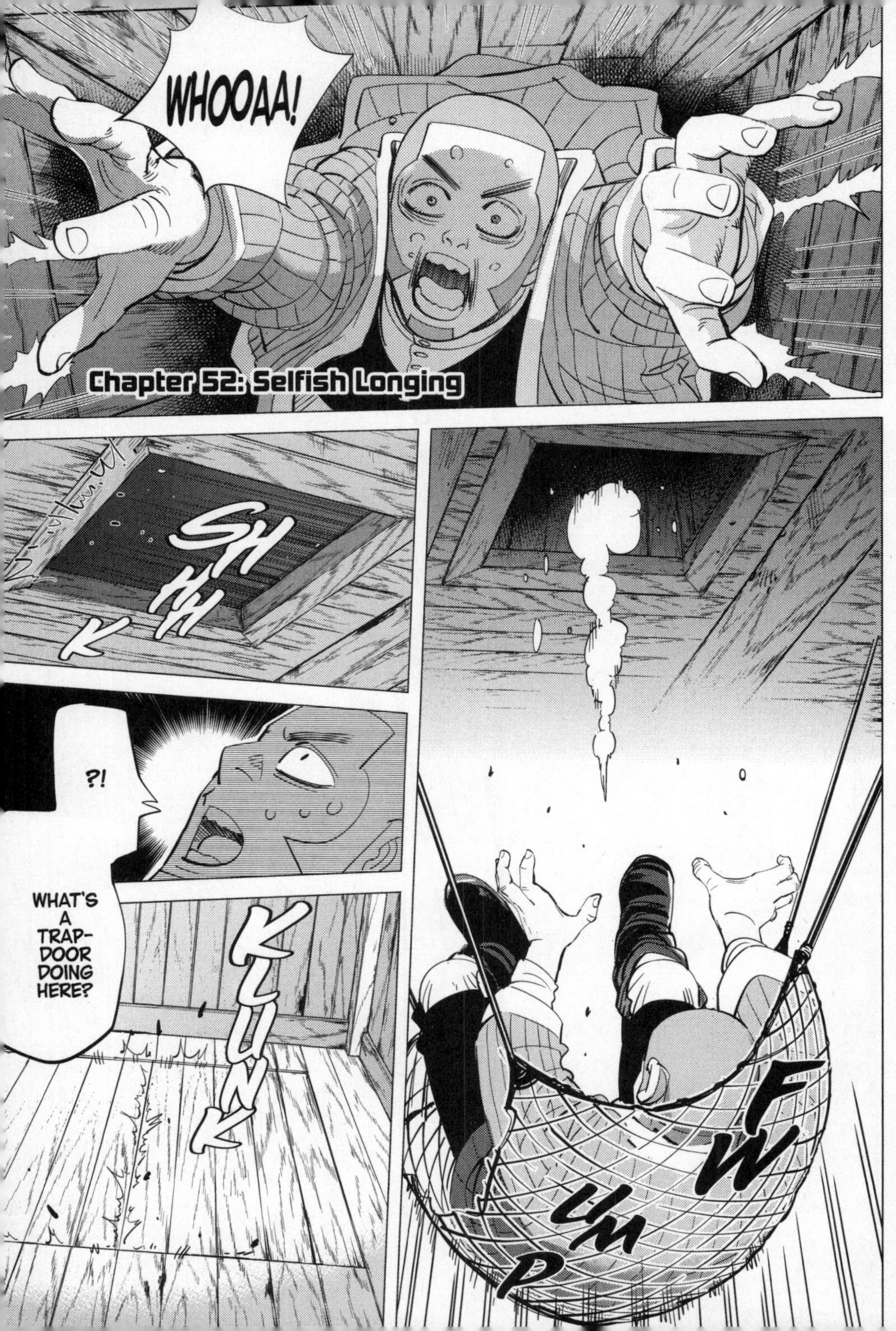
WHOOAA!
Chapter 52: Selfish Longing
FWUMP
SHHHK
?!
WHAT'S A TRAP-DOOR DOING HERE?
KLUNK

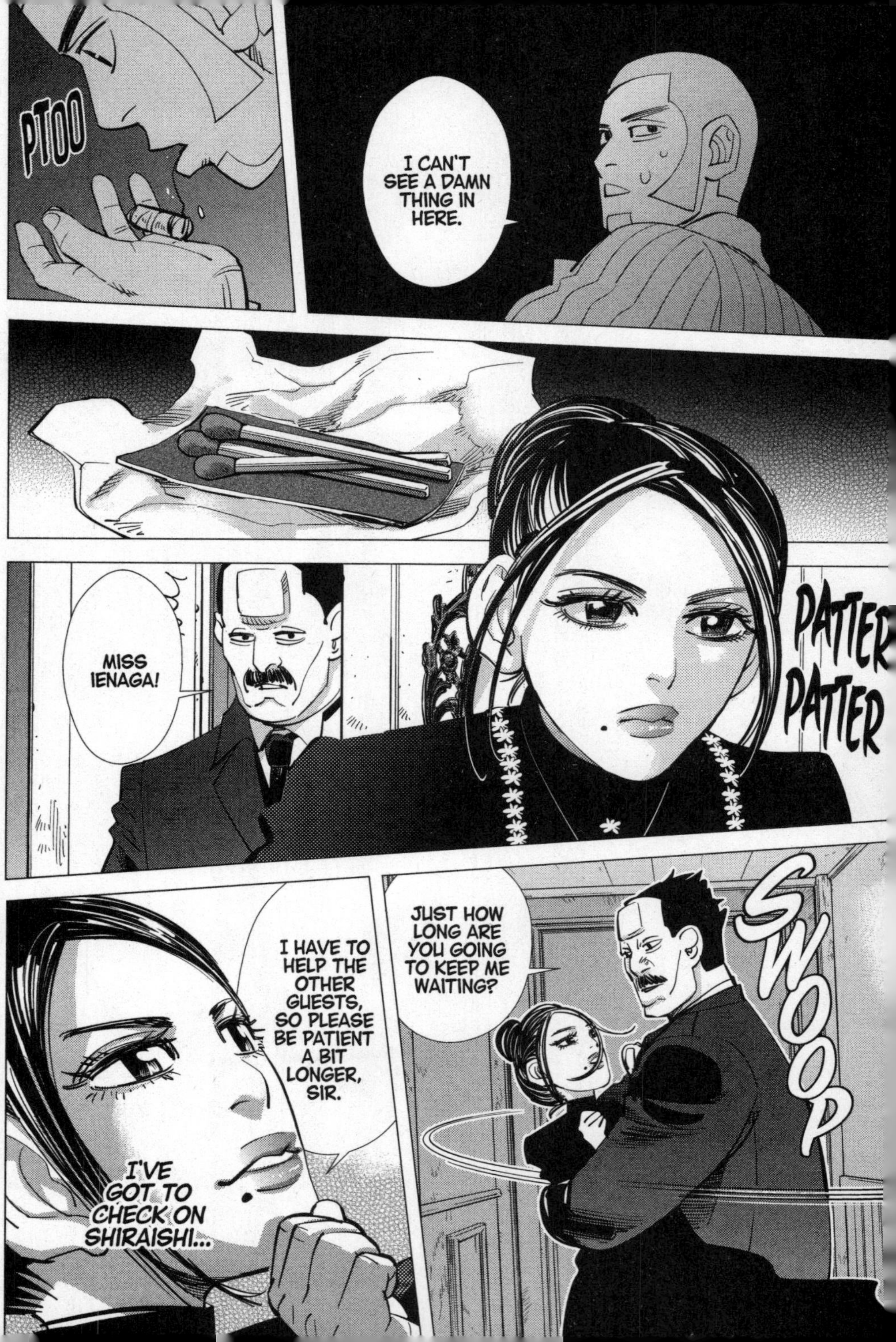
I CAN'T SEE A DAMN THING IN HERE.
PTOO
PATTER PATTER
MISS IENAGA!
SWOOP
JUST HOW LONG ARE YOU GOING TO KEEP ME WAITING?
I HAVE TO HELP THE OTHER GUESTS, SO PLEASE BE PATIENT A BIT LONGER, SIR.
I'VE GOT TO CHECK ON SHIRAISHI...

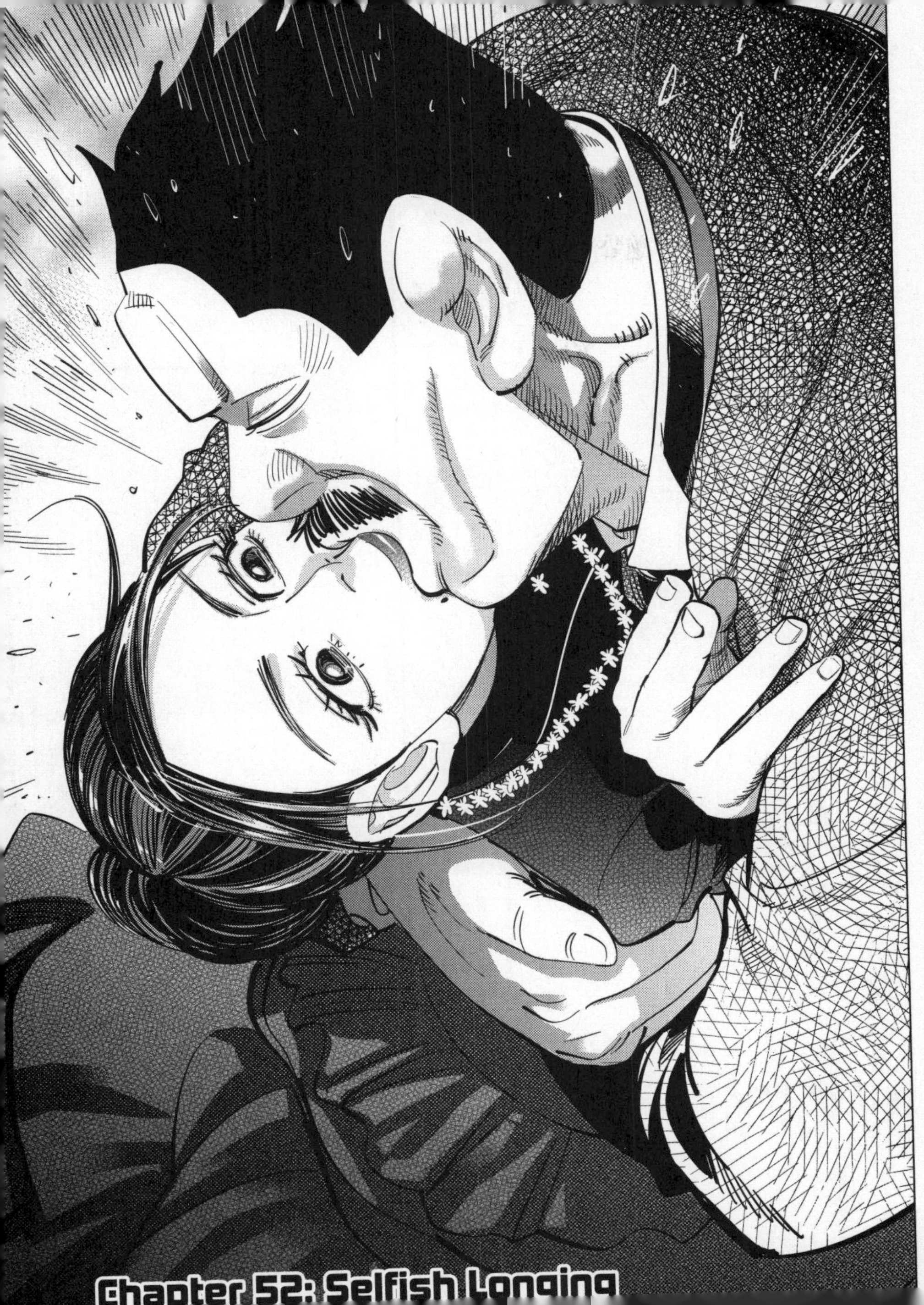

Chapter 52: Selfish Longing

LICK

DIDN'T YOU HEAR WHAT I SAID?

SHP

DRIBBLE

CRUMBLE

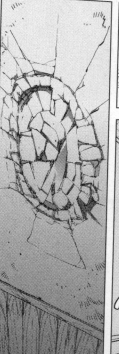

PATTER PATTER

SLAM

INCREDIBLE. I CAN'T TAKE IT ANYMORE...

I NEED TO STEP OUTSIDE TO COOL MY HEAD.

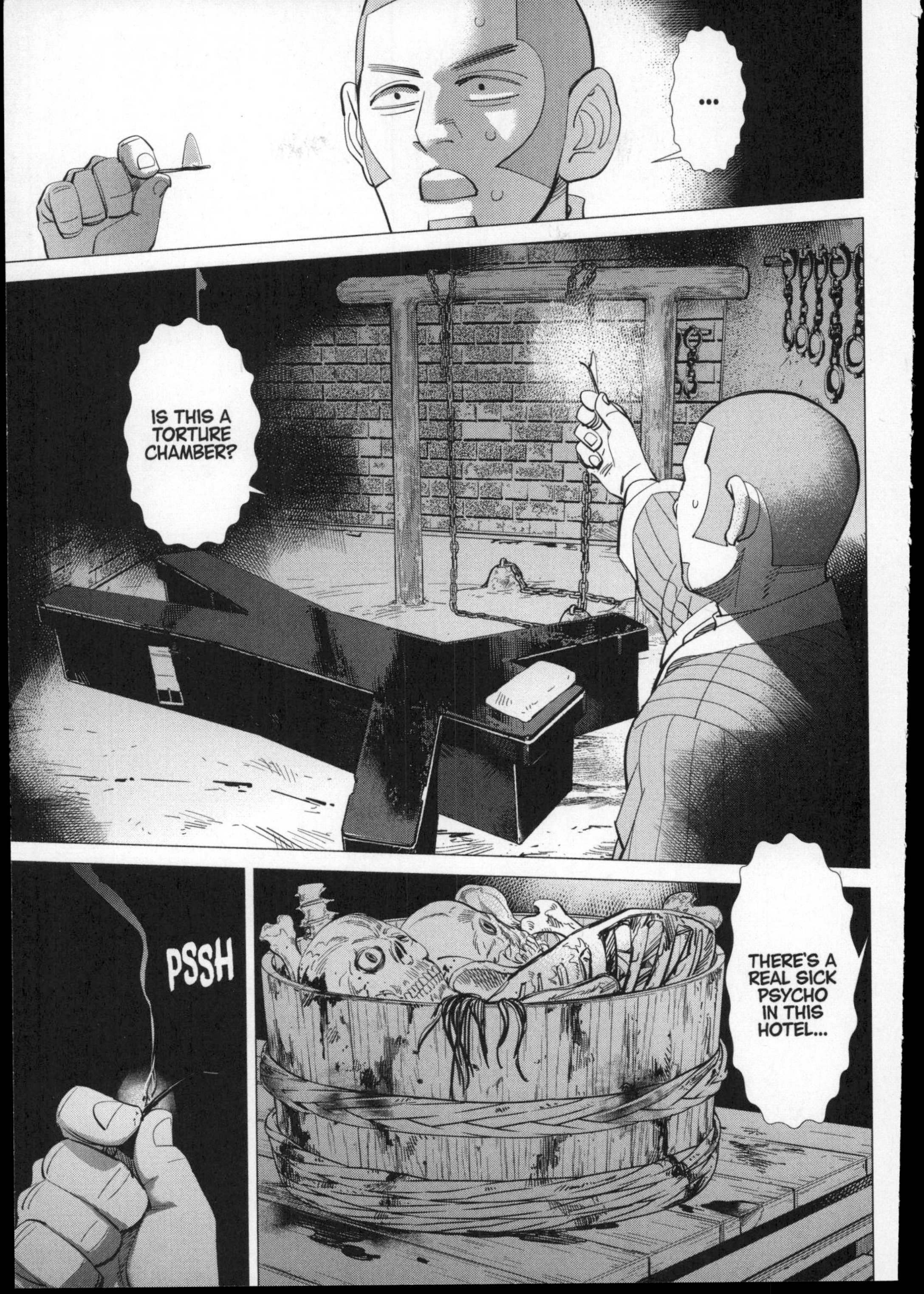
...
IS THIS A TORTURE CHAMBER?
THERE'S A REAL SICK PSYCHO IN THIS HOTEL...
PSSH

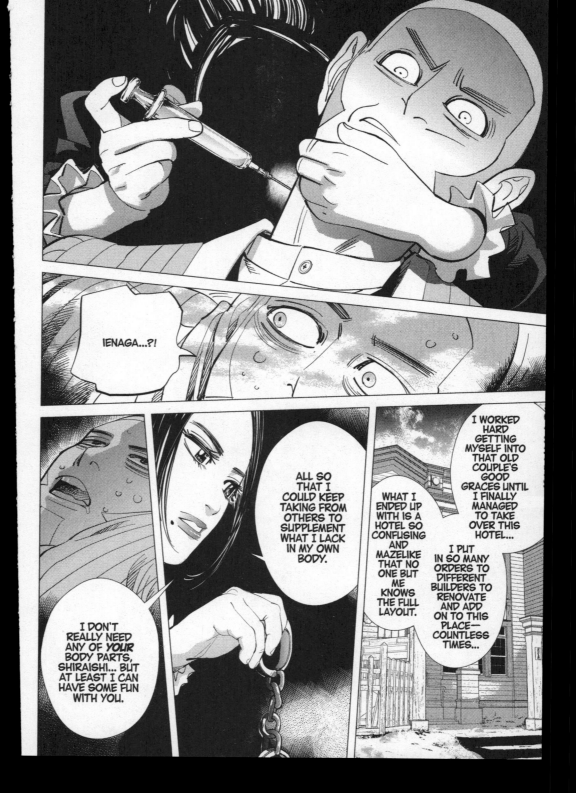

IENAGA...?!
I WORKED HARD GETTING MYSELF INTO THAT OLD COUPLE'S GOOD GRACES UNTIL I FINALLY MANAGED TO TAKE OVER THIS HOTEL...
I PUT IN SO MANY ORDERS TO DIFFERENT BUILDERS TO RENOVATE AND ADD ON TO THIS PLACE— COUNTLESS TIMES...
WHAT I ENDED UP WITH IS A HOTEL SO CONFUSING AND MAZELIKE THAT NO ONE BUT ME KNOWS THE FULL LAYOUT.
ALL SO THAT I COULD KEEP TAKING FROM OTHERS TO SUPPLEMENT WHAT I LACK IN MY OWN BODY.
I DON'T REALLY NEED ANY OF *YOUR* BODY PARTS, SHIRAISHI... BUT AT LEAST I CAN HAVE SOME FUN WITH YOU.

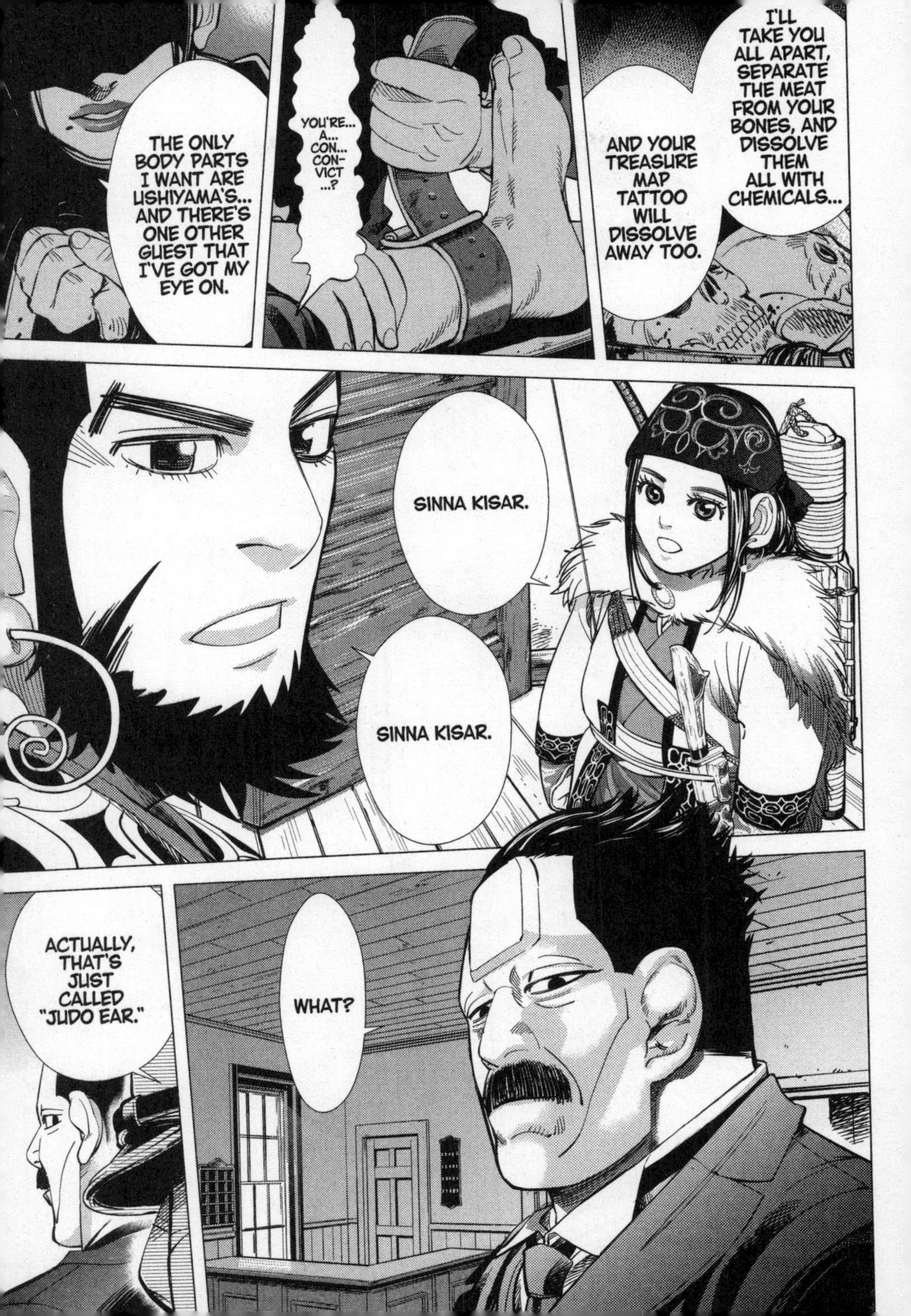
I'LL TAKE YOU ALL APART, SEPARATE THE MEAT FROM YOUR BONES, AND DISSOLVE THEM ALL WITH CHEMICALS...
AND YOUR TREASURE MAP TATTOO WILL DISSOLVE AWAY TOO.
YOU'RE... A... CON... CON-VICT ...?
THE ONLY BODY PARTS I WANT ARE USHIYAMA'S... AND THERE'S ONE OTHER GUEST THAT I'VE GOT MY EYE ON.
SINNA KISAR.
SINNA KISAR.
WHAT?
ACTUALLY, THAT'S JUST CALLED "JUDO EAR."

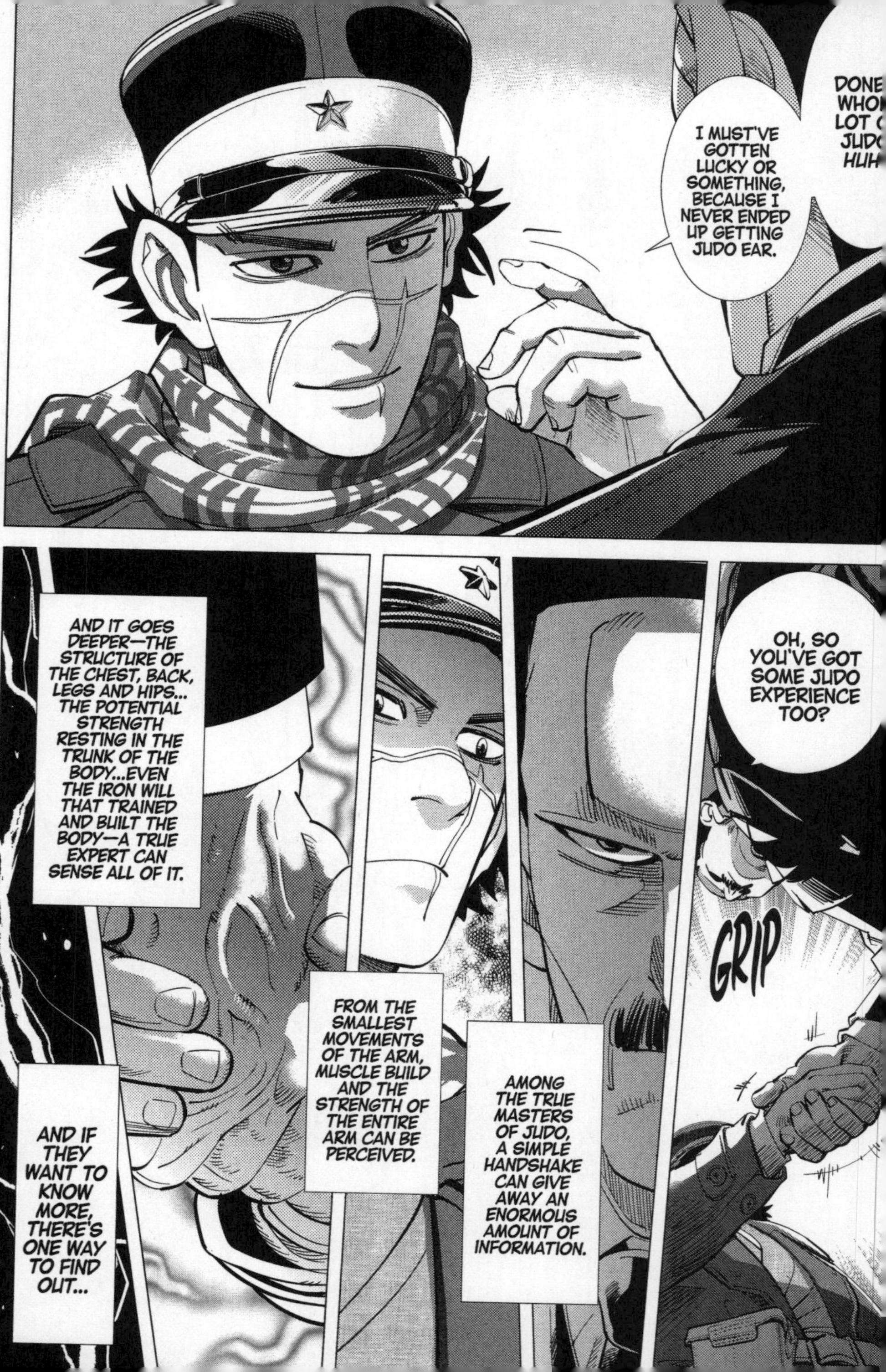

I MUST'VE GOTTEN LUCKY OR SOMETHING, BECAUSE I NEVER ENDED UP GETTING JUDO EAR.
OH, SO YOU'VE GOT SOME JUDO EXPERIENCE TOO?
GRIP
AMONG THE TRUE MASTERS OF JUDO, A SIMPLE HANDSHAKE CAN GIVE AWAY AN ENORMOUS AMOUNT OF INFORMATION.
FROM THE SMALLEST MOVEMENTS OF THE ARM, MUSCLE BUILD AND THE STRENGTH OF THE ENTIRE ARM CAN BE PERCEIVED.
AND IT GOES DEEPER—THE STRUCTURE OF THE CHEST, BACK, LEGS AND HIPS... THE POTENTIAL STRENGTH RESTING IN THE TRUNK OF THE BODY...EVEN THE IRON WILL THAT TRAINED AND BUILT THE BODY—A TRUE EXPERT CAN SENSE ALL OF IT.
AND IF THEY WANT TO KNOW MORE, THERE'S ONE WAY TO FIND OUT...

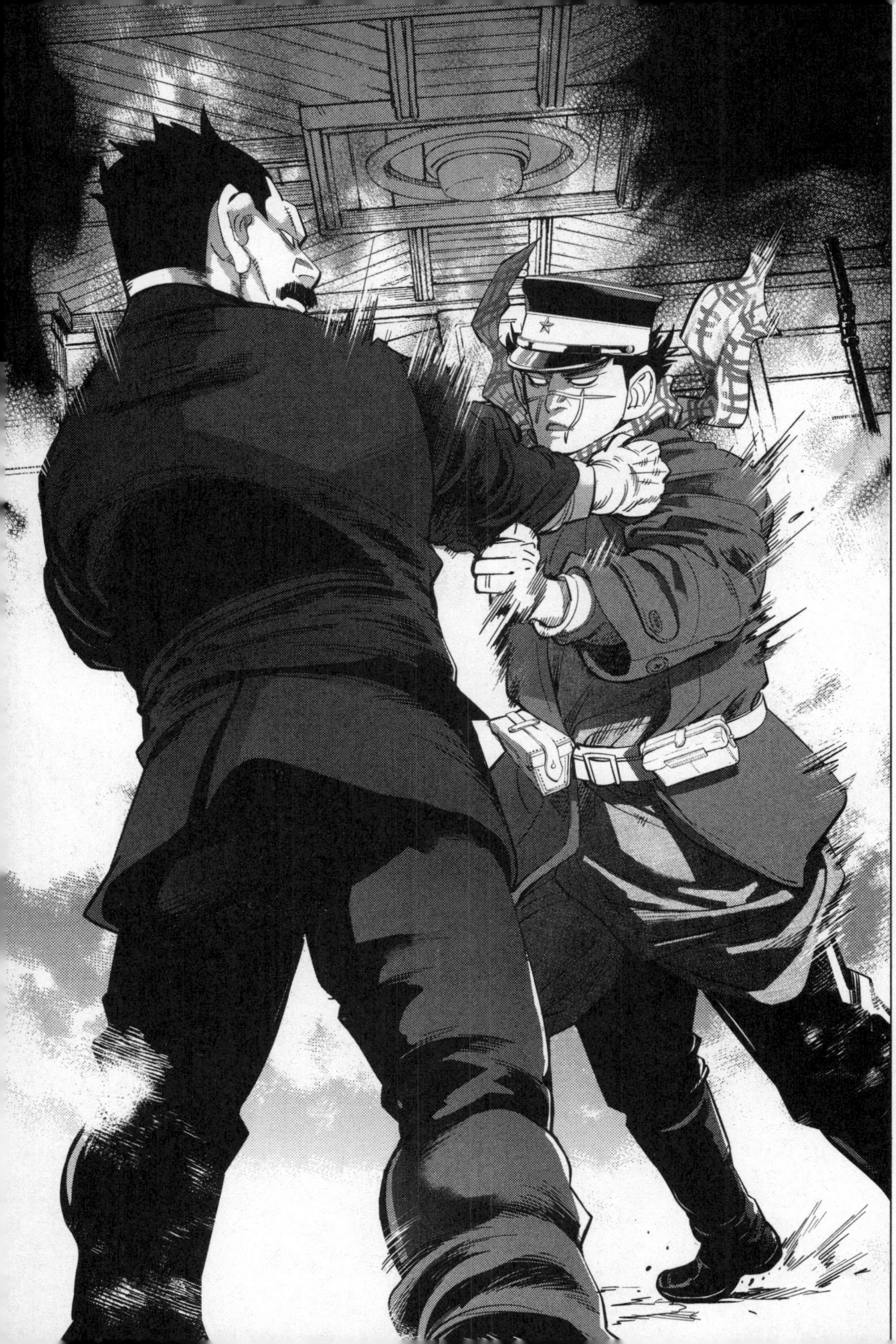

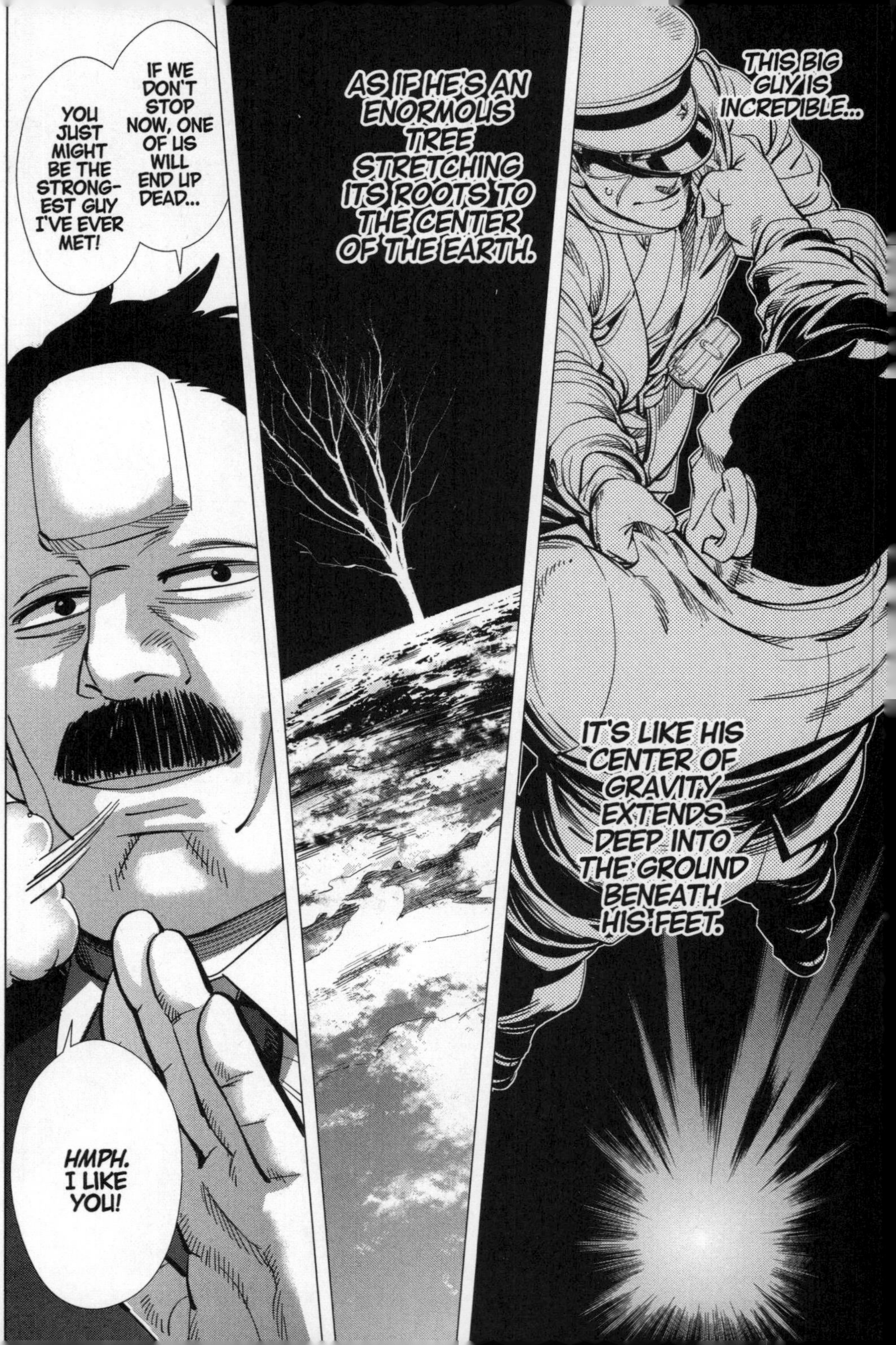
THIS BIG GUY IS INCREDIBLE...
IT'S LIKE HIS CENTER OF GRAVITY EXTENDS DEEP INTO THE GROUND BENEATH HIS FEET.
AS IF HE'S AN ENORMOUS TREE STRETCHING ITS ROOTS TO THE CENTER OF THE EARTH.
IF WE DON'T STOP NOW, ONE OF US WILL END UP DEAD...
YOU JUST MIGHT BE THE STRONG-EST GUY I'VE EVER MET!
HMPH. I LIKE YOU!

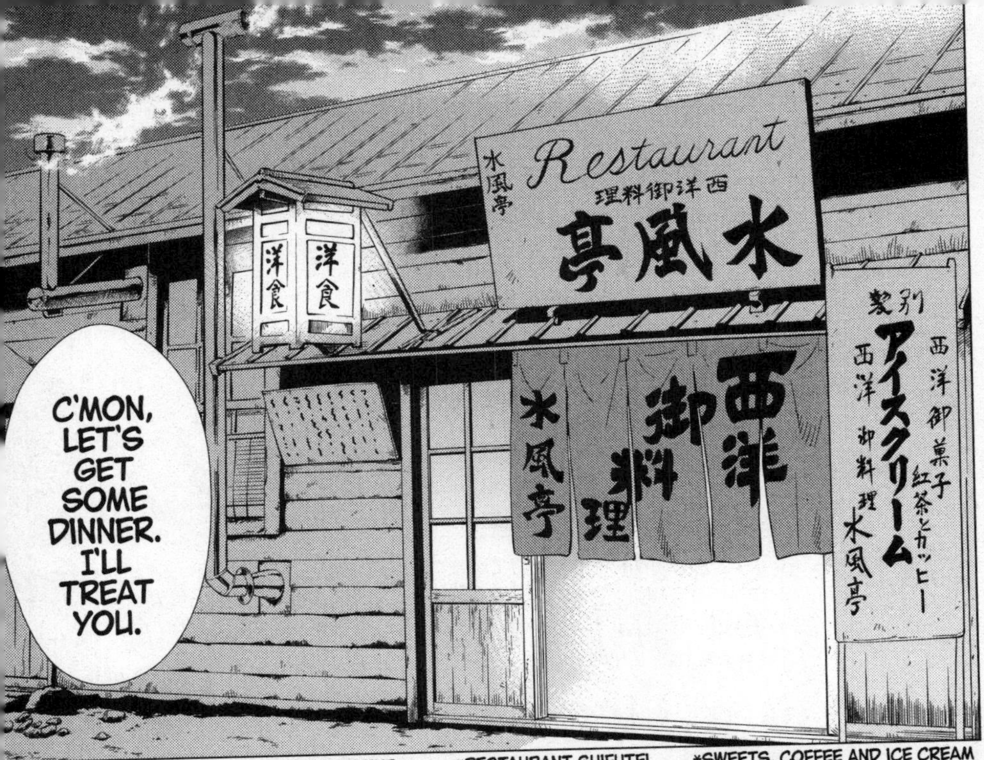
Restaurant
西洋御料理
水風亭
水風亭
洋食
洋食
西洋御料理
水風亭
西洋御菓子
アイスクリーム
紅茶とカッヒー
西洋御料理
水風亭
C'MON, LET'S GET SOME DINNER. I'LL TREAT YOU.

LAMP SIGN: WESTERN CUISINE *RESTAURANT SUIFUTEI *SWEETS, COFFEE AND ICE CREAM

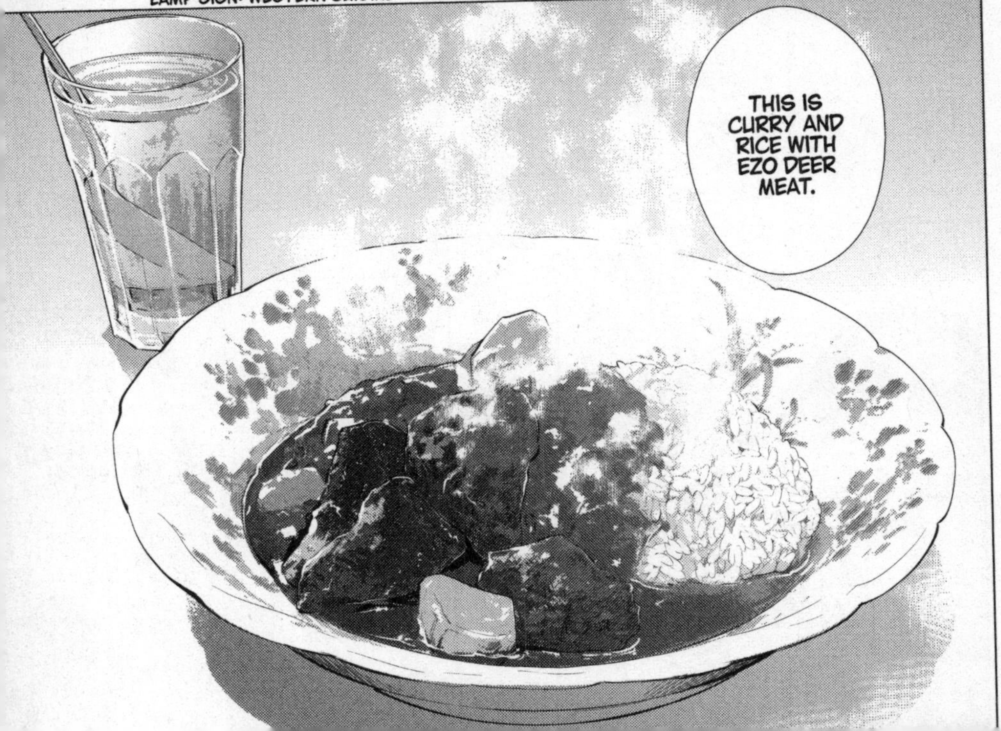
THIS IS CURRY AND RICE WITH EZO DEER MEAT.

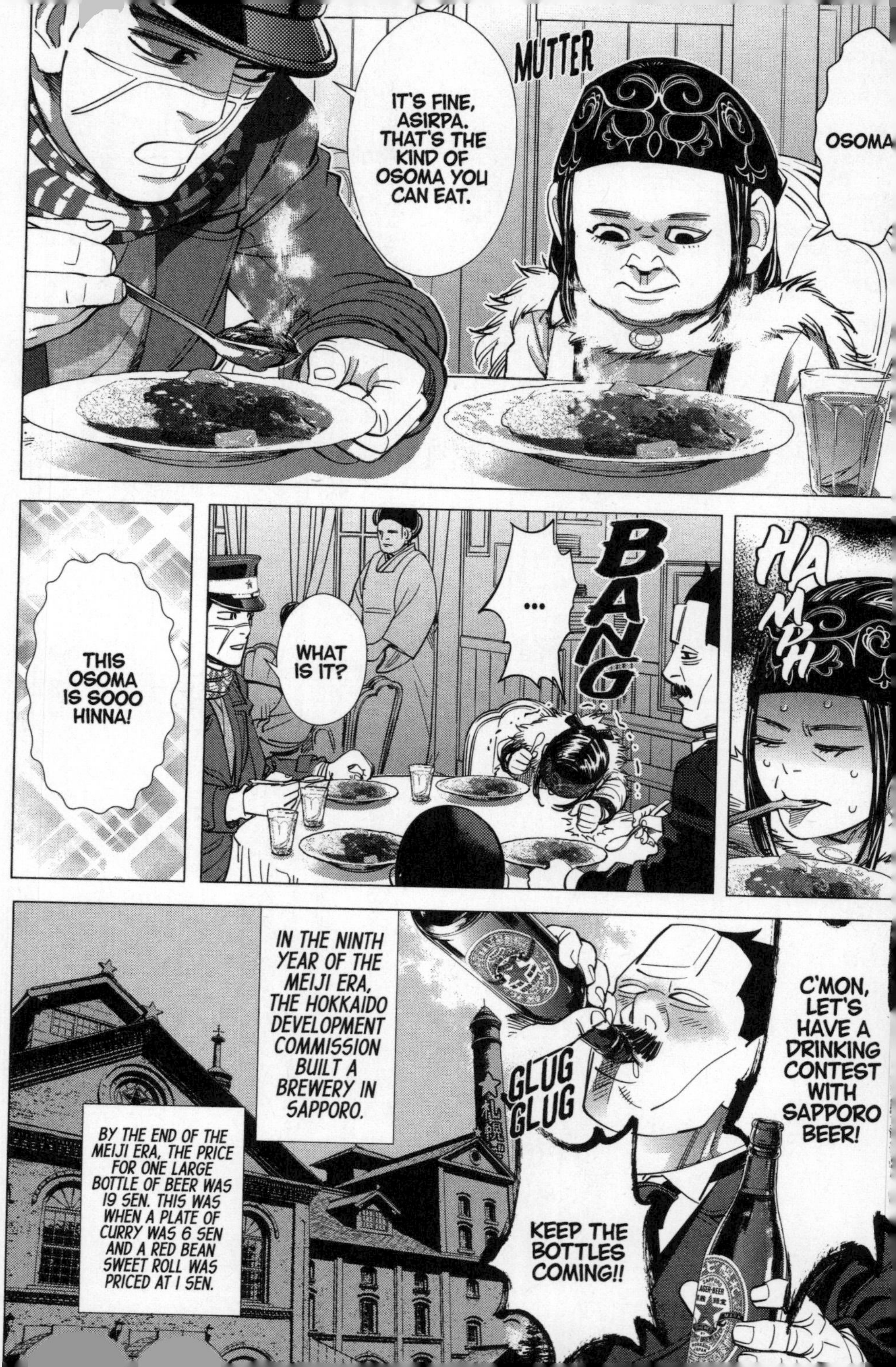
OSOMA
MUTTER
IT'S FINE, ASIRPA. THAT'S THE KIND OF OSOMA YOU CAN EAT.
HAMPH
BANG
...
WHAT IS IT?
THIS OSOMA IS SOOO HINNA!
C'MON, LET'S HAVE A DRINKING CONTEST WITH SAPPORO BEER!
GLUG GLUG
KEEP THE BOTTLES COMING!!
IN THE NINTH YEAR OF THE MEIJI ERA, THE HOKKAIDO DEVELOPMENT COMMISSION BUILT A BREWERY IN SAPPORO.
BY THE END OF THE MEIJI ERA, THE PRICE FOR ONE LARGE BOTTLE OF BEER WAS 19 SEN. THIS WAS WHEN A PLATE OF CURRY WAS 6 SEN AND A RED BEAN SWEET ROLL WAS PRICED AT 1 SEN.

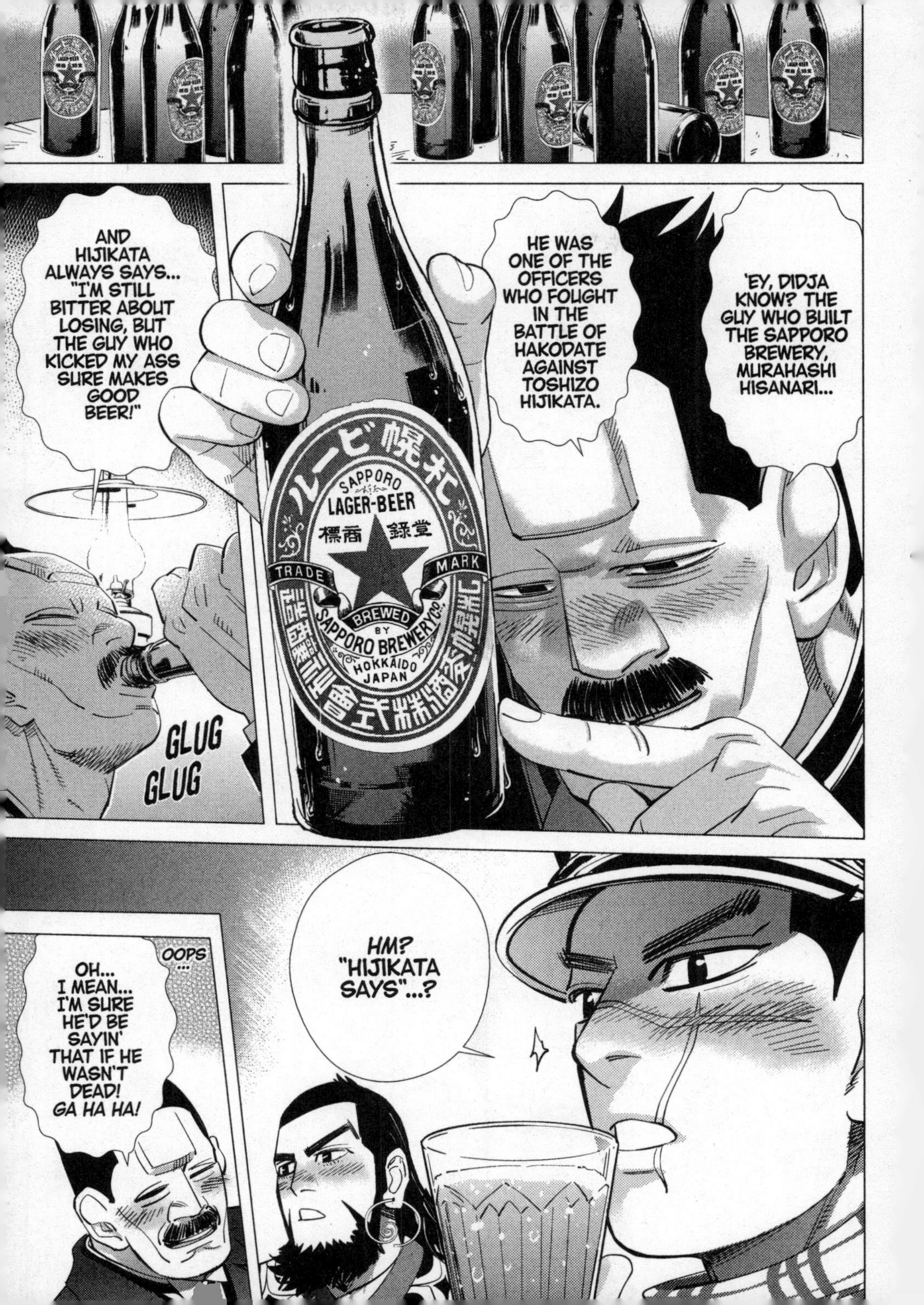

札幌ビール
SAPPORO
LAGER-BEER
登録商標
TRADE MARK
BREWED BY SAPPORO BREWERY Co.
HOKKAIDO JAPAN
'EY, DIDJA KNOW? THE GUY WHO BUILT THE SAPPORO BREWERY, MURAHASHI HISANARI...
HE WAS ONE OF THE OFFICERS WHO FOUGHT IN THE BATTLE OF HAKODATE AGAINST TOSHIZO HIJIKATA.
AND HIJIKATA ALWAYS SAYS... "I'M STILL BITTER ABOUT LOSING, BUT THE GUY WHO KICKED MY ASS SURE MAKES GOOD BEER!"
GLUG GLUG
HM? "HIJIKATA SAYS"...?
OOPS...
OH... I MEAN... I'M SURE HE'D BE SAYIN' THAT IF HE WASN'T DEAD! GA HA HA!

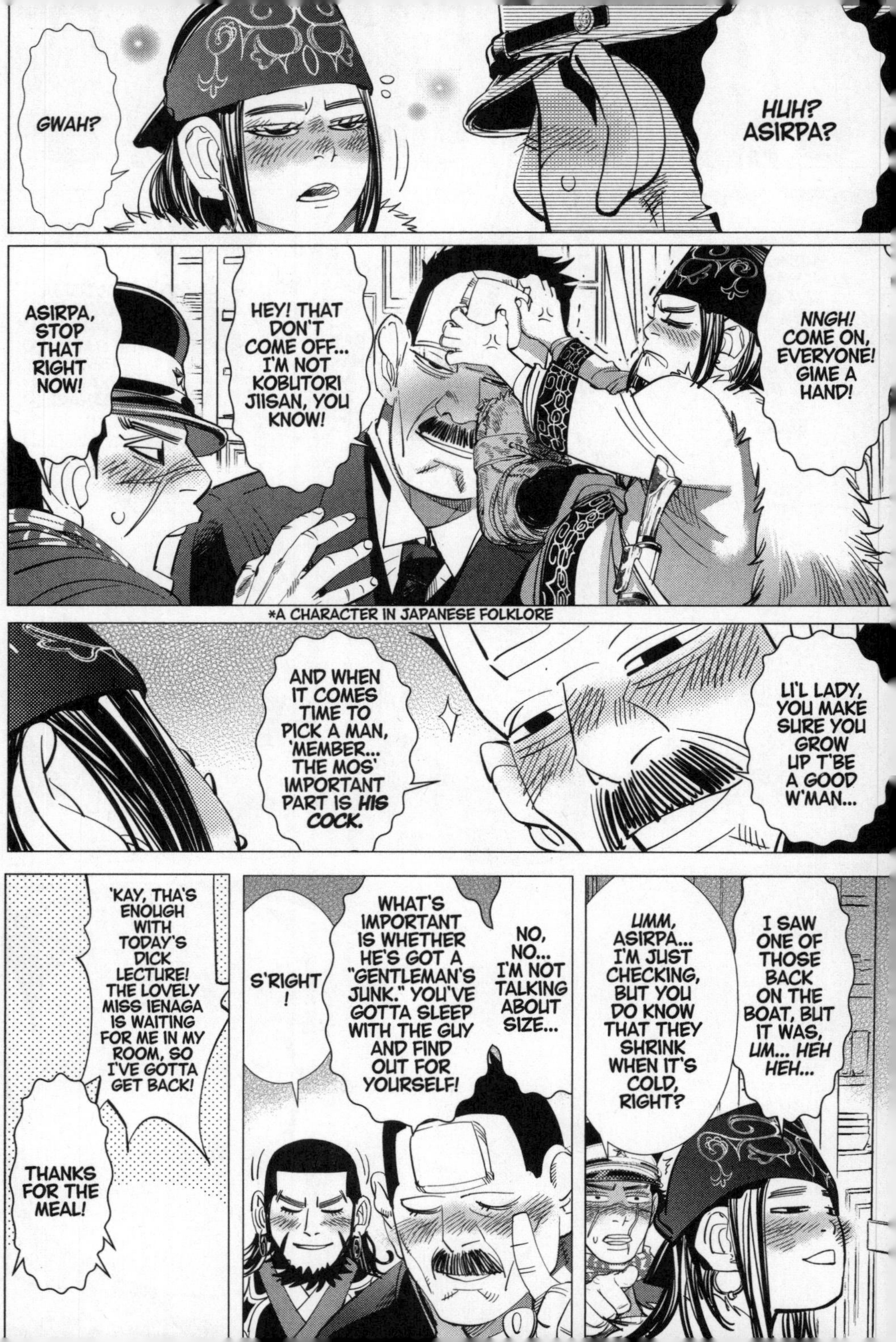
HUH? ASIRPA?
GWAH?
NNGH! COME ON, EVERYONE! GIME A HAND!
HEY! THAT DON'T COME OFF... I'M NOT KOBUTORI JIISAN, YOU KNOW!
ASIRPA, STOP THAT RIGHT NOW!
*A CHARACTER IN JAPANESE FOLKLORE
LI'L LADY, YOU MAKE SURE YOU GROW UP T'BE A GOOD W'MAN...
AND WHEN IT COMES TIME TO PICK A MAN, 'MEMBER... THE MOS' IMPORTANT PART IS HIS COCK.
I SAW ONE OF THOSE BACK ON THE BOAT, BUT IT WAS, UM... HEH HEH...
UMM, ASIRPA... I'M JUST CHECKING, BUT YOU DO KNOW THAT THEY SHRINK WHEN IT'S COLD, RIGHT?
NO, NO... I'M NOT TALKING ABOUT SIZE...
WHAT'S IMPORTANT IS WHETHER HE'S GOT A "GENTLEMAN'S JUNK." YOU'VE GOTTA SLEEP WITH THE GUY AND FIND OUT FOR YOURSELF!
S'RIGHT!
'KAY, THA'S ENOUGH WITH TODAY'S DICK LECTURE! THE LOVELY MISS IENAGA IS WAITING FOR ME IN MY ROOM, SO I'VE GOTTA GET BACK!
THANKS FOR THE MEAL!

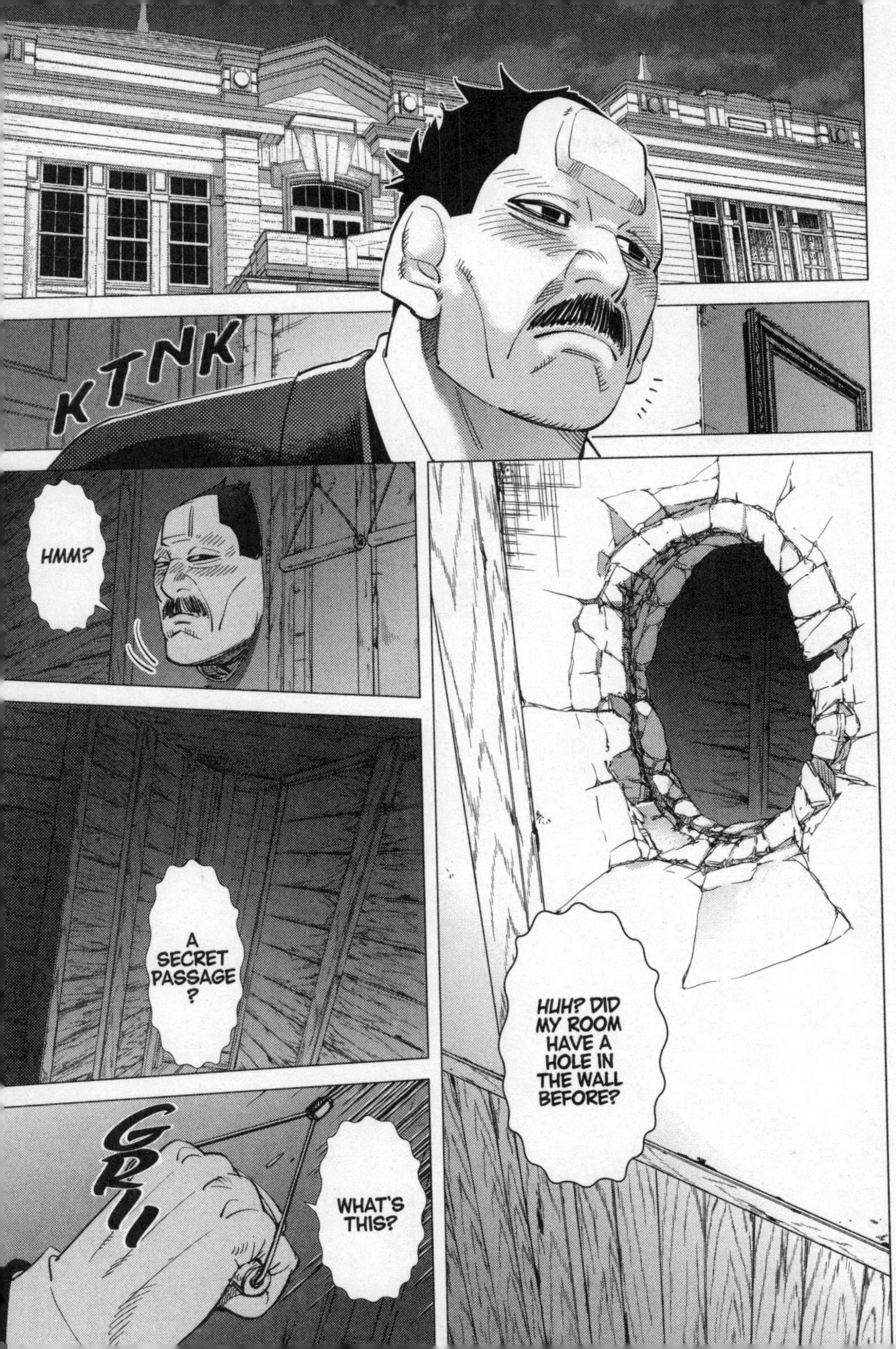
KTNK
HUH? DID MY ROOM HAVE A HOLE IN THE WALL BEFORE?
HMM?
A SECRET PASSAGE?
WHAT'S THIS?
GRI

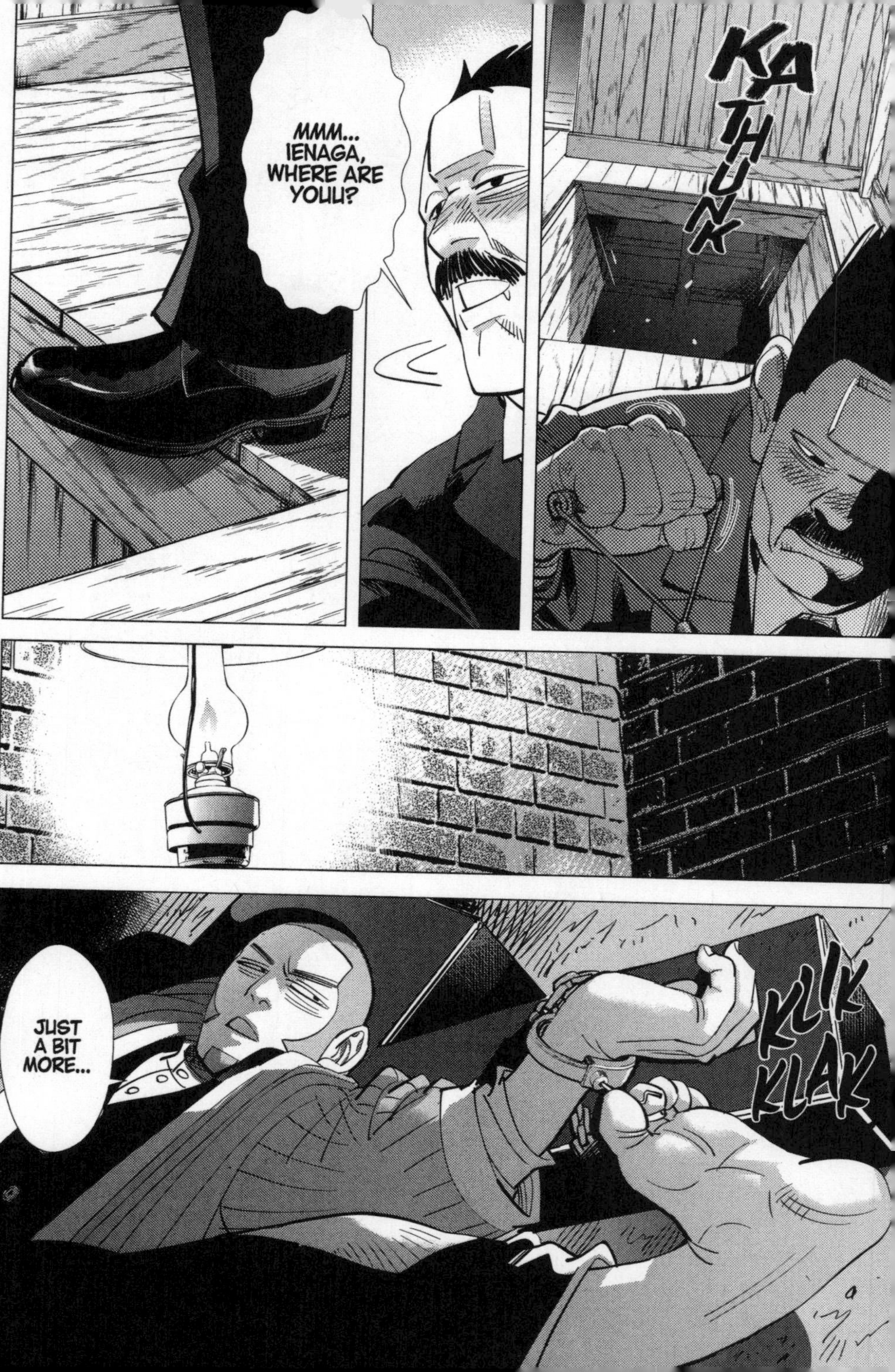
KA THUNK
MMM... IENAGA, WHERE ARE YOUU?
KLIK KLIK KLAK
JUST A BIT MORE...

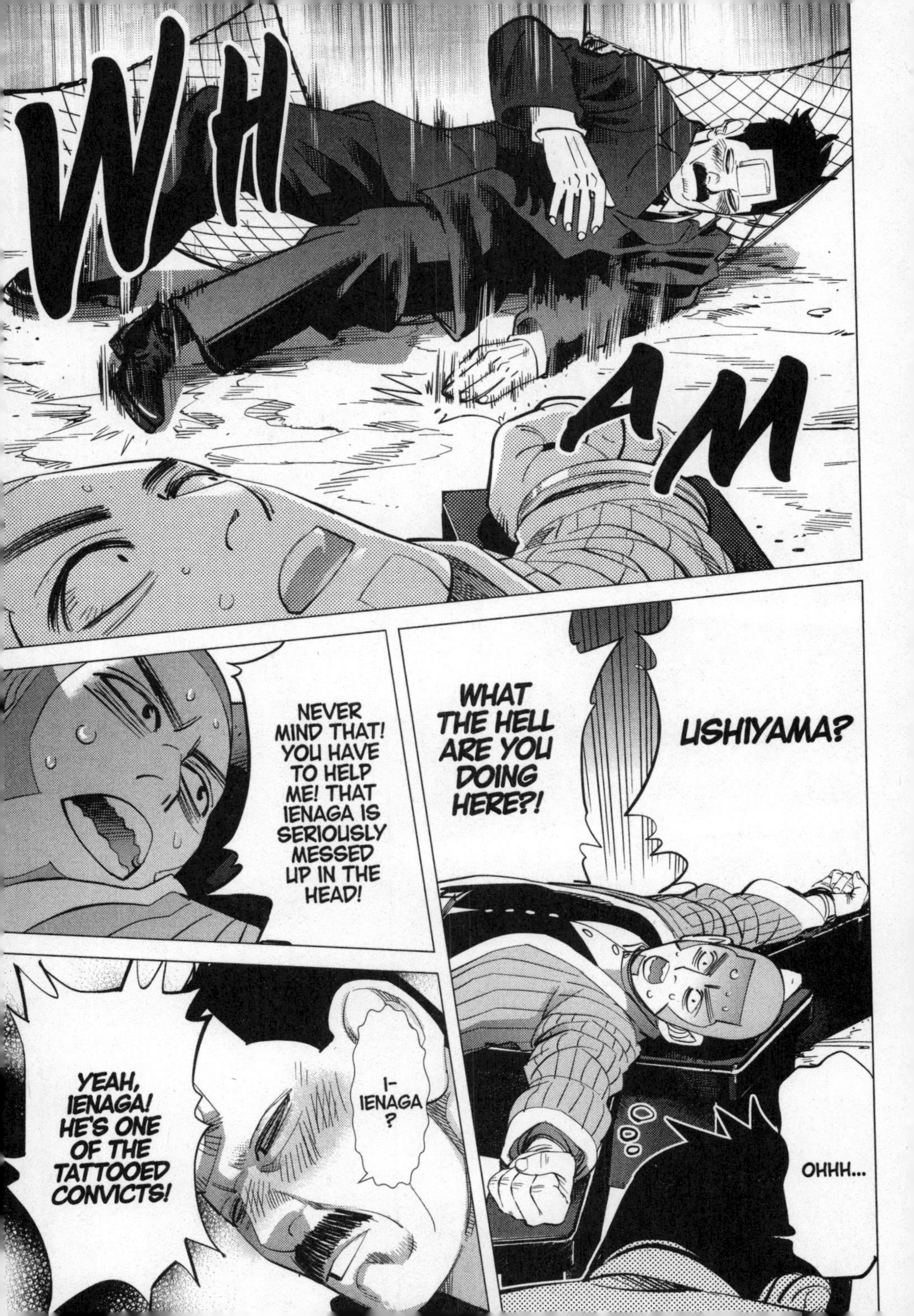
WHAM
USHIYAMA?
WHAT THE HELL ARE YOU DOING HERE?!
OHHH...
NEVER MIND THAT! YOU HAVE TO HELP ME! THAT IENAGA IS SERIOUSLY MESSED UP IN THE HEAD!
I-IENAGA?
YEAH, IENAGA! HE'S ONE OF THE TATTOOED CONVICTS!

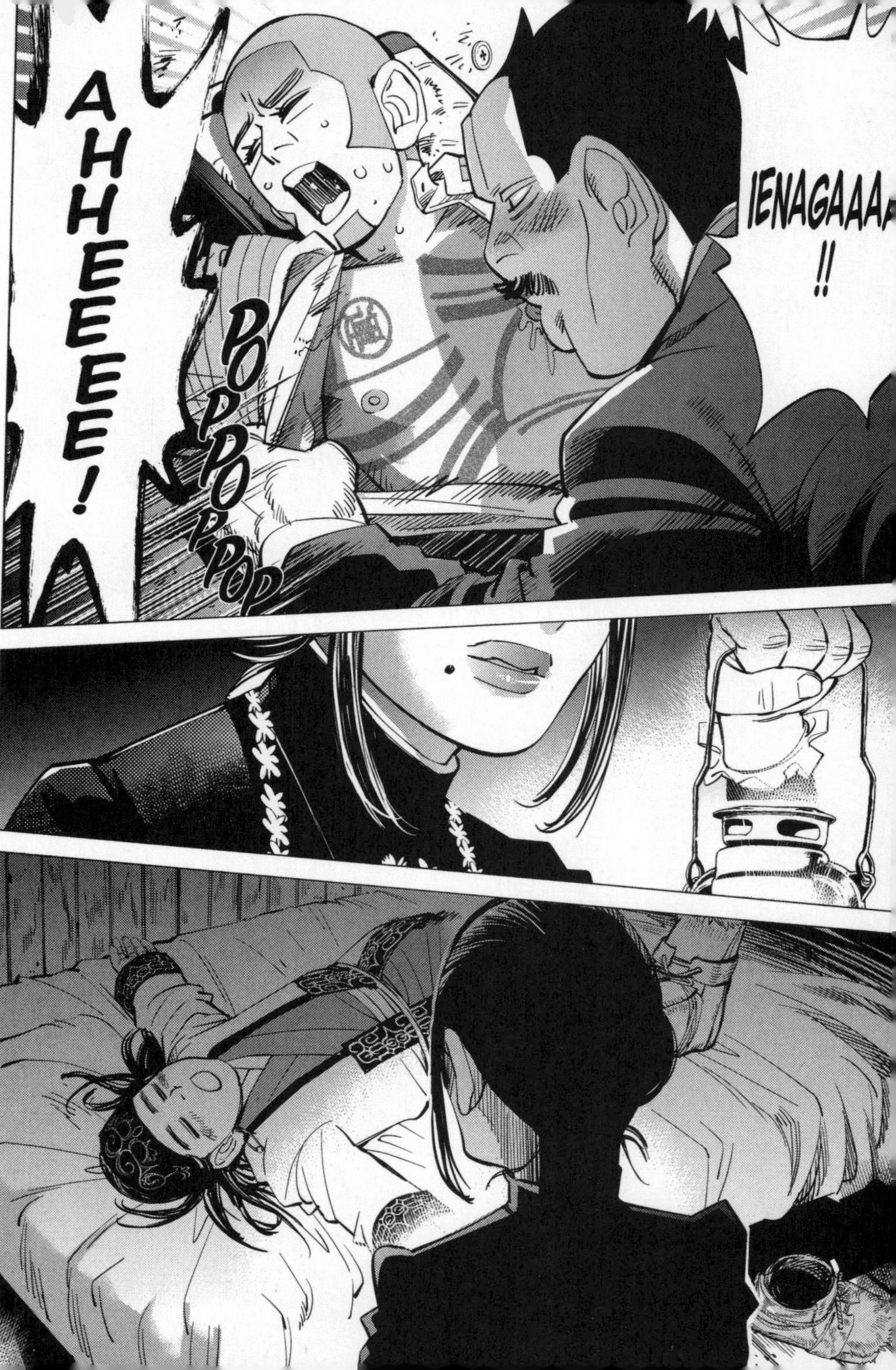
IENAGAAAA
!!
AHHEEEEE!
POPPOPPOP

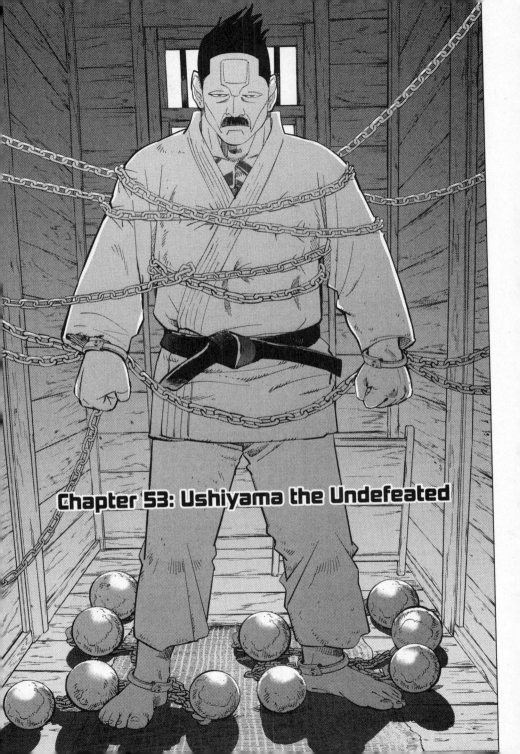

Chapter 53: Ushiyama the Undefeated

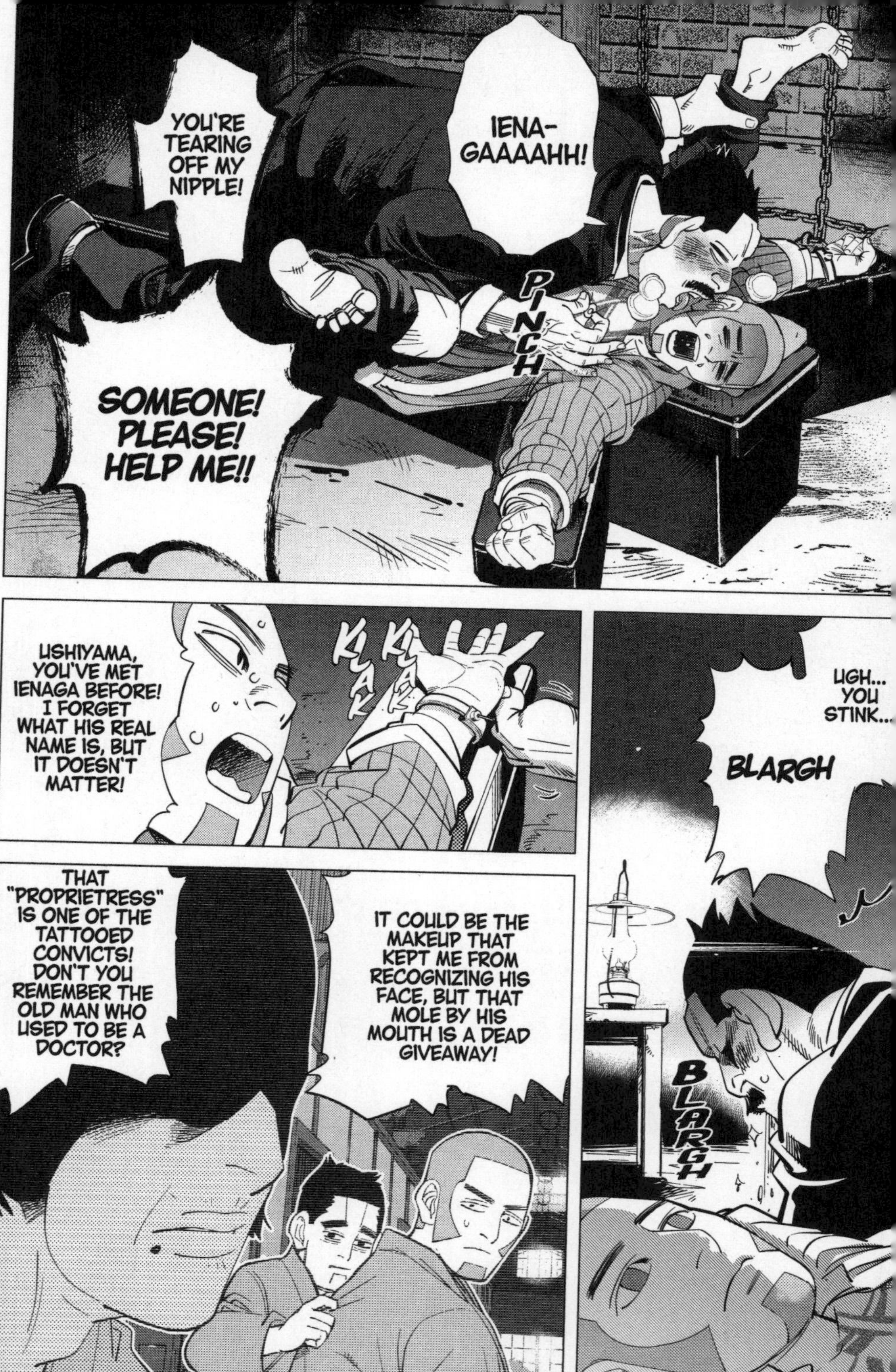
IENA-GAAAAHH!
YOU'RE TEARING OFF MY NIPPLE!
PINCH
SOMEONE! PLEASE! HELP ME!!
UGH... YOU STINK...
BLARGH
BLARGH
KLAK KLAK
USHIYAMA, YOU'VE MET IENAGA BEFORE! I FORGET WHAT HIS REAL NAME IS, BUT IT DOESN'T MATTER!
IT COULD BE THE MAKEUP THAT KEPT ME FROM RECOGNIZING HIS FACE, BUT THAT MOLE BY HIS MOUTH IS A DEAD GIVEAWAY!
THAT "PROPRIETRESS" IS ONE OF THE TATTOOED CONVICTS! DON'T YOU REMEMBER THE OLD MAN WHO USED TO BE A DOCTOR?

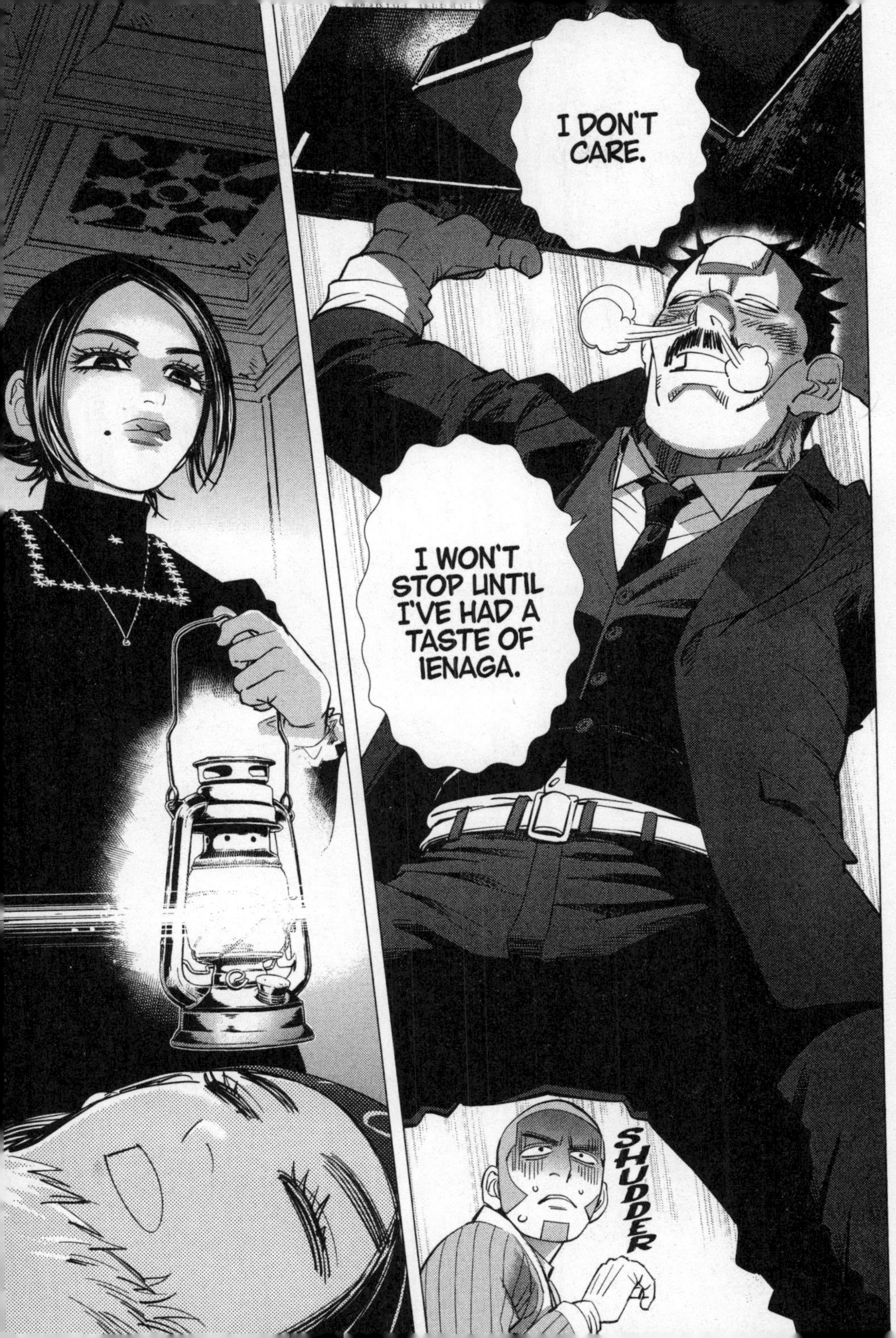
I DON'T CARE.
I WON'T STOP UNTIL I'VE HAD A TASTE OF IENAGA.
SHUDDER

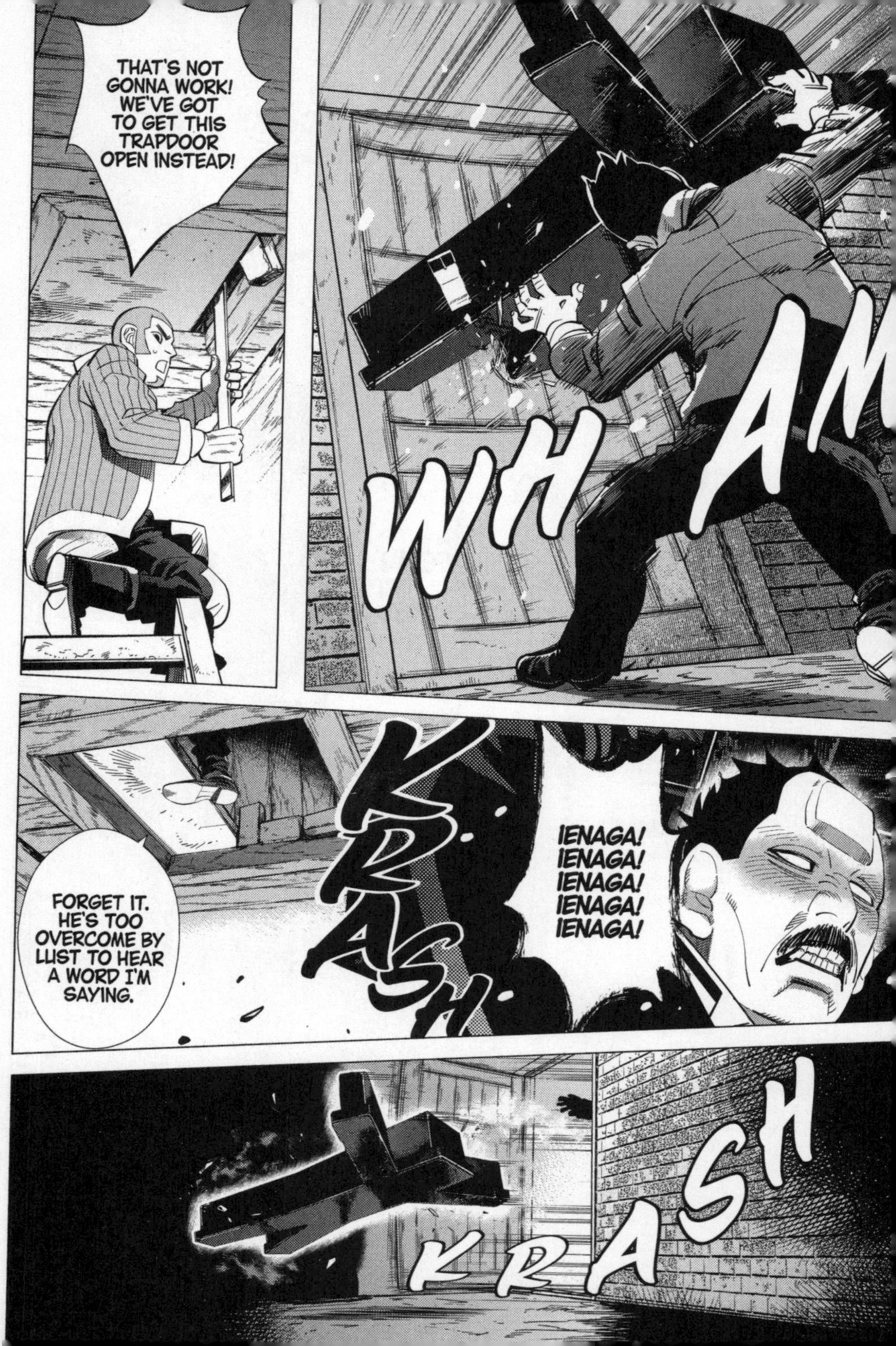
WHAM
THAT'S NOT GONNA WORK! WE'VE GOT TO GET THIS TRAPDOOR OPEN INSTEAD!
IENAGA! IENAGA! IENAGA! IENAGA! IENAGA!
KRASH
FORGET IT. HE'S TOO OVERCOME BY LUST TO HEAR A WORD I'M SAYING.
KRASH

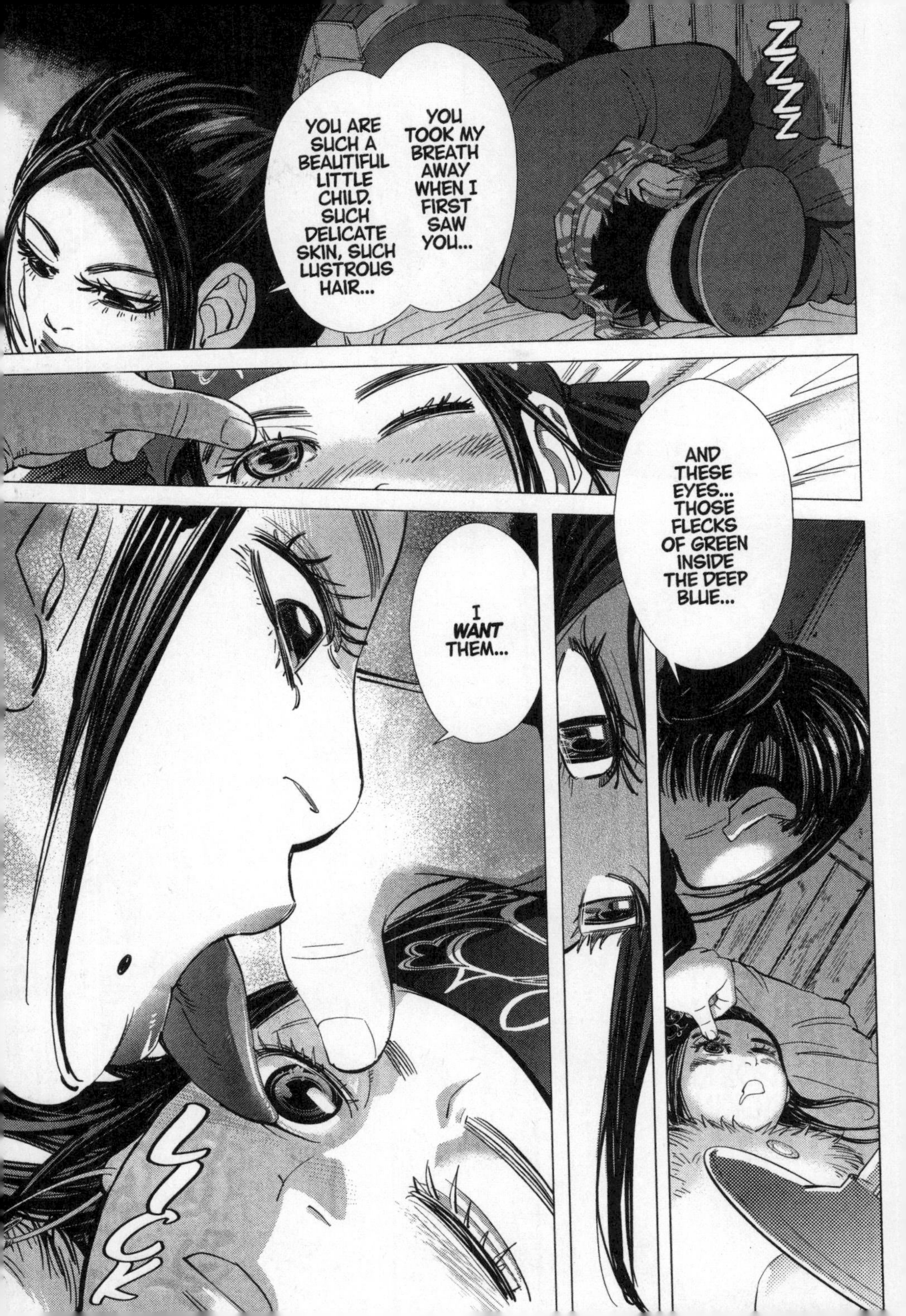
ZZZZ
YOU TOOK MY BREATH AWAY WHEN I FIRST SAW YOU...
YOU ARE SUCH A BEAUTIFUL LITTLE CHILD. SUCH DELICATE SKIN, SUCH LUSTROUS HAIR...
AND THESE EYES... THOSE FLECKS OF GREEN INSIDE THE DEEP BLUE...
I *WANT* THEM...
LICK

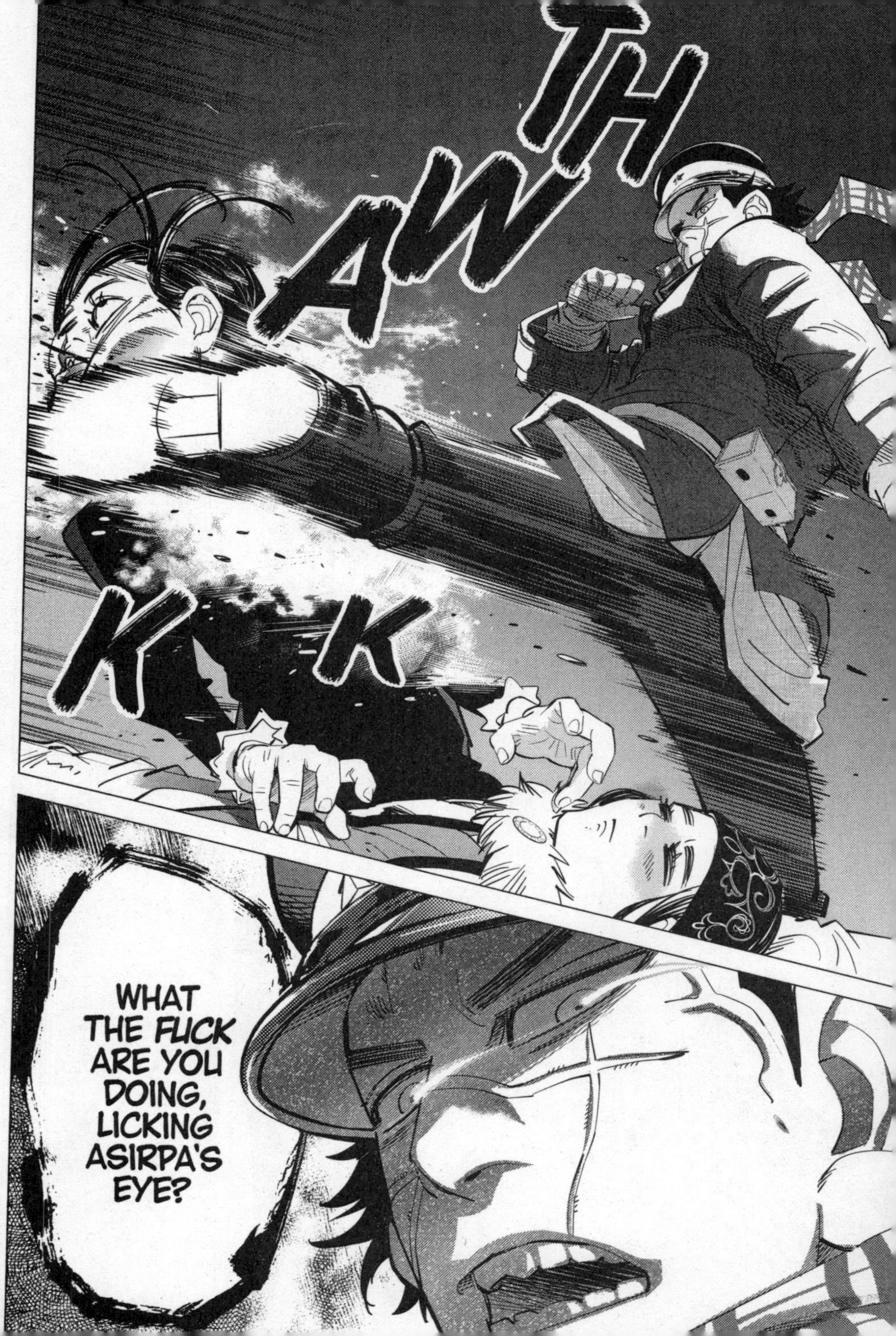
THWAK
K K
WHAT THE FUCK ARE YOU DOING, LICKING ASIRPA'S EYE?

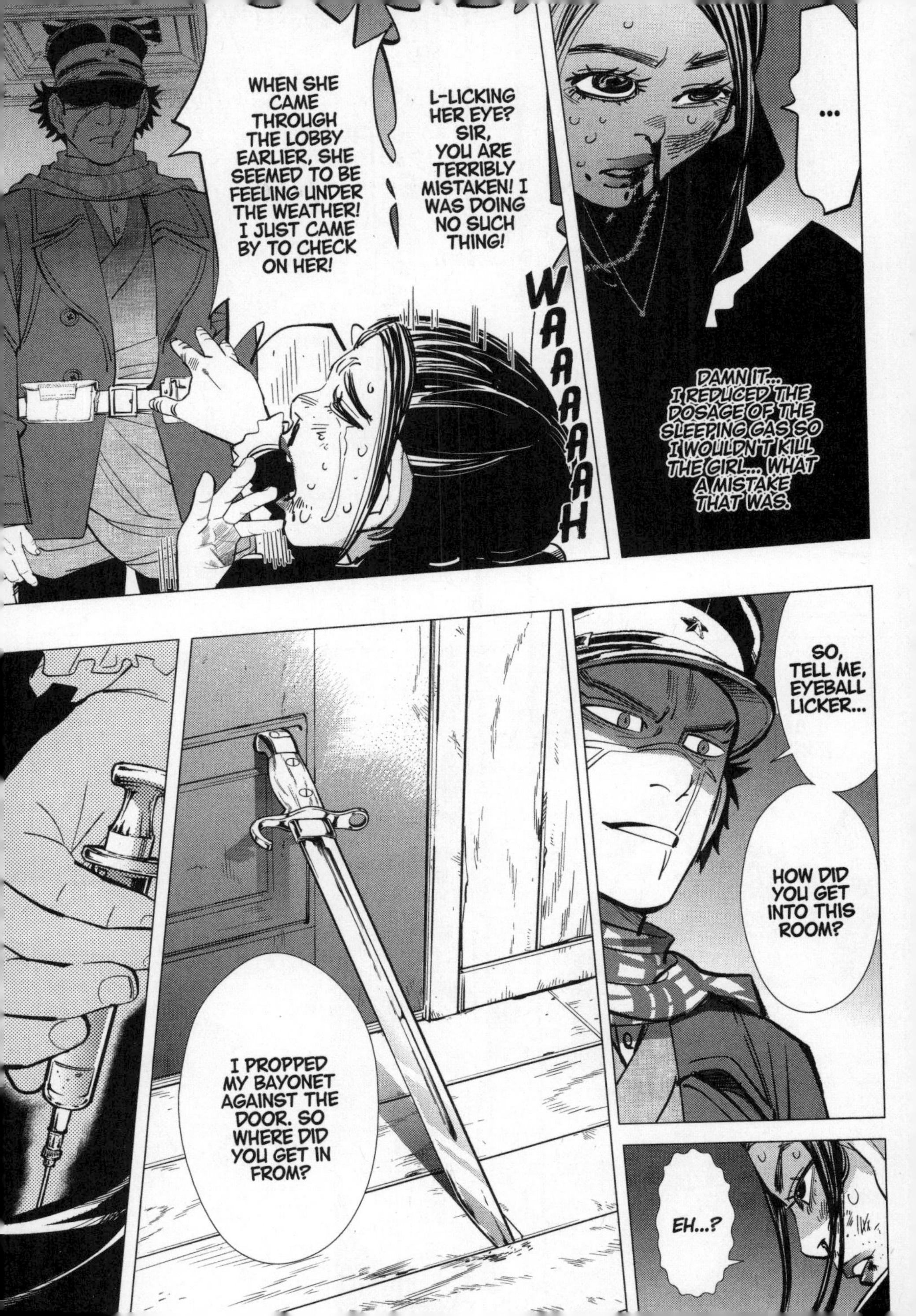
...
DAMN IT... I REDUCED THE DOSAGE OF THE SLEEPING GAS SO I WOULDN'T KILL THE GIRL... WHAT A MISTAKE THAT WAS.
L-LICKING HER EYE? SIR, YOU ARE TERRIBLY MISTAKEN! I WAS DOING NO SUCH THING!
WHEN SHE CAME THROUGH THE LOBBY EARLIER, SHE SEEMED TO BE FEELING UNDER THE WEATHER! I JUST CAME BY TO CHECK ON HER!
WAAAAAAAH
SO, TELL ME, EYEBALL LICKER...
HOW DID YOU GET INTO THIS ROOM?
EH...?
I PROPPED MY BAYONET AGAINST THE DOOR. SO WHERE DID YOU GET IN FROM?

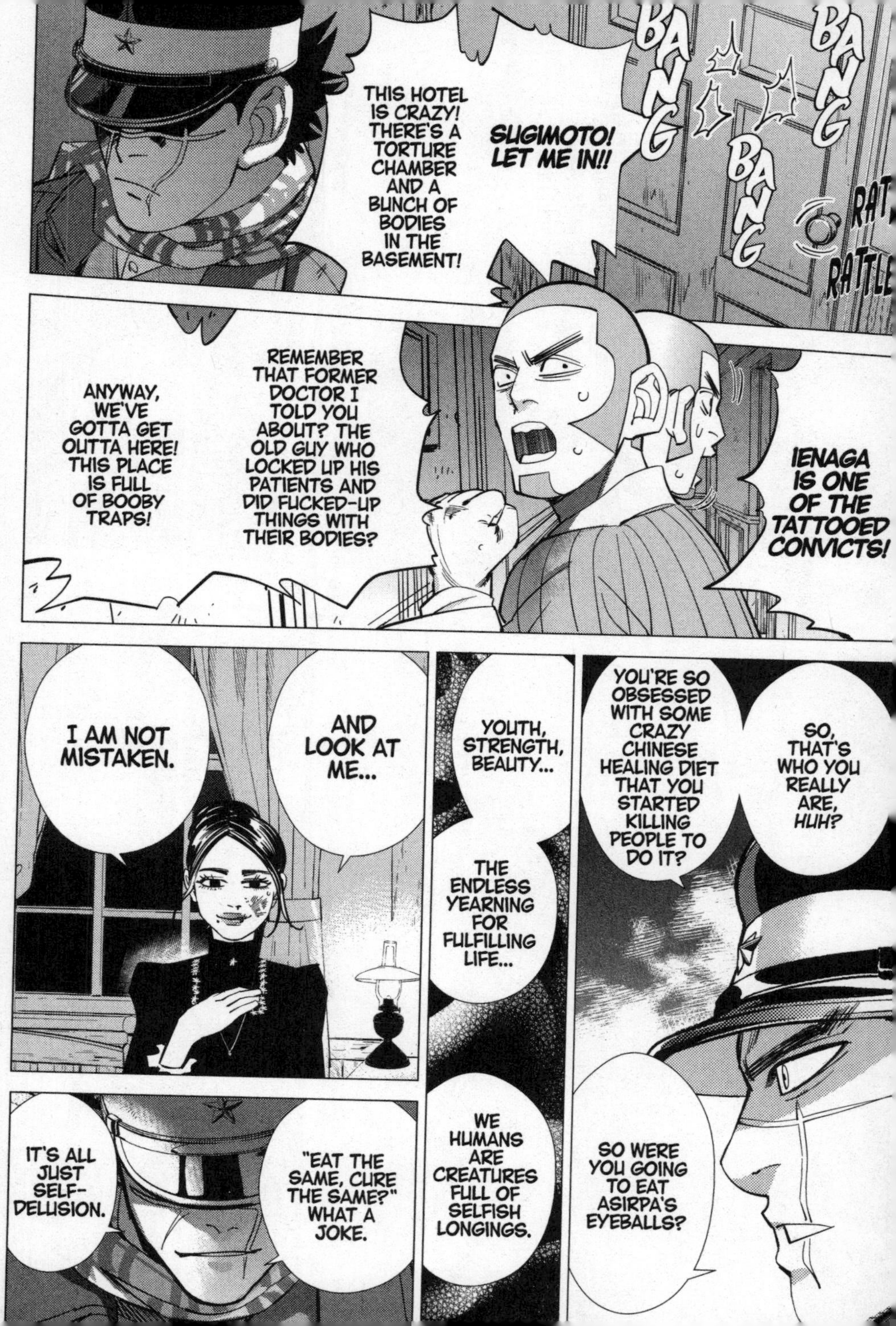
BANG BANG
BANG BANG
RAT RATTLE
SUGIMOTO! LET ME IN!!
THIS HOTEL IS CRAZY! THERE'S A TORTURE CHAMBER AND A BUNCH OF BODIES IN THE BASEMENT!
IENAGA IS ONE OF THE TATTOOED CONVICTS!
REMEMBER THAT FORMER DOCTOR I TOLD YOU ABOUT? THE OLD GUY WHO LOCKED UP HIS PATIENTS AND DID FUCKED-UP THINGS WITH THEIR BODIES?
ANYWAY, WE'VE GOTTA GET OUTTA HERE! THIS PLACE IS FULL OF BOOBY TRAPS!
SO, THAT'S WHO YOU REALLY ARE, HUH?
YOU'RE SO OBSESSED WITH SOME CRAZY CHINESE HEALING DIET THAT YOU STARTED KILLING PEOPLE TO DO IT?
SO WERE YOU GOING TO EAT ASIRPA'S EYEBALLS?
YOUTH, STRENGTH, BEAUTY...
THE ENDLESS YEARNING FOR FULFILLING LIFE...
WE HUMANS ARE CREATURES FULL OF SELFISH LONGINGS.
AND LOOK AT ME...
I AM NOT MISTAKEN.
"EAT THE SAME, CURE THE SAME?" WHAT A JOKE.
IT'S ALL JUST SELF-DELUSION.

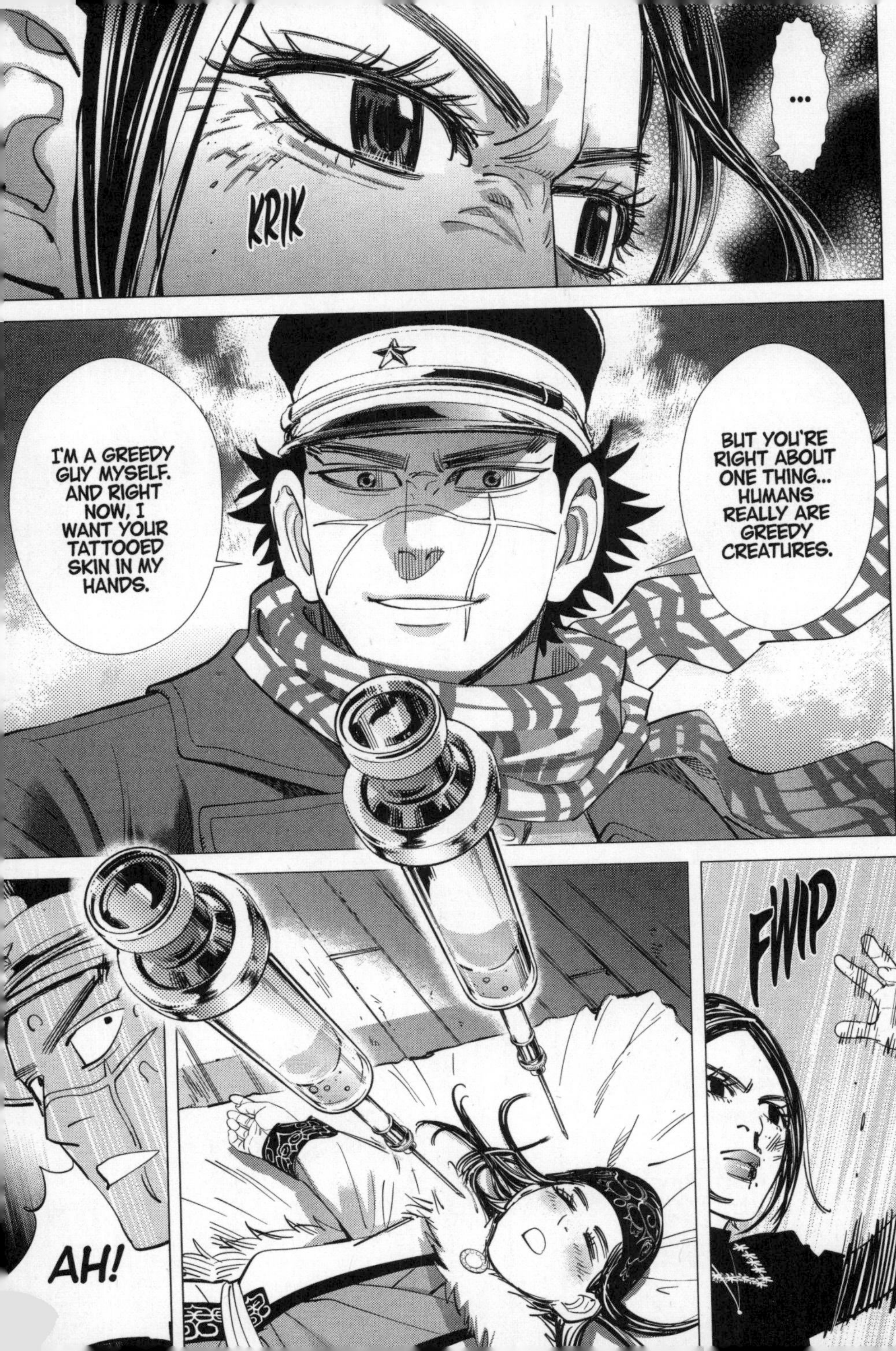
...
KRIK
BUT YOU'RE RIGHT ABOUT ONE THING... HUMANS REALLY ARE GREEDY CREATURES.
I'M A GREEDY GUY MYSELF. AND RIGHT NOW, I WANT YOUR TATTOOED SKIN IN MY HANDS.
FWIP
AH!

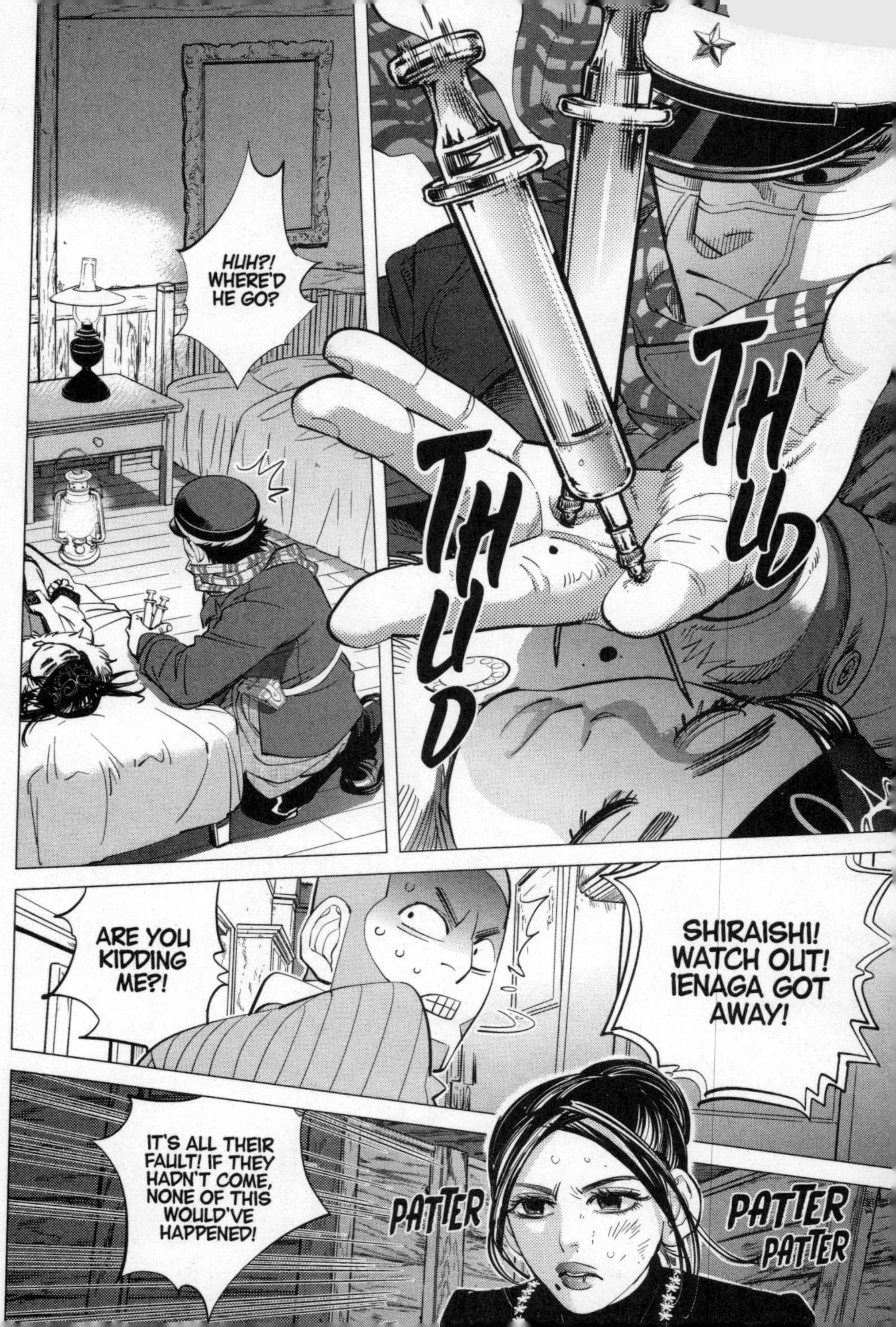
THUD
THUD
HUH?! WHERE'D HE GO?
SHIRAISHI! WATCH OUT! IENAGA GOT AWAY!
ARE YOU KIDDING ME?!
PATTER PATTER
IT'S ALL THEIR FAULT! IF THEY HADN'T COME, NONE OF THIS WOULD'VE HAPPENED!
PATTER

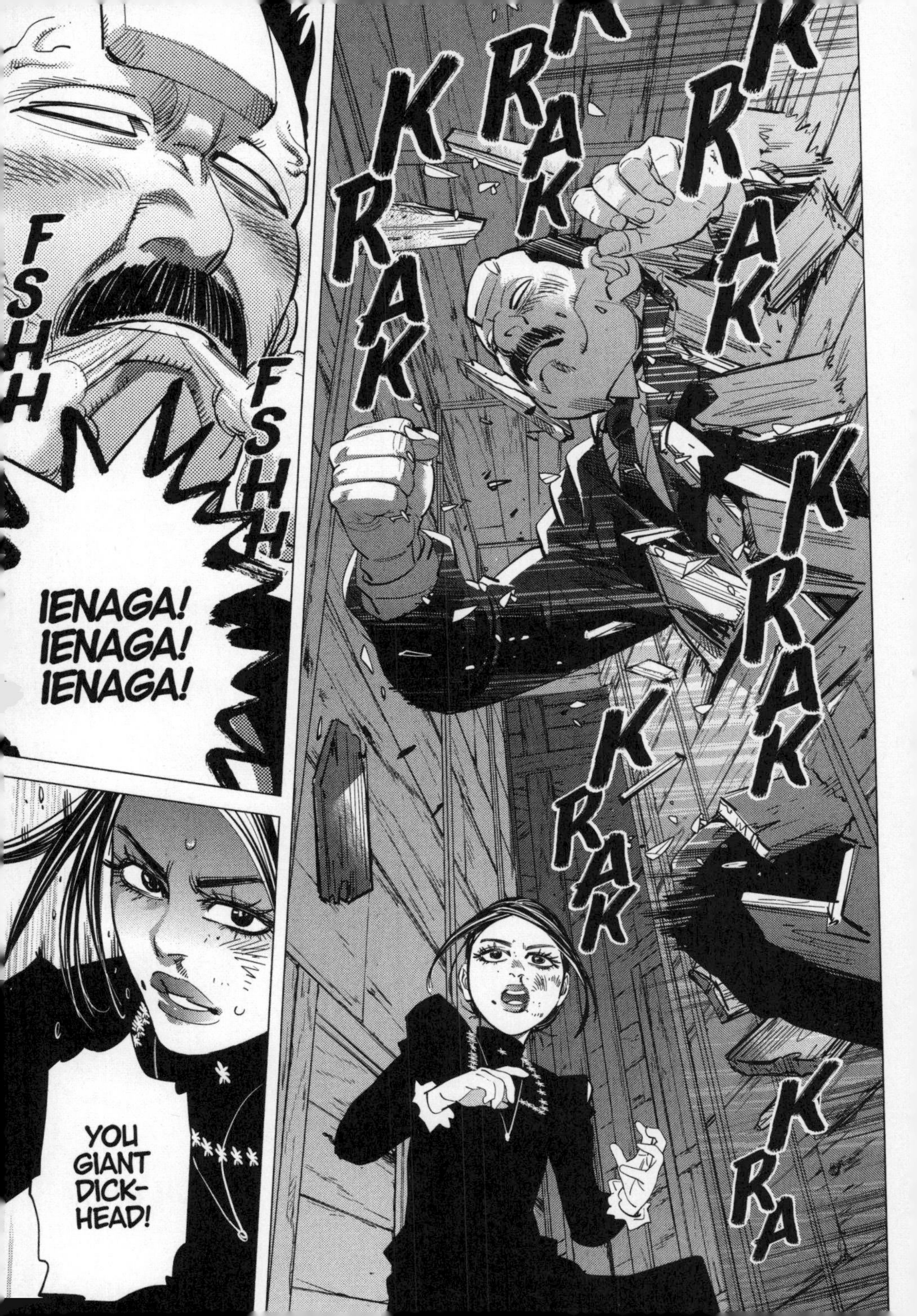
KRAK
KRAK
KRAK
KRAK
KRAK
KRAK
KRAK
KRA
FSHH
FSHH
IENAGA! IENAGA! IENAGA!
YOU GIANT DICK-HEAD!

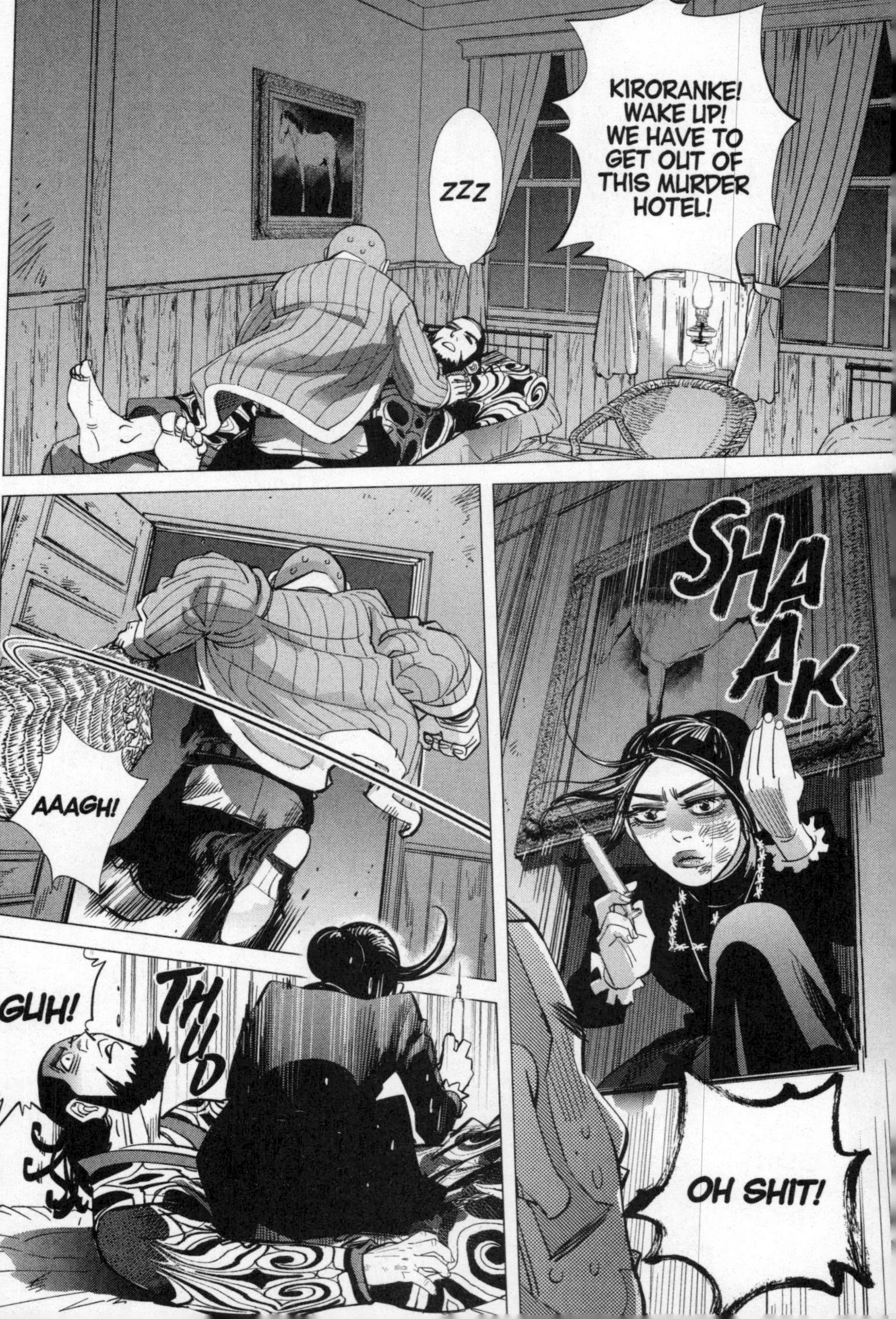
KIRORANKE! WAKE UP! WE HAVE TO GET OUT OF THIS MURDER HOTEL!
ZZZ
SHAAK
OH SHIT!
AAAGH!
THUD
GUH!

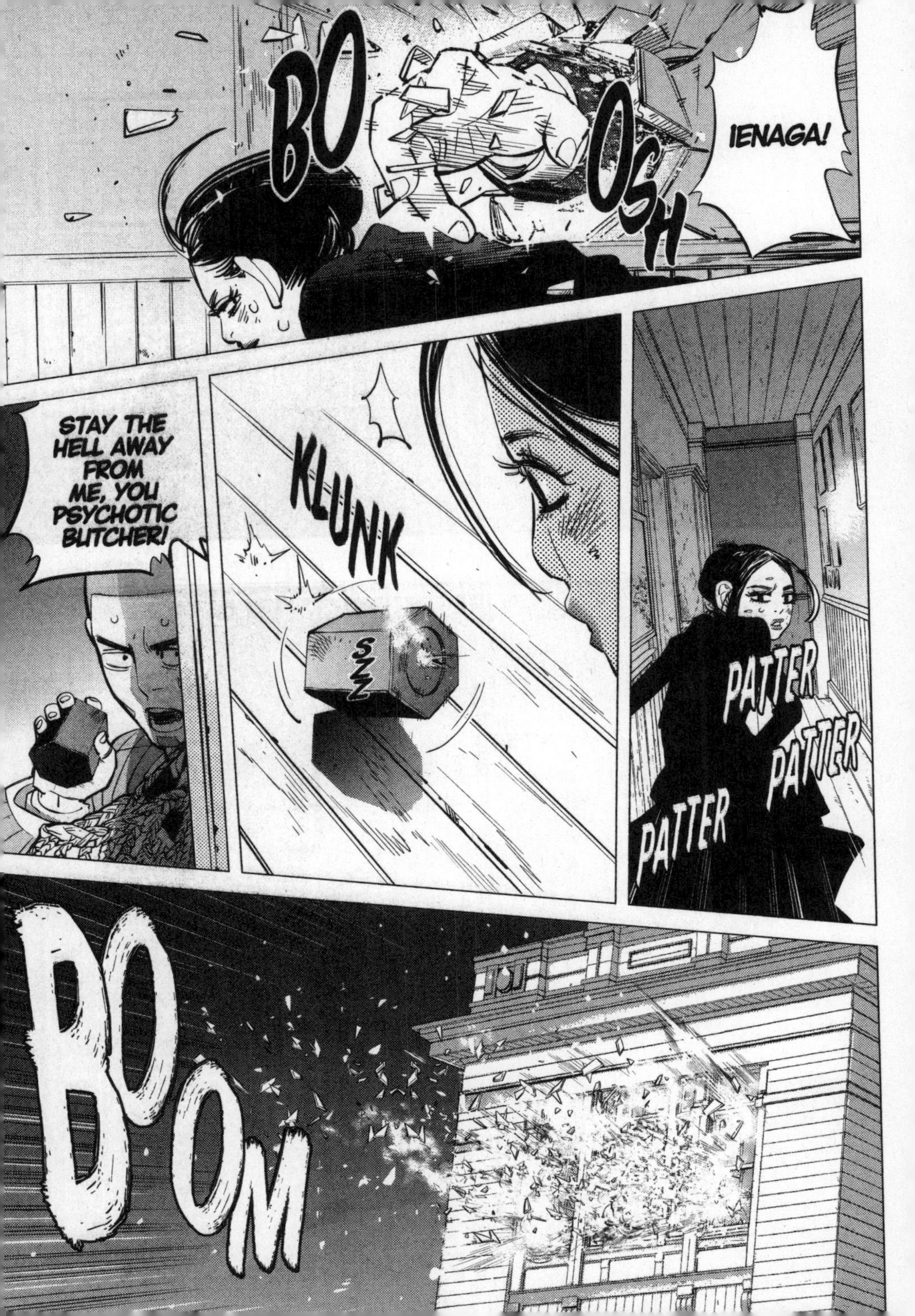
IENAGA!
BOOSH
PATTER PATTER PATTER
KLUNK
SZZ
STAY THE HELL AWAY FROM ME, YOU PSYCHOTIC BUTCHER!
BOOM

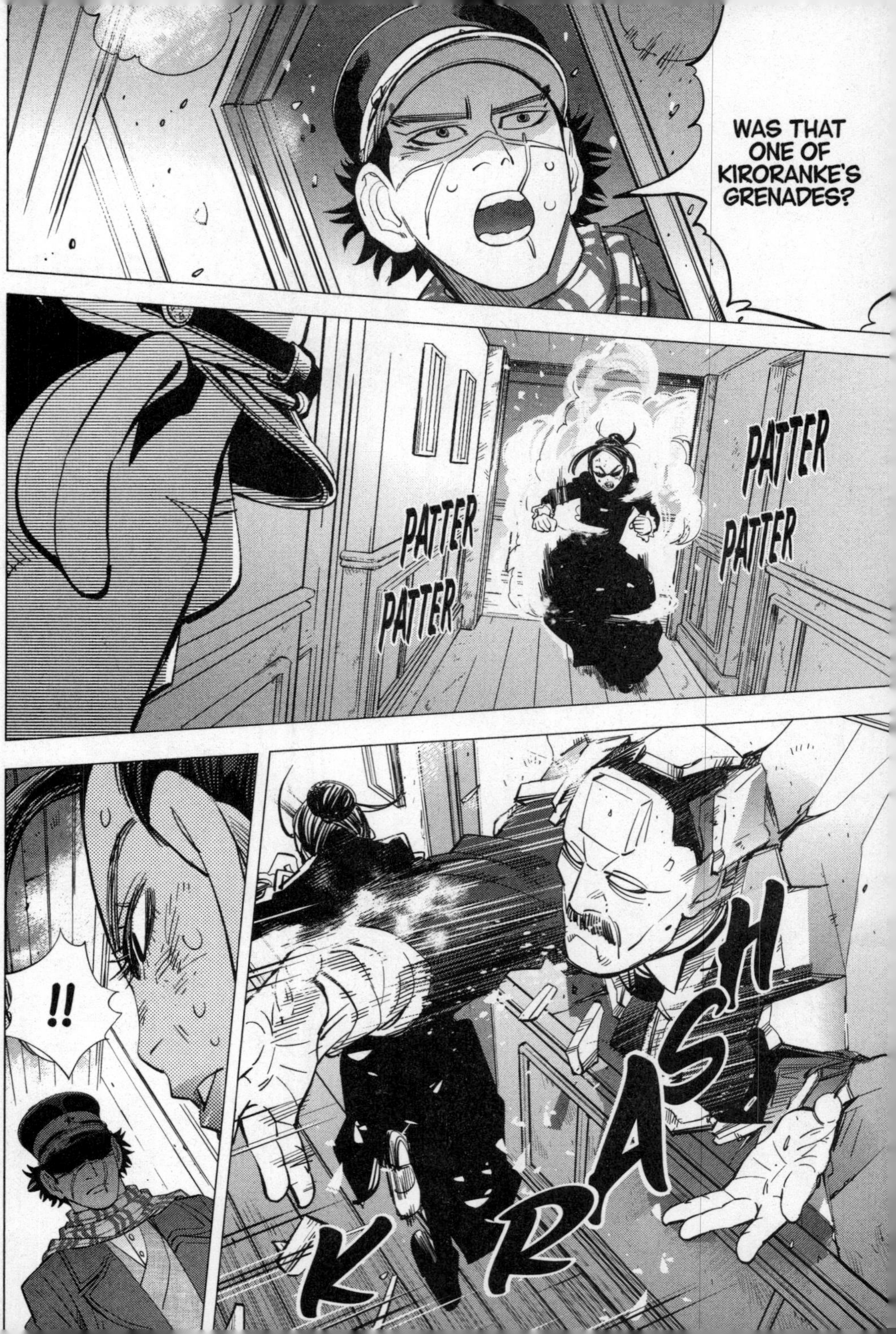
WAS THAT ONE OF KIRORANKE'S GRENADES?
PATTER PATTER
PATTER PATTER
KRASH
!!

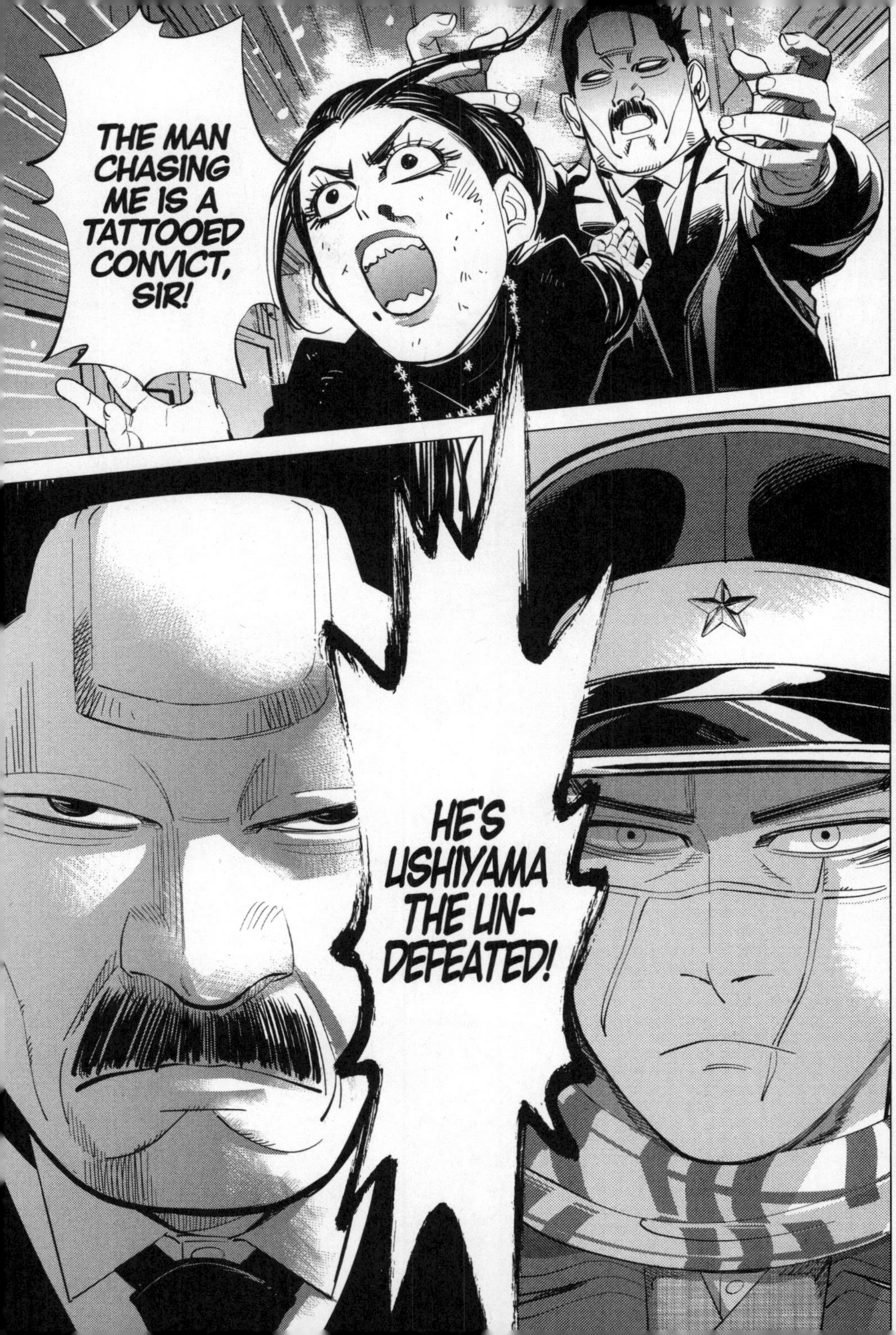
THE MAN CHASING ME IS A TATTOOED CONVICT, SIR!
HE'S USHIYAMA THE UN-DEFEATED!

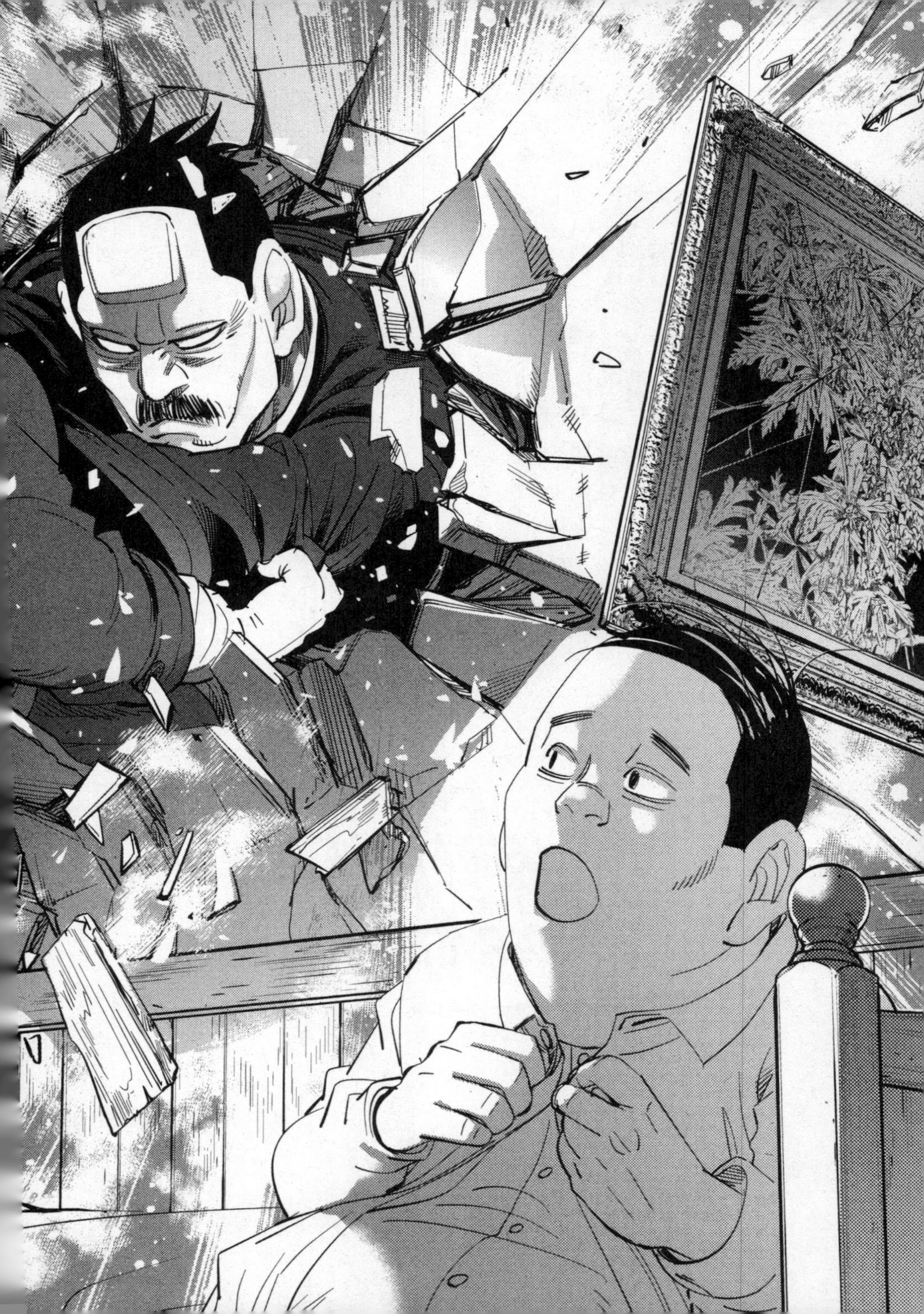

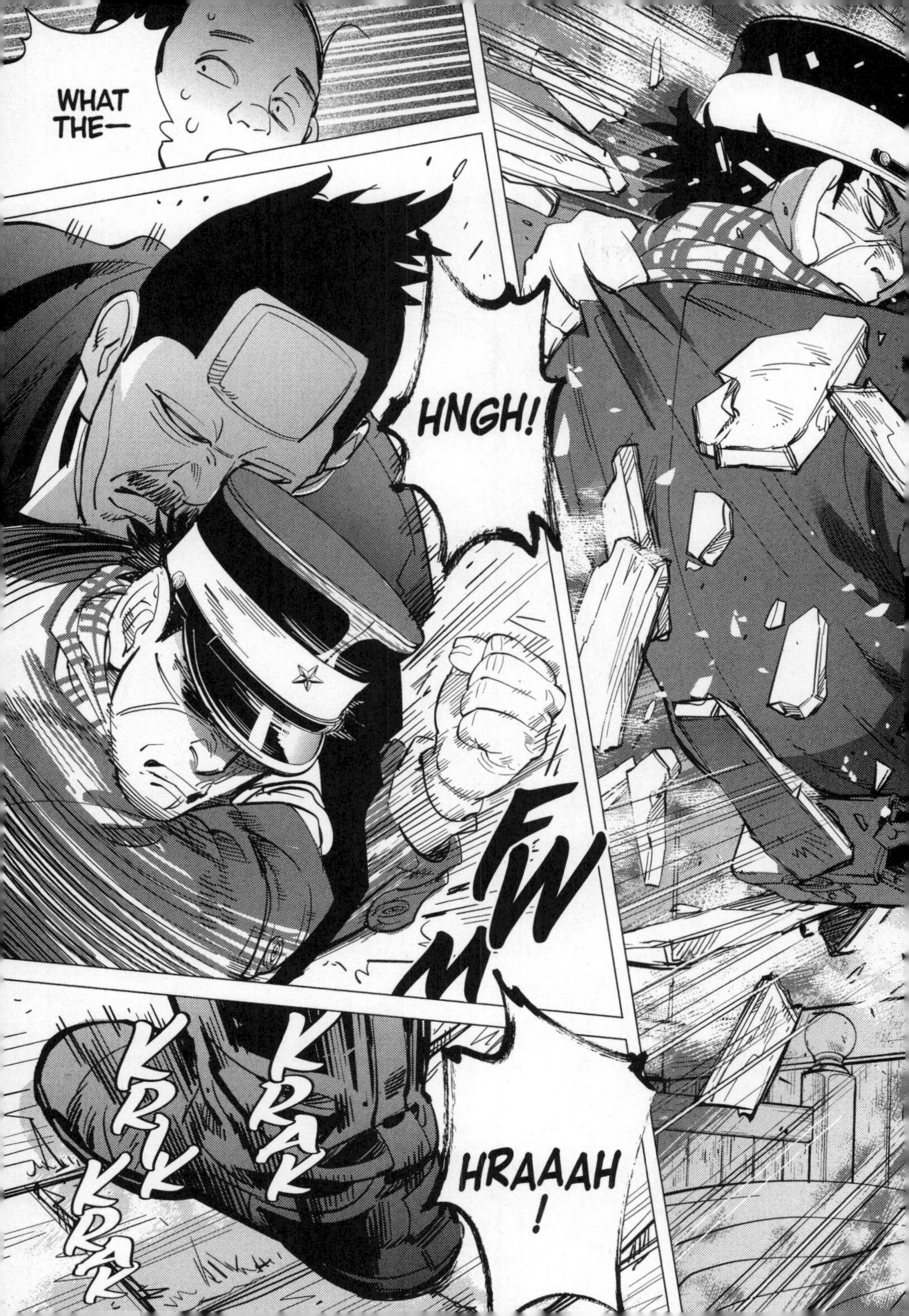
HNGH!
WHAT THE—
FWM
HRAAAH!
KRAK
KRIK KRAK

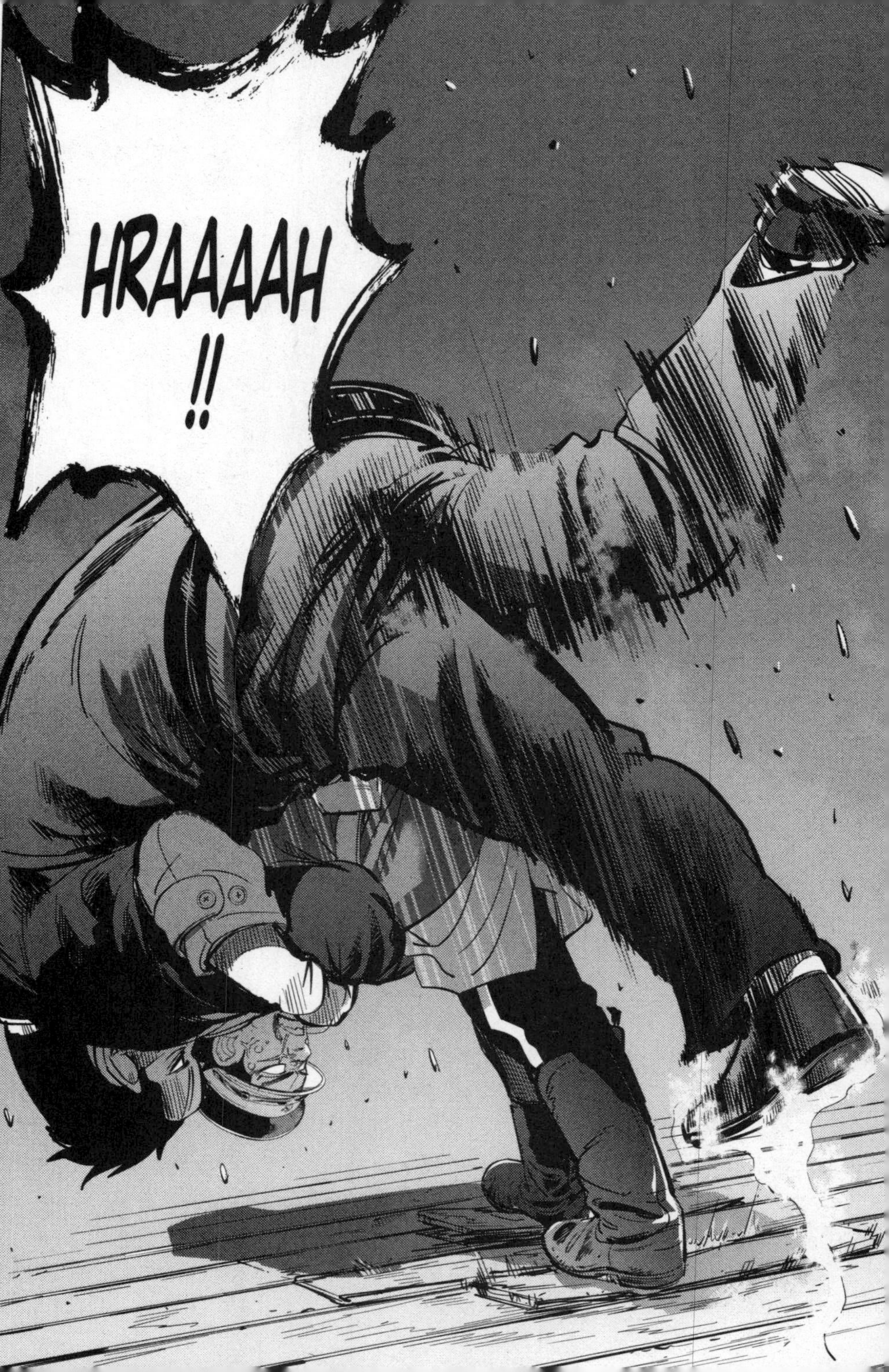
HRAAAAH
!!

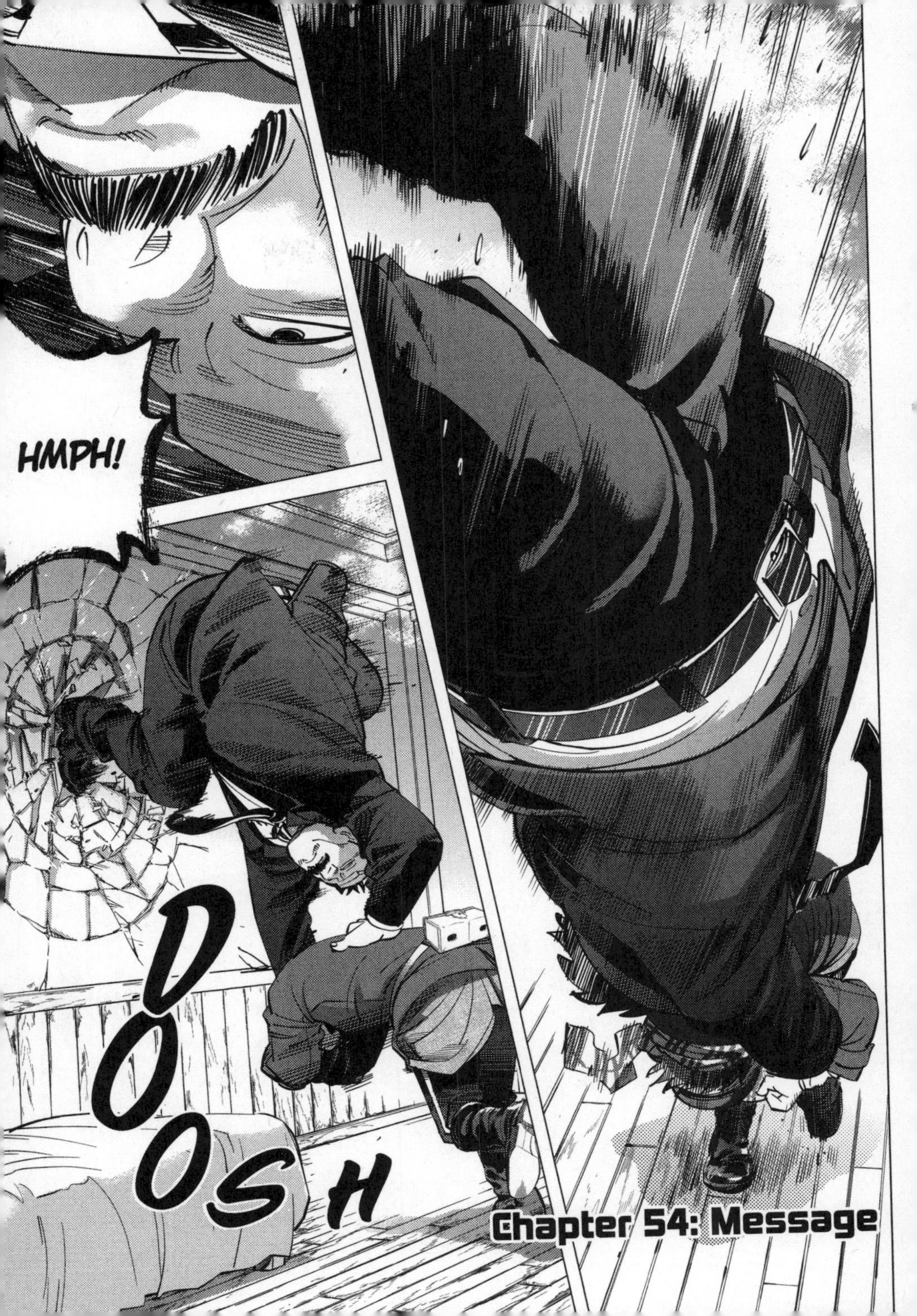
HMPH!
DOOOSH
Chapter 54: Message

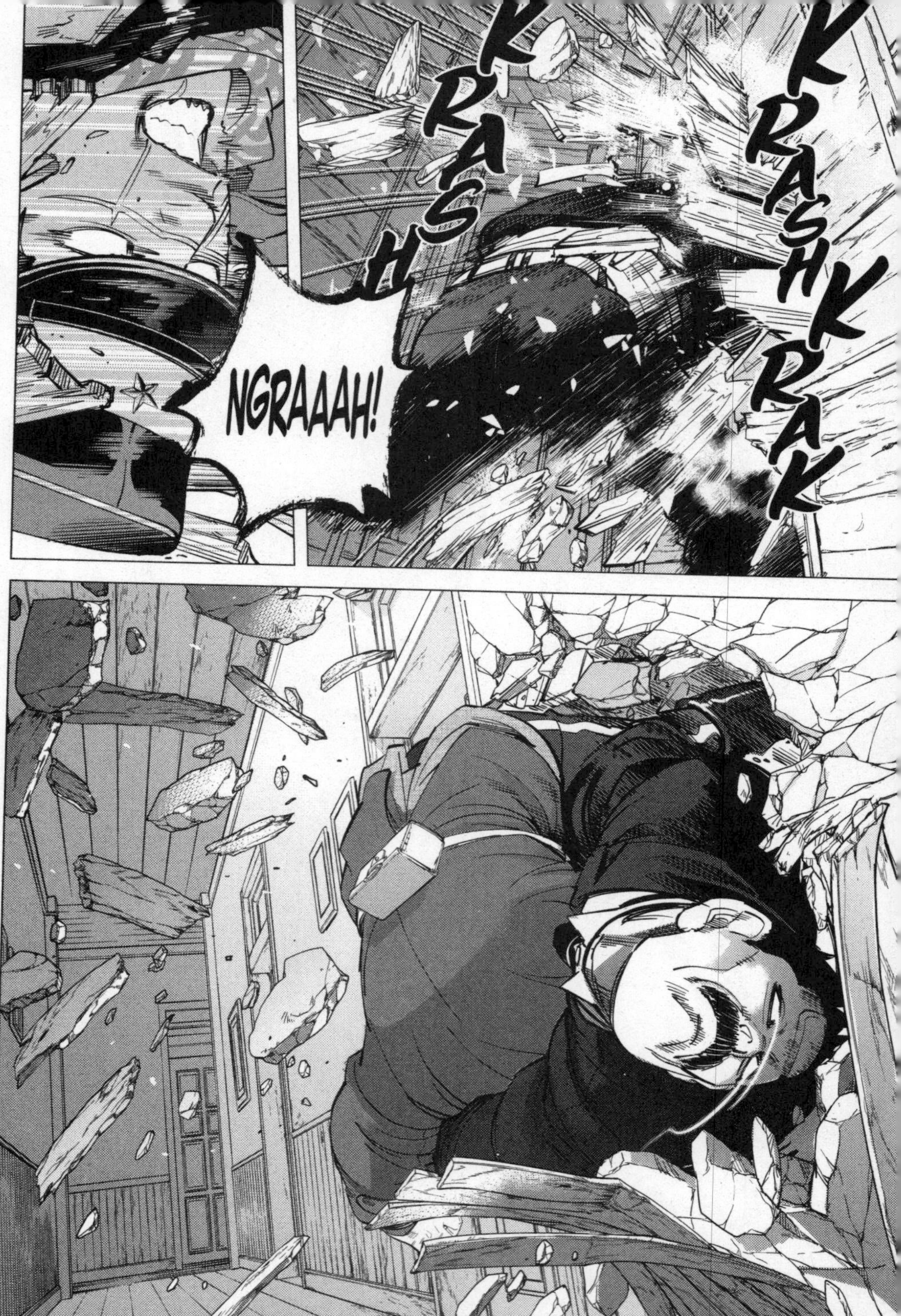
KRASHKRAK
KRASH
NGRAAAH!

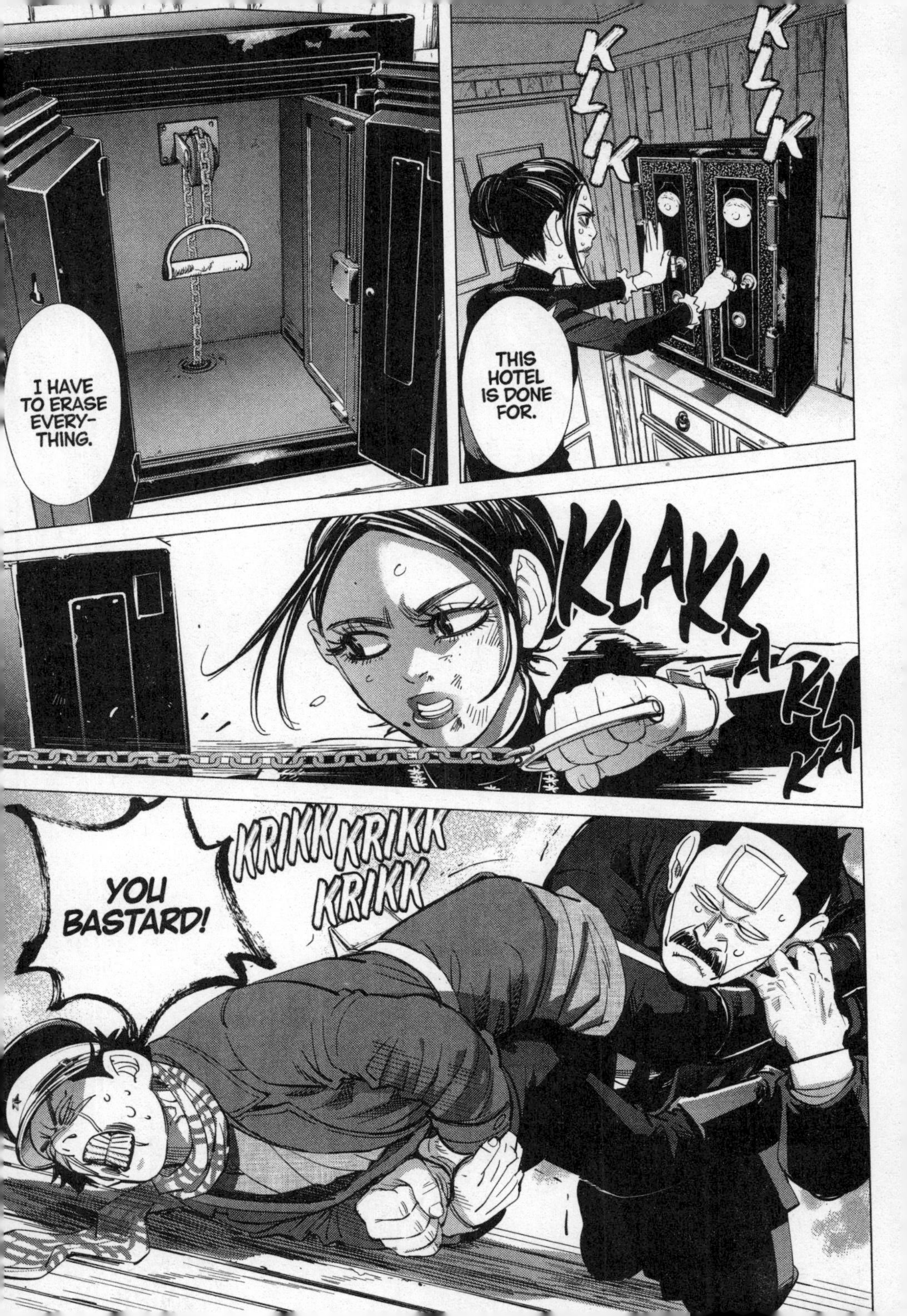
KLIK
KLIK
THIS HOTEL IS DONE FOR.
I HAVE TO ERASE EVERY-THING.
KLAKK
AKLAKA
KRIKK KRIKK KRIKK
YOU BASTARD!

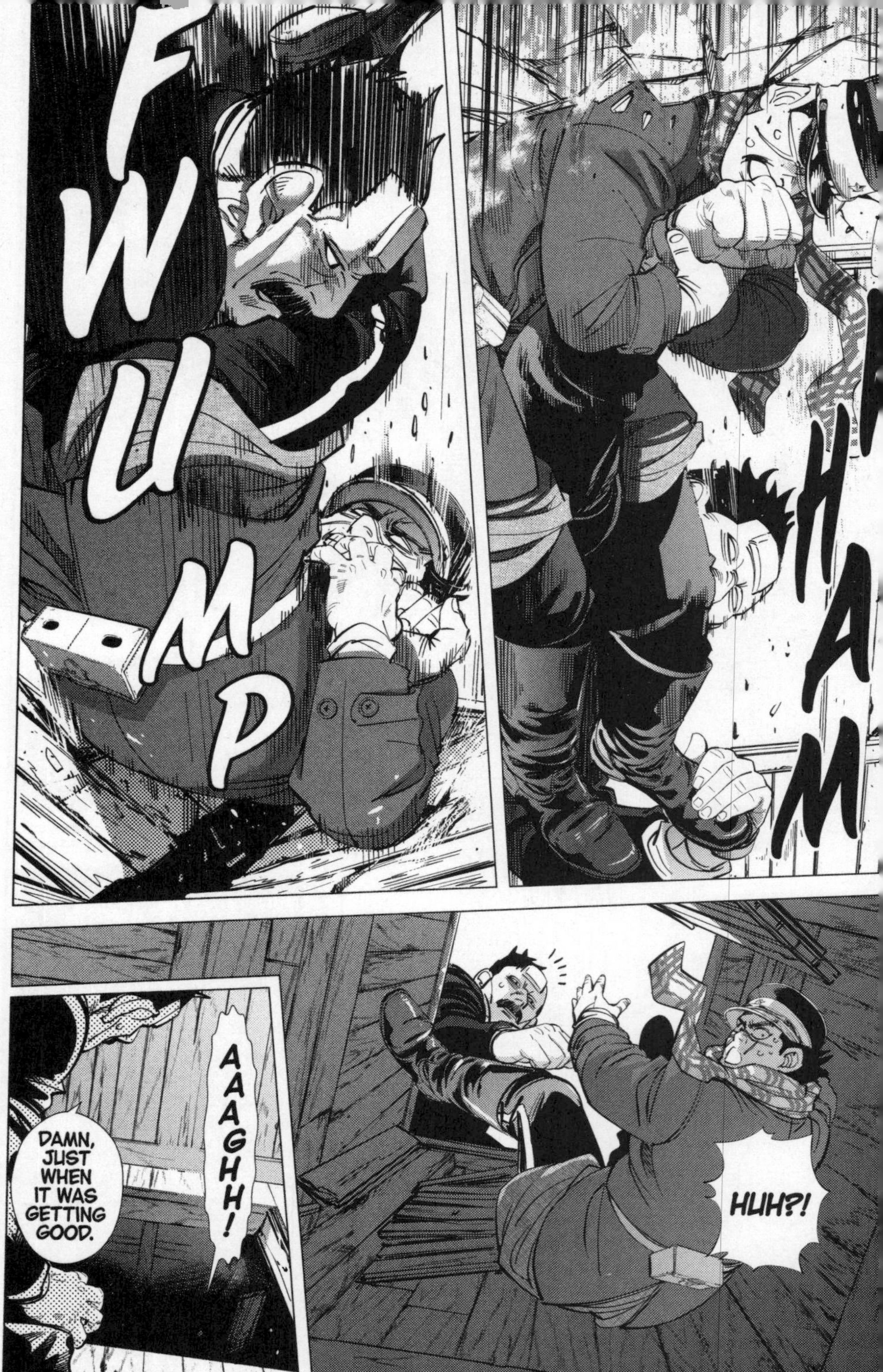
WHAM
FWUMP
HUH?!
AAAAGHH!
DAMN, JUST WHEN IT WAS GETTING GOOD.

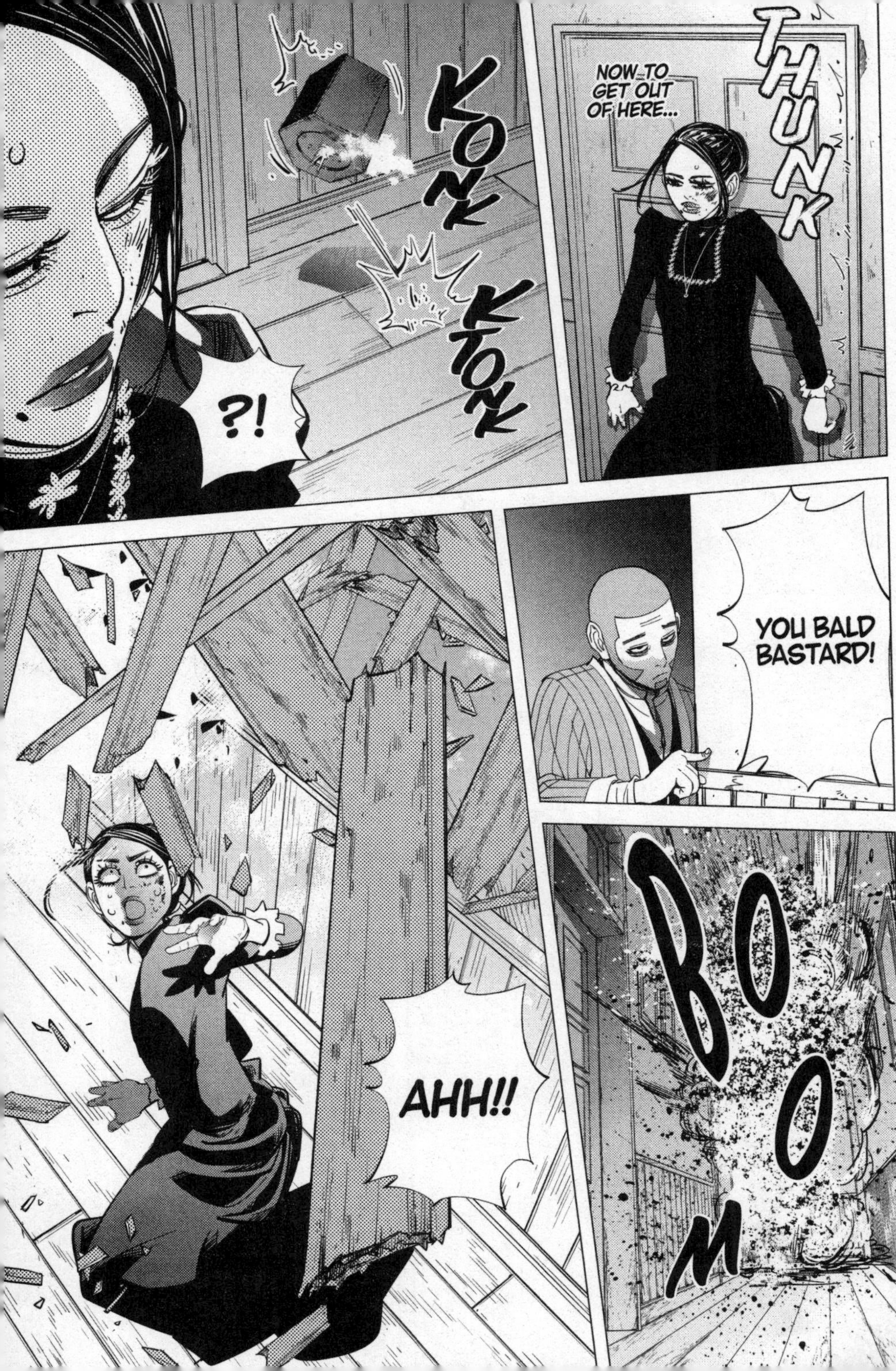
THUNK
NOW TO GET OUT OF HERE...
KONK
KTONK
?!
YOU BALD BASTARD!
BOOM
AHH!!

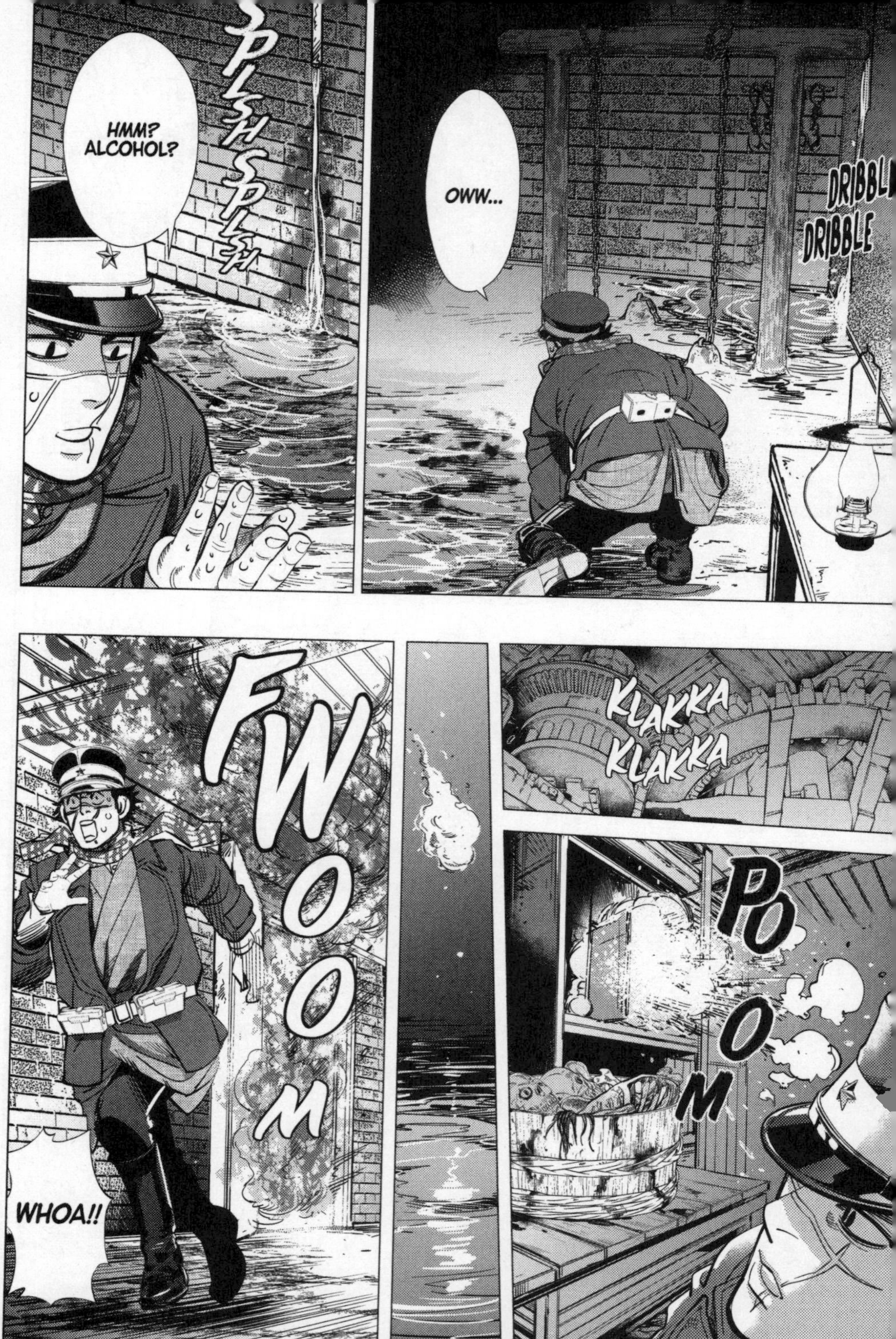

OWW...
DRIBBL
DRIBBLE
HMM? ALCOHOL?
SPLSH SPLSH
KLAKKA KLAKKA
POOOM
FWOOOM
WHOA!!

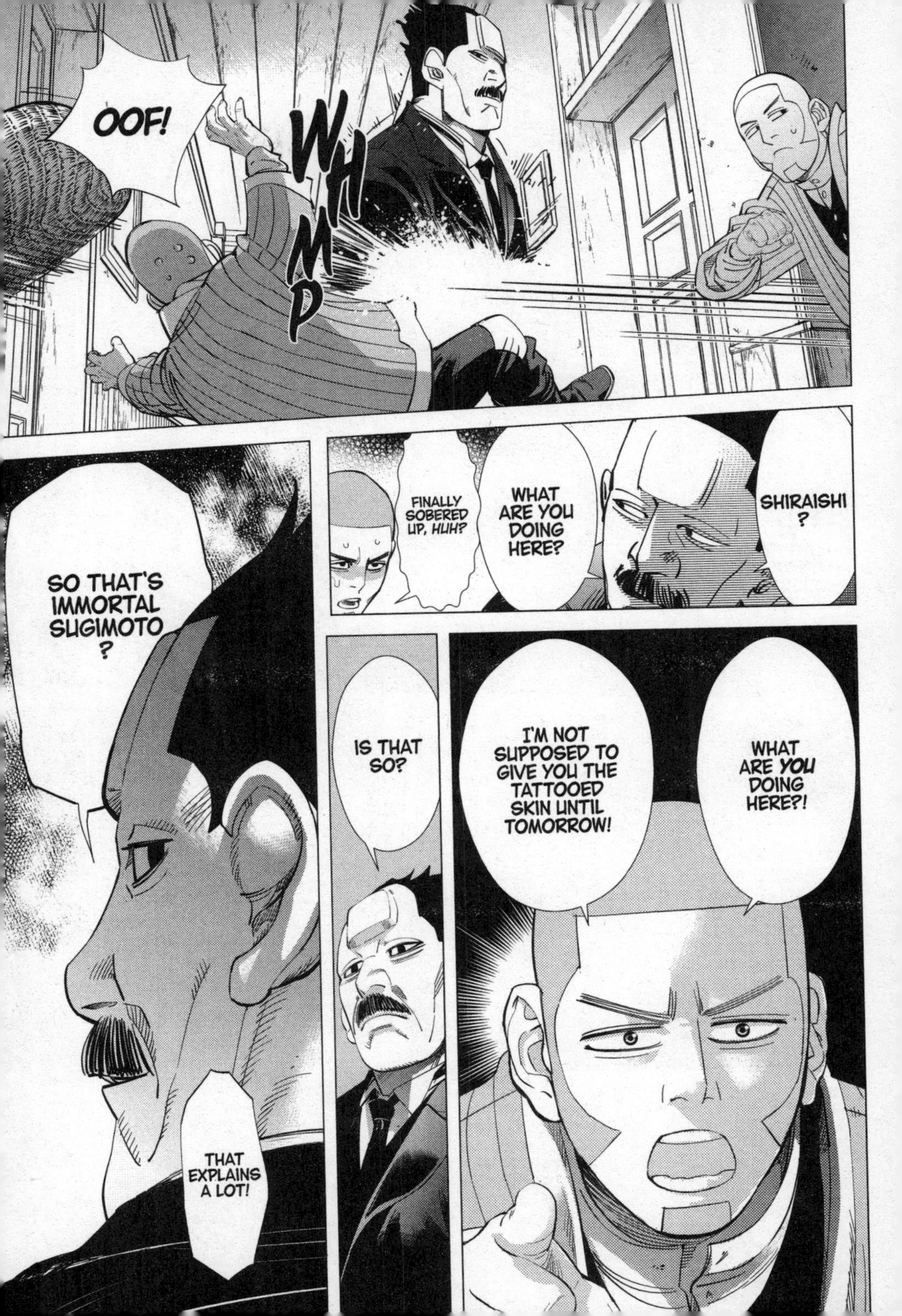
WHMP
OOF!
SHIRAISHI?
WHAT ARE YOU DOING HERE?
FINALLY SOBERED UP, HUH?
WHAT ARE YOU DOING HERE?!
I'M NOT SUPPOSED TO GIVE YOU THE TATTOOED SKIN UNTIL TOMORROW!
IS THAT SO?
SO THAT'S IMMORTAL SUGIMOTO?
THAT EXPLAINS A LOT!

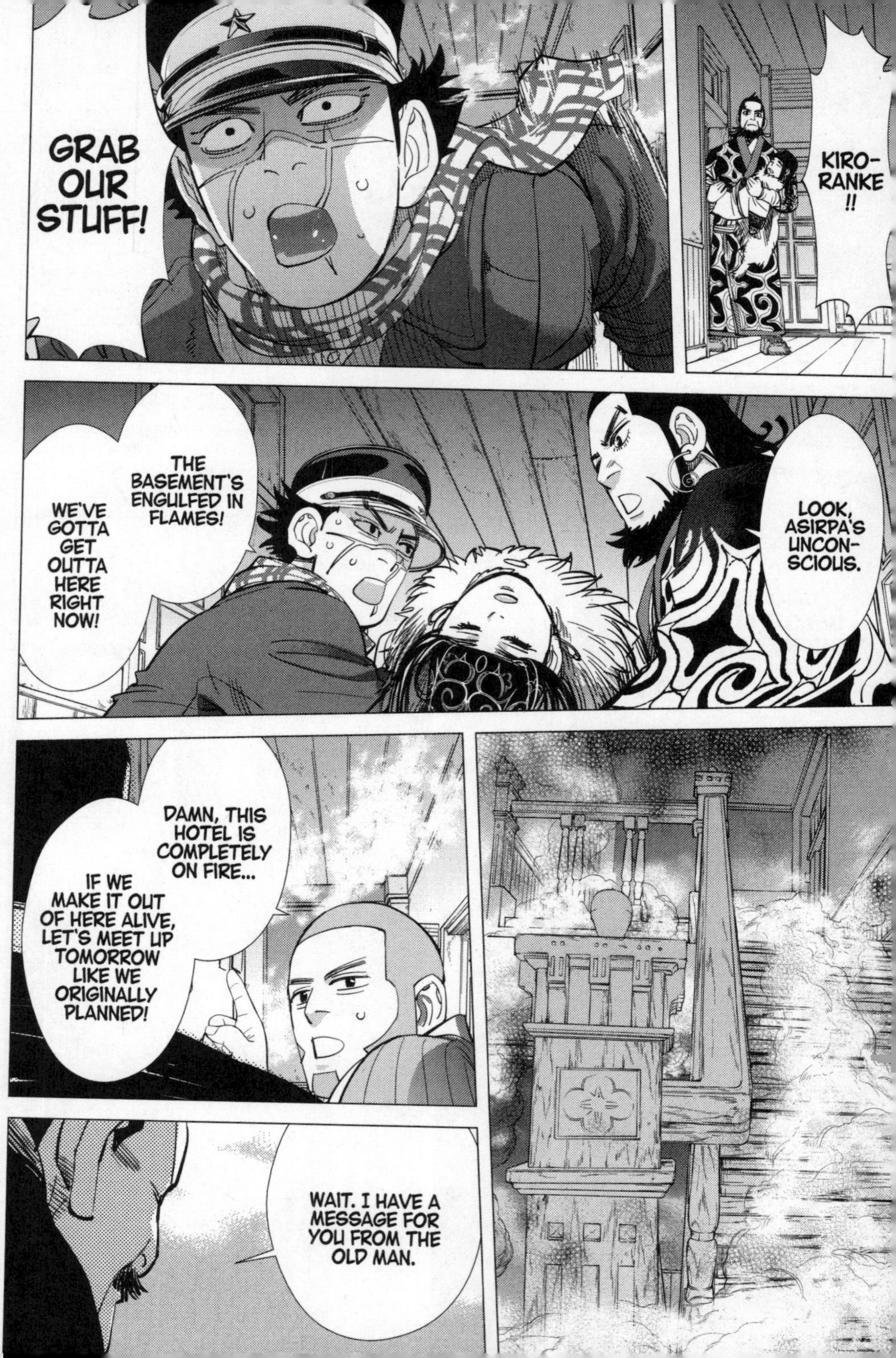
KIRO-RANKE!!
GRAB OUR STUFF!
LOOK, ASIRPA'S UNCON-SCIOUS.
THE BASEMENT'S ENGULFED IN FLAMES!
WE'VE GOTTA GET OUTTA HERE RIGHT NOW!
DAMN, THIS HOTEL IS COMPLETELY ON FIRE...
IF WE MAKE IT OUT OF HERE ALIVE, LET'S MEET UP TOMORROW LIKE WE ORIGINALLY PLANNED!
WAIT. I HAVE A MESSAGE FOR YOU FROM THE OLD MAN.

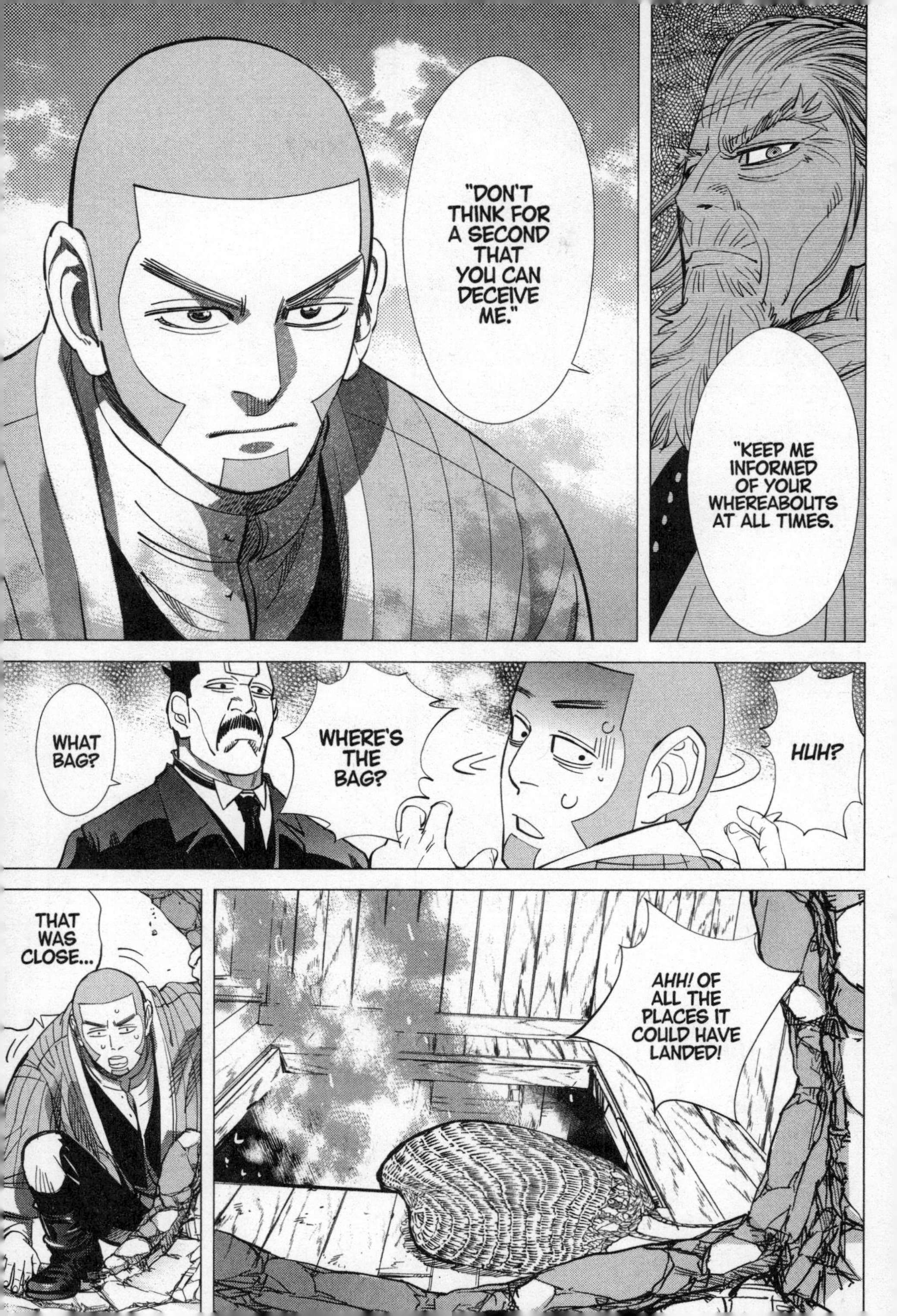
"KEEP ME INFORMED OF YOUR WHEREABOUTS AT ALL TIMES.
"DON'T THINK FOR A SECOND THAT YOU CAN DECEIVE ME."
HUH?
WHERE'S THE BAG?
WHAT BAG?
AHH! OF ALL THE PLACES IT COULD HAVE LANDED!
THAT WAS CLOSE...

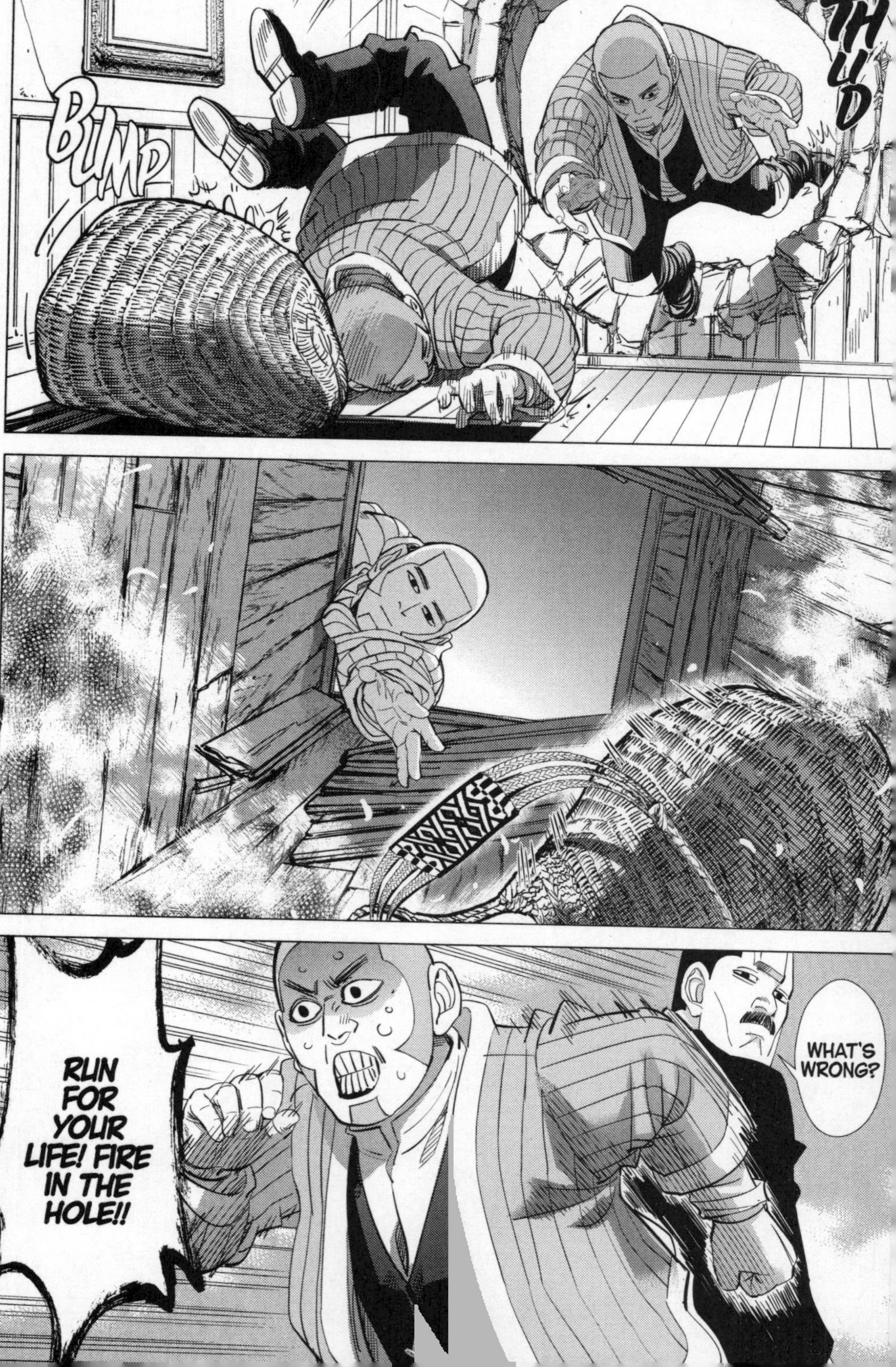
THUD
BUMP
WHAT'S WRONG?
RUN FOR YOUR LIFE! FIRE IN THE HOLE!!

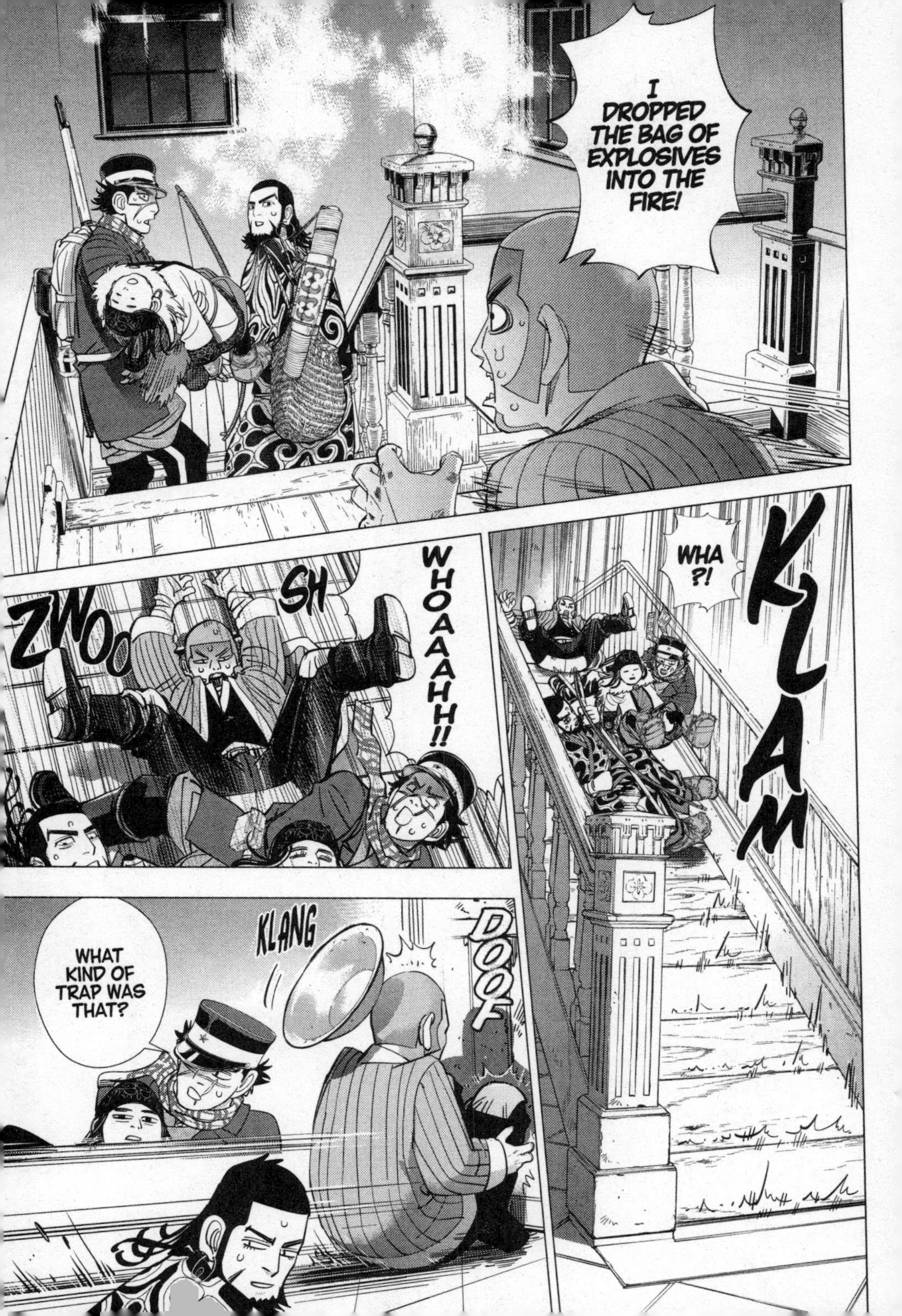
I DROPPED THE BAG OF EXPLOSIVES INTO THE FIRE!
KLAM
WHA ?!
WHOAAAAHH!!
ZWOOSH
DOOF
KLANG
WHAT KIND OF TRAP WAS THAT?

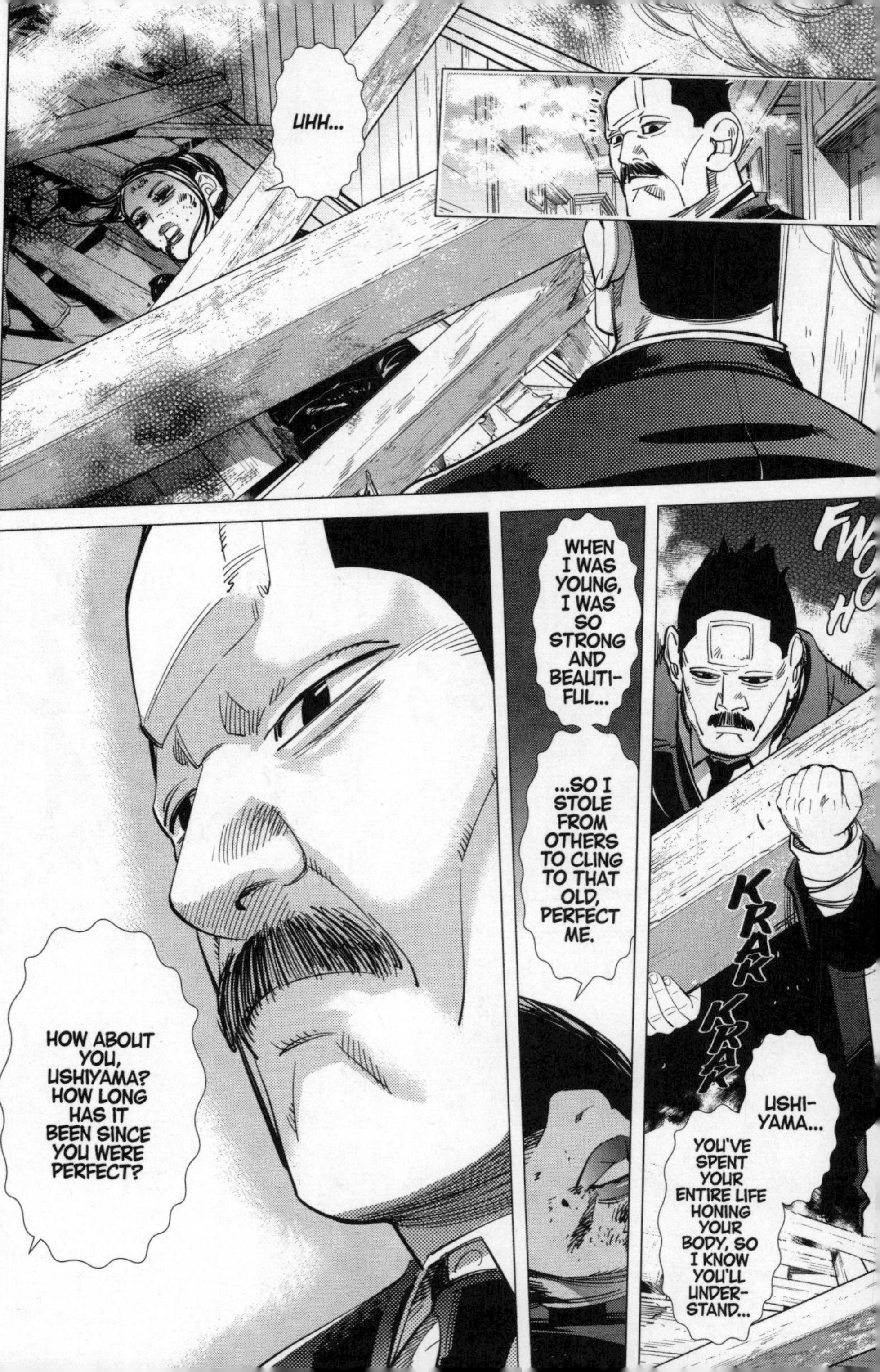
UHH...
FWOOH
KRAK KRAK
USHI-YAMA... YOU'VE SPENT YOUR ENTIRE LIFE HONING YOUR BODY, SO I KNOW YOU'LL UNDER-STAND...
WHEN I WAS YOUNG, I WAS SO STRONG AND BEAUTI-FUL...
...SO I STOLE FROM OTHERS TO CLING TO THAT OLD, PERFECT ME.
HOW ABOUT YOU, USHIYAMA? HOW LONG HAS IT BEEN SINCE YOU WERE PERFECT?

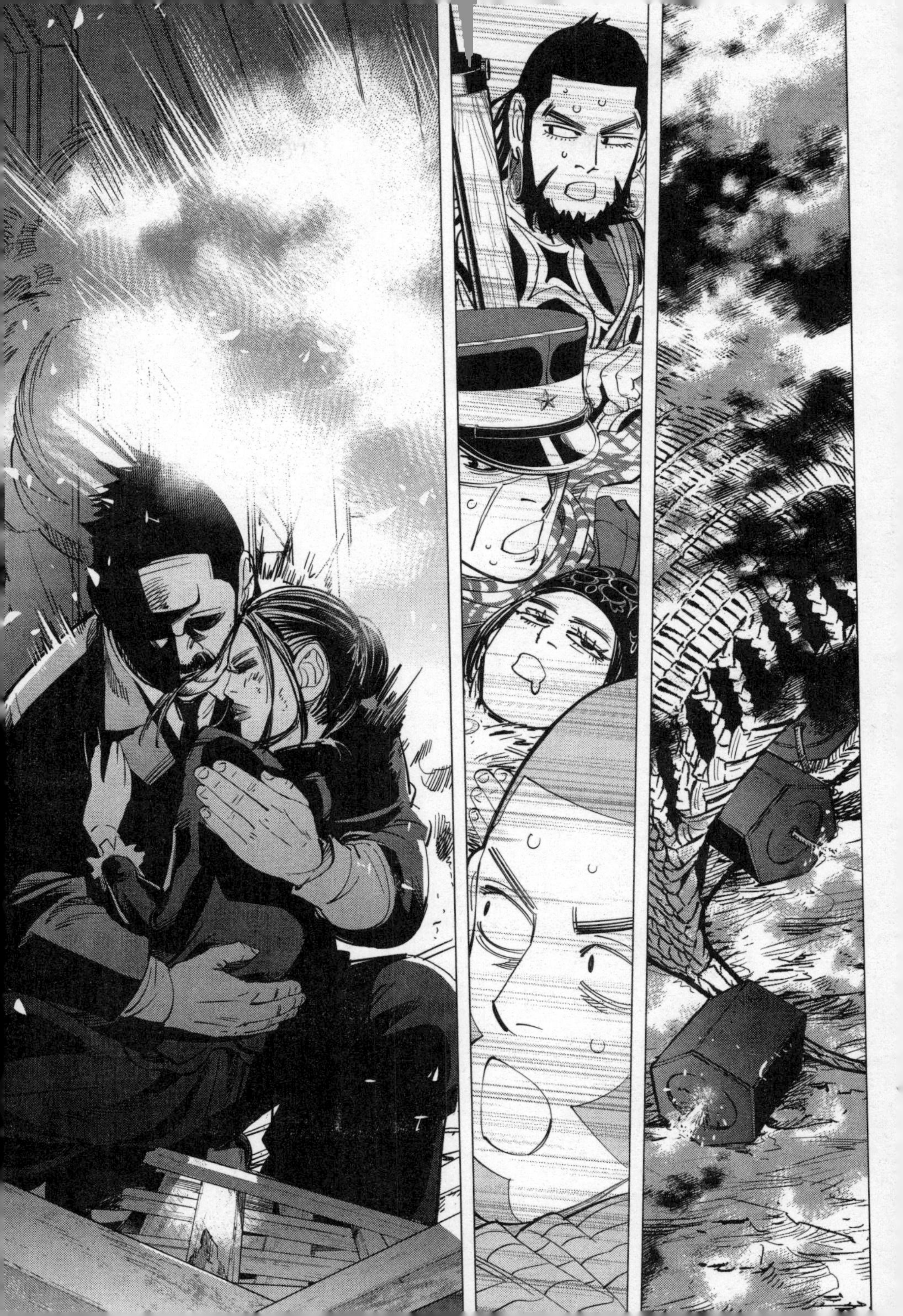

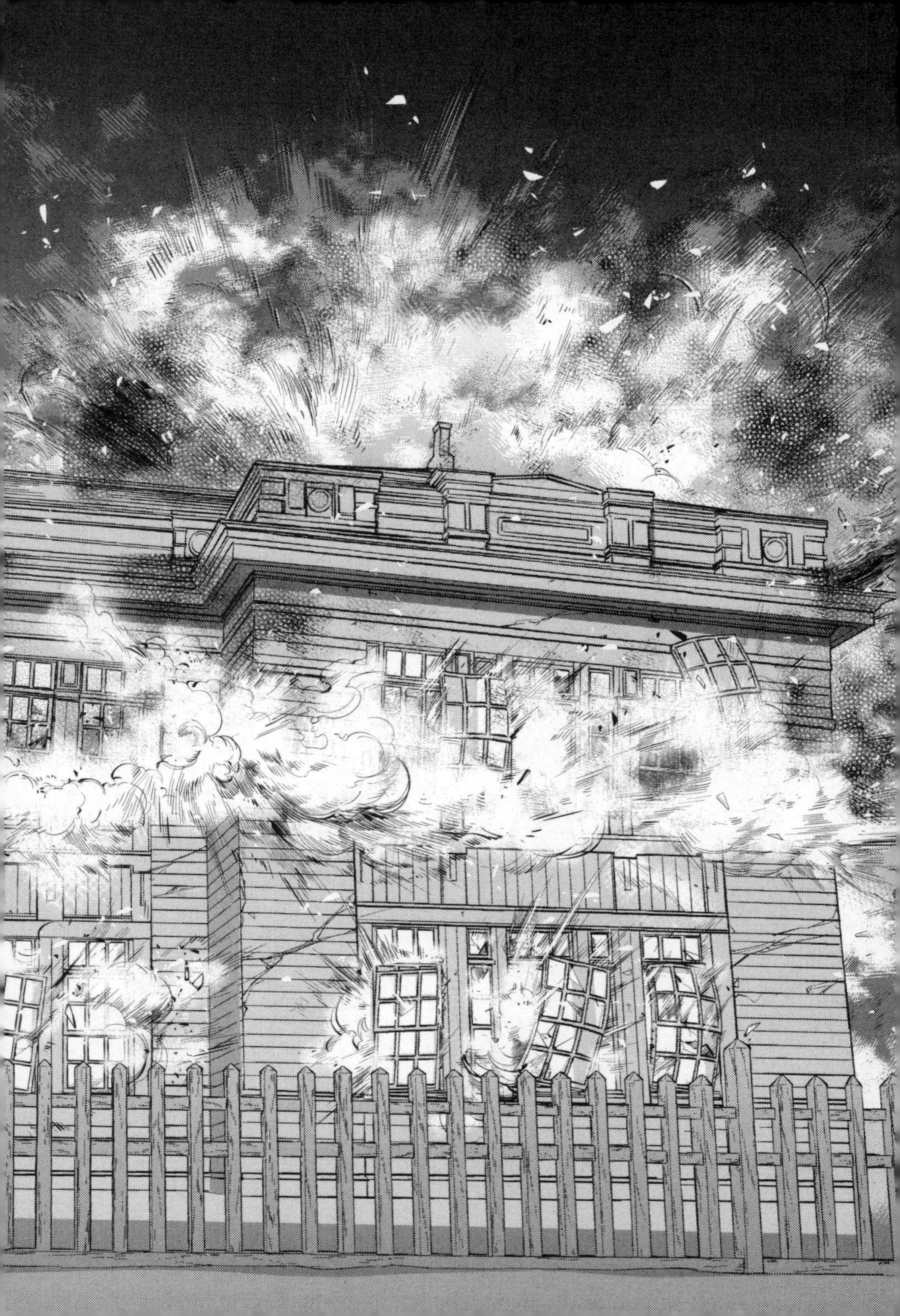

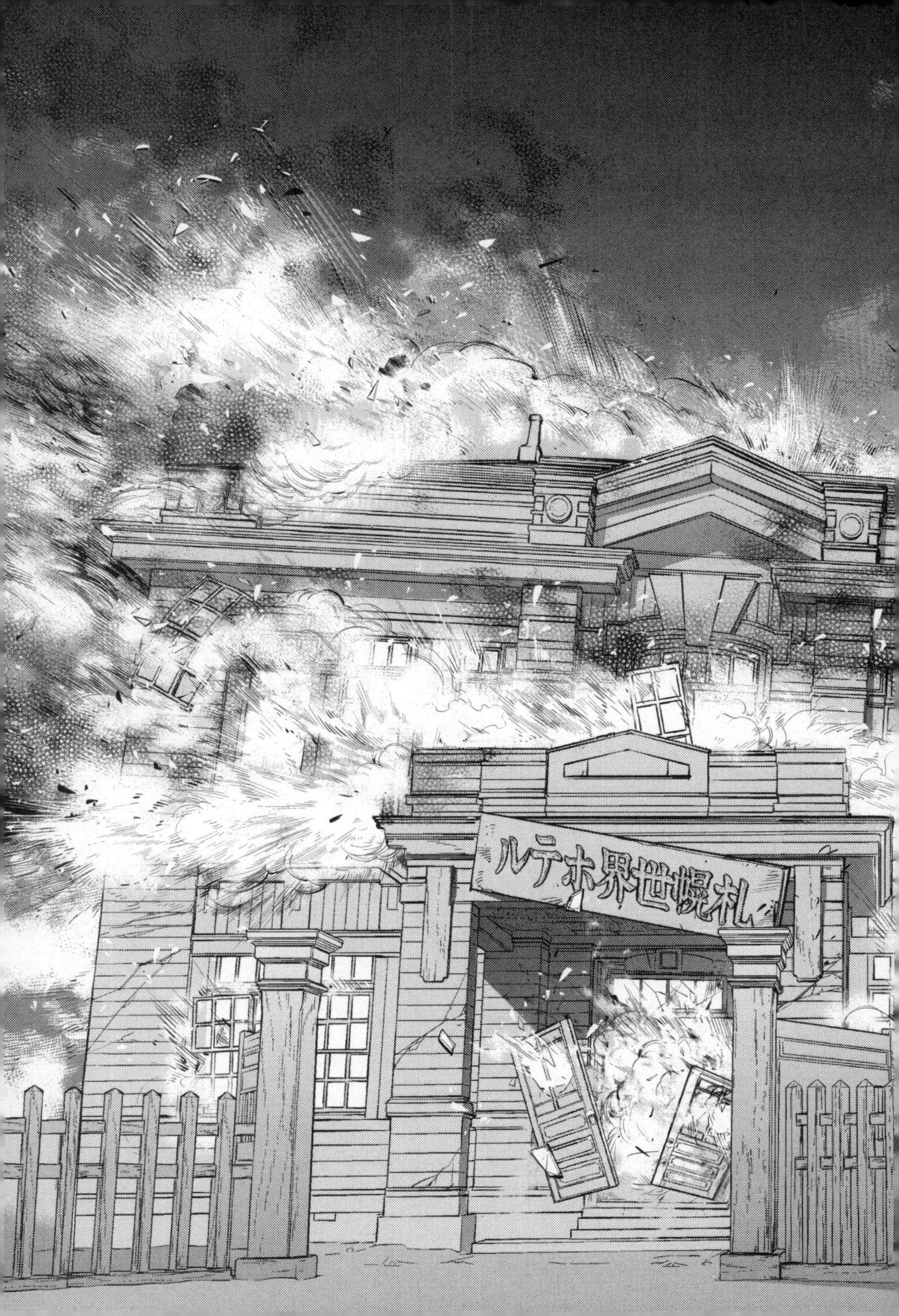
札幌世界ホテル

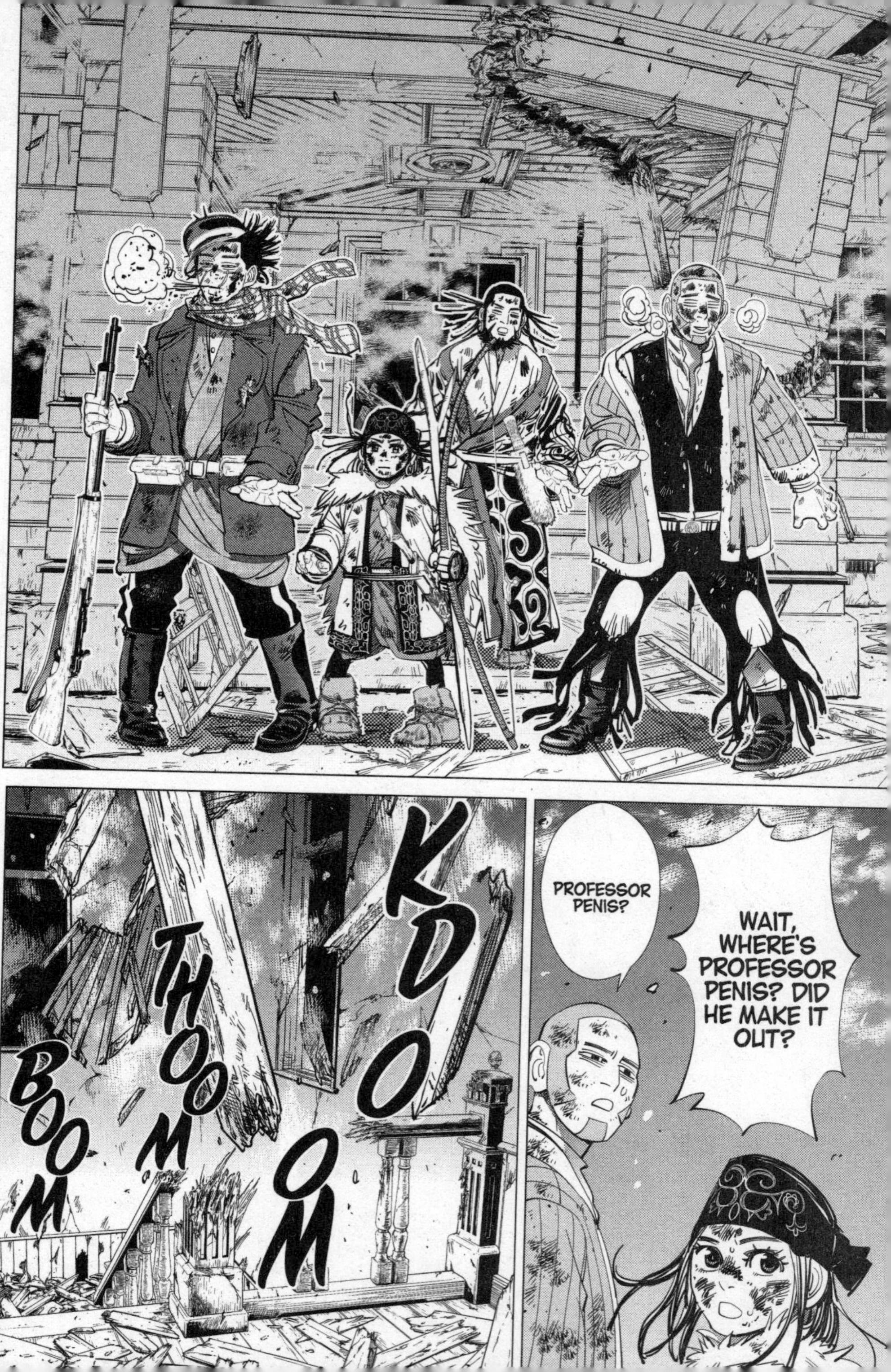

WAIT, WHERE'S PROFESSOR PENIS? DID HE MAKE IT OUT?
PROFESSOR PENIS?
KDOOOM
THOOOM
BOOOM

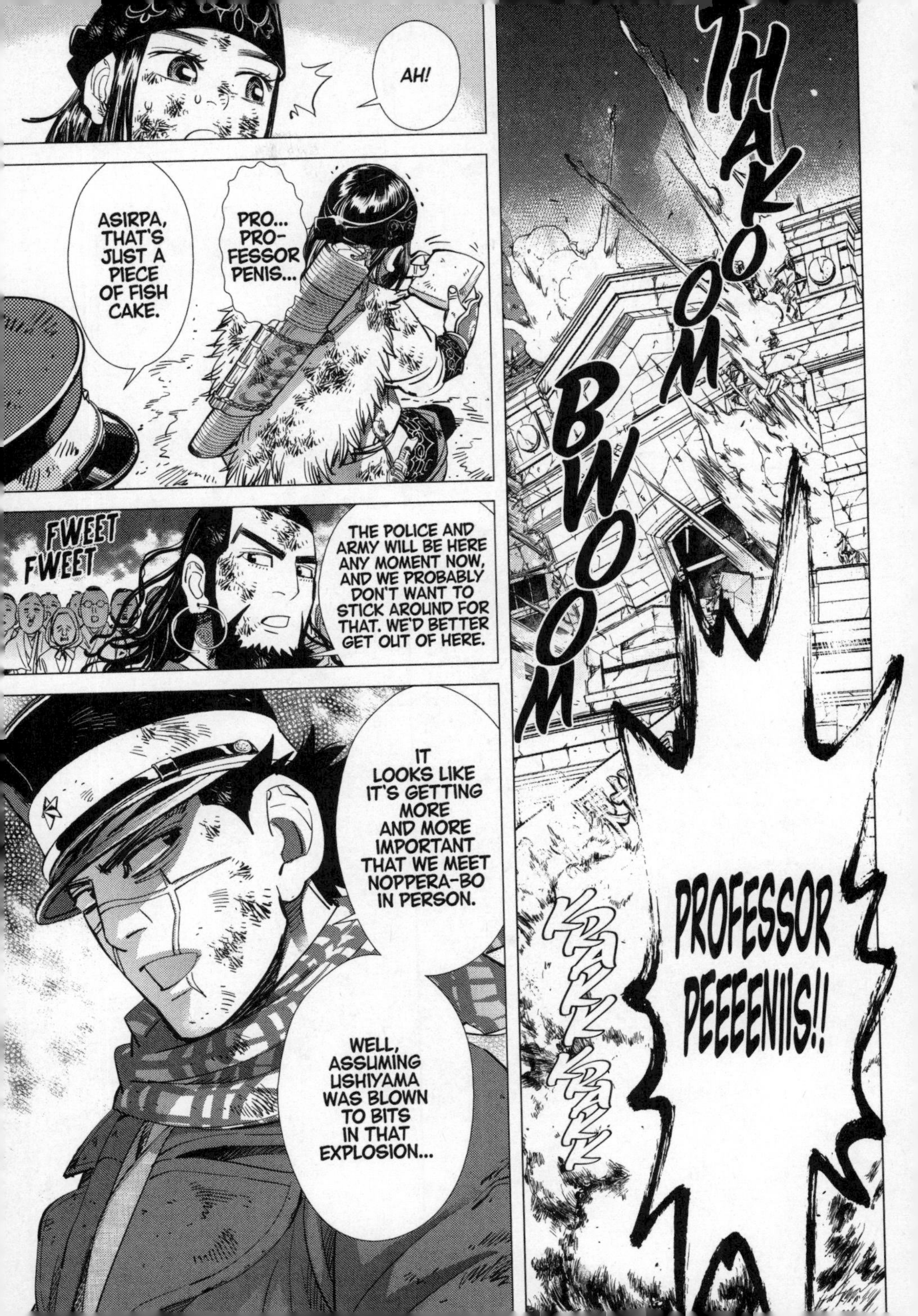
THAKOOM
BWOOOM
KRAK KRAK
PROFESSOR PEEEENIIS!!
AH!
PRO... PRO-FESSOR PENIS...
ASIRPA, THAT'S JUST A PIECE OF FISH CAKE.
THE POLICE AND ARMY WILL BE HERE ANY MOMENT NOW, AND WE PROBABLY DON'T WANT TO STICK AROUND FOR THAT. WE'D BETTER GET OUT OF HERE.
FWEET FWEET
IT LOOKS LIKE IT'S GETTING MORE AND MORE IMPORTANT THAT WE MEET NOPPERA-BO IN PERSON.
WELL, ASSUMING USHIYAMA WAS BLOWN TO BITS IN THAT EXPLOSION...

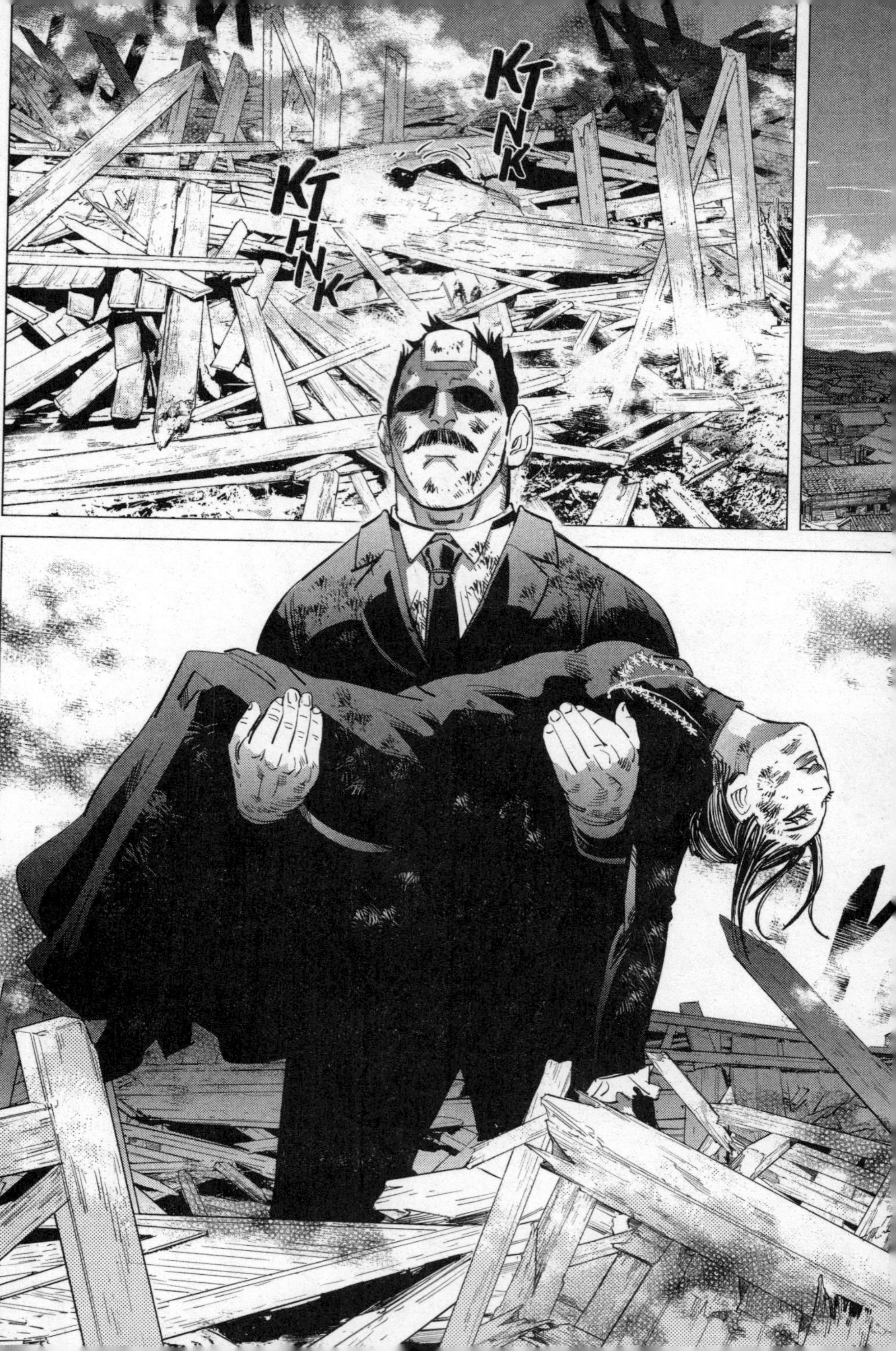
KTNK
KTHNK

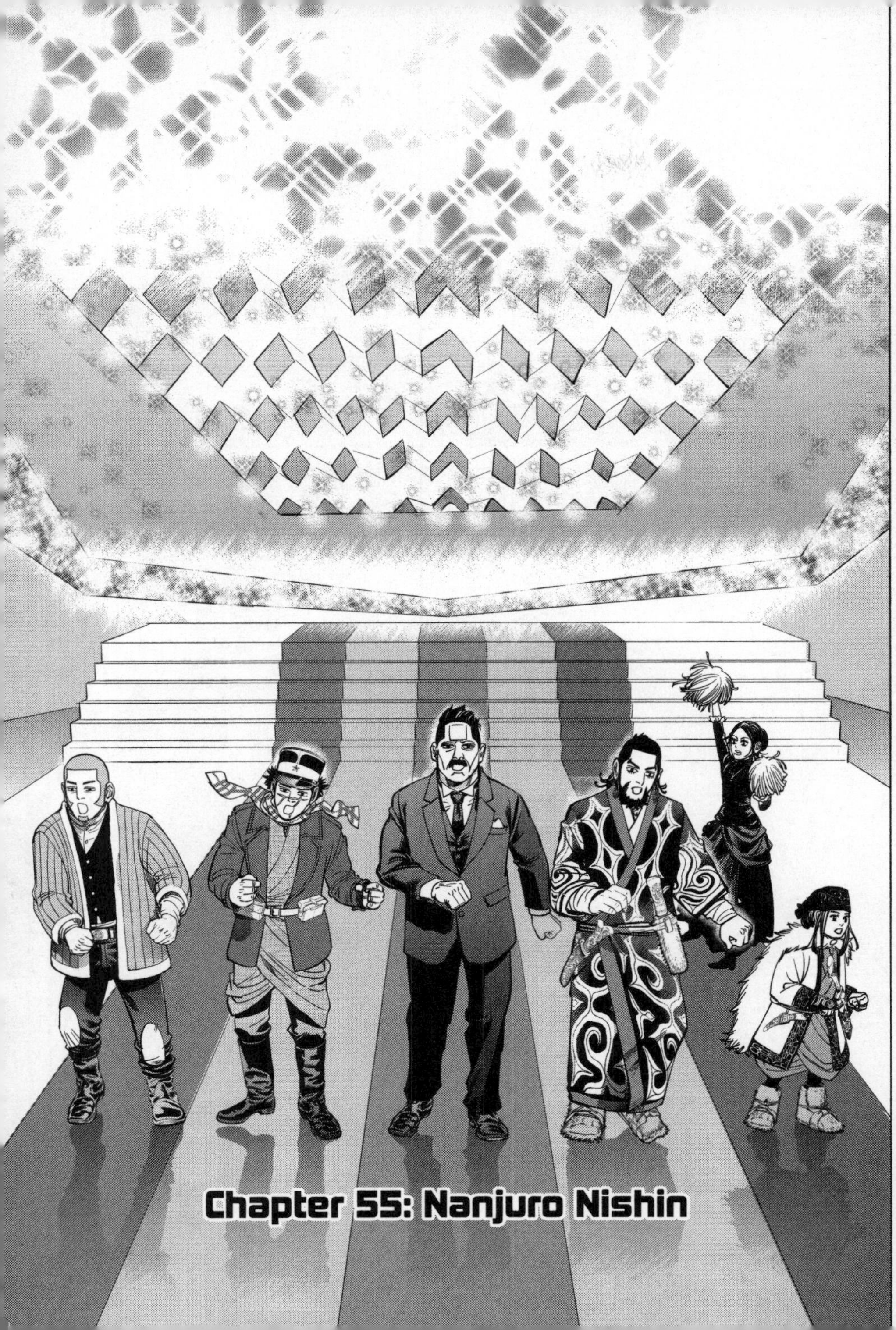
Chapter 55: Nanjuro Nishin

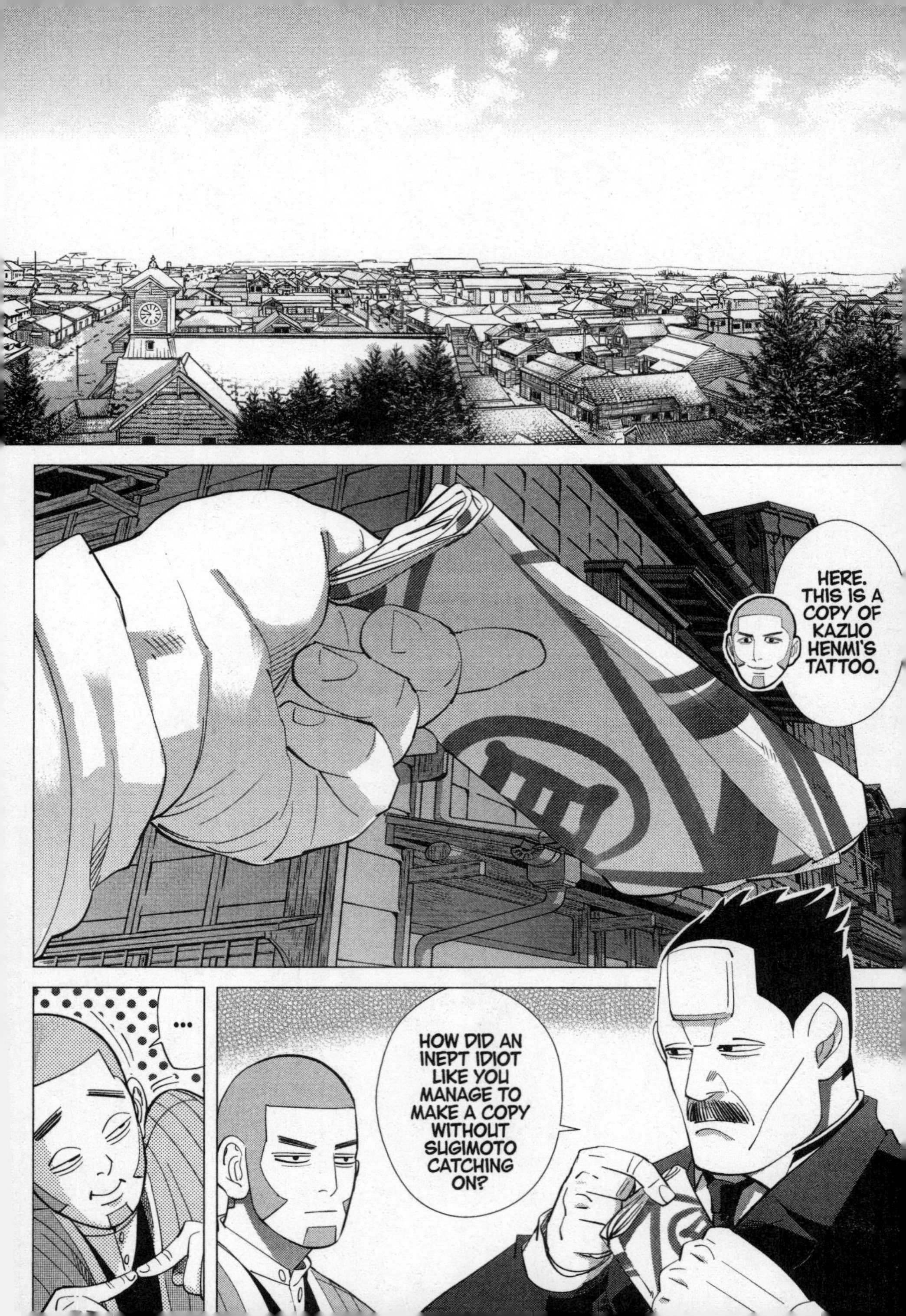
HERE. THIS IS A COPY OF KAZUO HENMI'S TATTOO.
HOW DID AN INEPT IDIOT LIKE YOU MANAGE TO MAKE A COPY WITHOUT SUGIMOTO CATCHING ON?
...

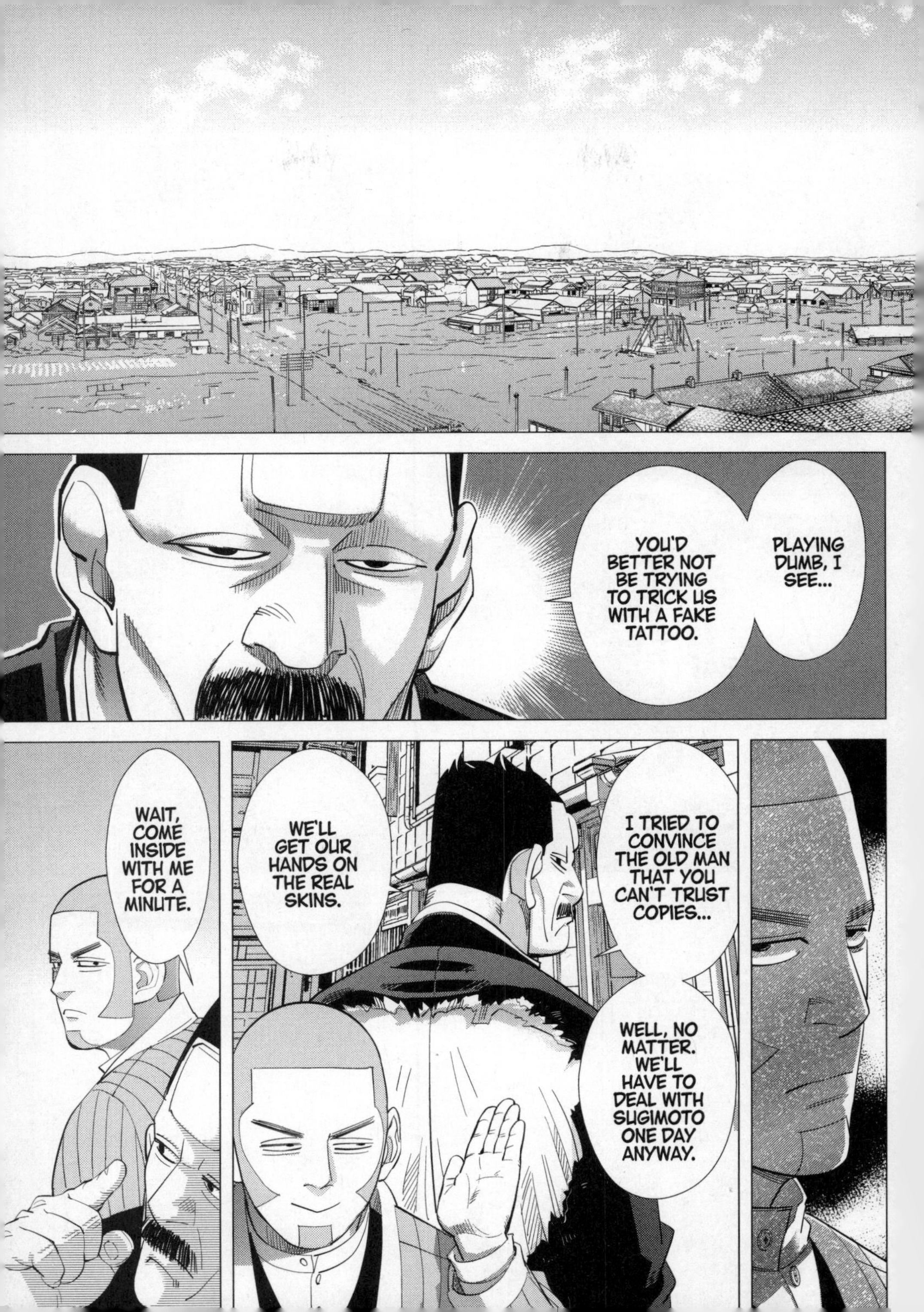
PLAYING DUMB, I SEE...
YOU'D BETTER NOT BE TRYING TO TRICK US WITH A FAKE TATTOO.
I TRIED TO CONVINCE THE OLD MAN THAT YOU CAN'T TRUST COPIES...
WELL, NO MATTER. WE'LL HAVE TO DEAL WITH SUGIMOTO ONE DAY ANYWAY.
WE'LL GET OUR HANDS ON THE REAL SKINS.
WAIT, COME INSIDE WITH ME FOR A MINUTE.

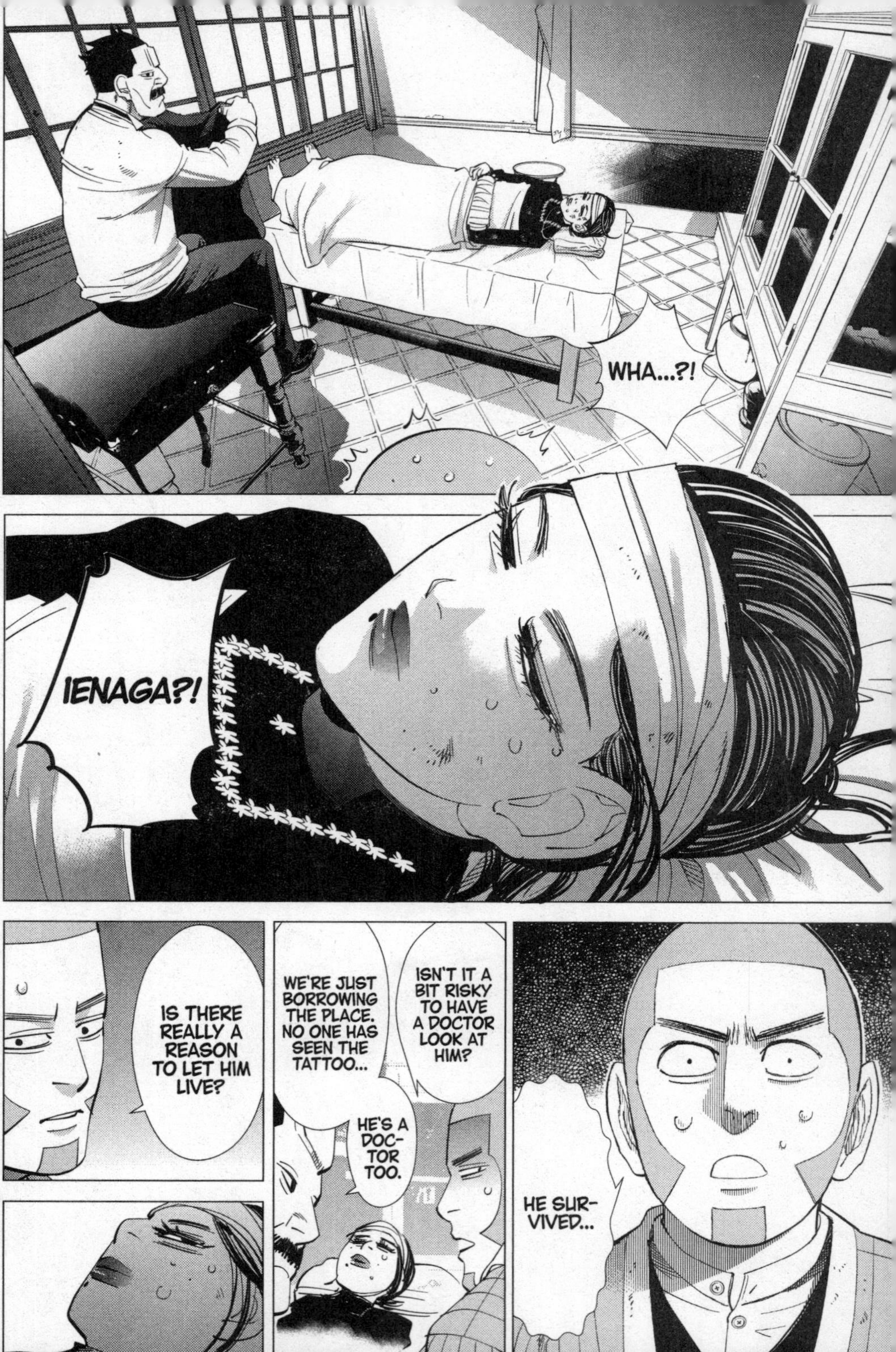
WHA...?!
IENAGA?!
HE SURVIVED...
ISN'T IT A BIT RISKY TO HAVE A DOCTOR LOOK AT HIM?
WE'RE JUST BORROWING THE PLACE. NO ONE HAS SEEN THE TATTOO...
HE'S A DOCTOR TOO.
IS THERE REALLY A REASON TO LET HIM LIVE?

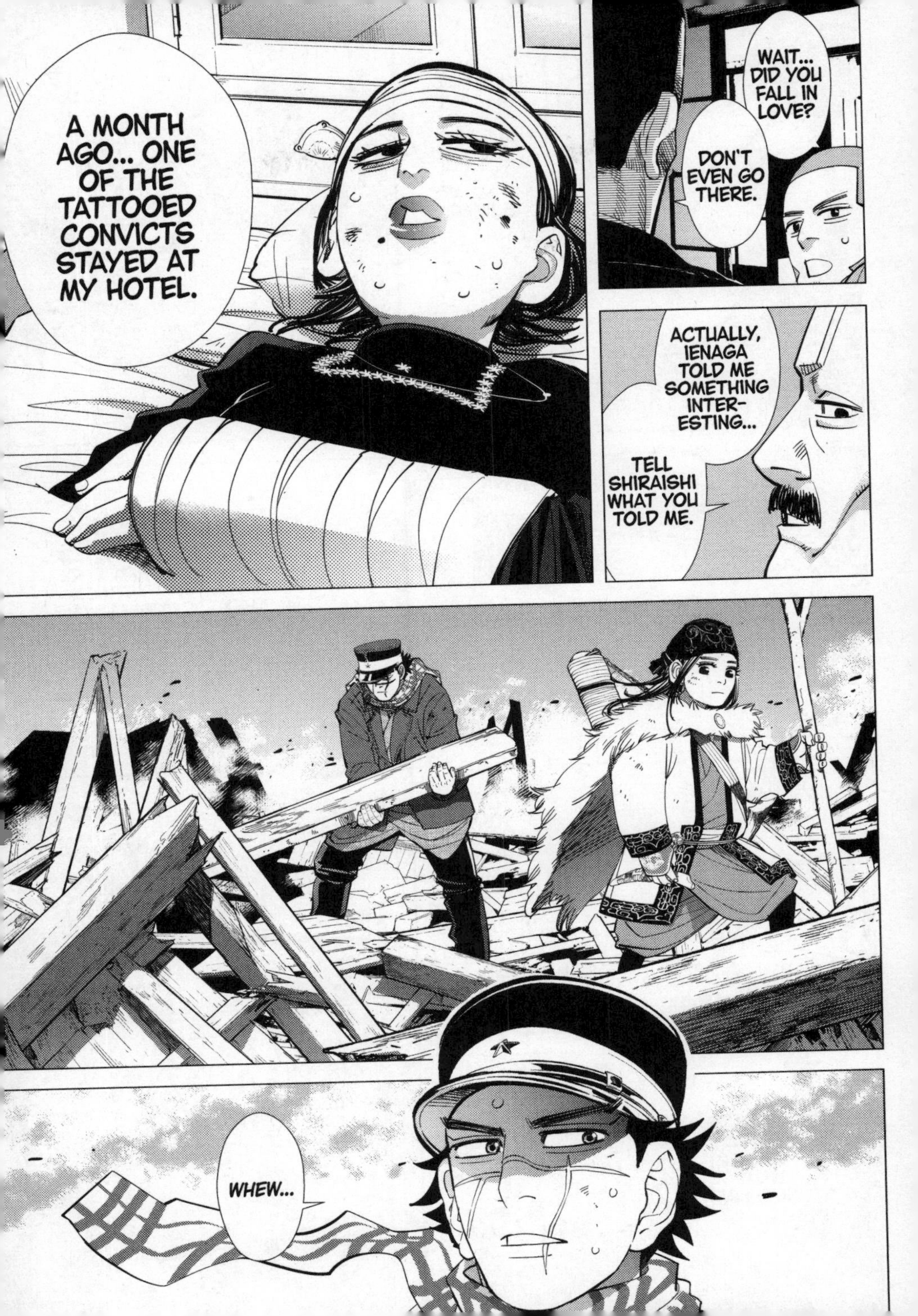
WAIT... DID YOU FALL IN LOVE?
DON'T EVEN GO THERE.
ACTUALLY, IENAGA TOLD ME SOMETHING INTER-ESTING...
TELL SHIRAISHI WHAT YOU TOLD ME.
A MONTH AGO... ONE OF THE TATTOOED CONVICTS STAYED AT MY HOTEL.
WHEW...

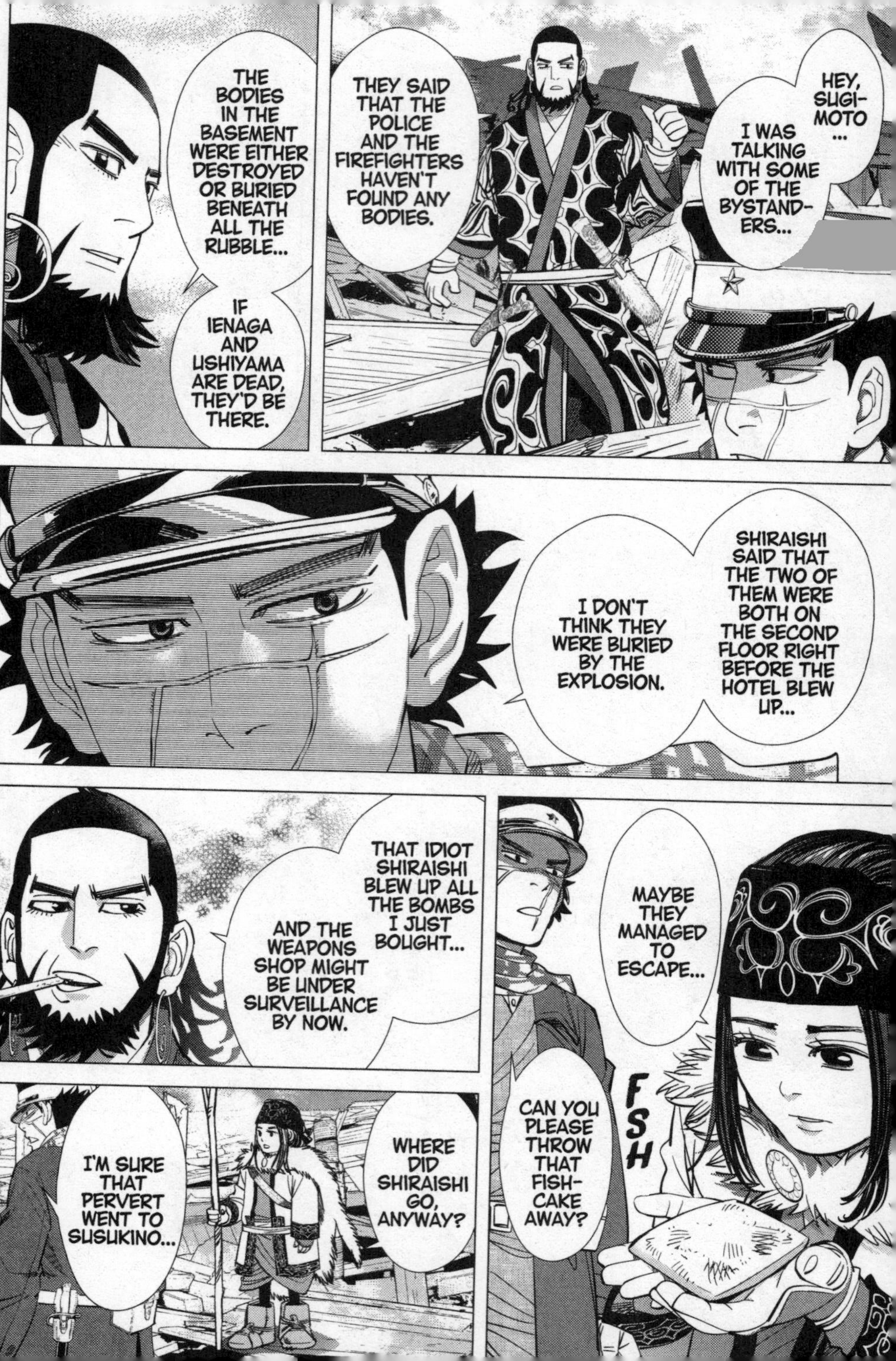
HEY, SUGI-MOTO...
I WAS TALKING WITH SOME OF THE BYSTAND-ERS...
THEY SAID THAT THE POLICE AND THE FIREFIGHTERS HAVEN'T FOUND ANY BODIES.
THE BODIES IN THE BASEMENT WERE EITHER DESTROYED OR BURIED BENEATH ALL THE RUBBLE...
IF IENAGA AND USHIYAMA ARE DEAD, THEY'D BE THERE.
SHIRAISHI SAID THAT THE TWO OF THEM WERE BOTH ON THE SECOND FLOOR RIGHT BEFORE THE HOTEL BLEW UP...
I DON'T THINK THEY WERE BURIED BY THE EXPLOSION.
MAYBE THEY MANAGED TO ESCAPE...
THAT IDIOT SHIRAISHI BLEW UP ALL THE BOMBS I JUST BOUGHT...
AND THE WEAPONS SHOP MIGHT BE UNDER SURVEILLANCE BY NOW.
FSH
CAN YOU PLEASE THROW THAT FISH-CAKE AWAY?
WHERE DID SHIRAISHI GO, ANYWAY?
I'M SURE THAT PERVERT WENT TO SUSUKINO...

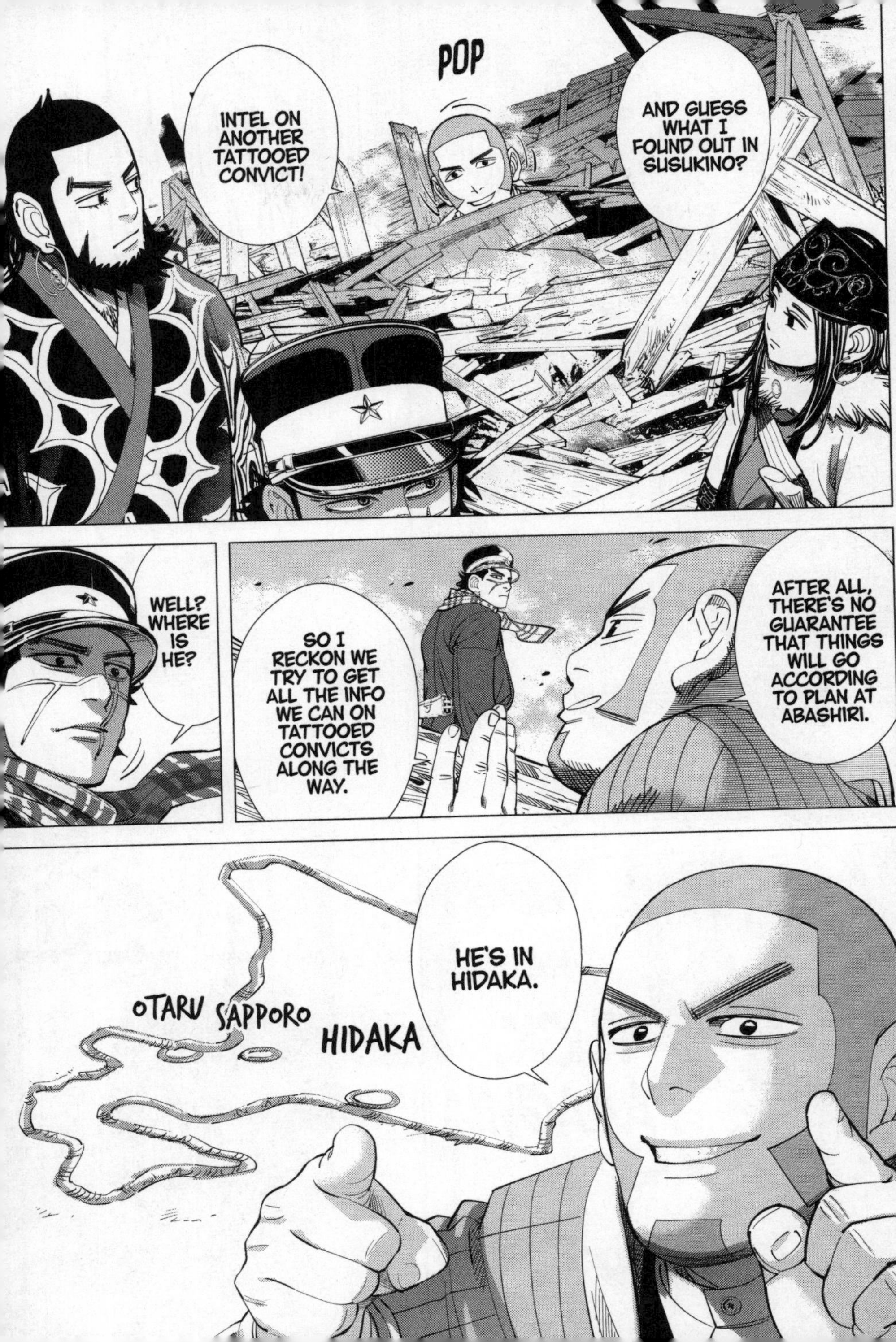
POP
AND GUESS WHAT I FOUND OUT IN SUSUKINO?
INTEL ON ANOTHER TATTOOED CONVICT!
AFTER ALL, THERE'S NO GUARANTEE THAT THINGS WILL GO ACCORDING TO PLAN AT ABASHIRI.
SO I RECKON WE TRY TO GET ALL THE INFO WE CAN ON TATTOOED CONVICTS ALONG THE WAY.
WELL? WHERE IS HE?
HE'S IN HIDAKA.
OTARU
SAPPORO
HIDAKA

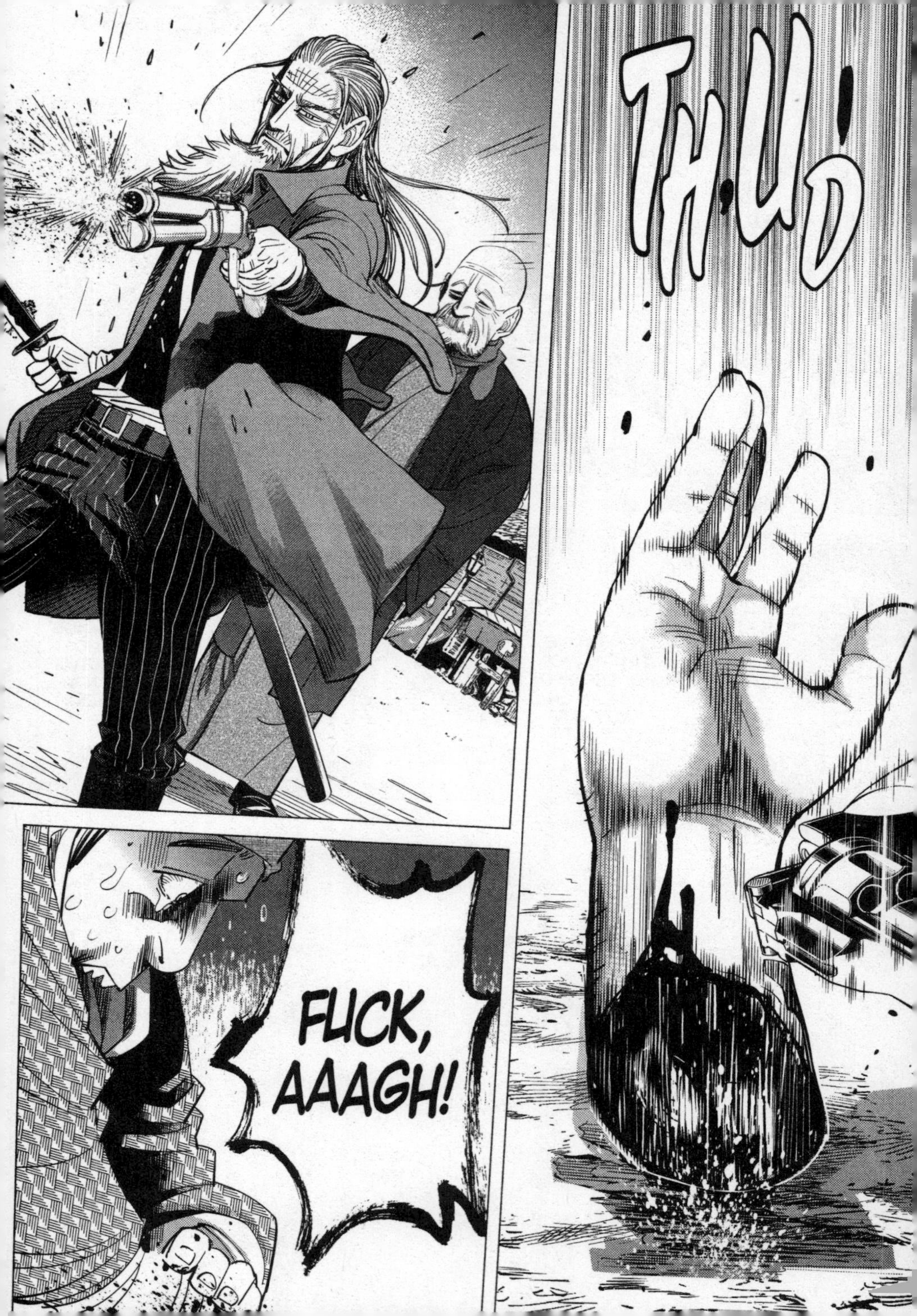
THUD
FUCK, AAAGH!

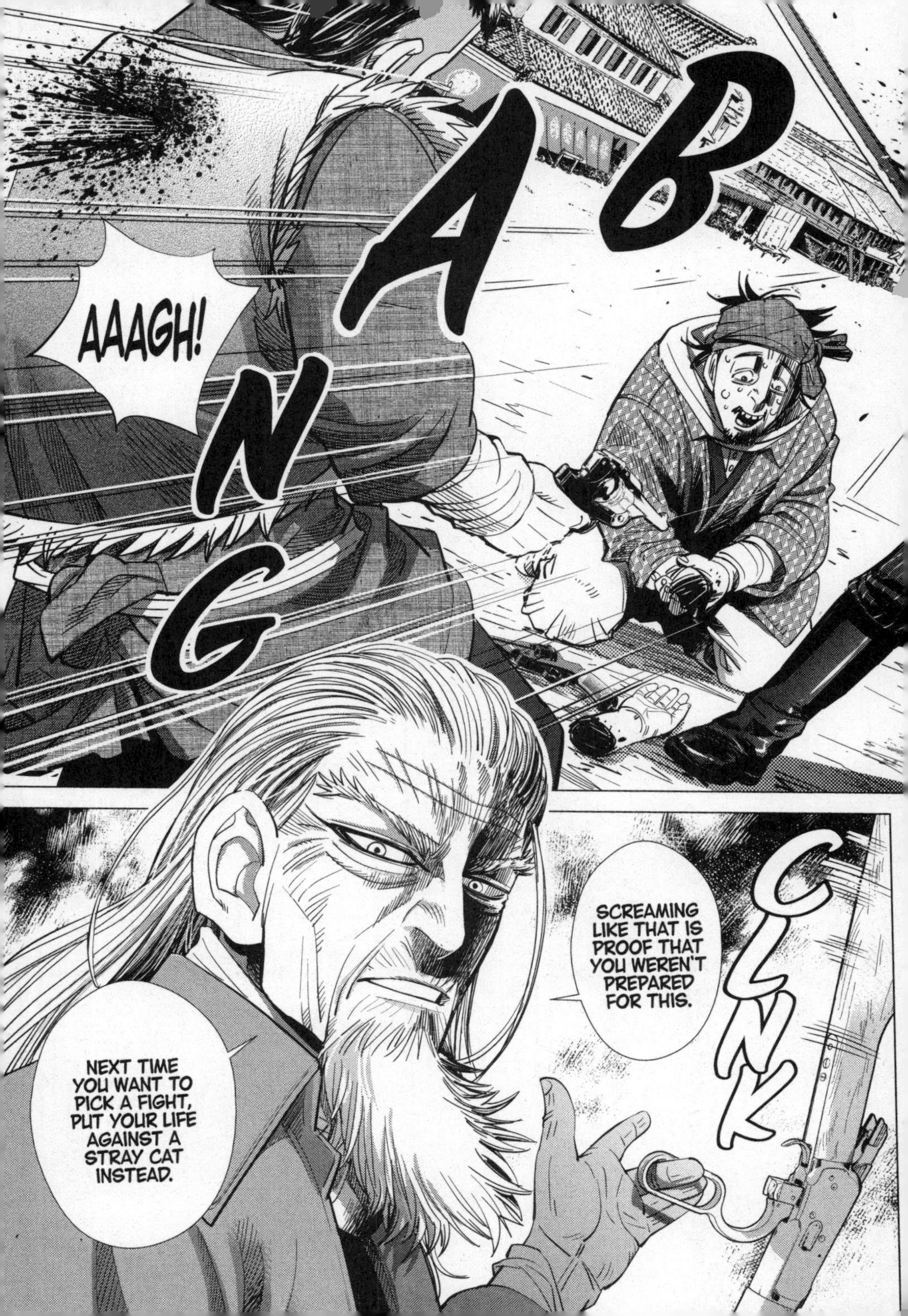
BANG
AAAGH!
SCREAMING LIKE THAT IS PROOF THAT YOU WEREN'T PREPARED FOR THIS.
CLINK
NEXT TIME YOU WANT TO PICK A FIGHT, PUT YOUR LIFE AGAINST A STRAY CAT INSTEAD.

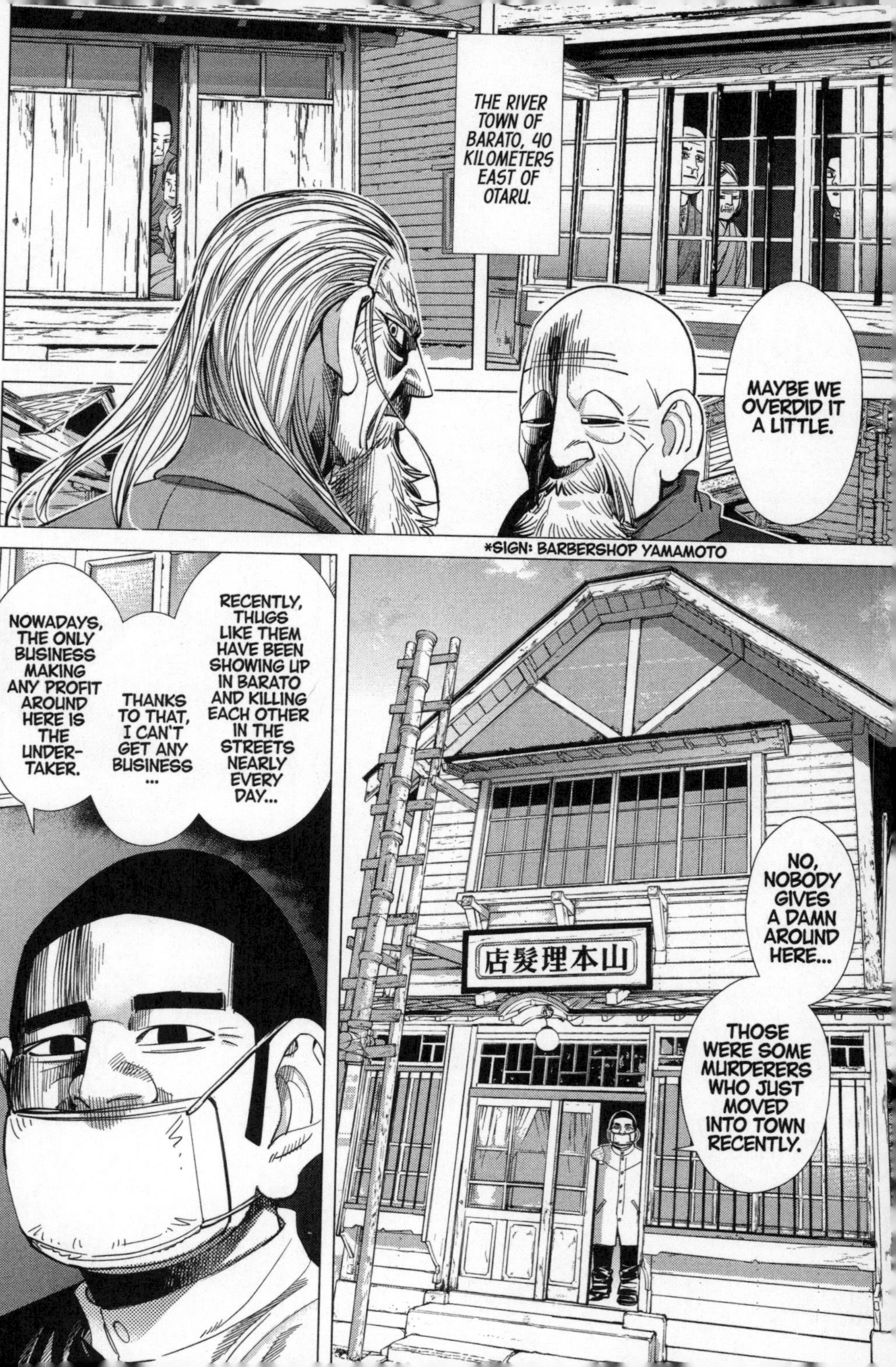
THE RIVER TOWN OF BARATO, 40 KILOMETERS EAST OF OTARU.
MAYBE WE OVERDID IT A LITTLE.
*SIGN: BARBERSHOP YAMAMOTO
山本理髪店
NO, NOBODY GIVES A DAMN AROUND HERE...
THOSE WERE SOME MURDERERS WHO JUST MOVED INTO TOWN RECENTLY.
RECENTLY, THUGS LIKE THEM HAVE BEEN SHOWING UP IN BARATO AND KILLING EACH OTHER IN THE STREETS NEARLY EVERY DAY...
THANKS TO THAT, I CAN'T GET ANY BUSINESS...
NOWADAYS, THE ONLY BUSINESS MAKING ANY PROFIT AROUND HERE IS THE UNDER-TAKER.

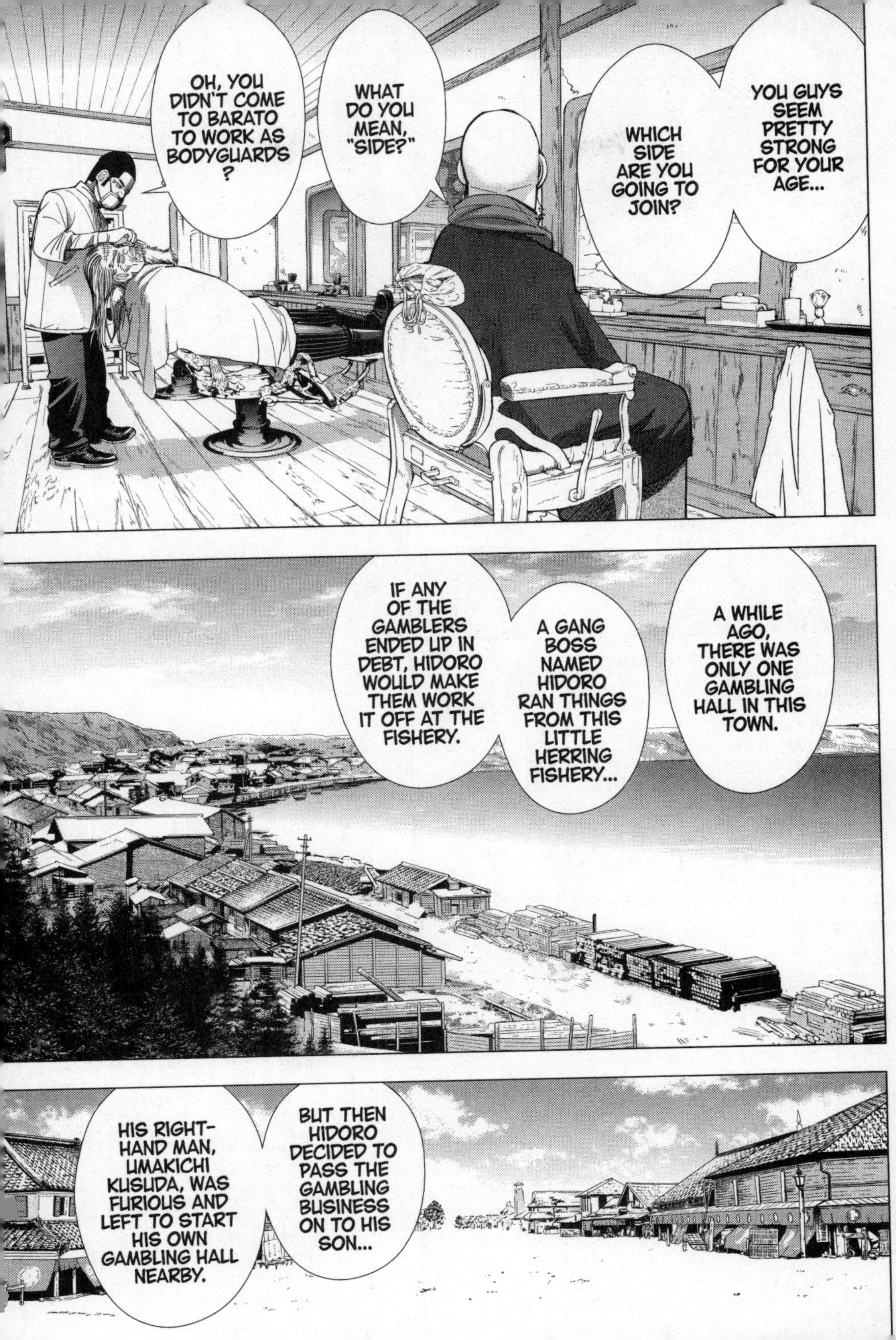
YOU GUYS SEEM PRETTY STRONG FOR YOUR AGE...
WHICH SIDE ARE YOU GOING TO JOIN?
WHAT DO YOU MEAN, "SIDE?"
OH, YOU DIDN'T COME TO BARATO TO WORK AS BODYGUARDS?
A WHILE AGO, THERE WAS ONLY ONE GAMBLING HALL IN THIS TOWN.
A GANG BOSS NAMED HIDORO RAN THINGS FROM THIS LITTLE HERRING FISHERY...
IF ANY OF THE GAMBLERS ENDED UP IN DEBT, HIDORO WOULD MAKE THEM WORK IT OFF AT THE FISHERY.
BUT THEN HIDORO DECIDED TO PASS THE GAMBLING BUSINESS ON TO HIS SON...
HIS RIGHT-HAND MAN, UMAKICHI KUSUDA, WAS FURIOUS AND LEFT TO START HIS OWN GAMBLING HALL NEARBY.

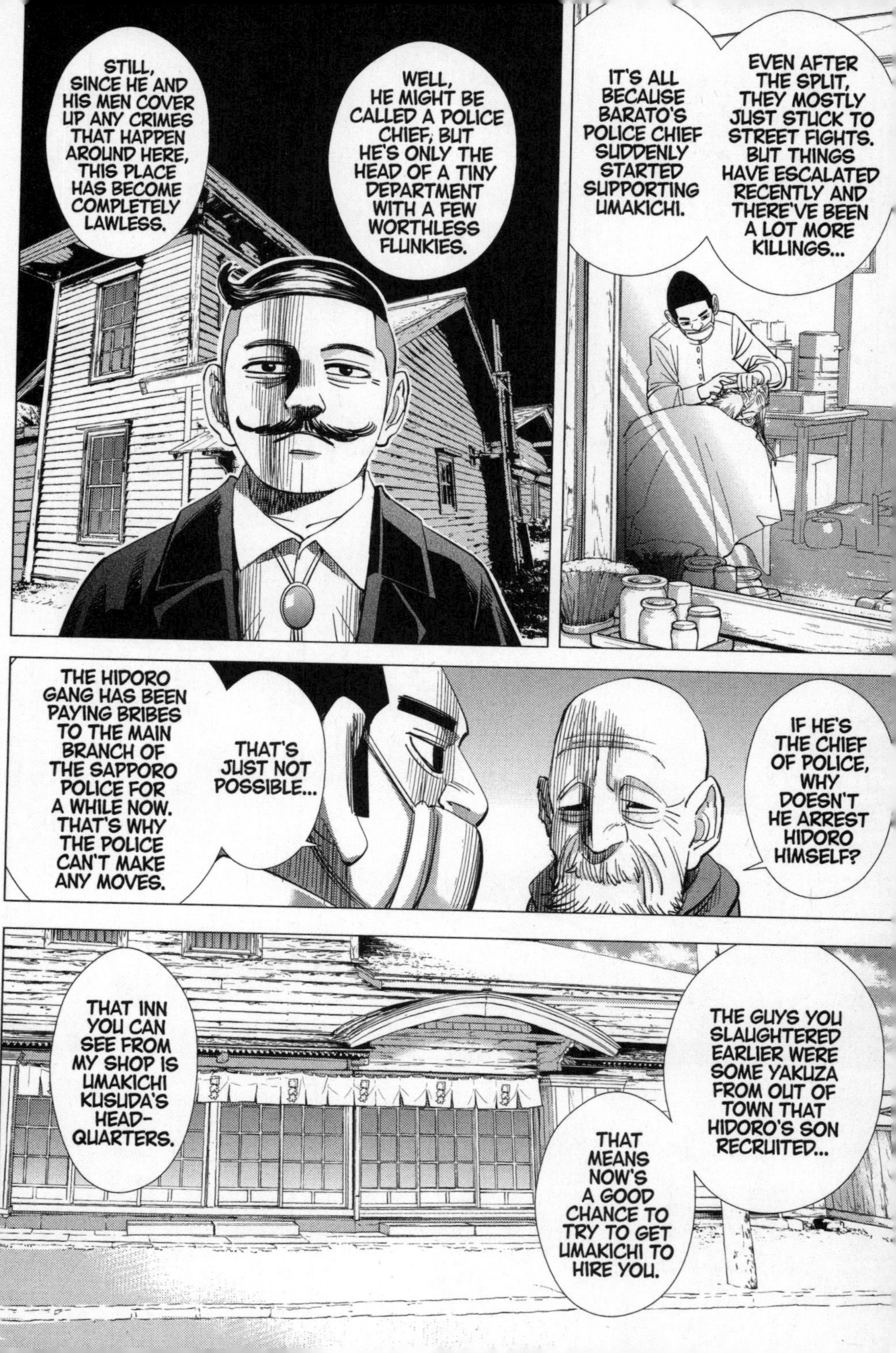
EVEN AFTER THE SPLIT, THEY MOSTLY JUST STUCK TO STREET FIGHTS. BUT THINGS HAVE ESCALATED RECENTLY AND THERE'VE BEEN A LOT MORE KILLINGS...
IT'S ALL BECAUSE BARATO'S POLICE CHIEF SUDDENLY STARTED SUPPORTING UMAKICHI.
WELL, HE MIGHT BE CALLED A POLICE CHIEF, BUT HE'S ONLY THE HEAD OF A TINY DEPARTMENT WITH A FEW WORTHLESS FLUNKIES.
STILL, SINCE HE AND HIS MEN COVER UP ANY CRIMES THAT HAPPEN AROUND HERE, THIS PLACE HAS BECOME COMPLETELY LAWLESS.
IF HE'S THE CHIEF OF POLICE, WHY DOESN'T HE ARREST HIDORO HIMSELF?
THAT'S JUST NOT POSSIBLE...
THE HIDORO GANG HAS BEEN PAYING BRIBES TO THE MAIN BRANCH OF THE SAPPORO POLICE FOR A WHILE NOW. THAT'S WHY THE POLICE CAN'T MAKE ANY MOVES.
THE GUYS YOU SLAUGHTERED EARLIER WERE SOME YAKUZA FROM OUT OF TOWN THAT HIDORO'S SON RECRUITED...
THAT INN YOU CAN SEE FROM MY SHOP IS UMAKICHI KUSUDA'S HEAD-QUARTERS.
THAT MEANS NOW'S A GOOD CHANCE TO TRY TO GET UMAKICHI TO HIRE YOU.

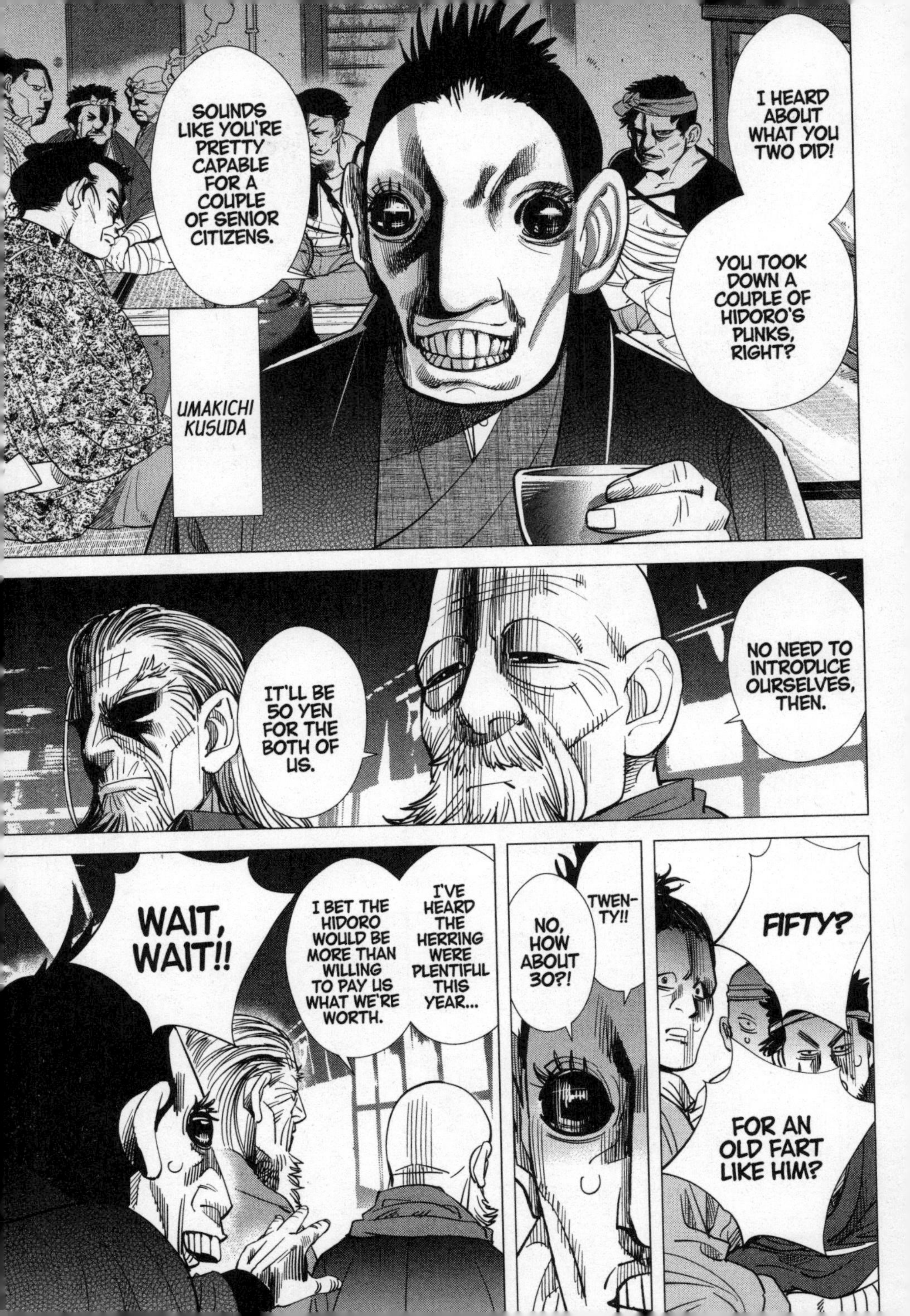
I HEARD ABOUT WHAT YOU TWO DID!
YOU TOOK DOWN A COUPLE OF HIDORO'S PUNKS, RIGHT?
SOUNDS LIKE YOU'RE PRETTY CAPABLE FOR A COUPLE OF SENIOR CITIZENS.
UMAKICHI KUSUDA
NO NEED TO INTRODUCE OURSELVES, THEN.
IT'LL BE 50 YEN FOR THE BOTH OF US.
FIFTY?
FOR AN OLD FART LIKE HIM?
TWEN-TY!!
NO, HOW ABOUT 30?!
I'VE HEARD THE HERRING WERE PLENTIFUL THIS YEAR...
I BET THE HIDORO WOULD BE MORE THAN WILLING TO PAY US WHAT WE'RE WORTH.
WAIT, WAIT!!

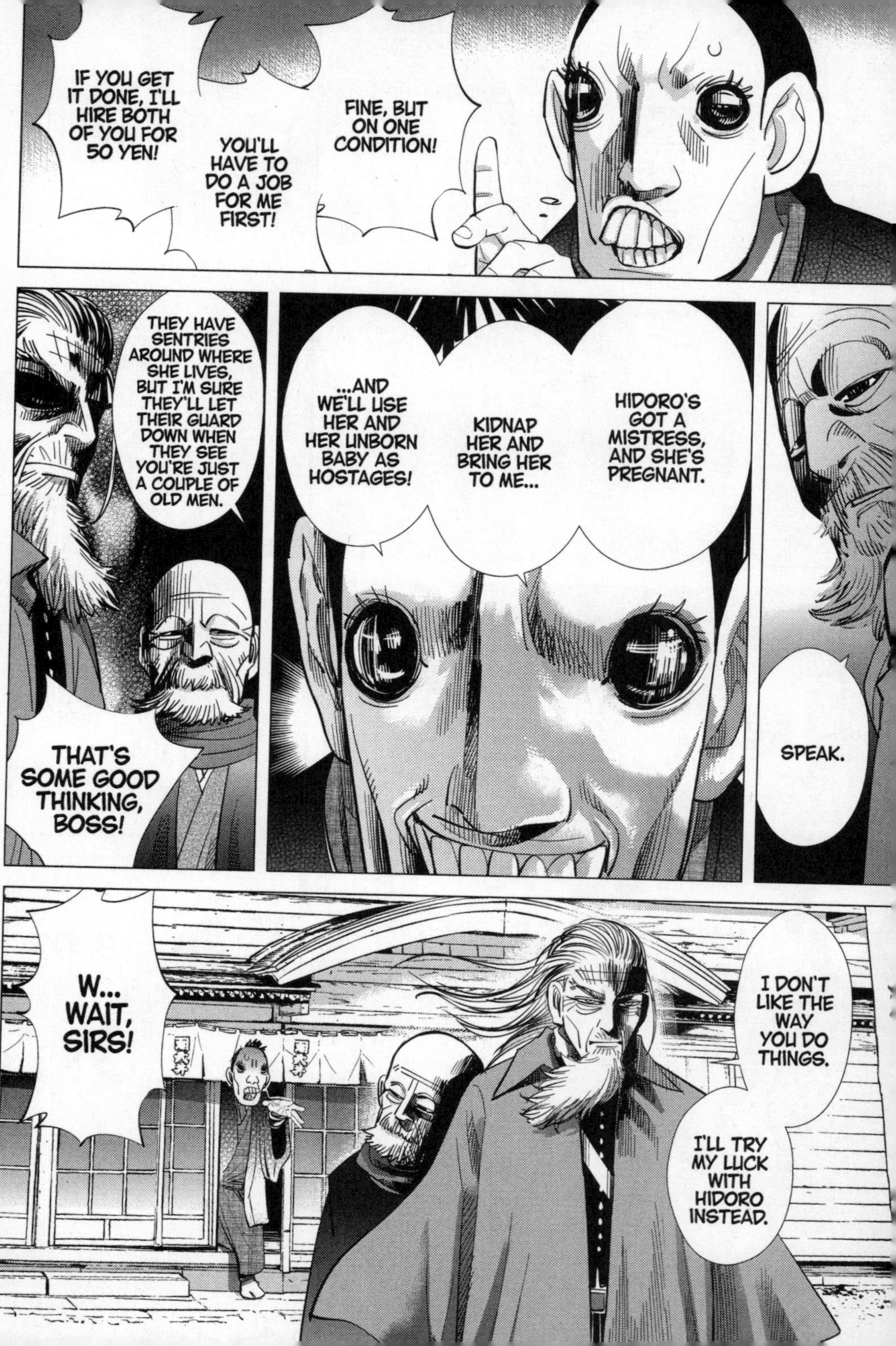
FINE, BUT ON ONE CONDITION!
YOU'LL HAVE TO DO A JOB FOR ME FIRST!
IF YOU GET IT DONE, I'LL HIRE BOTH OF YOU FOR 50 YEN!
SPEAK.
HIDORO'S GOT A MISTRESS, AND SHE'S PREGNANT.
KIDNAP HER AND BRING HER TO ME...
...AND WE'LL USE HER AND HER UNBORN BABY AS HOSTAGES!
THEY HAVE SENTRIES AROUND WHERE SHE LIVES, BUT I'M SURE THEY'LL LET THEIR GUARD DOWN WHEN THEY SEE YOU'RE JUST A COUPLE OF OLD MEN.
THAT'S SOME GOOD THINKING, BOSS!
I DON'T LIKE THE WAY YOU DO THINGS.
I'LL TRY MY LUCK WITH HIDORO INSTEAD.
W... WAIT, SIRS!

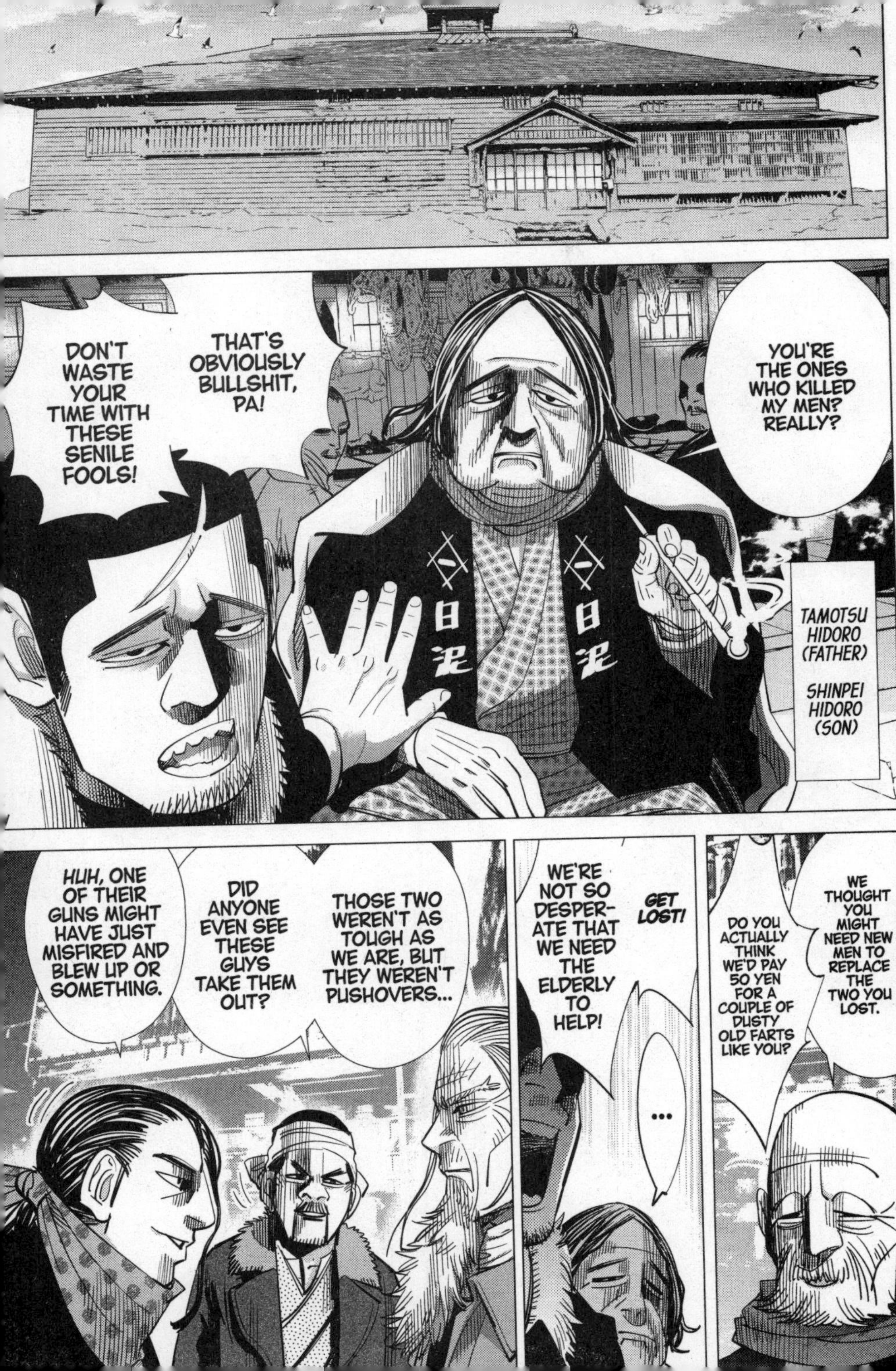
YOU'RE THE ONES WHO KILLED MY MEN? REALLY?
TAMOTSU HIDORO (FATHER)
SHINPEI HIDORO (SON)
THAT'S OBVIOUSLY BULLSHIT, PA!
DON'T WASTE YOUR TIME WITH THESE SENILE FOOLS!
WE THOUGHT YOU MIGHT NEED NEW MEN TO REPLACE THE TWO YOU LOST.
DO YOU ACTUALLY THINK WE'D PAY 50 YEN FOR A COUPLE OF DUSTY OLD FARTS LIKE YOU?
GET LOST!
WE'RE NOT SO DESPERATE THAT WE NEED THE ELDERLY TO HELP!
...
THOSE TWO WEREN'T AS TOUGH AS WE ARE, BUT THEY WEREN'T PUSHOVERS...
DID ANYONE EVEN SEE THESE GUYS TAKE THEM OUT?
HUH, ONE OF THEIR GUNS MIGHT HAVE JUST MISFIRED AND BLEW UP OR SOMETHING.

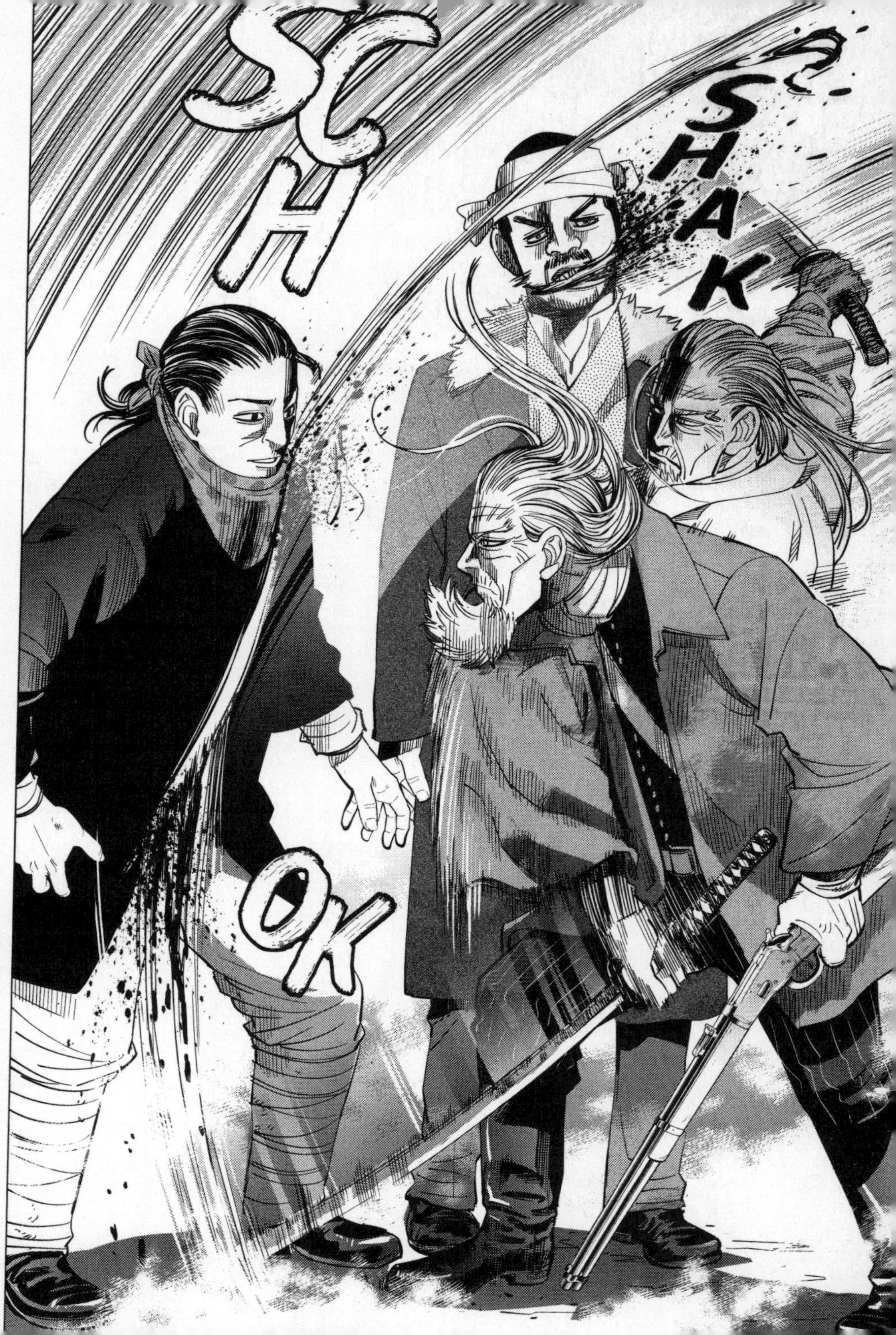
SHAK
SCHOK

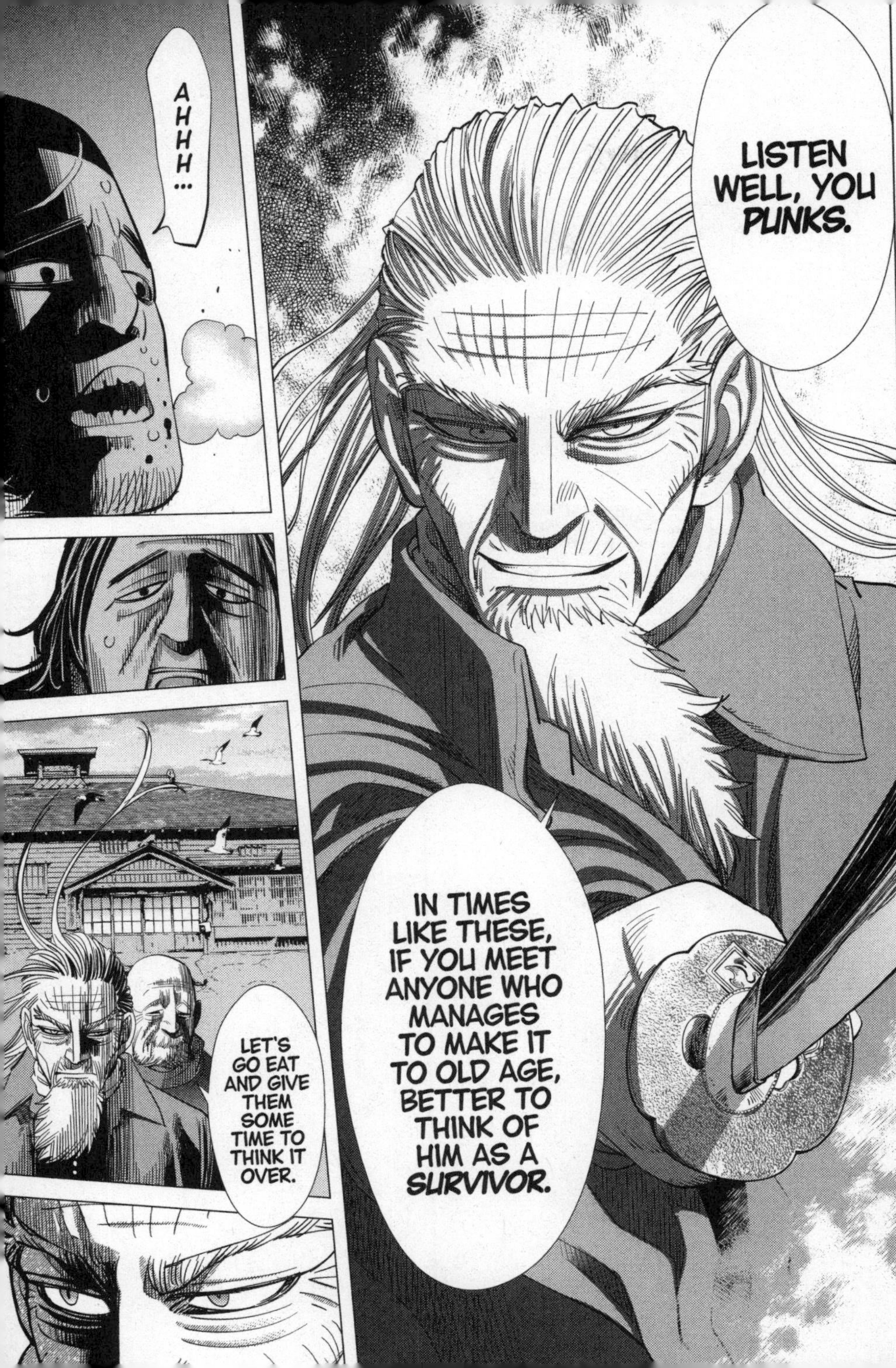
LISTEN WELL, YOU PUNKS.
IN TIMES LIKE THESE, IF YOU MEET ANYONE WHO MANAGES TO MAKE IT TO OLD AGE, BETTER TO THINK OF HIM AS A SURVIVOR.
AHHH...
LET'S GO EAT AND GIVE THEM SOME TIME TO THINK IT OVER.

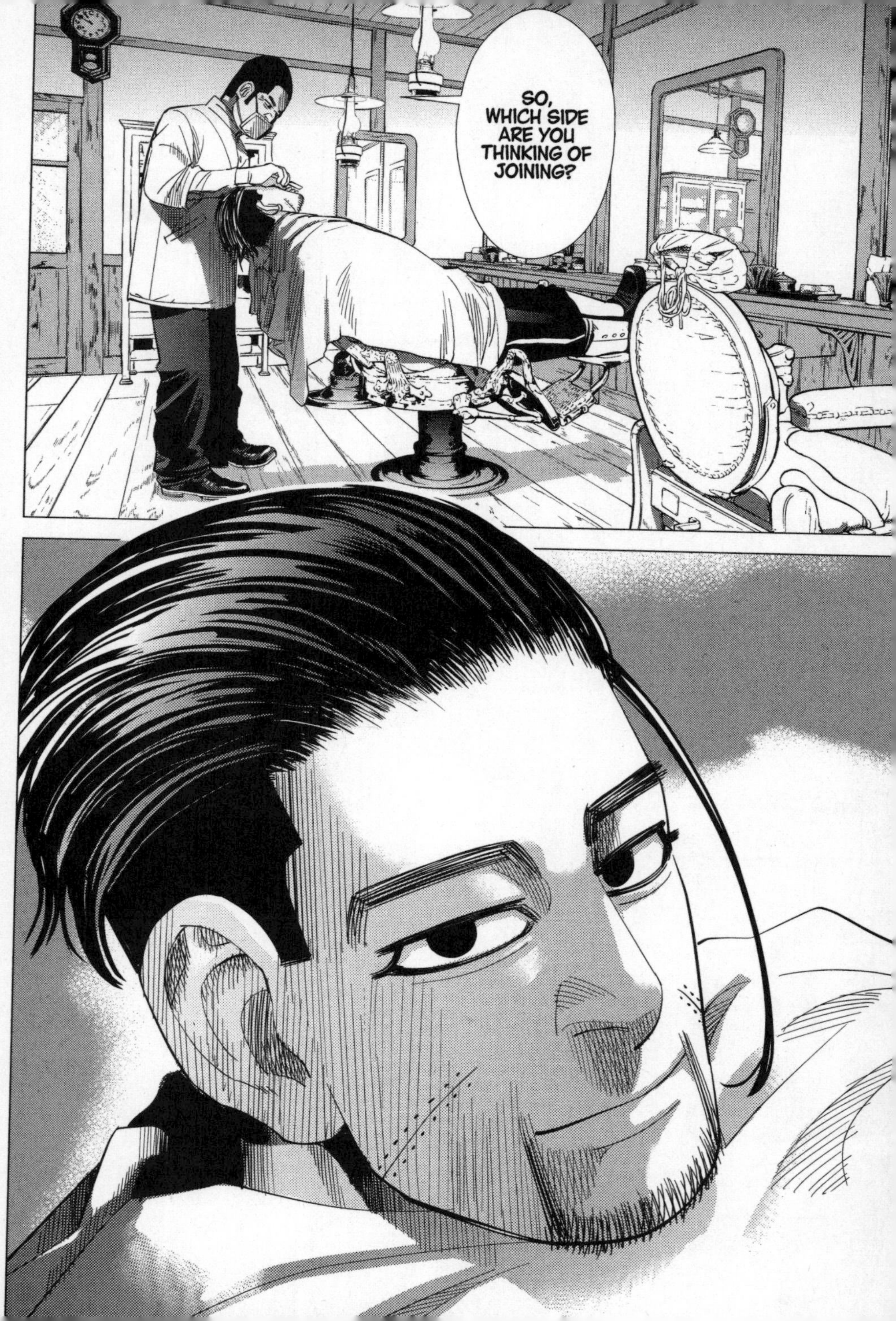
SO, WHICH SIDE ARE YOU THINKING OF JOINING?

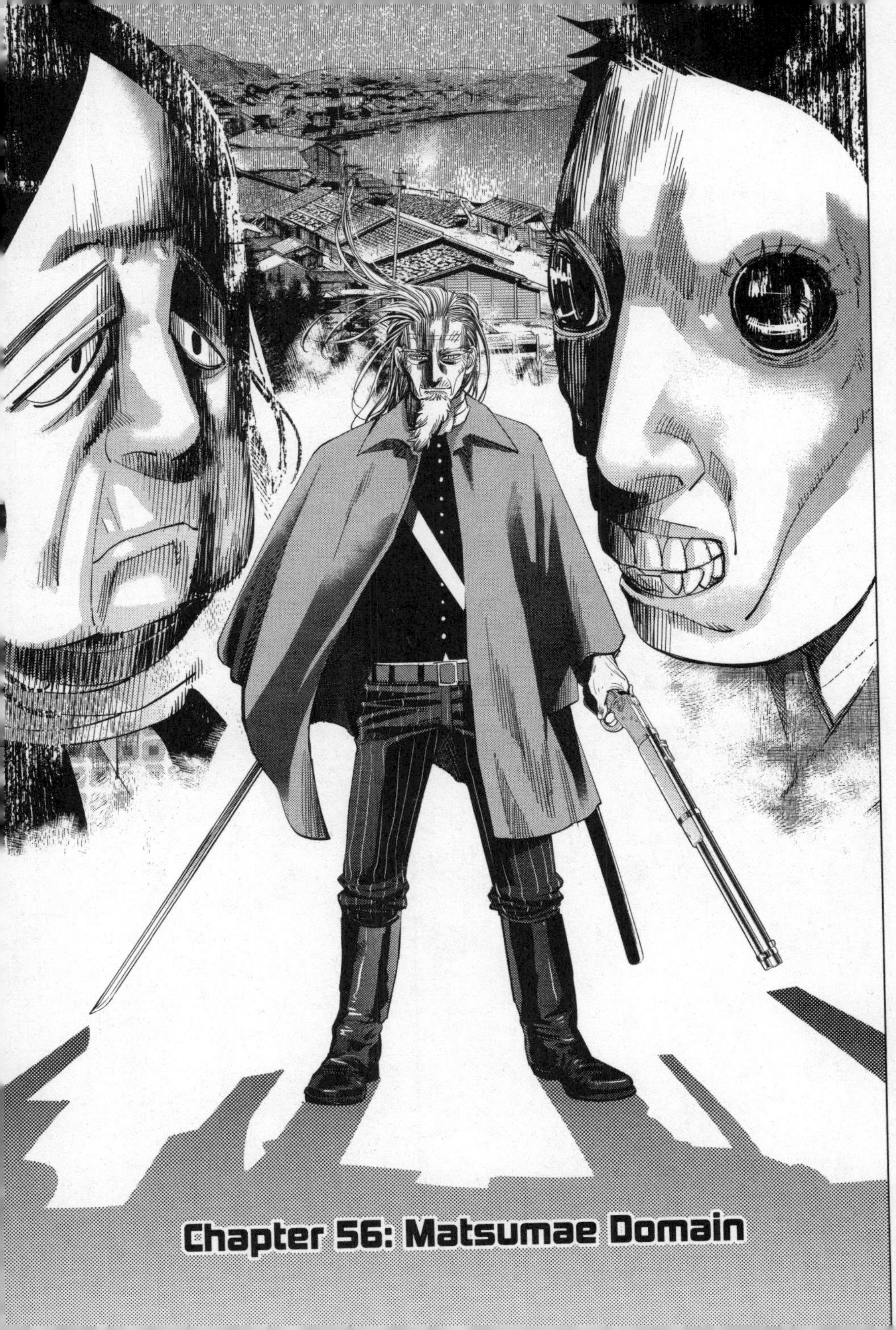

Chapter 56: Matsumae Domain

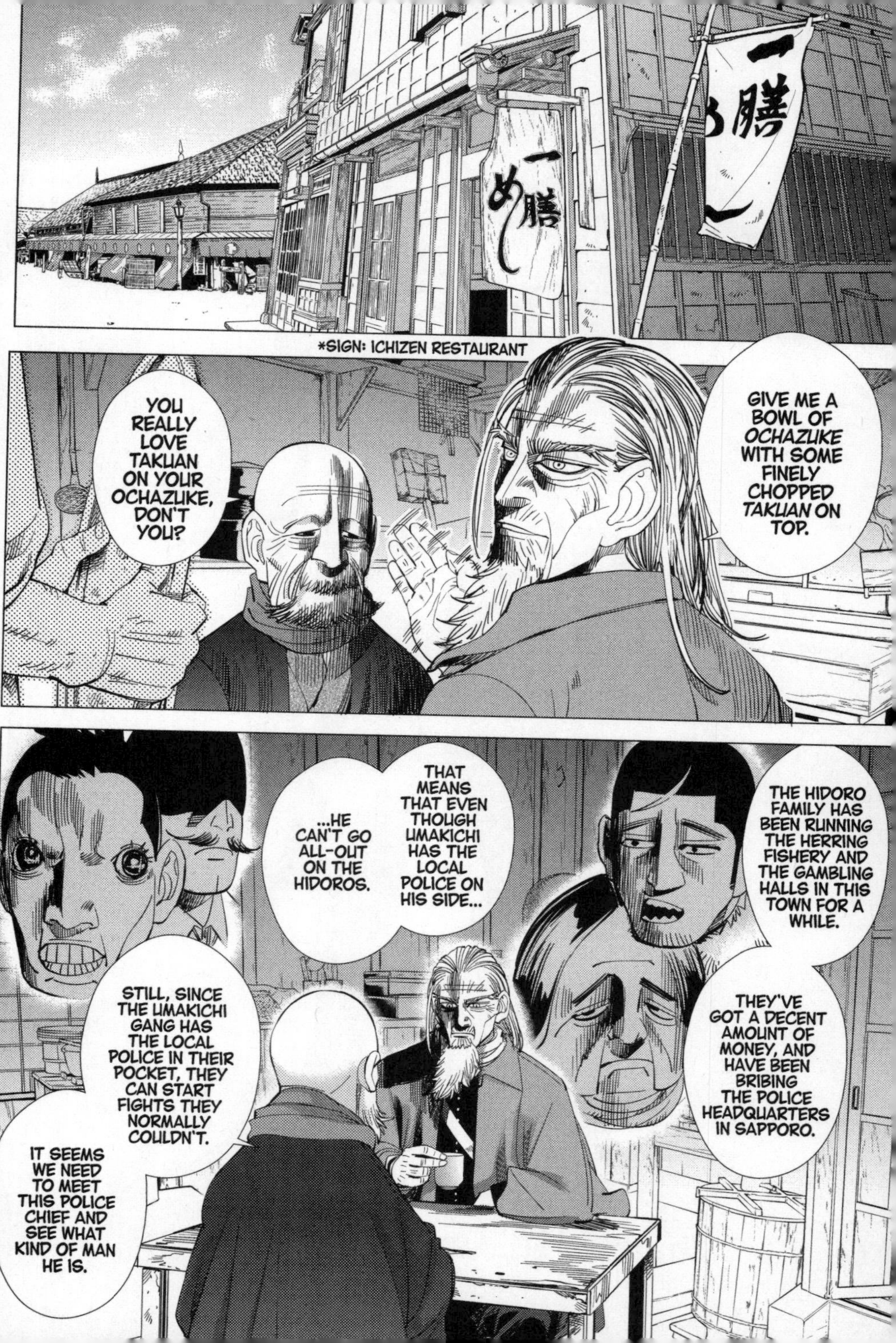
一膳めし
*SIGN: ICHIZEN RESTAURANT
GIVE ME A BOWL OF OCHAZUKE WITH SOME FINELY CHOPPED TAKUAN ON TOP.
YOU REALLY LOVE TAKUAN ON YOUR OCHAZUKE, DON'T YOU?
THE HIDORO FAMILY HAS BEEN RUNNING THE HERRING FISHERY AND THE GAMBLING HALLS IN THIS TOWN FOR A WHILE.
THAT MEANS THAT EVEN THOUGH UMAKICHI HAS THE LOCAL POLICE ON HIS SIDE...
...HE CAN'T GO ALL-OUT ON THE HIDOROS.
THEY'VE GOT A DECENT AMOUNT OF MONEY, AND HAVE BEEN BRIBING THE POLICE HEADQUARTERS IN SAPPORO.
STILL, SINCE THE UMAKICHI GANG HAS THE LOCAL POLICE IN THEIR POCKET, THEY CAN START FIGHTS THEY NORMALLY COULDN'T.
IT SEEMS WE NEED TO MEET THIS POLICE CHIEF AND SEE WHAT KIND OF MAN HE IS.

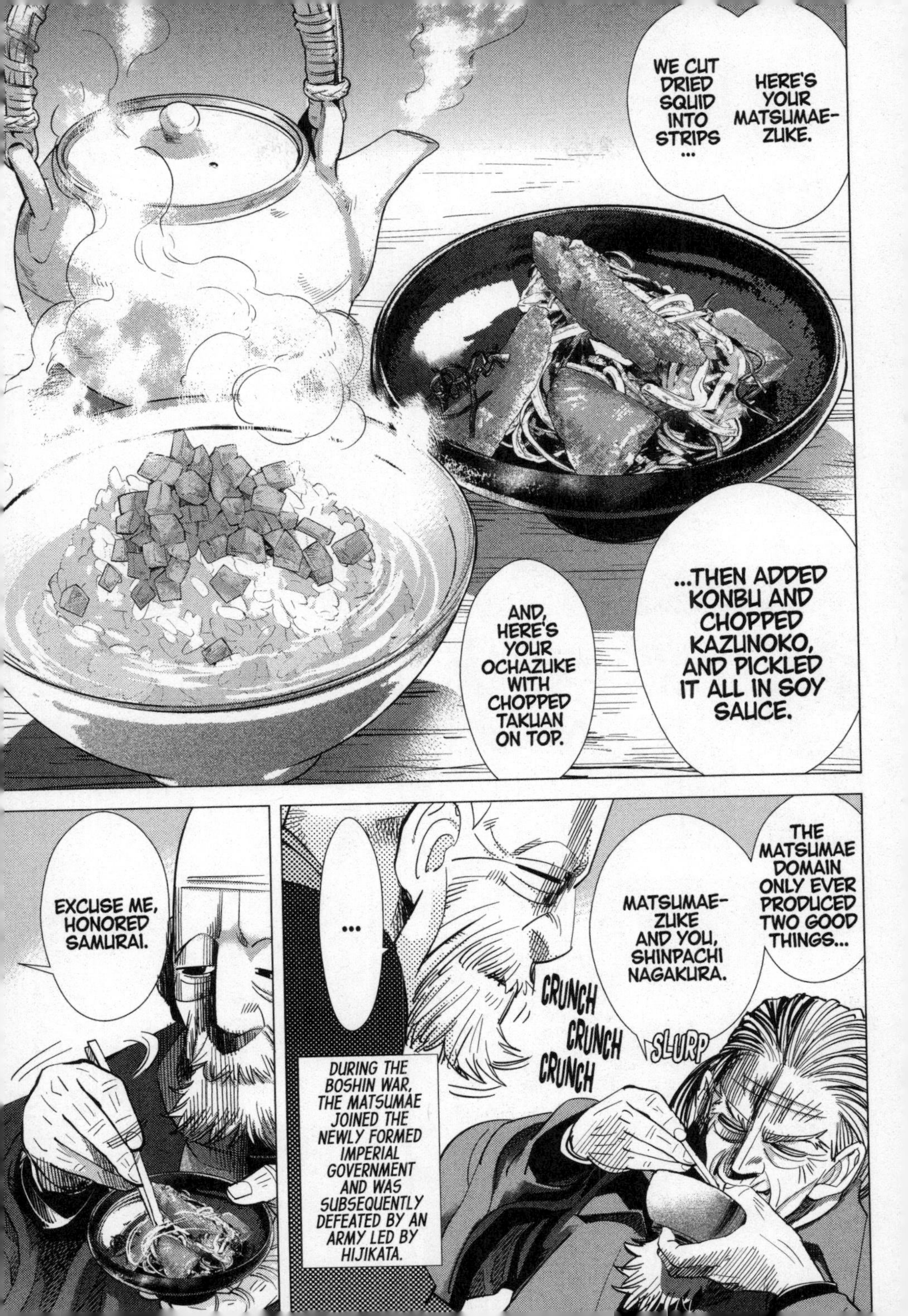
HERE'S YOUR MATSUMAE-ZUKE.
WE CUT DRIED SQUID INTO STRIPS...
...THEN ADDED KONBU AND CHOPPED KAZUNOKO, AND PICKLED IT ALL IN SOY SAUCE.
AND, HERE'S YOUR OCHAZUKE WITH CHOPPED TAKUAN ON TOP.
THE MATSUMAE DOMAIN ONLY EVER PRODUCED TWO GOOD THINGS...
MATSUMAE-ZUKE AND YOU, SHINPACHI NAGAKURA.
...
SLURP
CRUNCH
CRUNCH
CRUNCH
DURING THE BOSHIN WAR, THE MATSUMAE JOINED THE NEWLY FORMED IMPERIAL GOVERNMENT AND WAS SUBSEQUENTLY DEFEATED BY AN ARMY LED BY HIJIKATA.
EXCUSE ME, HONORED SAMURAI.

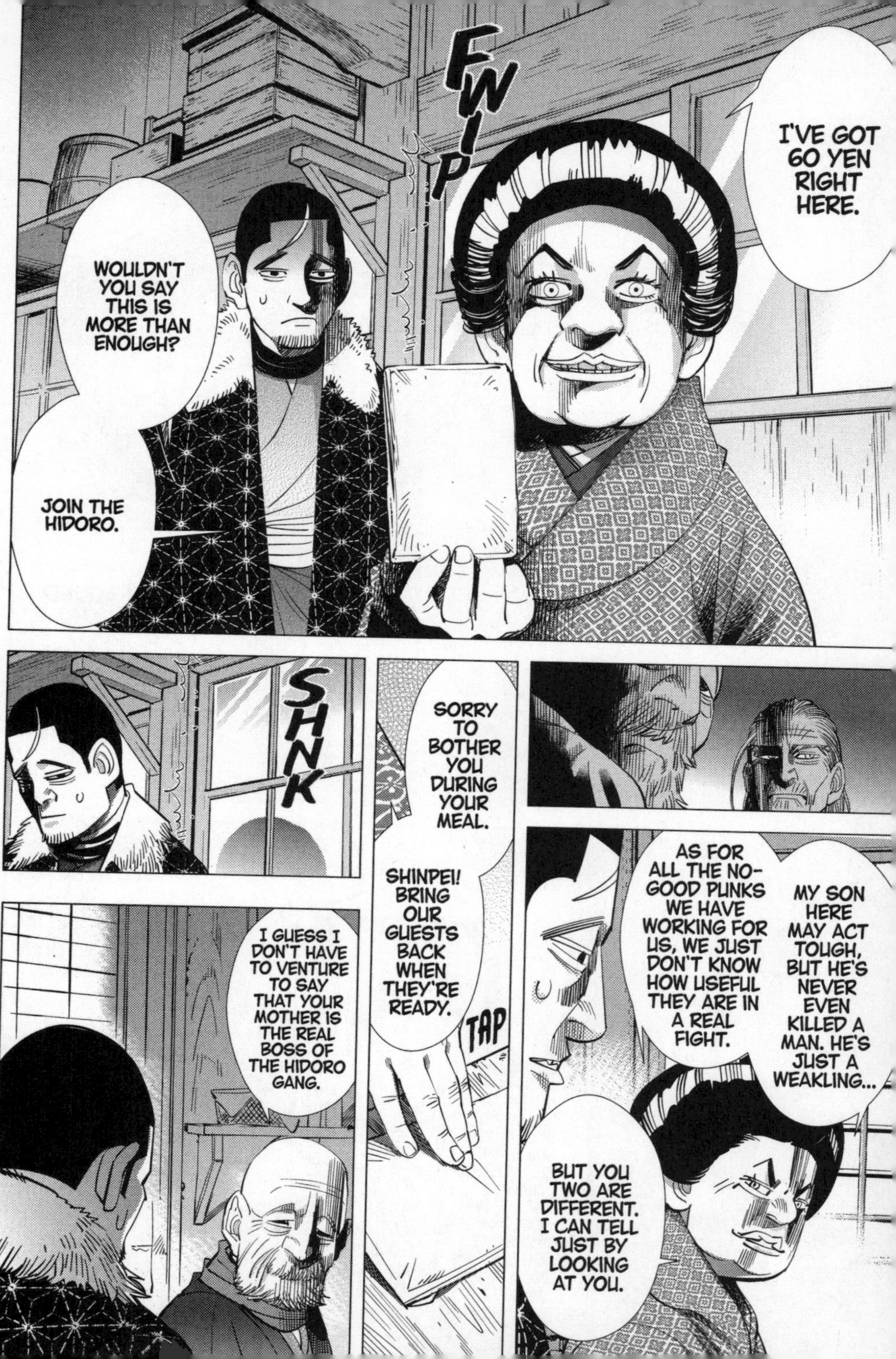
I'VE GOT 60 YEN RIGHT HERE.
FWIP
WOULDN'T YOU SAY THIS IS MORE THAN ENOUGH?
JOIN THE HIDORO.
MY SON HERE MAY ACT TOUGH, BUT HE'S NEVER EVEN KILLED A MAN. HE'S JUST A WEAKLING...
AS FOR ALL THE NO-GOOD PUNKS WE HAVE WORKING FOR US, WE JUST DON'T KNOW HOW USEFUL THEY ARE IN A REAL FIGHT.
BUT YOU TWO ARE DIFFERENT. I CAN TELL JUST BY LOOKING AT YOU.
SORRY TO BOTHER YOU DURING YOUR MEAL.
SHINPEI! BRING OUR GUESTS BACK WHEN THEY'RE READY.
TAP
SHNK
I GUESS I DON'T HAVE TO VENTURE TO SAY THAT YOUR MOTHER IS THE REAL BOSS OF THE HIDORO GANG.

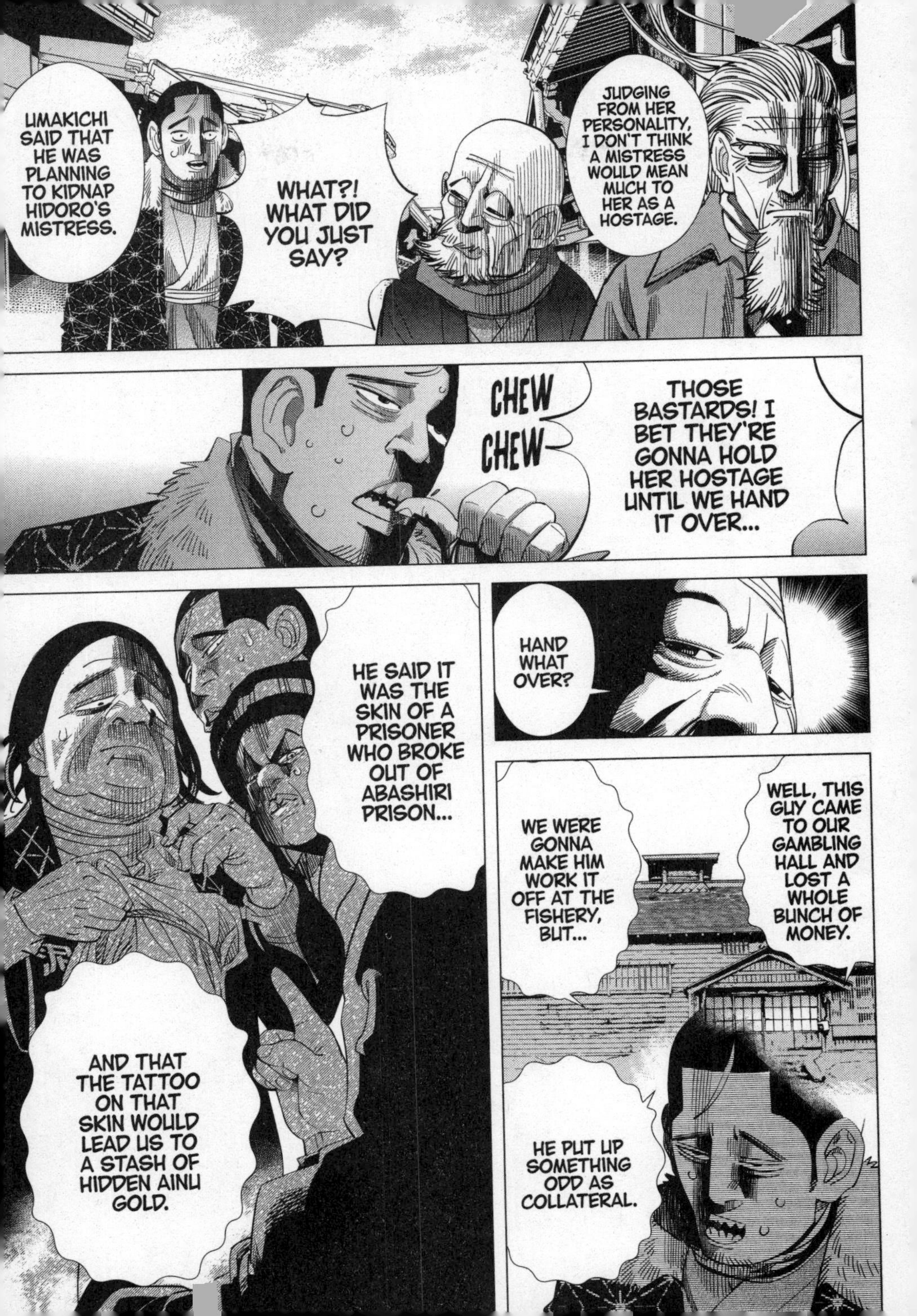
JUDGING FROM HER PERSONALITY, I DON'T THINK A MISTRESS WOULD MEAN MUCH TO HER AS A HOSTAGE.
WHAT?! WHAT DID YOU JUST SAY?
UMAKICHI SAID THAT HE WAS PLANNING TO KIDNAP HIDORO'S MISTRESS.
THOSE BASTARDS! I BET THEY'RE GONNA HOLD HER HOSTAGE UNTIL WE HAND IT OVER...
CHEW CHEW
HAND WHAT OVER?
WELL, THIS GUY CAME TO OUR GAMBLING HALL AND LOST A WHOLE BUNCH OF MONEY.
WE WERE GONNA MAKE HIM WORK IT OFF AT THE FISHERY, BUT...
HE PUT UP SOMETHING ODD AS COLLATERAL.
HE SAID IT WAS THE SKIN OF A PRISONER WHO BROKE OUT OF ABASHIRI PRISON...
AND THAT THE TATTOO ON THAT SKIN WOULD LEAD US TO A STASH OF HIDDEN AINU GOLD.

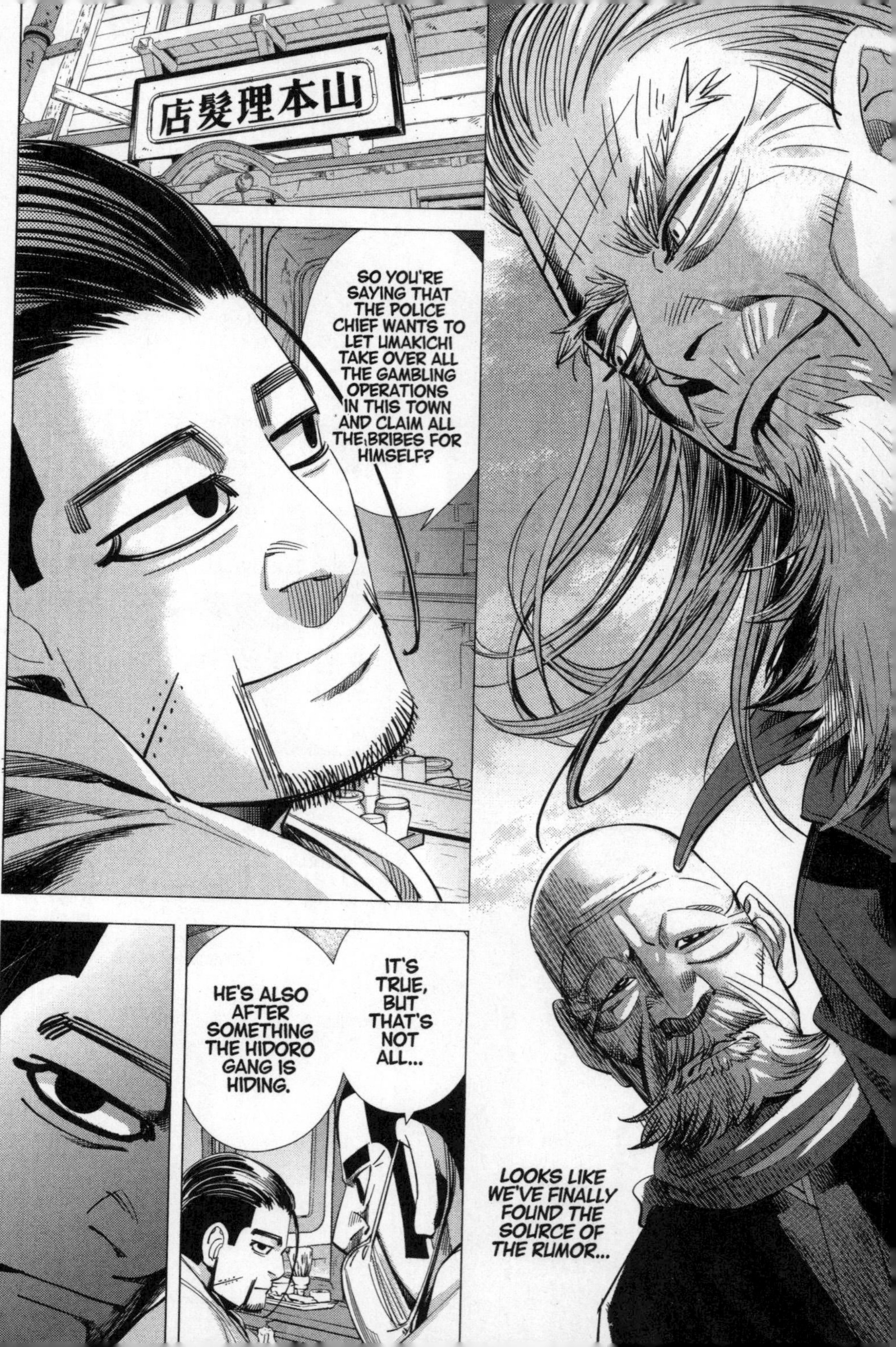
LOOKS LIKE WE'VE FINALLY FOUND THE SOURCE OF THE RUMOR...
山本理髪店
SO YOU'RE SAYING THAT THE POLICE CHIEF WANTS TO LET UMAKICHI TAKE OVER ALL THE GAMBLING OPERATIONS IN THIS TOWN AND CLAIM ALL THE BRIBES FOR HIMSELF?
IT'S TRUE, BUT THAT'S NOT ALL...
HE'S ALSO AFTER SOMETHING THE HIDORO GANG IS HIDING.

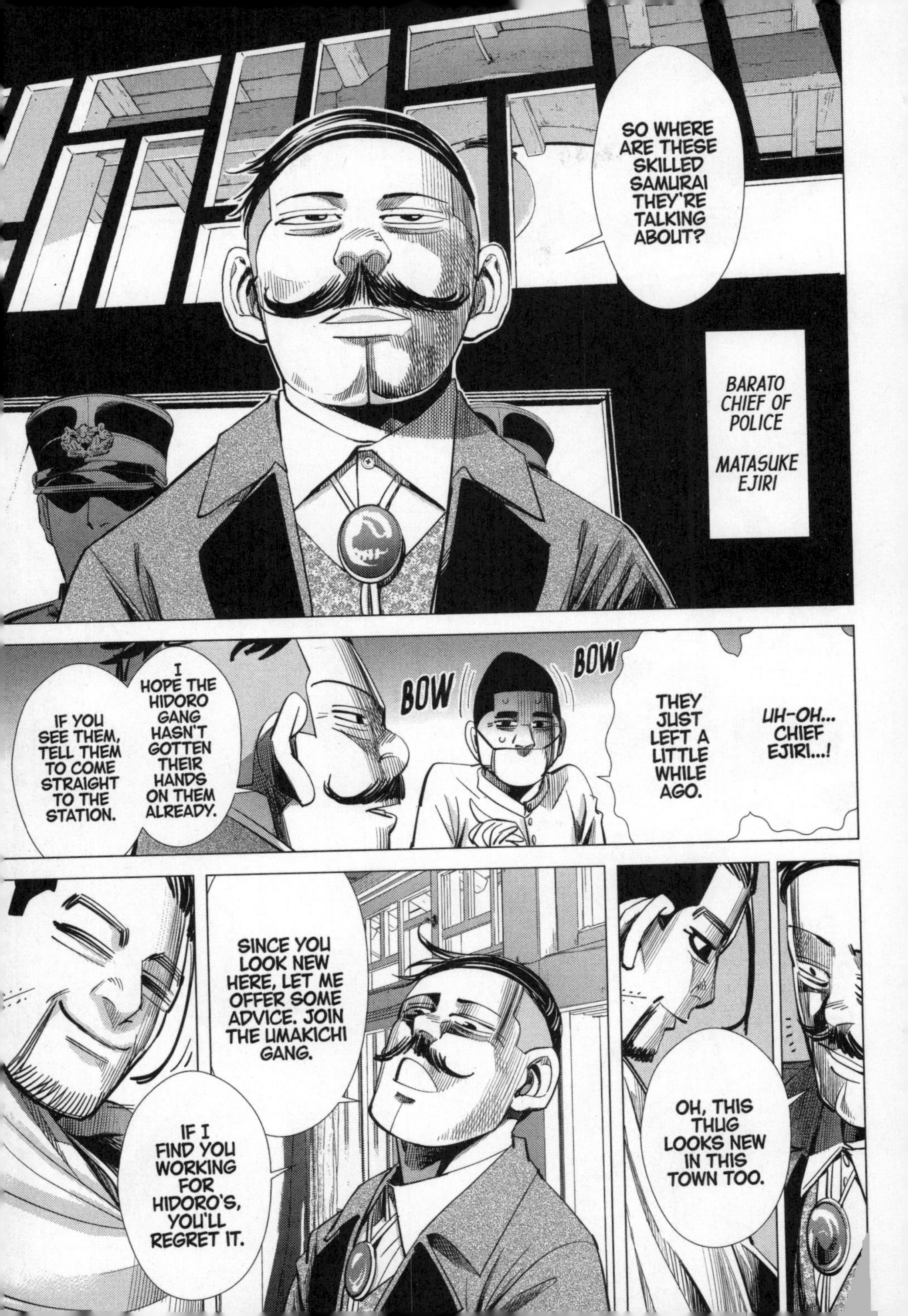
SO WHERE ARE THESE SKILLED SAMURAI THEY'RE TALKING ABOUT?
BARATO CHIEF OF POLICE
MATASUKE EJIRI
UH-OH... CHIEF EJIRI...!
BOW
BOW
THEY JUST LEFT A LITTLE WHILE AGO.
I HOPE THE HIDORO GANG HASN'T GOTTEN THEIR HANDS ON THEM ALREADY.
IF YOU SEE THEM, TELL THEM TO COME STRAIGHT TO THE STATION.
OH, THIS THUG LOOKS NEW IN THIS TOWN TOO.
SINCE YOU LOOK NEW HERE, LET ME OFFER SOME ADVICE. JOIN THE UMAKICHI GANG.
IF I FIND YOU WORKING FOR HIDORO'S, YOU'LL REGRET IT.

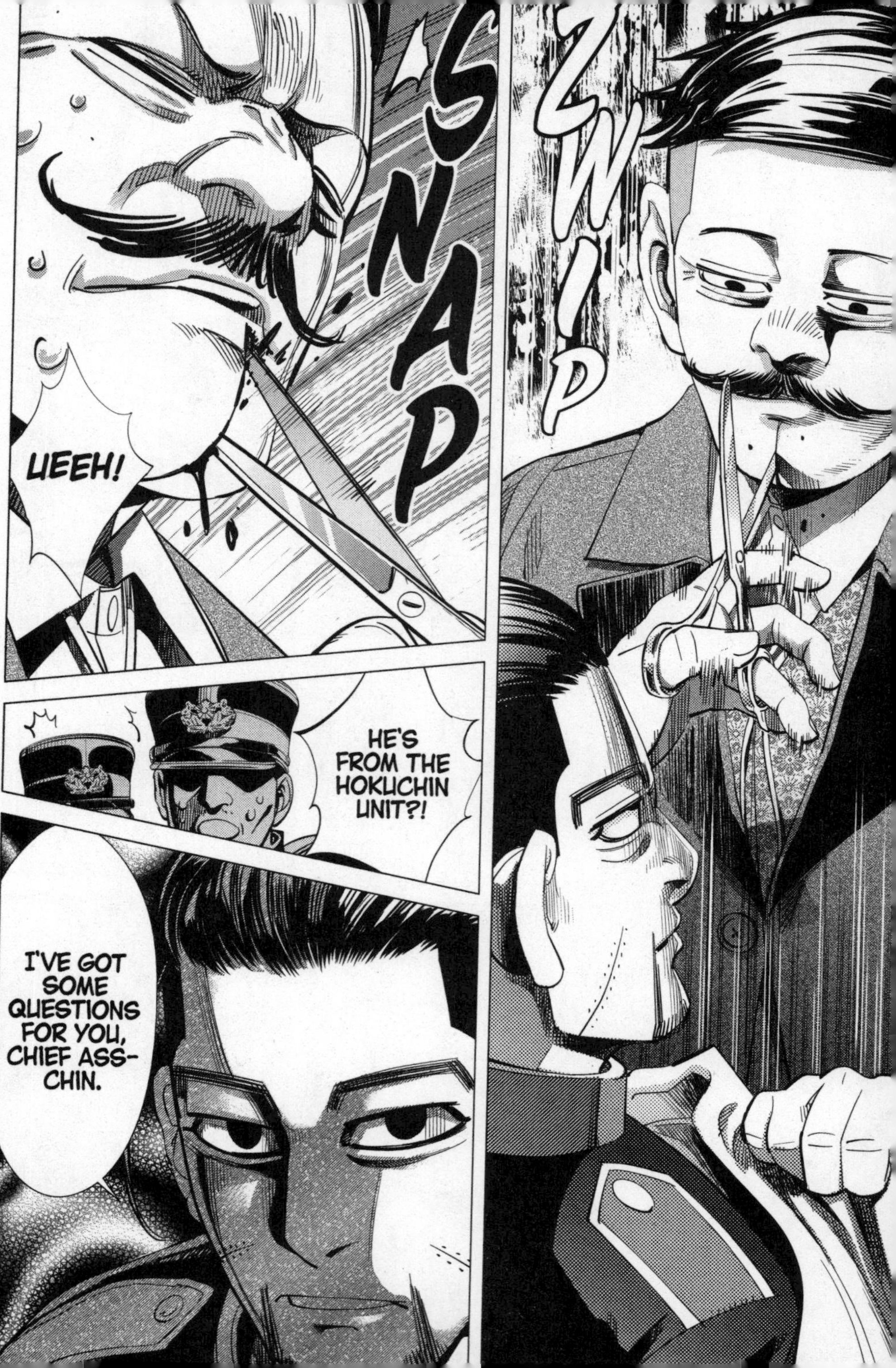
SWIP
SNAP
UEEH!
HE'S FROM THE HOKUCHIN UNIT?!
I'VE GOT SOME QUESTIONS FOR YOU, CHIEF ASS-CHIN.

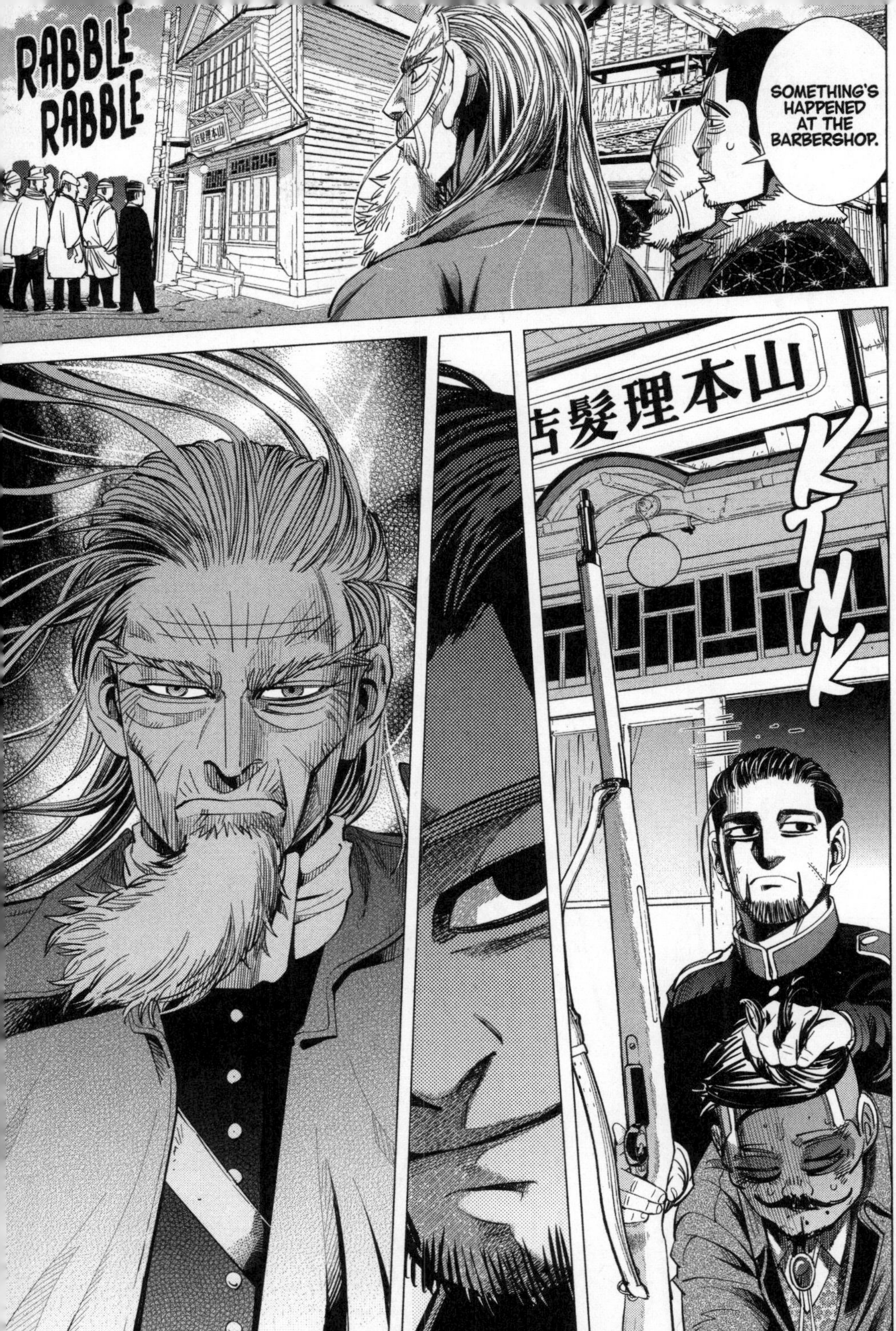
SOMETHING'S HAPPENED AT THE BARBERSHOP.
RABBLE RABBLE
KINK

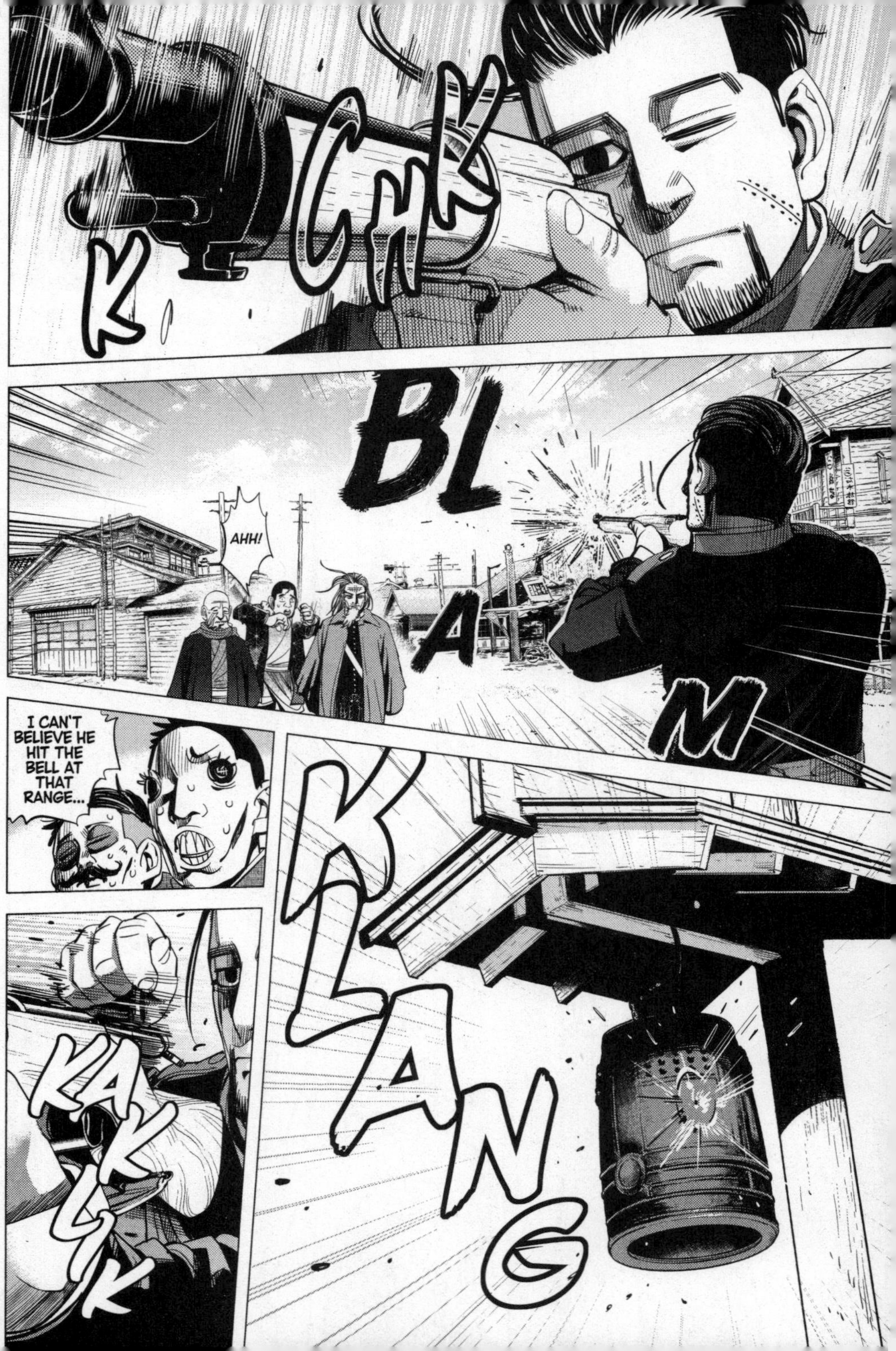
CHK
K
BLAM
AHH!
KLANG
I CAN'T BELIEVE HE HIT THE BELL AT THAT RANGE...
KA KLIK

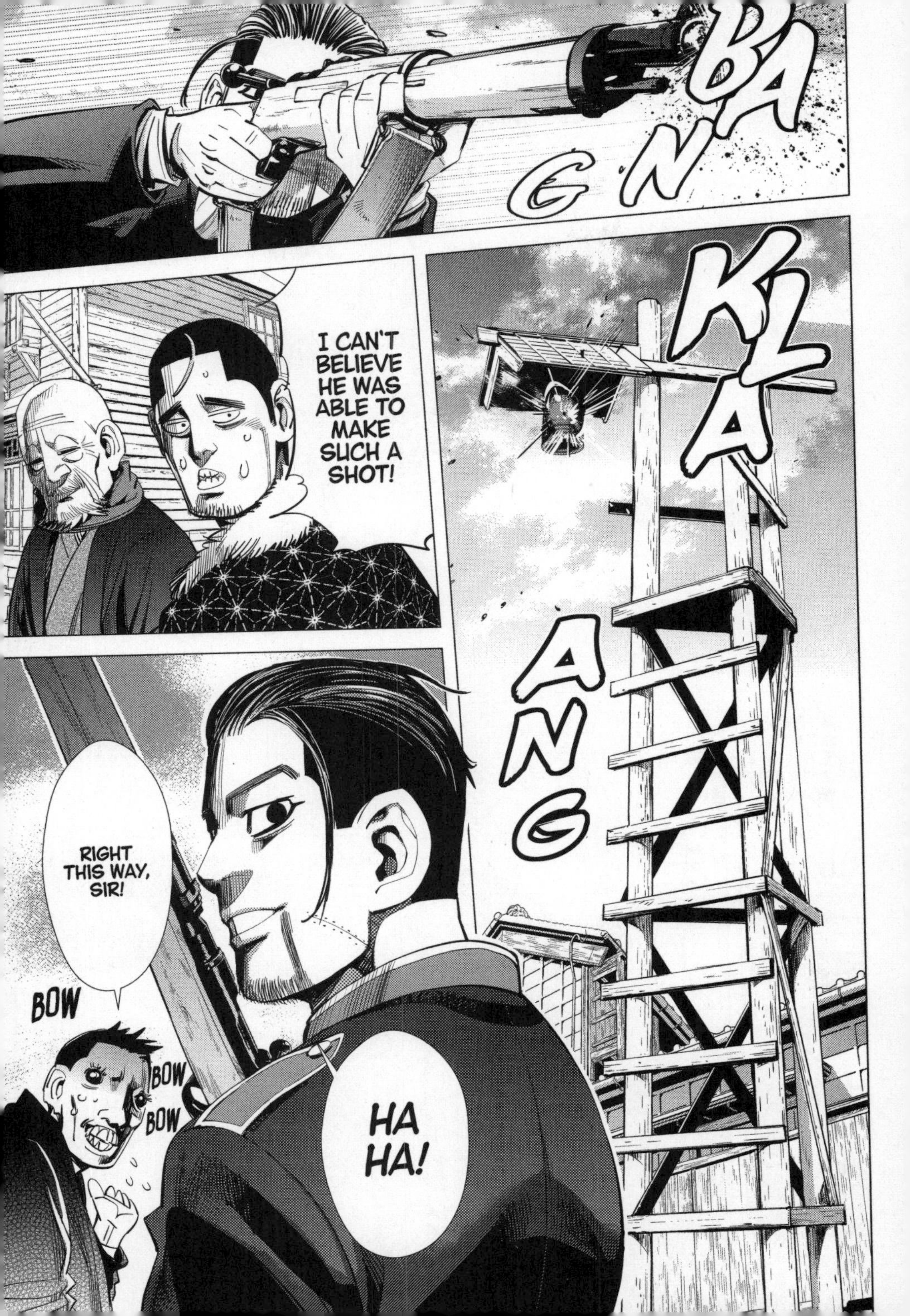
BANG
KLAANG
I CAN'T BELIEVE HE WAS ABLE TO MAKE SUCH A SHOT!
RIGHT THIS WAY, SIR!
BOW
BOW
BOW
HA HA!

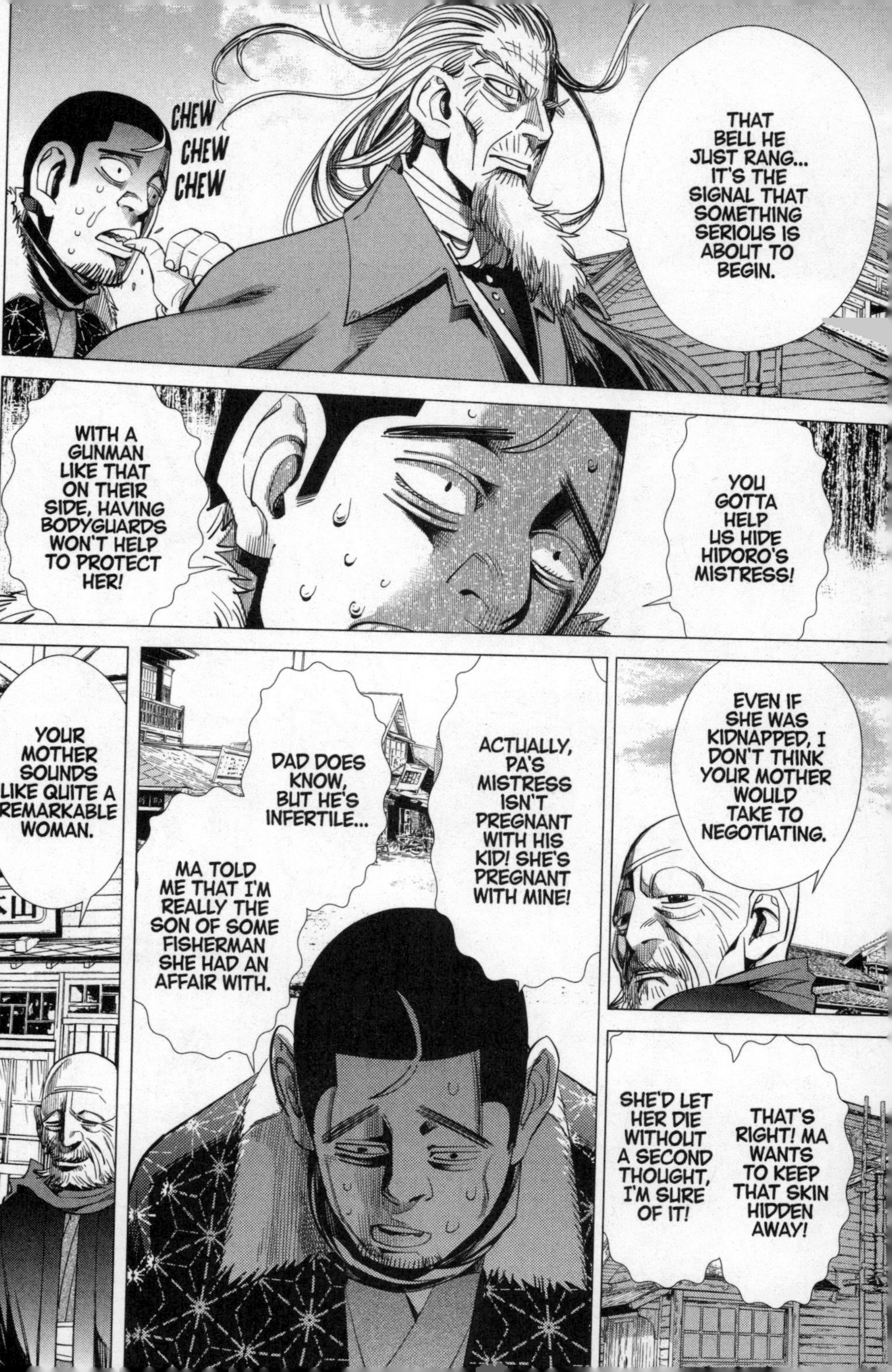
THAT BELL HE JUST RANG... IT'S THE SIGNAL THAT SOMETHING SERIOUS IS ABOUT TO BEGIN.
CHEW CHEW CHEW
YOU GOTTA HELP US HIDE HIDORO'S MISTRESS!
WITH A GUNMAN LIKE THAT ON THEIR SIDE, HAVING BODYGUARDS WON'T HELP TO PROTECT HER!
EVEN IF SHE WAS KIDNAPPED, I DON'T THINK YOUR MOTHER WOULD TAKE TO NEGOTIATING.
THAT'S RIGHT! MA WANTS TO KEEP THAT SKIN HIDDEN AWAY!
SHE'D LET HER DIE WITHOUT A SECOND THOUGHT, I'M SURE OF IT!
ACTUALLY, PA'S MISTRESS ISN'T PREGNANT WITH HIS KID! SHE'S PREGNANT WITH MINE!
DAD DOES KNOW, BUT HE'S INFERTILE...
MA TOLD ME THAT I'M REALLY THE SON OF SOME FISHERMAN SHE HAD AN AFFAIR WITH.
YOUR MOTHER SOUNDS LIKE QUITE A REMARKABLE WOMAN.

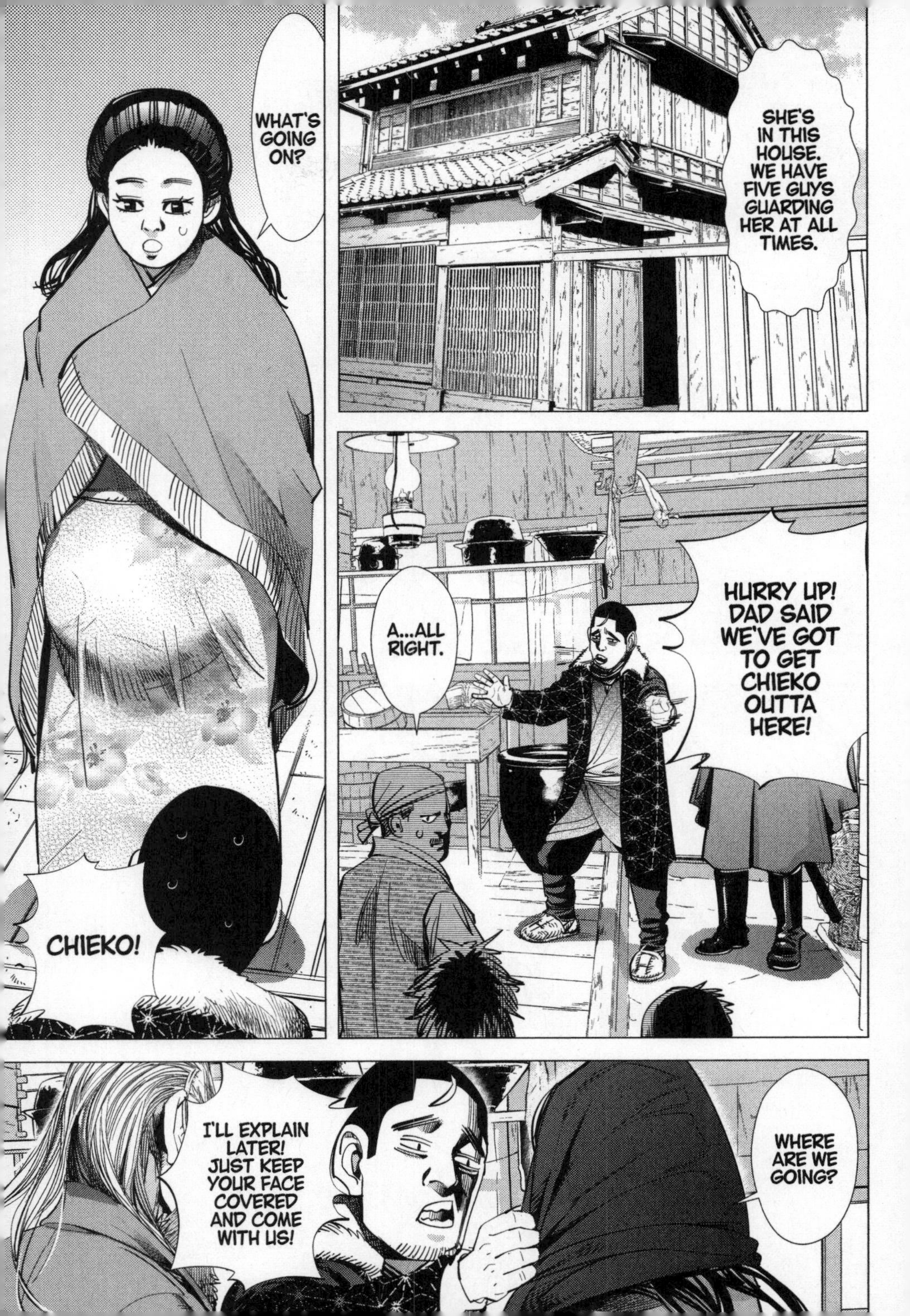
SHE'S IN THIS HOUSE. WE HAVE FIVE GUYS GUARDING HER AT ALL TIMES.
HURRY UP! DAD SAID WE'VE GOT TO GET CHIEKO OUTTA HERE!
A...ALL RIGHT.
WHAT'S GOING ON?
CHIEKO!
WHERE ARE WE GOING?
I'LL EXPLAIN LATER! JUST KEEP YOUR FACE COVERED AND COME WITH US!

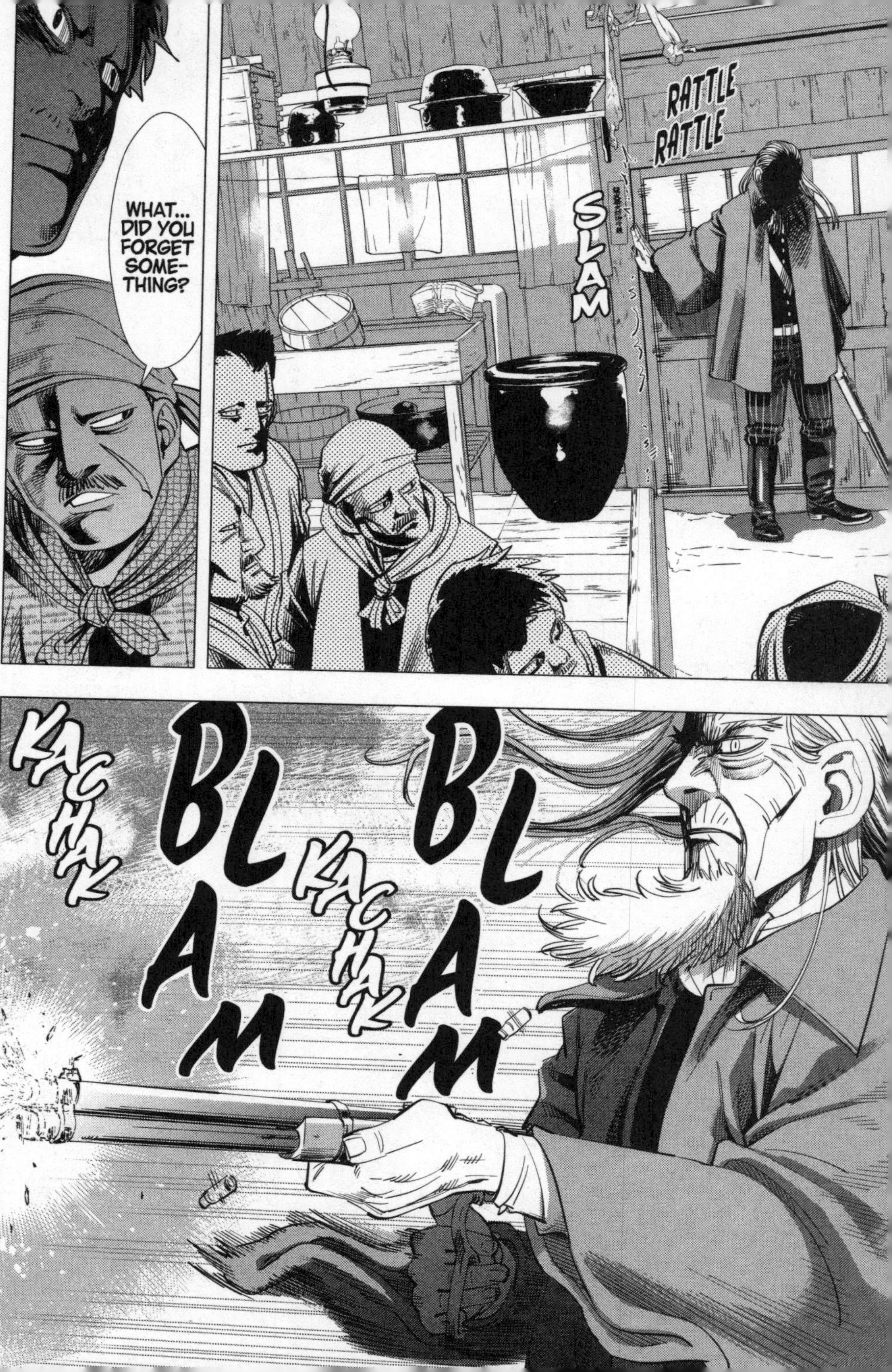
RATTLE RATTLE
SLAM
WHAT... DID YOU FORGET SOME-THING?
BLAM
KACHAK
BLAM
KACHAK

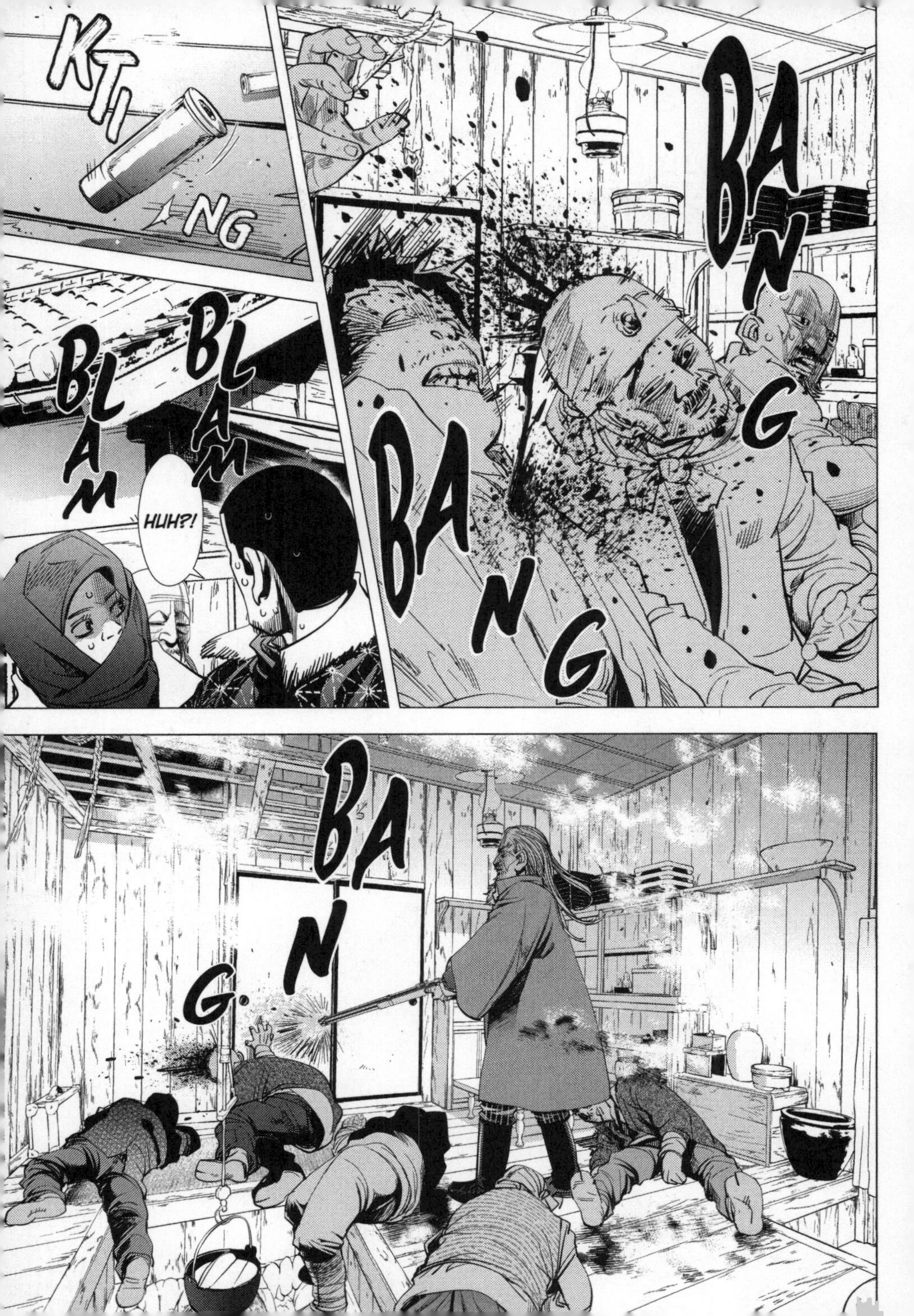
BANG
BANG
KTIING
BLAM
BLAM
HUH?!
BANG.

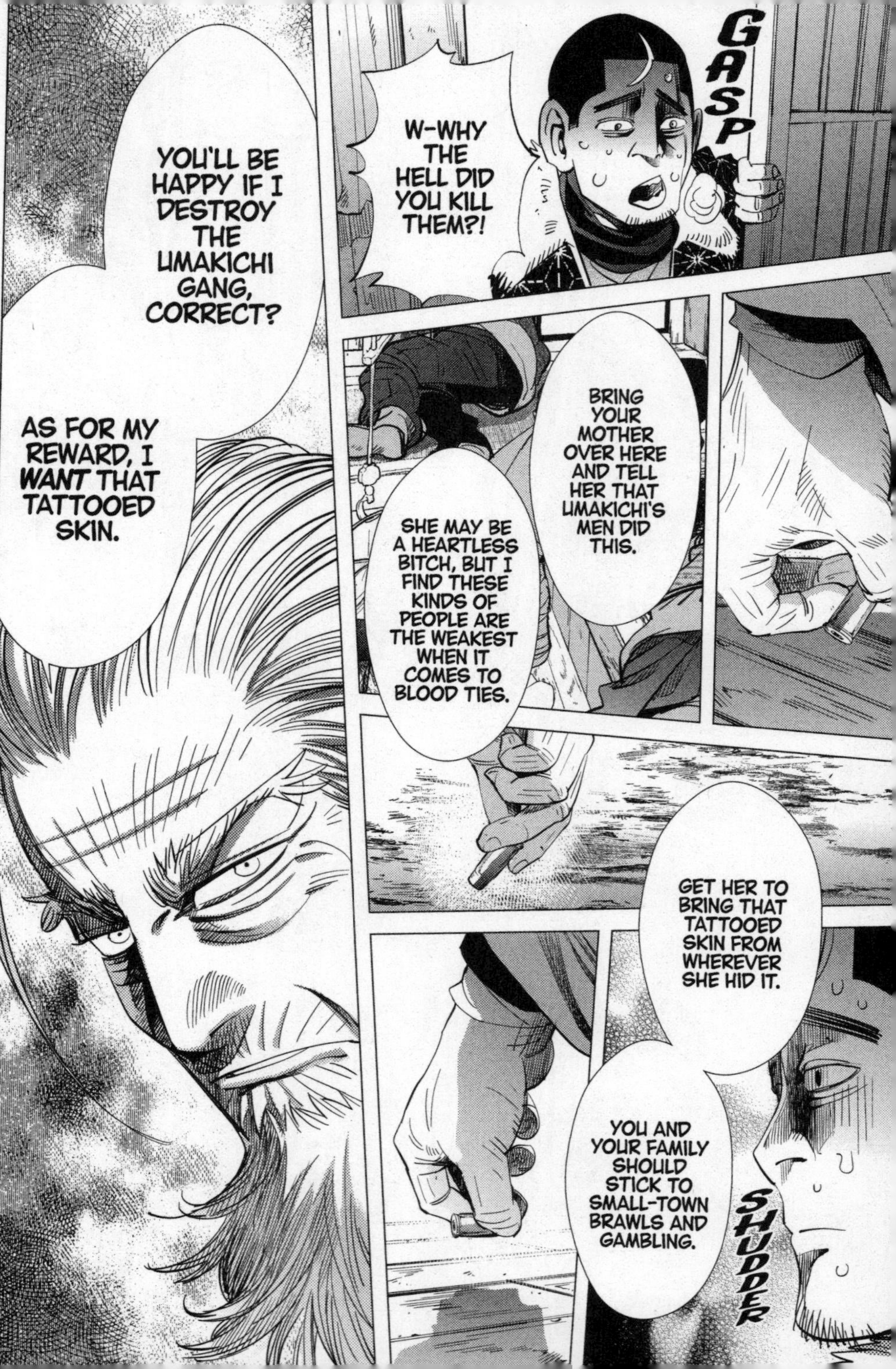
GASP
W-WHY THE HELL DID YOU KILL THEM?!
BRING YOUR MOTHER OVER HERE AND TELL HER THAT UMAKICHI'S MEN DID THIS.
SHE MAY BE A HEARTLESS BITCH, BUT I FIND THESE KINDS OF PEOPLE ARE THE WEAKEST WHEN IT COMES TO BLOOD TIES.
GET HER TO BRING THAT TATTOOED SKIN FROM WHEREVER SHE HID IT.
YOU AND YOUR FAMILY SHOULD STICK TO SMALL-TOWN BRAWLS AND GAMBLING.
SHUDDER
YOU'LL BE HAPPY IF I DESTROY THE UMAKICHI GANG, CORRECT?
AS FOR MY REWARD, I *WANT* THAT TATTOOED SKIN.

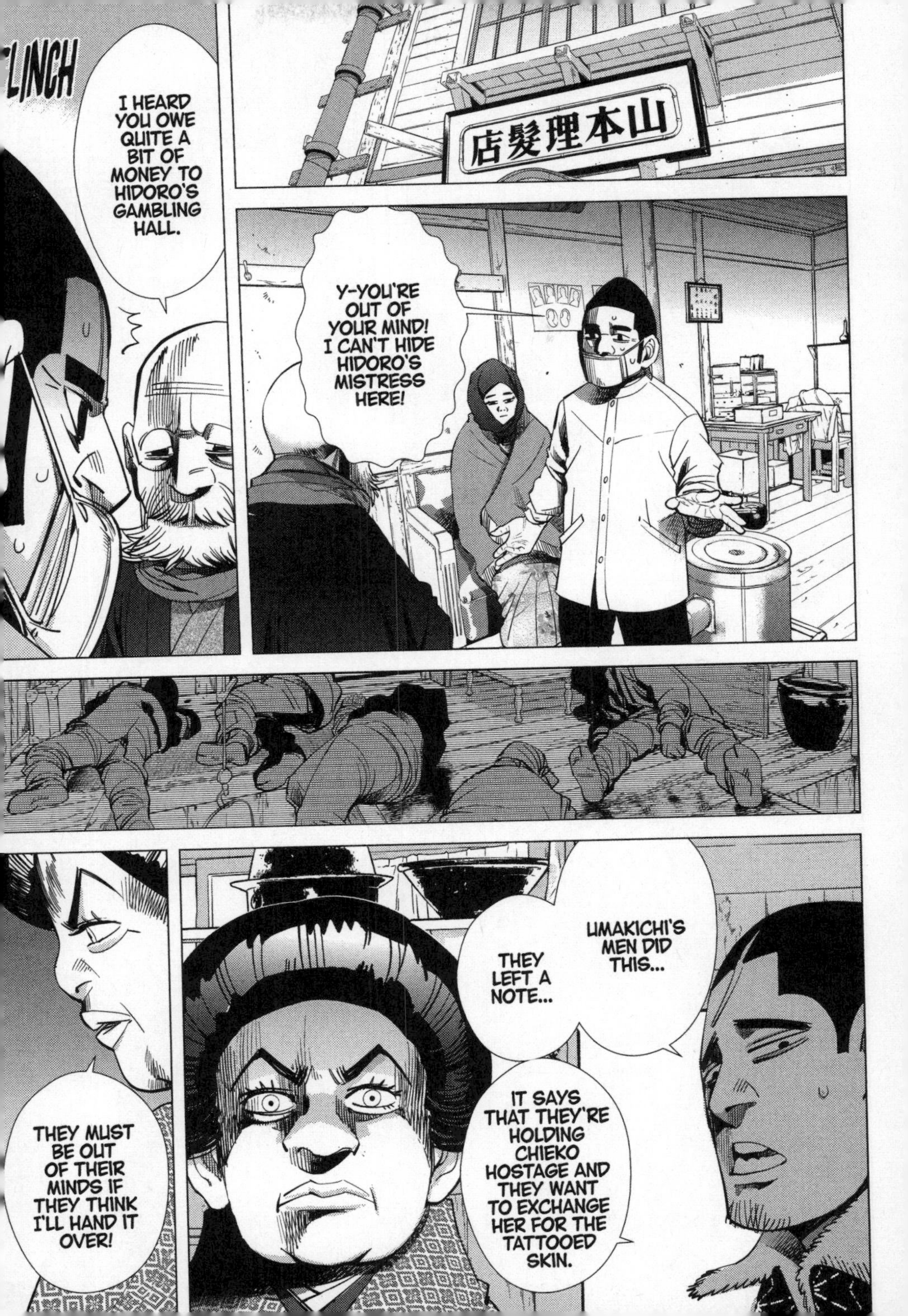

山本理髪店
Y-YOU'RE OUT OF YOUR MIND! I CAN'T HIDE HIDORO'S MISTRESS HERE!
LINCH
I HEARD YOU OWE QUITE A BIT OF MONEY TO HIDORO'S GAMBLING HALL.
UMAKICHI'S MEN DID THIS...
THEY LEFT A NOTE...
IT SAYS THAT THEY'RE HOLDING CHIEKO HOSTAGE AND THEY WANT TO EXCHANGE HER FOR THE TATTOOED SKIN.
THEY MUST BE OUT OF THEIR MINDS IF THEY THINK I'LL HAND IT OVER!

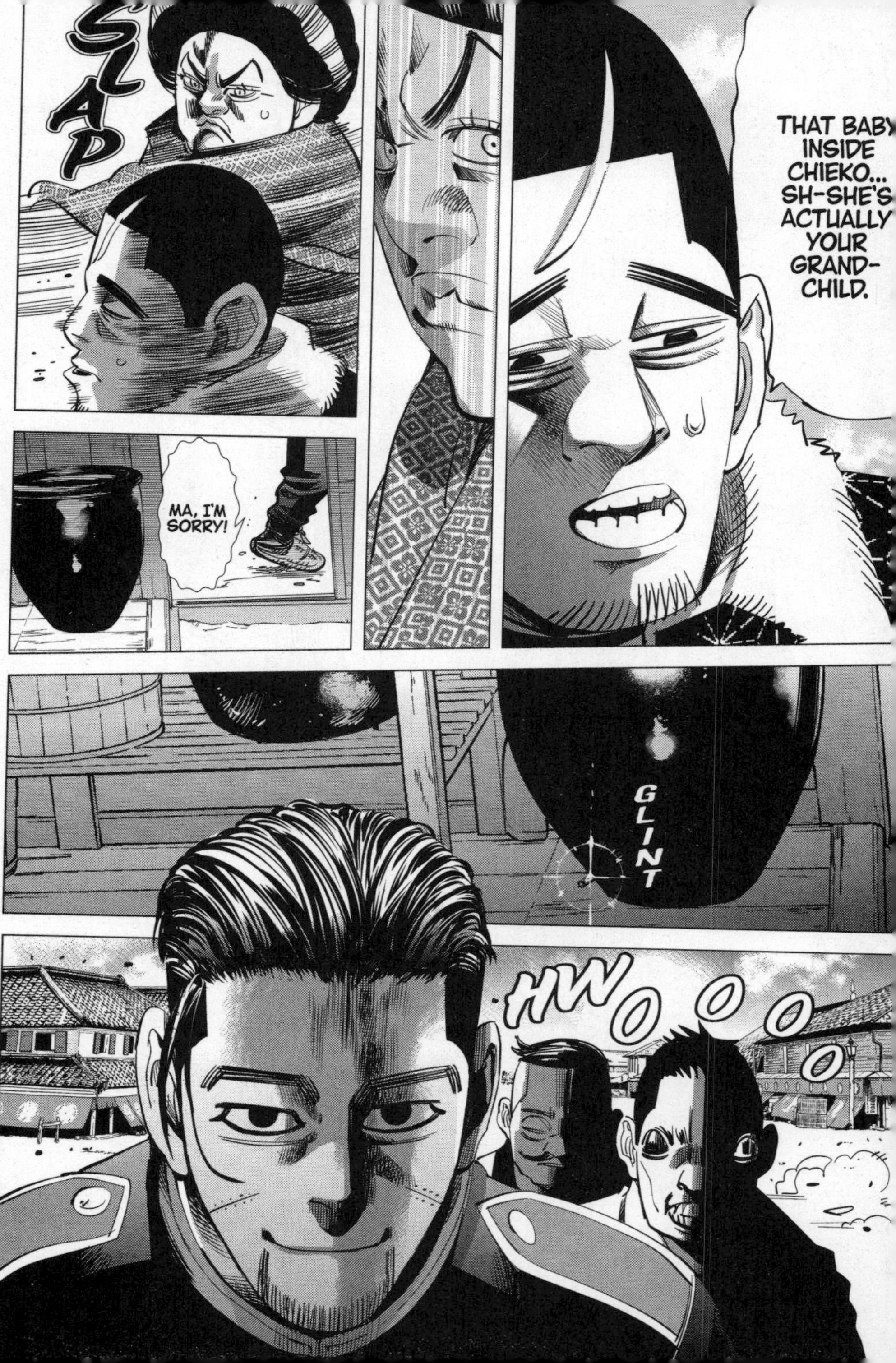
THAT BABY INSIDE CHIEKO... SH-SHE'S ACTUALLY YOUR GRANDCHILD.
SLAP
MA, I'M SORRY!
GLINT
HWOOOOO

Chapter 57: Bubble

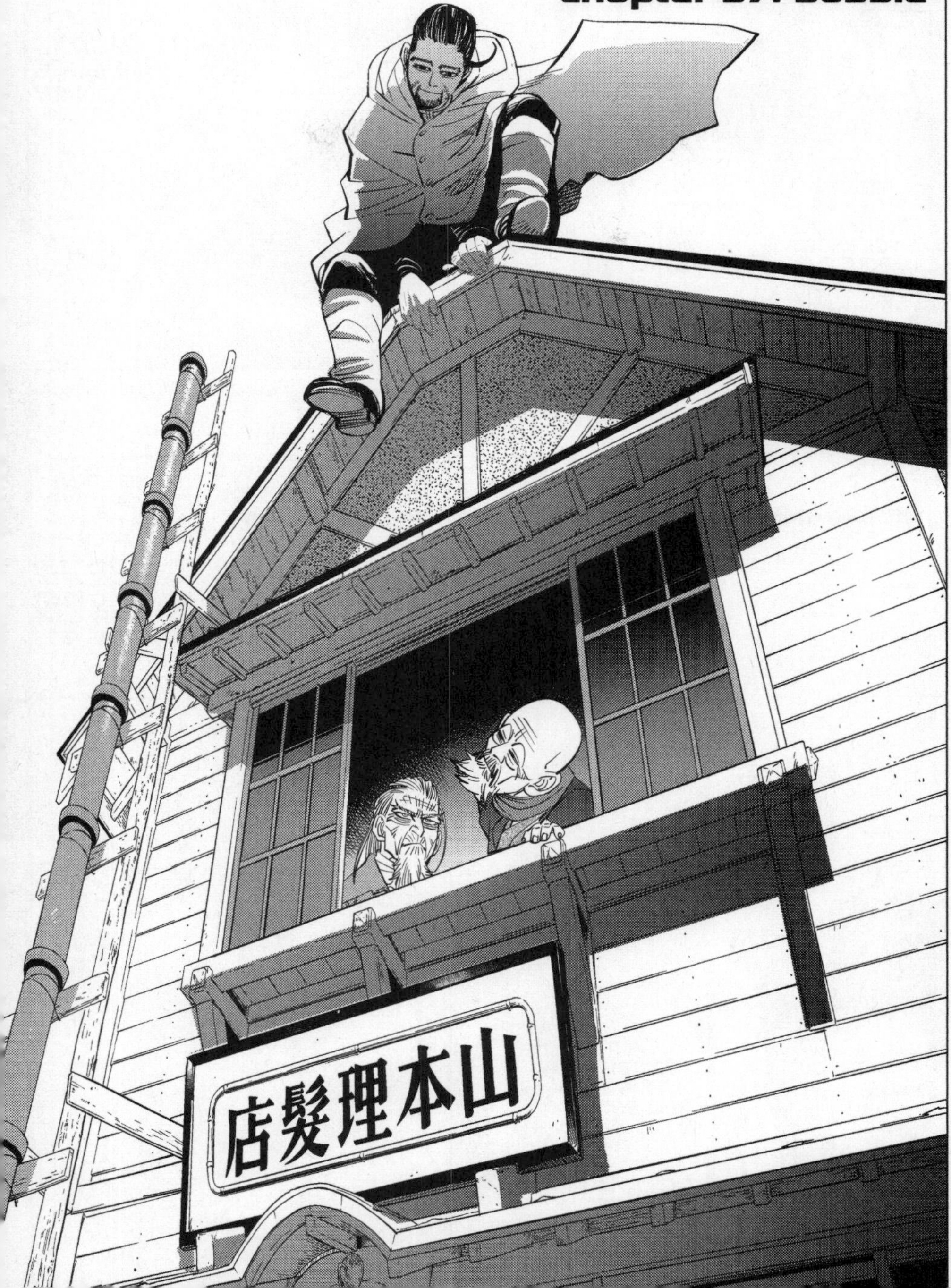
店髮理本山

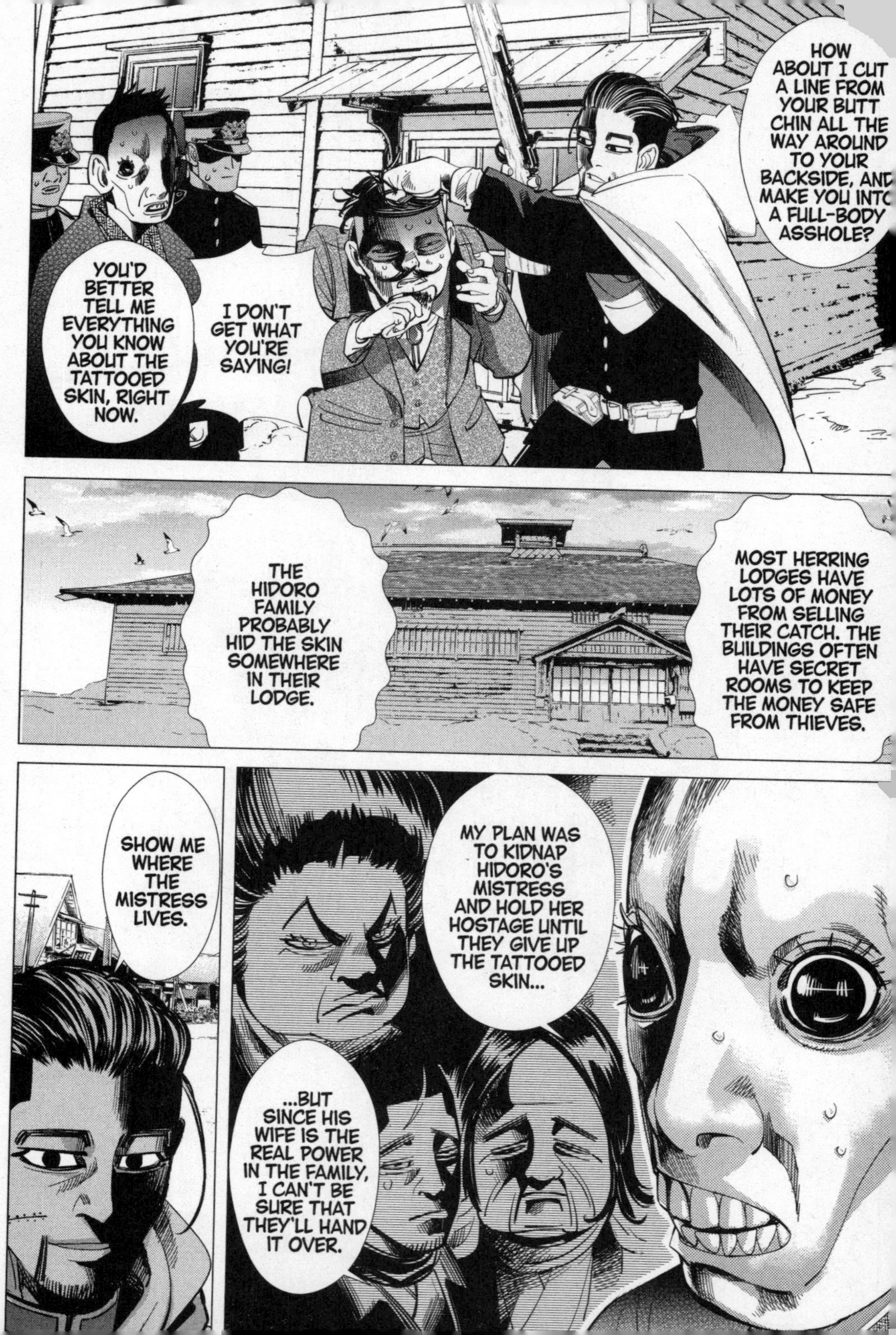
HOW ABOUT I CUT A LINE FROM YOUR BUTT CHIN ALL THE WAY AROUND TO YOUR BACKSIDE, AND MAKE YOU INTO A FULL-BODY ASSHOLE?
I DON'T GET WHAT YOU'RE SAYING!
YOU'D BETTER TELL ME EVERYTHING YOU KNOW ABOUT THE TATTOOED SKIN, RIGHT NOW.
MOST HERRING LODGES HAVE LOTS OF MONEY FROM SELLING THEIR CATCH. THE BUILDINGS OFTEN HAVE SECRET ROOMS TO KEEP THE MONEY SAFE FROM THIEVES.
THE HIDORO FAMILY PROBABLY HID THE SKIN SOMEWHERE IN THEIR LODGE.
MY PLAN WAS TO KIDNAP HIDORO'S MISTRESS AND HOLD HER HOSTAGE UNTIL THEY GIVE UP THE TATTOOED SKIN...
...BUT SINCE HIS WIFE IS THE REAL POWER IN THE FAMILY, I CAN'T BE SURE THAT THEY'LL HAND IT OVER.
SHOW ME WHERE THE MISTRESS LIVES.

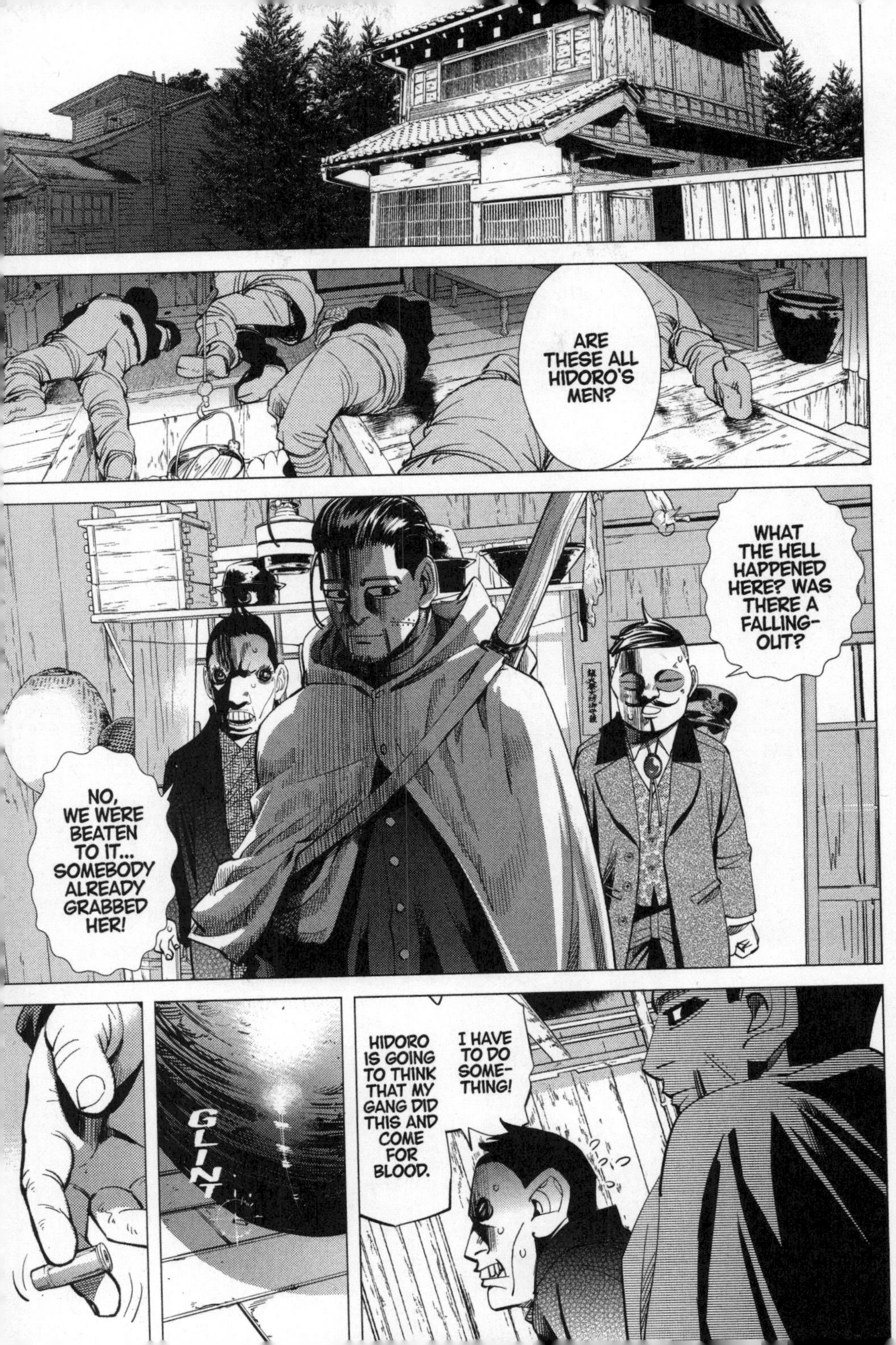
ARE THESE ALL HIDORO'S MEN?
WHAT THE HELL HAPPENED HERE? WAS THERE A FALLING-OUT?
NO, WE WERE BEATEN TO IT... SOMEBODY ALREADY GRABBED HER!
I HAVE TO DO SOME-THING!
HIDORO IS GOING TO THINK THAT MY GANG DID THIS AND COME FOR BLOOD.
GLINT

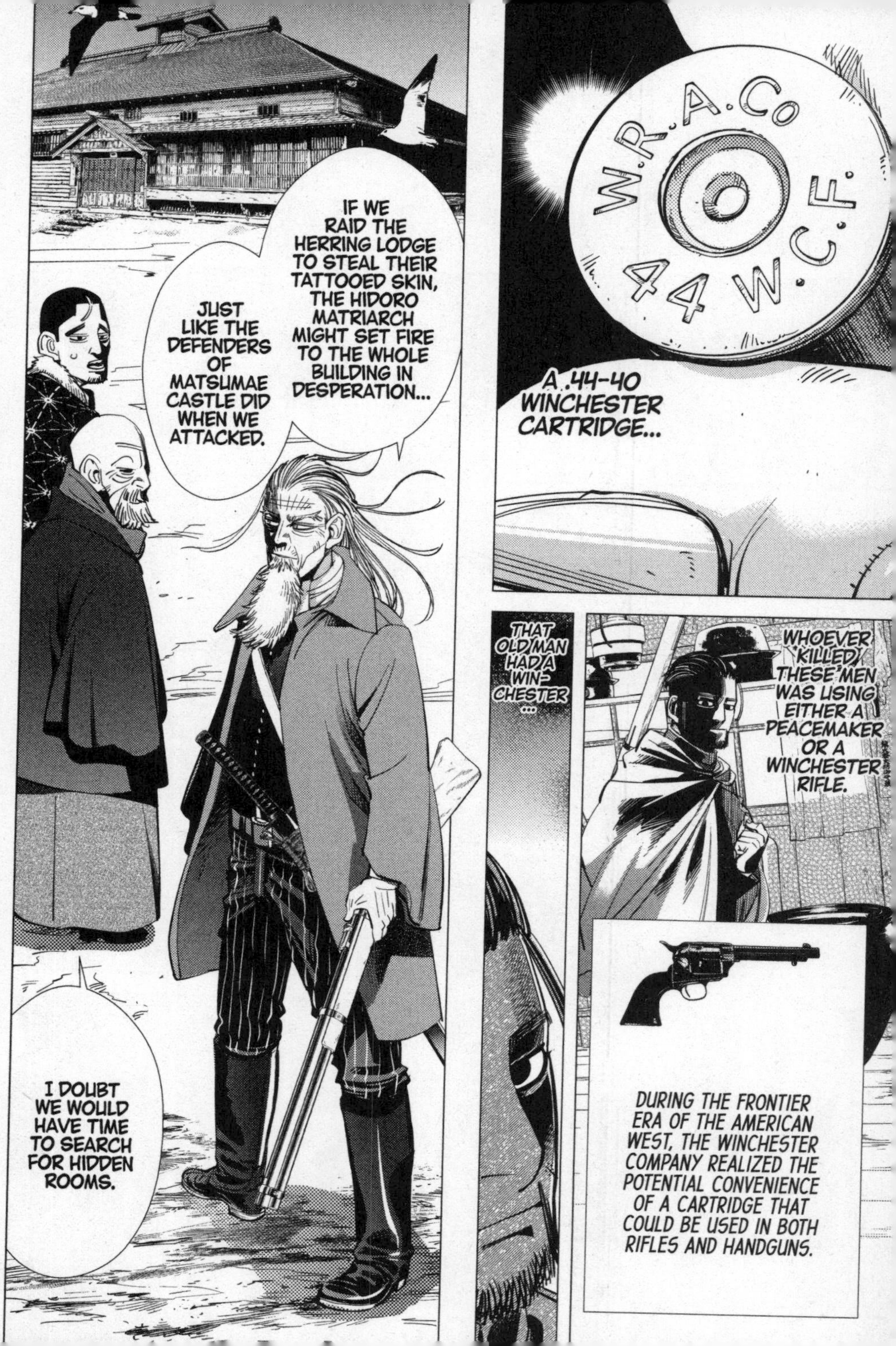
W.R.A.Co
44 W.C.F.
A .44-40 WINCHESTER CARTRIDGE...
WHOEVER KILLED THESE MEN WAS USING EITHER A PEACEMAKER OR A WINCHESTER RIFLE.
THAT OLD MAN HAD A WIN-CHESTER...
DURING THE FRONTIER ERA OF THE AMERICAN WEST, THE WINCHESTER COMPANY REALIZED THE POTENTIAL CONVENIENCE OF A CARTRIDGE THAT COULD BE USED IN BOTH RIFLES AND HANDGUNS.
IF WE RAID THE HERRING LODGE TO STEAL THEIR TATTOOED SKIN, THE HIDORO MATRIARCH MIGHT SET FIRE TO THE WHOLE BUILDING IN DESPERATION...
JUST LIKE THE DEFENDERS OF MATSUMAE CASTLE DID WHEN WE ATTACKED.
I DOUBT WE WOULD HAVE TIME TO SEARCH FOR HIDDEN ROOMS.

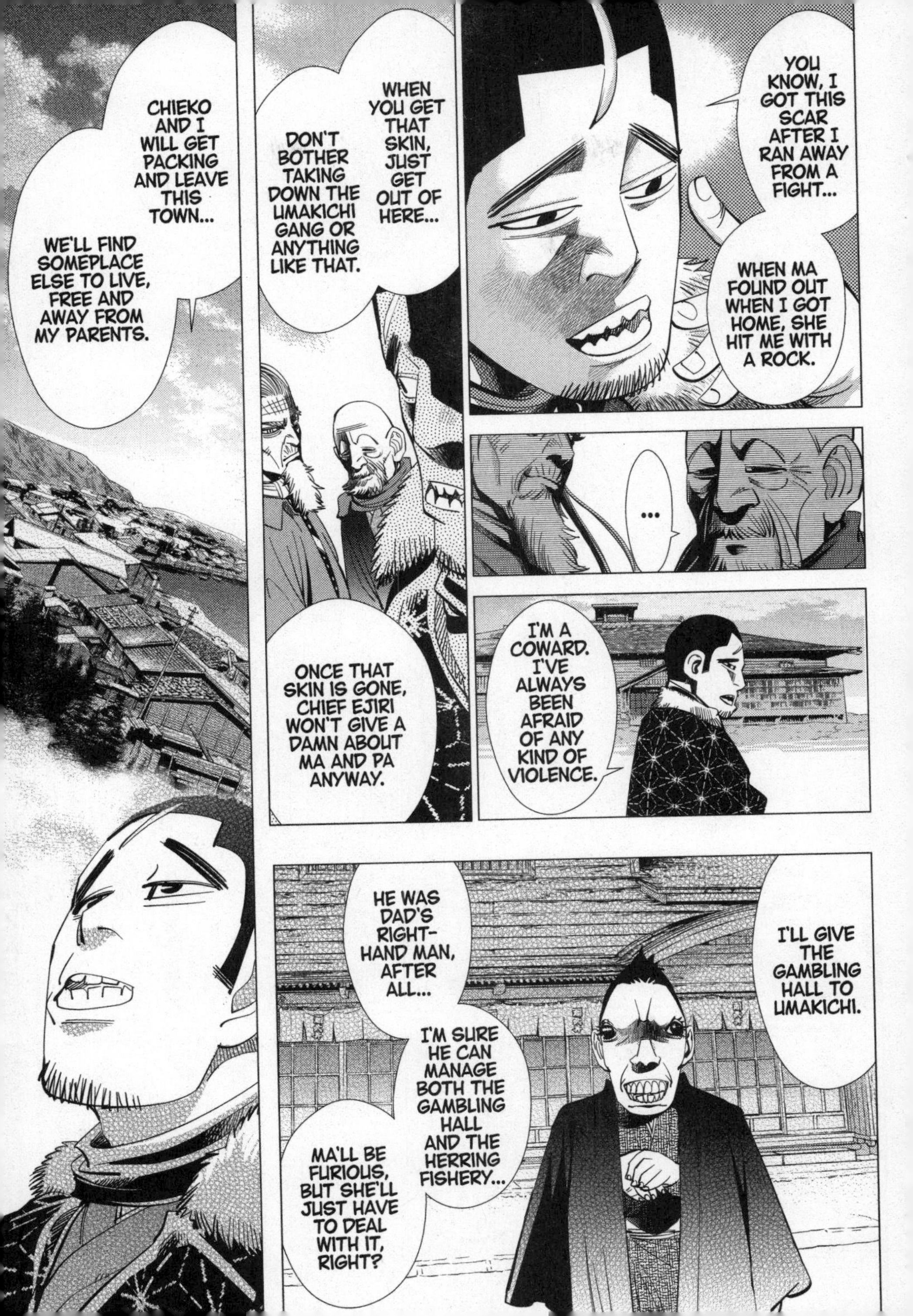
YOU KNOW, I GOT THIS SCAR AFTER I RAN AWAY FROM A FIGHT...
WHEN MA FOUND OUT WHEN I GOT HOME, SHE HIT ME WITH A ROCK.
...
I'M A COWARD. I'VE ALWAYS BEEN AFRAID OF ANY KIND OF VIOLENCE.
WHEN YOU GET THAT SKIN, JUST GET OUT OF HERE...
DON'T BOTHER TAKING DOWN THE UMAKICHI GANG OR ANYTHING LIKE THAT.
ONCE THAT SKIN IS GONE, CHIEF EJIRI WON'T GIVE A DAMN ABOUT MA AND PA ANYWAY.
I'LL GIVE THE GAMBLING HALL TO UMAKICHI.
HE WAS DAD'S RIGHT-HAND MAN, AFTER ALL...
I'M SURE HE CAN MANAGE BOTH THE GAMBLING HALL AND THE HERRING FISHERY...
MA'LL BE FURIOUS, BUT SHE'LL JUST HAVE TO DEAL WITH IT, RIGHT?
CHIEKO AND I WILL GET PACKING AND LEAVE THIS TOWN...
WE'LL FIND SOMEPLACE ELSE TO LIVE, FREE AND AWAY FROM MY PARENTS.

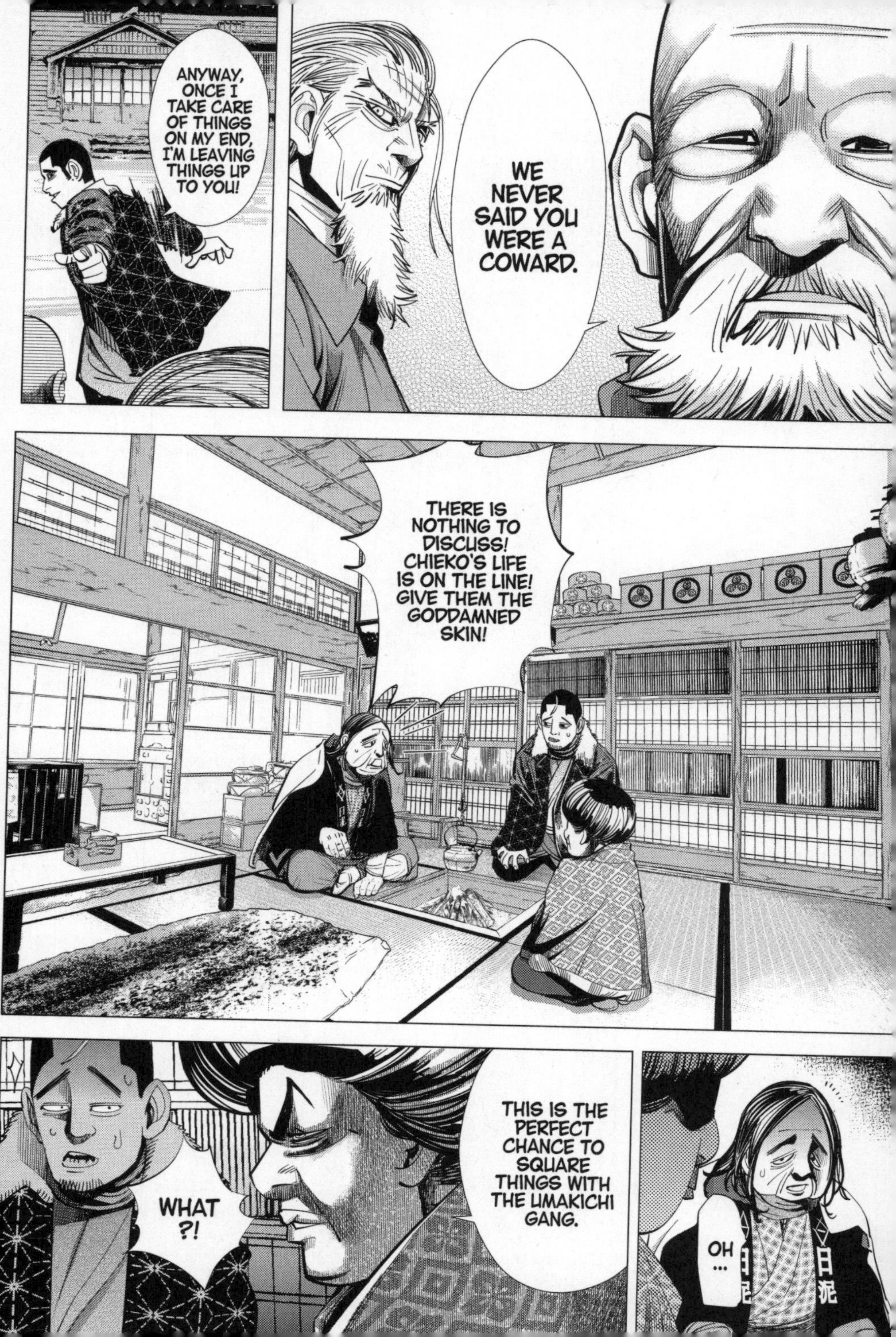
WE NEVER SAID YOU WERE A COWARD.
ANYWAY, ONCE I TAKE CARE OF THINGS ON MY END, I'M LEAVING THINGS UP TO YOU!
THERE IS NOTHING TO DISCUSS! CHIEKO'S LIFE IS ON THE LINE! GIVE THEM THE GODDAMNED SKIN!
OH ...
THIS IS THE PERFECT CHANCE TO SQUARE THINGS WITH THE UMAKICHI GANG.
WHAT ?!

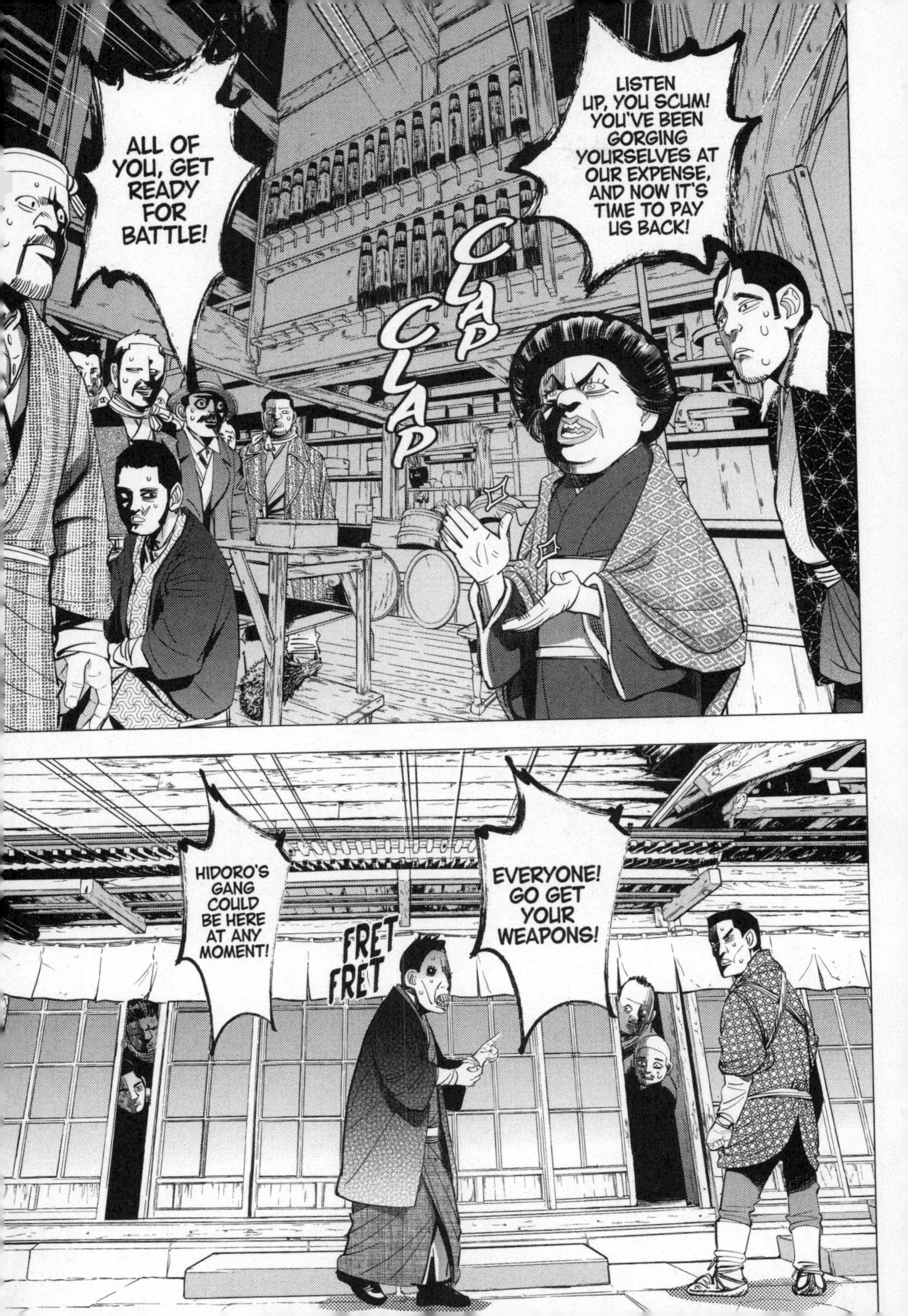
LISTEN UP, YOU SCUM! YOU'VE BEEN GORGING YOURSELVES AT OUR EXPENSE, AND NOW IT'S TIME TO PAY US BACK!
CLAP CLAP
ALL OF YOU, GET READY FOR BATTLE!
EVERYONE! GO GET YOUR WEAPONS!
FRET FRET
HIDORO'S GANG COULD BE HERE AT ANY MOMENT!

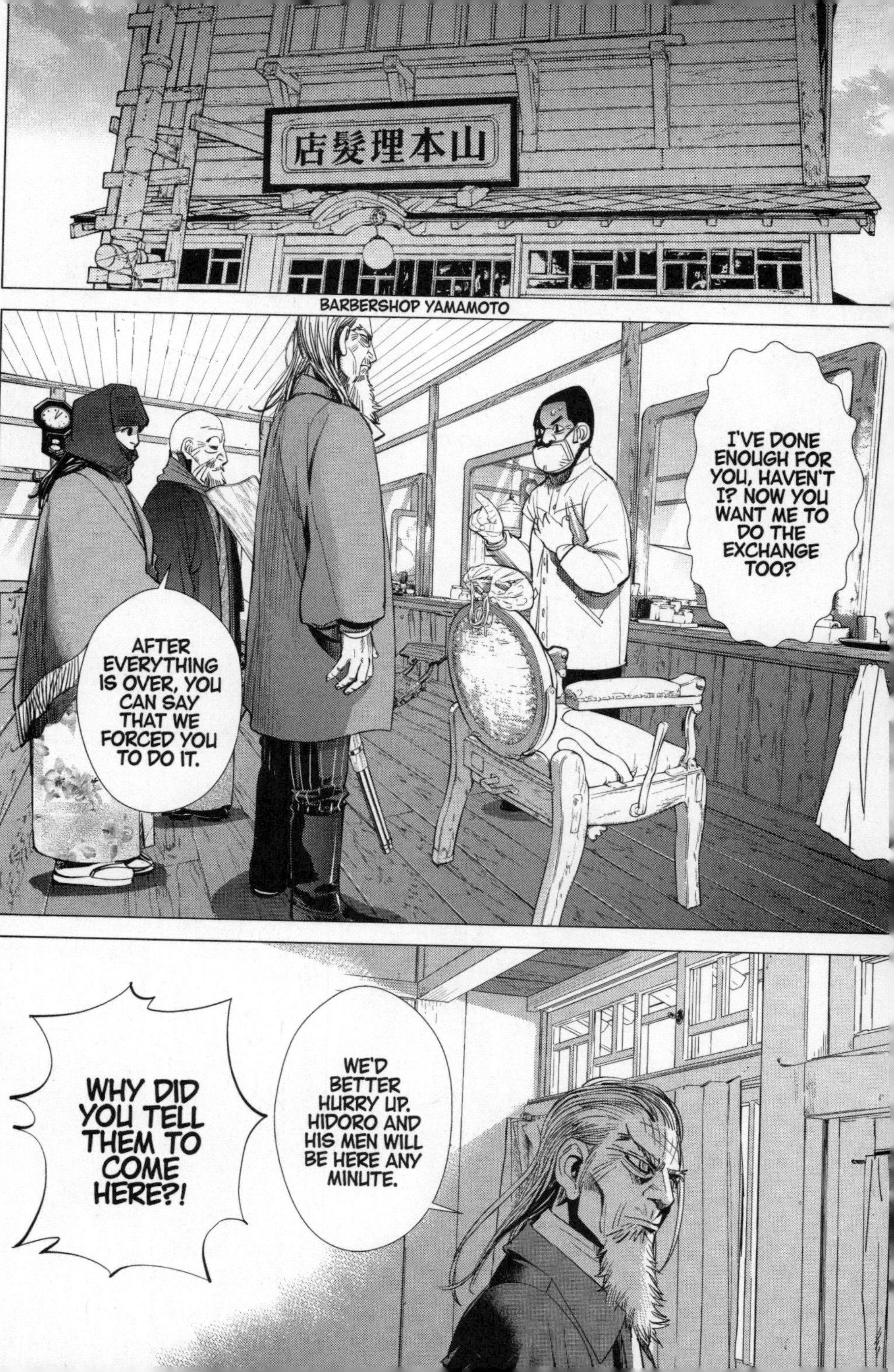
山本理髪店
BARBERSHOP YAMAMOTO
I'VE DONE ENOUGH FOR YOU, HAVEN'T I? NOW YOU WANT ME TO DO THE EXCHANGE TOO?
AFTER EVERYTHING IS OVER, YOU CAN SAY THAT WE FORCED YOU TO DO IT.
WE'D BETTER HURRY UP. HIDORO AND HIS MEN WILL BE HERE ANY MINUTE.
WHY DID YOU TELL THEM TO COME HERE?!

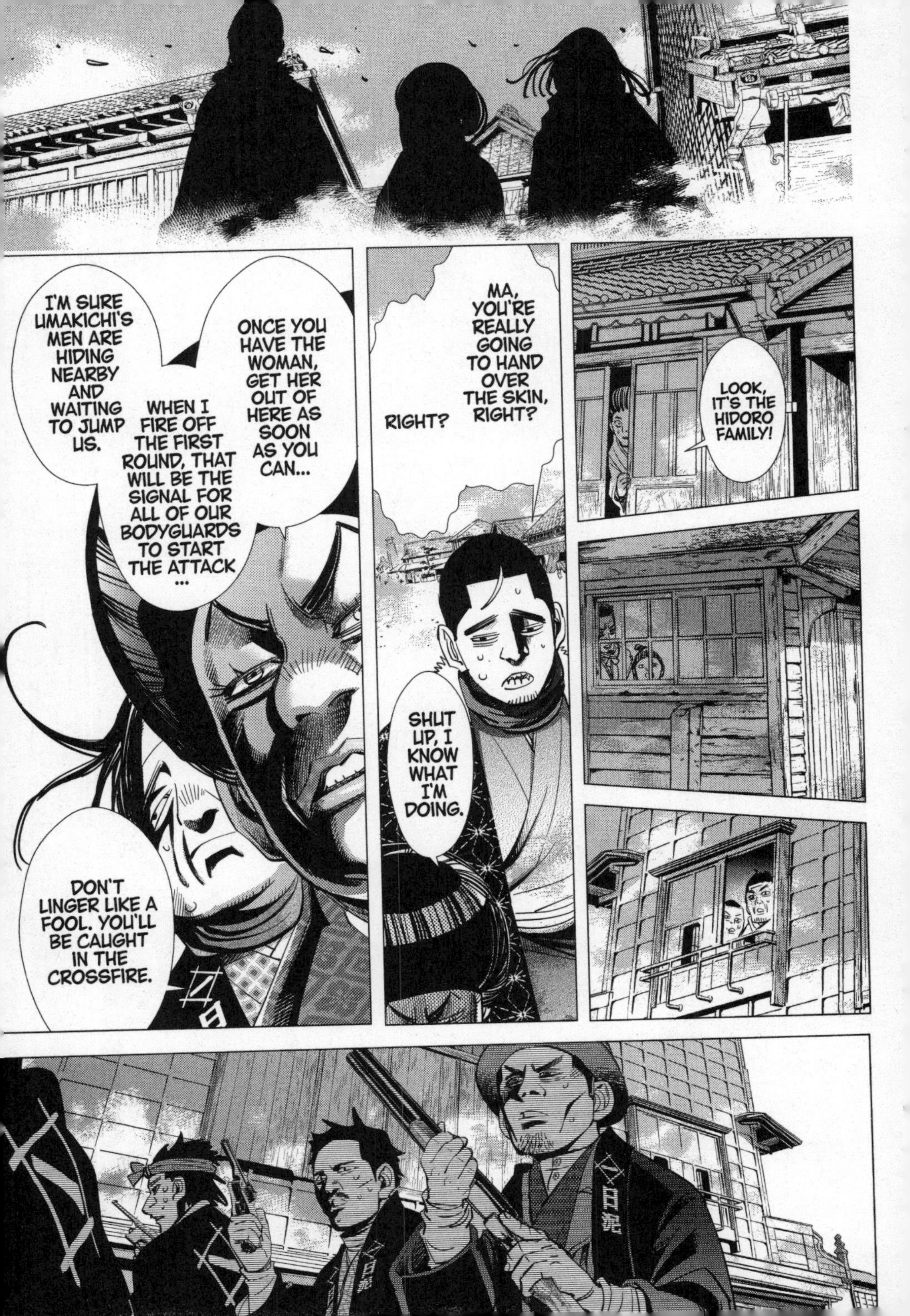
LOOK, IT'S THE HIDORO FAMILY!
MA, YOU'RE REALLY GOING TO HAND OVER THE SKIN, RIGHT?
RIGHT?
SHUT UP, I KNOW WHAT I'M DOING.
ONCE YOU HAVE THE WOMAN, GET HER OUT OF HERE AS SOON AS YOU CAN...
I'M SURE UMAKICHI'S MEN ARE HIDING NEARBY AND WAITING TO JUMP US.
WHEN I FIRE OFF THE FIRST ROUND, THAT WILL BE THE SIGNAL FOR ALL OF OUR BODYGUARDS TO START THE ATTACK...
DON'T LINGER LIKE A FOOL. YOU'LL BE CAUGHT IN THE CROSSFIRE.

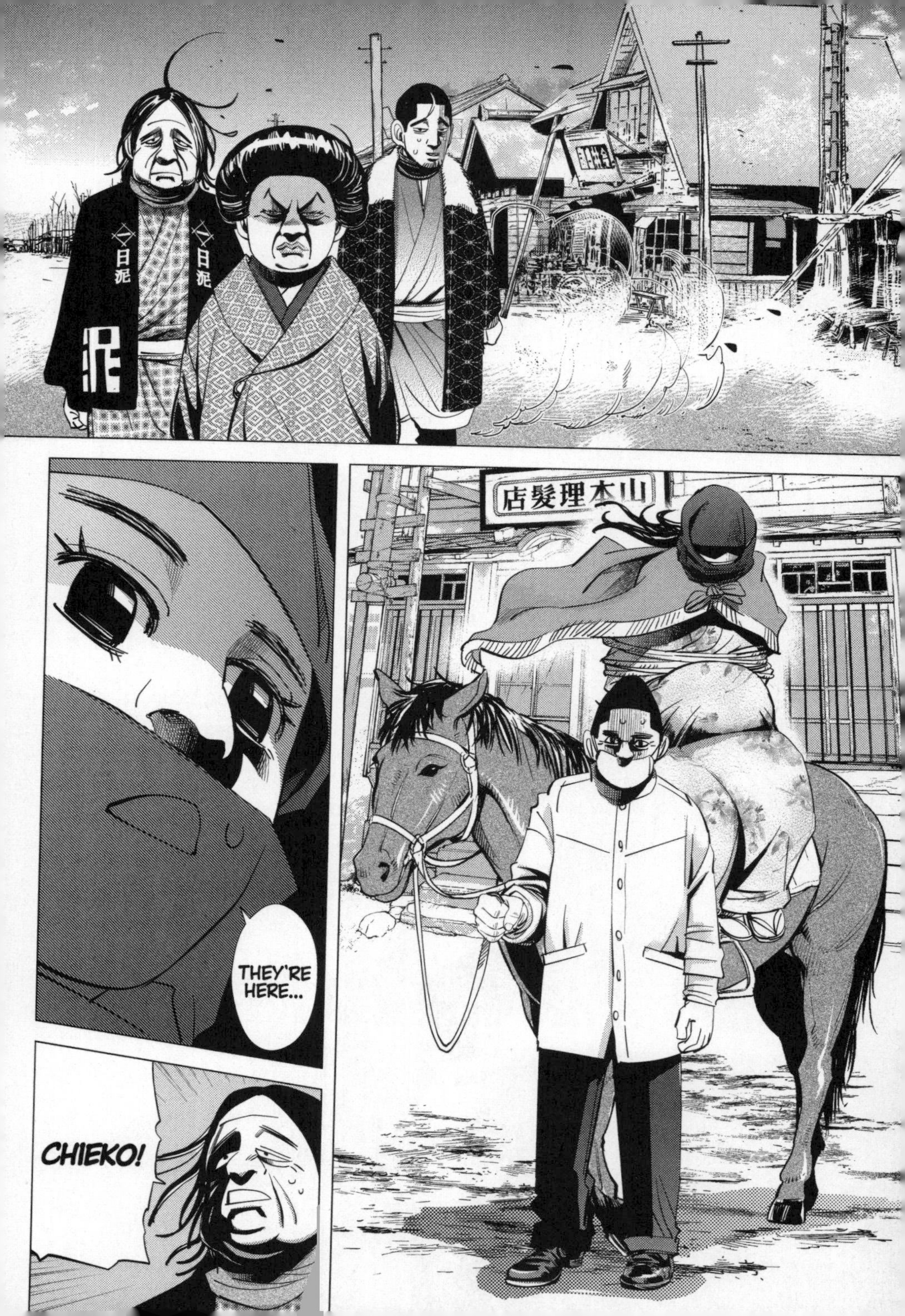
山本理髪店
THEY'RE HERE...
CHIEKO!

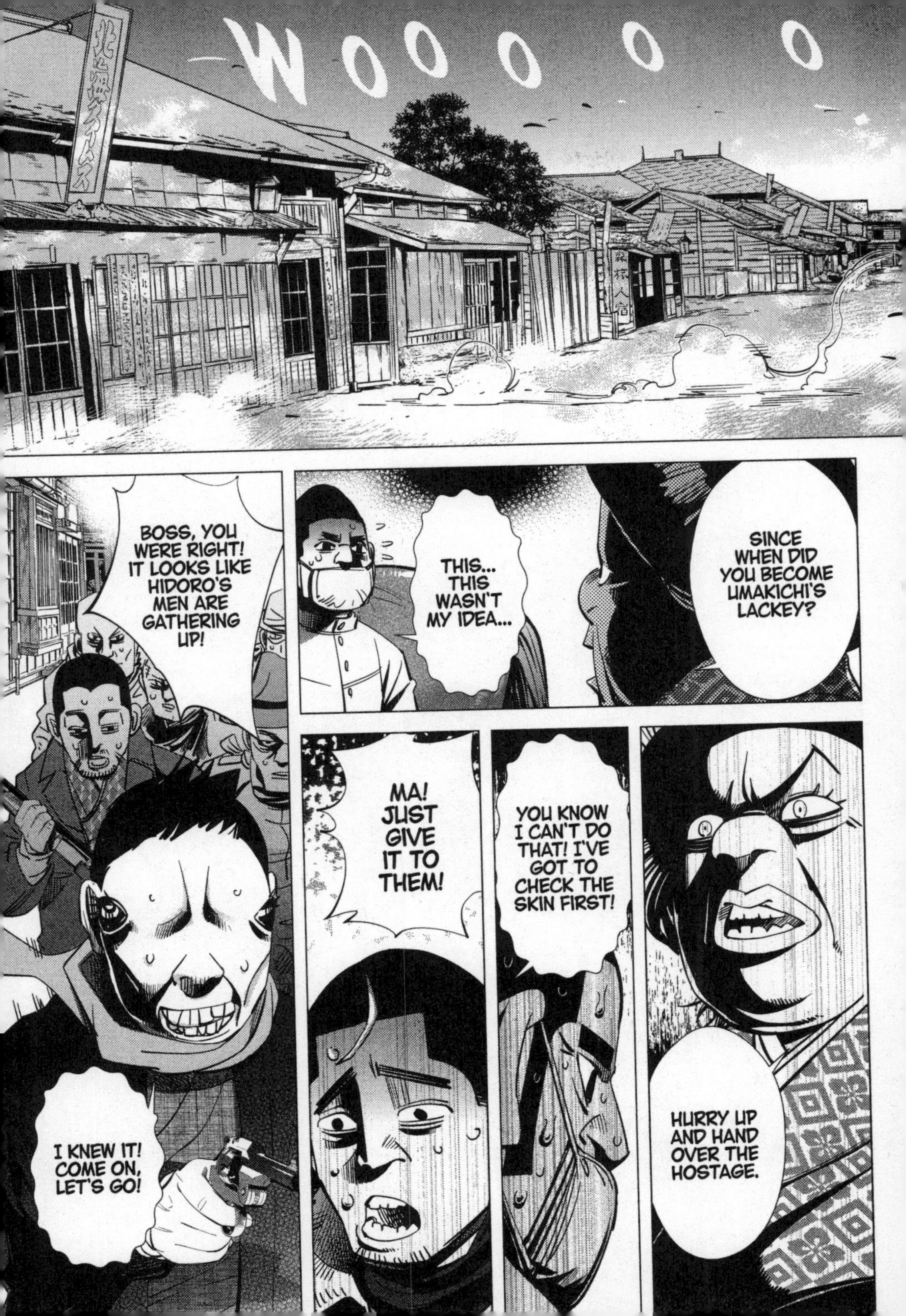
WOOOOO
SINCE WHEN DID YOU BECOME UMAKICHI'S LACKEY?
THIS... THIS WASN'T MY IDEA...
HURRY UP AND HAND OVER THE HOSTAGE.
YOU KNOW I CAN'T DO THAT! I'VE GOT TO CHECK THE SKIN FIRST!
MA! JUST GIVE IT TO THEM!
BOSS, YOU WERE RIGHT! IT LOOKS LIKE HIDORO'S MEN ARE GATHERING UP!
I KNEW IT! COME ON, LET'S GO!

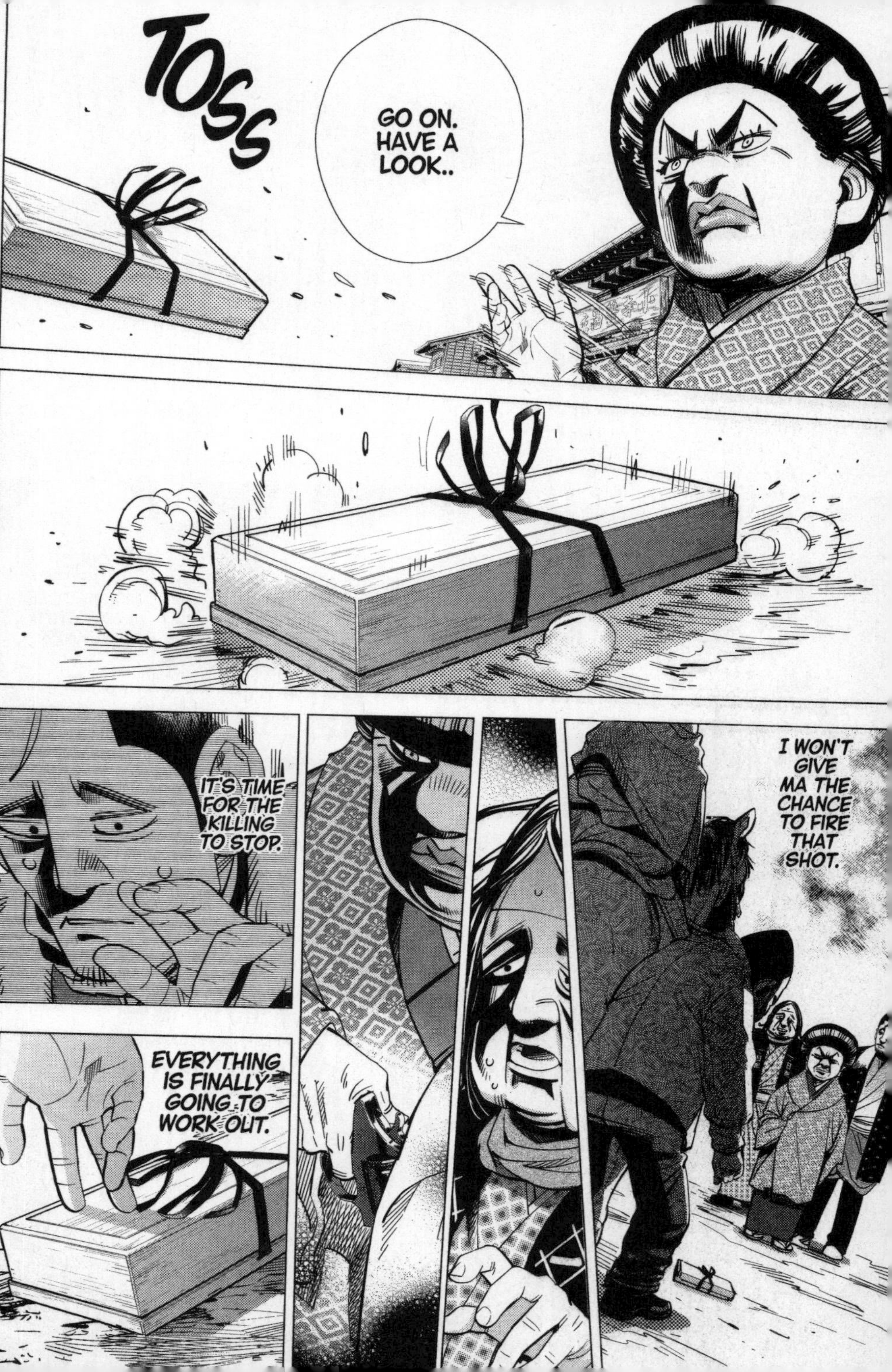
GO ON. HAVE A LOOK..
TOSS
I WON'T GIVE MA THE CHANCE TO FIRE THAT SHOT.
IT'S TIME FOR THE KILLING TO STOP.
EVERYTHING IS FINALLY GOING TO WORK OUT.

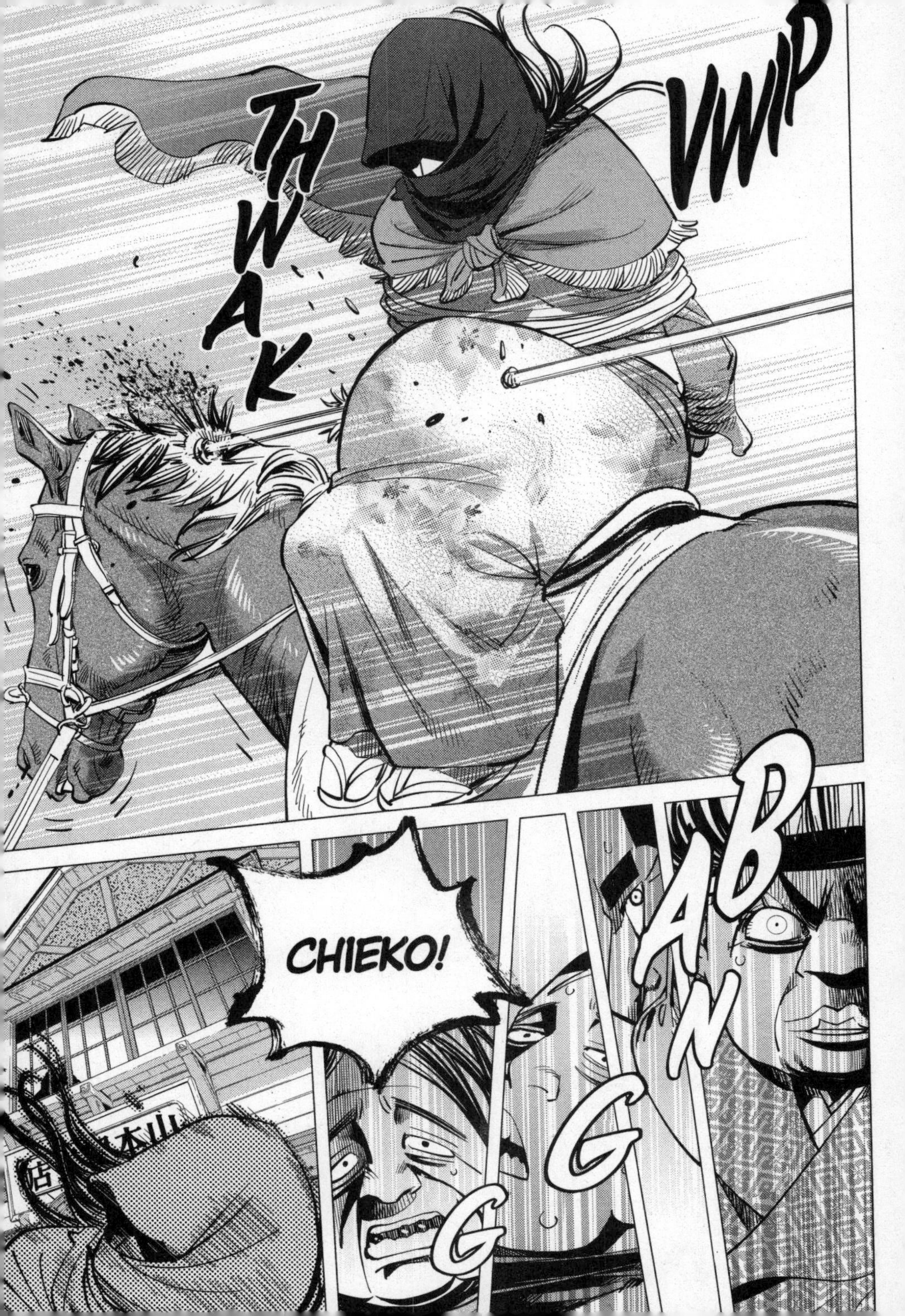
VWIP
THWAK
BANGG
CHIEKO!

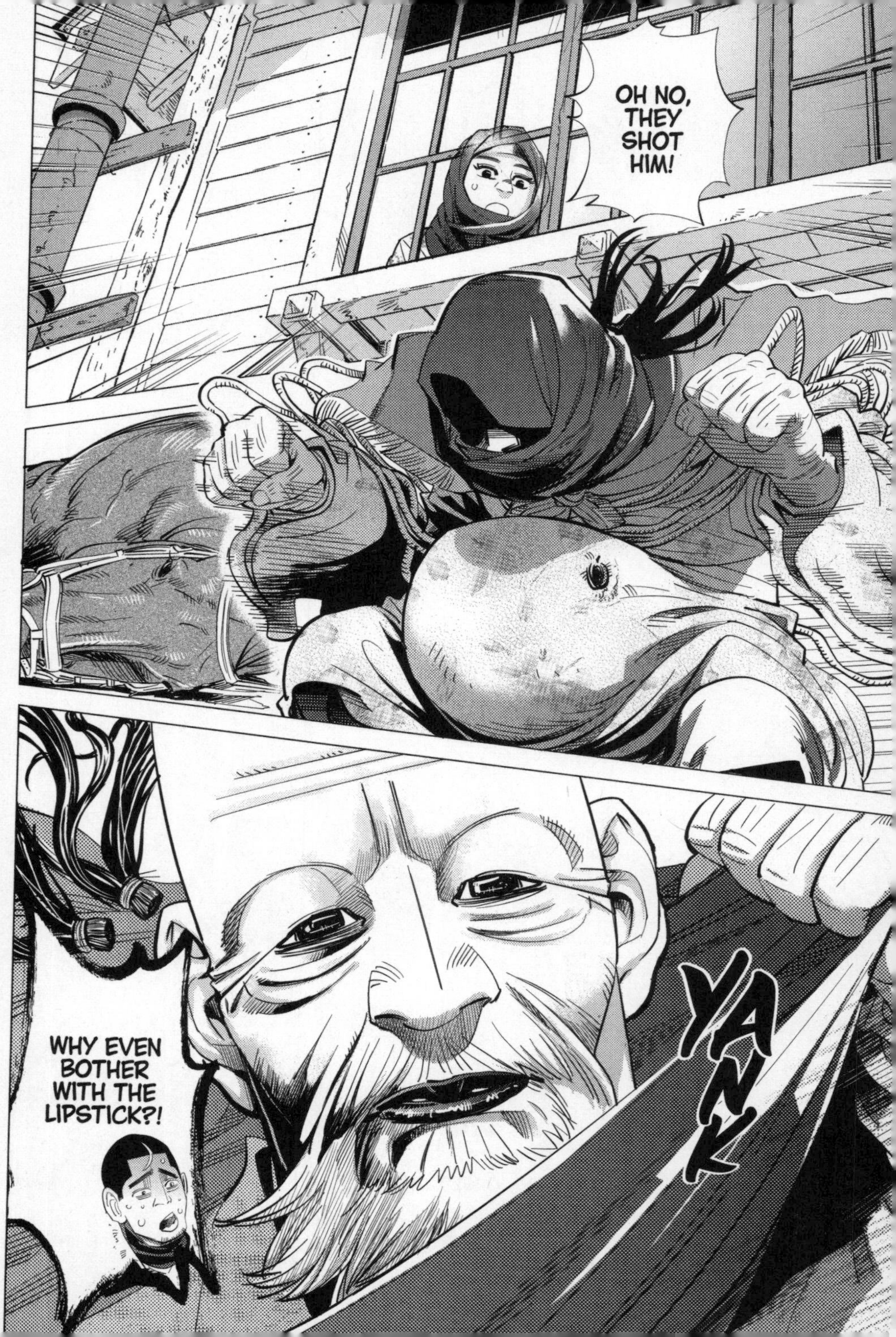
OH NO, THEY SHOT HIM!
YANK
WHY EVEN BOTHER WITH THE LIPSTICK?!

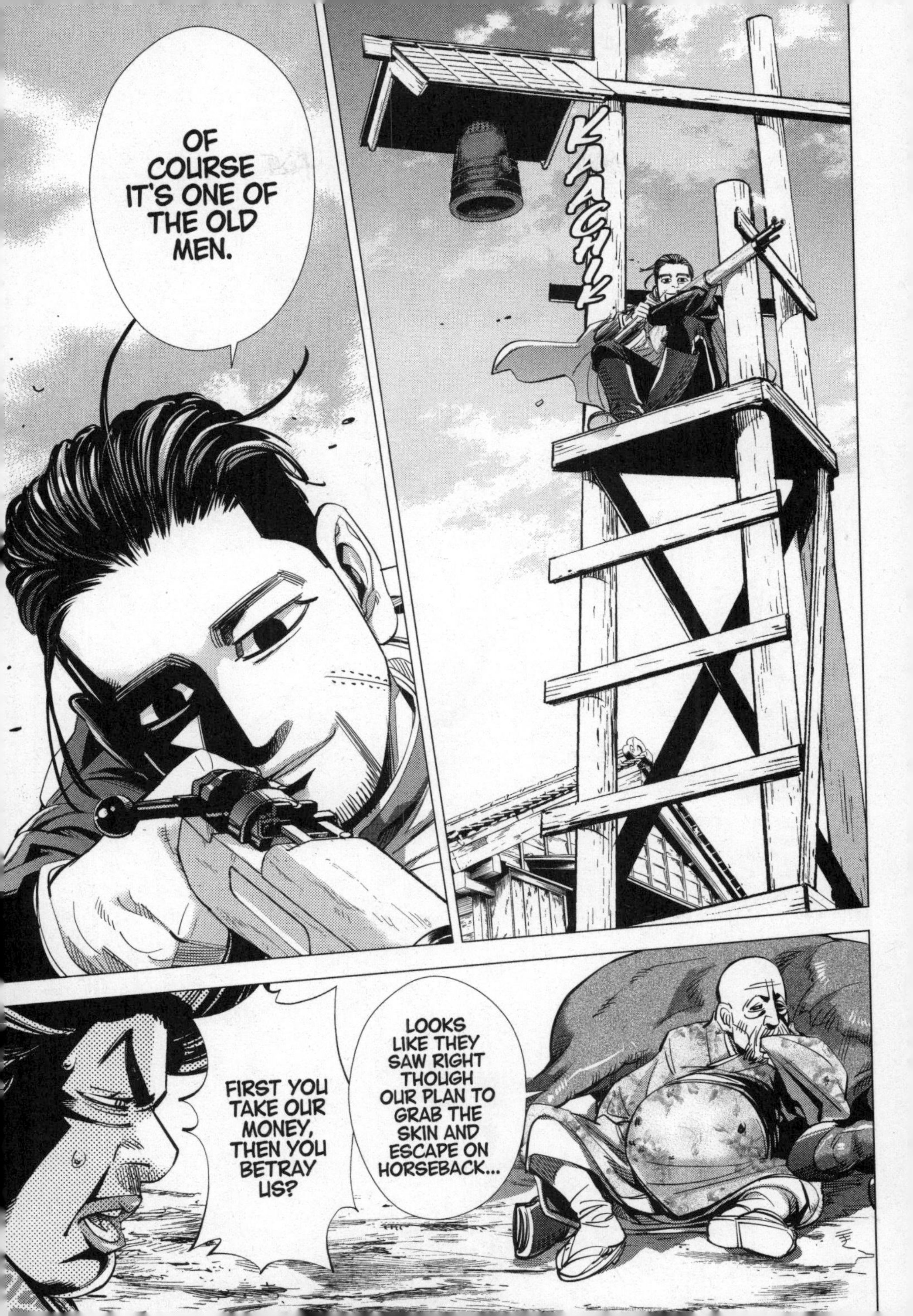
KACHIK
OF COURSE IT'S ONE OF THE OLD MEN.
LOOKS LIKE THEY SAW RIGHT THOUGH OUR PLAN TO GRAB THE SKIN AND ESCAPE ON HORSEBACK...
FIRST YOU TAKE OUR MONEY, THEN YOU BETRAY US?

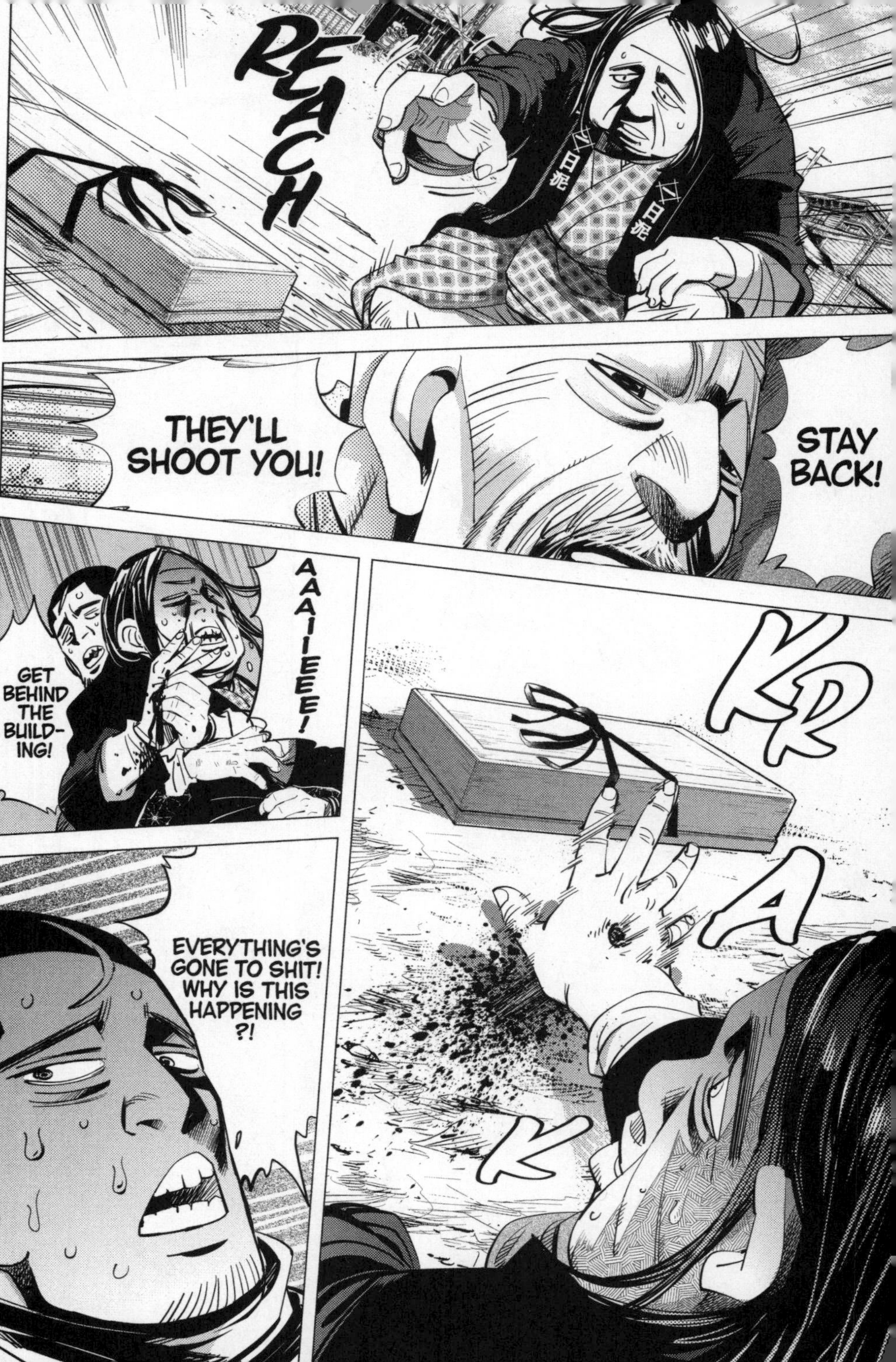
REACH
STAY BACK!
THEY'LL SHOOT YOU!
KRAK
AAAIIEEEE!
GET BEHIND THE BUILDING!
EVERYTHING'S GONE TO SHIT! WHY IS THIS HAPPENING?!

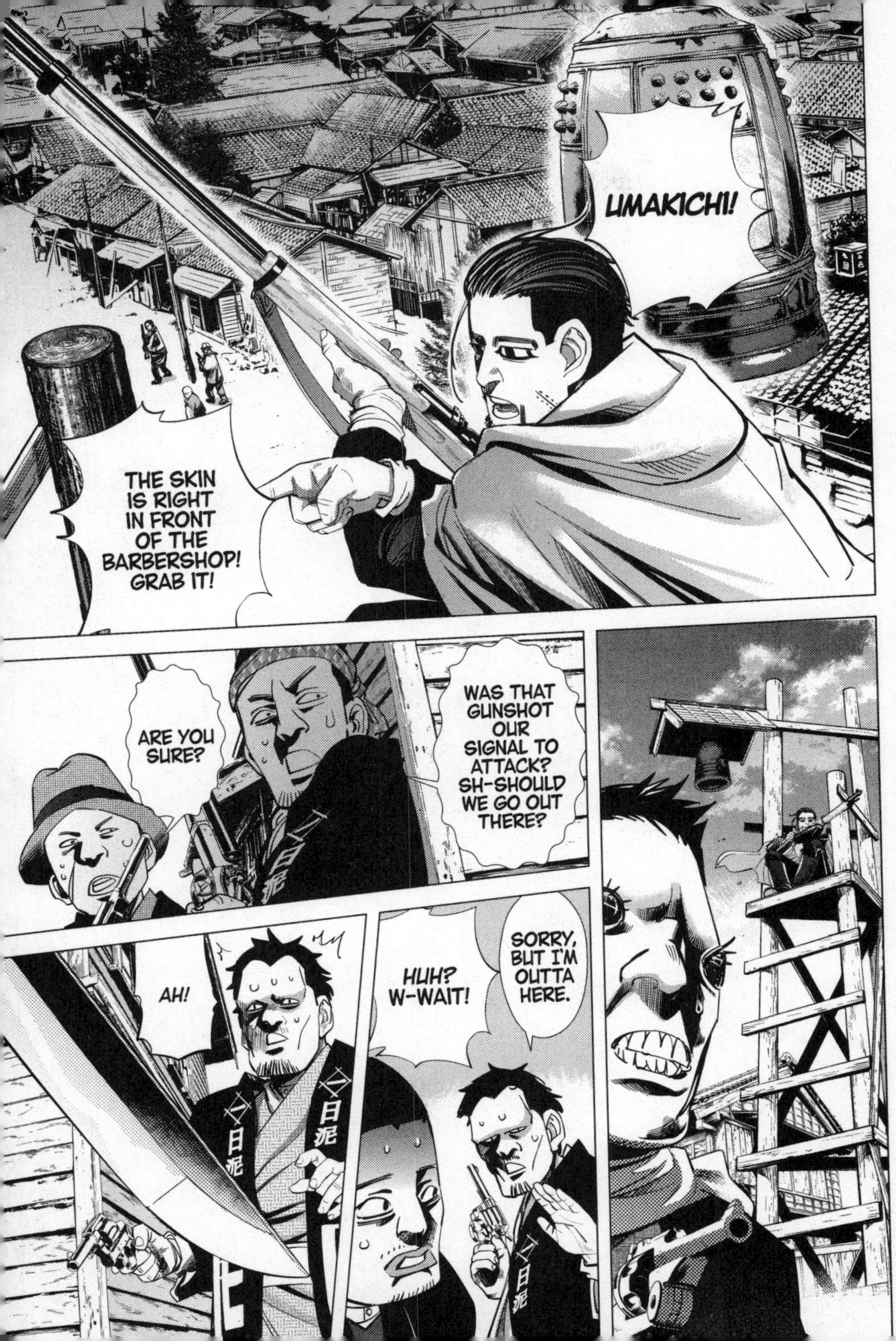
UMAKICHI!
THE SKIN IS RIGHT IN FRONT OF THE BARBERSHOP! GRAB IT!
WAS THAT GUNSHOT OUR SIGNAL TO ATTACK? SH-SHOULD WE GO OUT THERE?
ARE YOU SURE?
SORRY, BUT I'M OUTTA HERE.
HUH? W-WAIT!
AH!

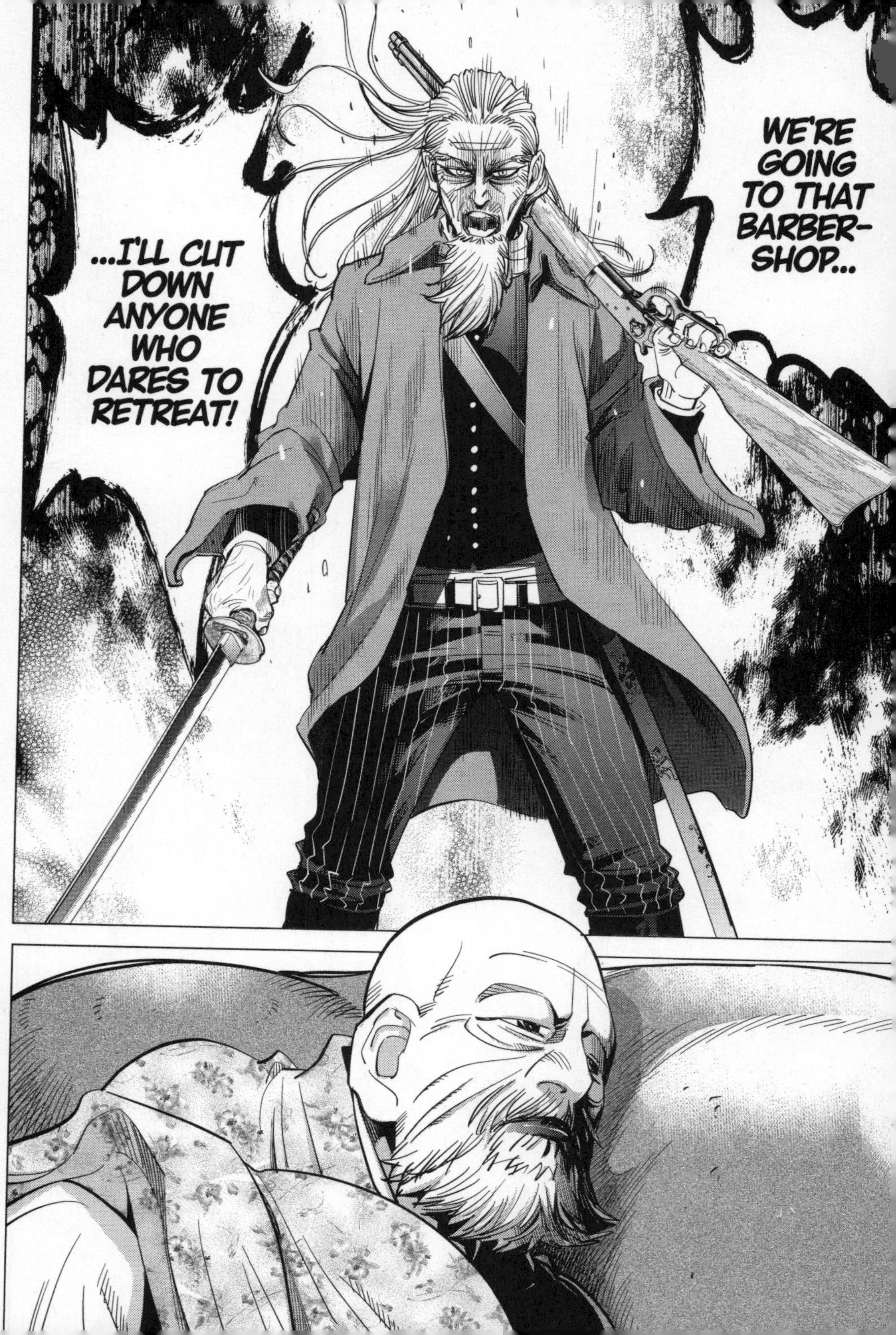
WE'RE GOING TO THAT BARBER-SHOP...
...I'LL CUT DOWN ANYONE WHO DARES TO RETREAT!

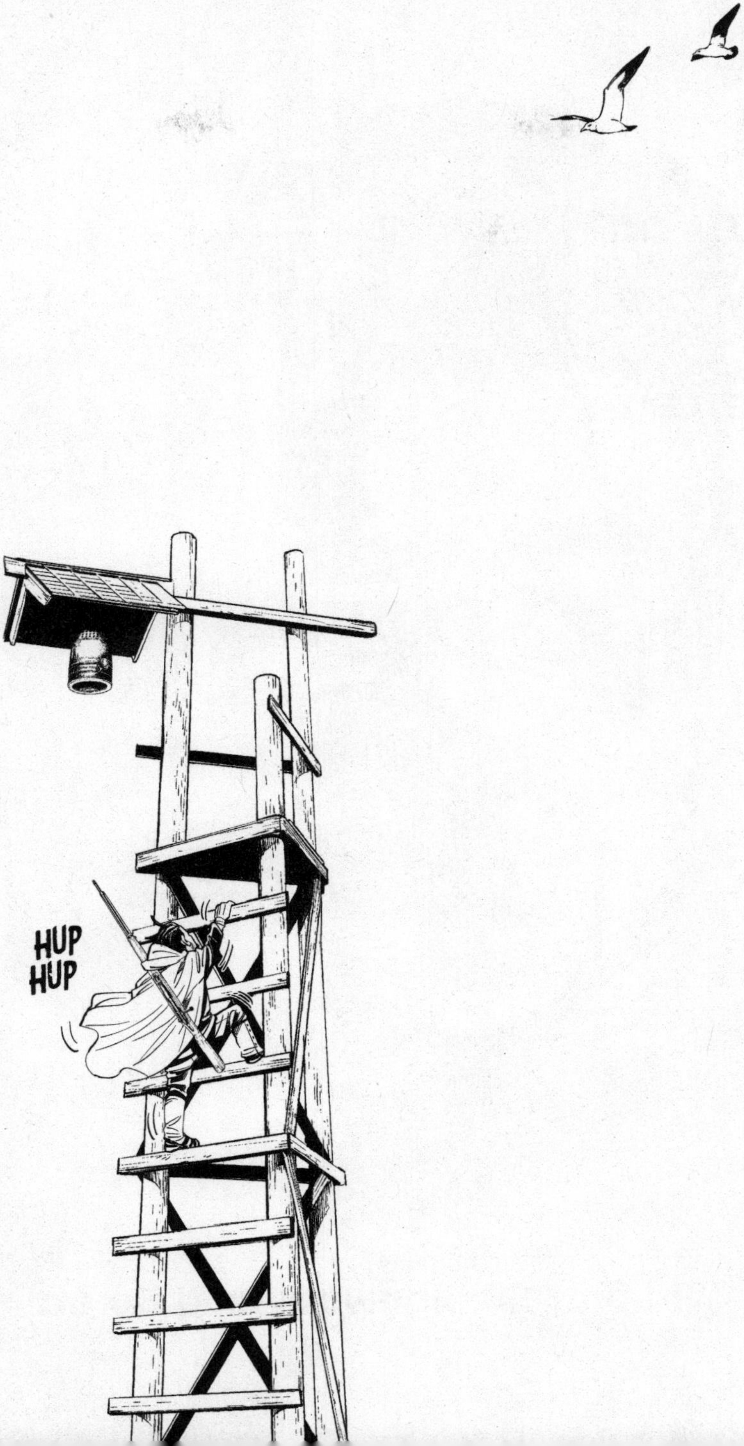
HUP HUP

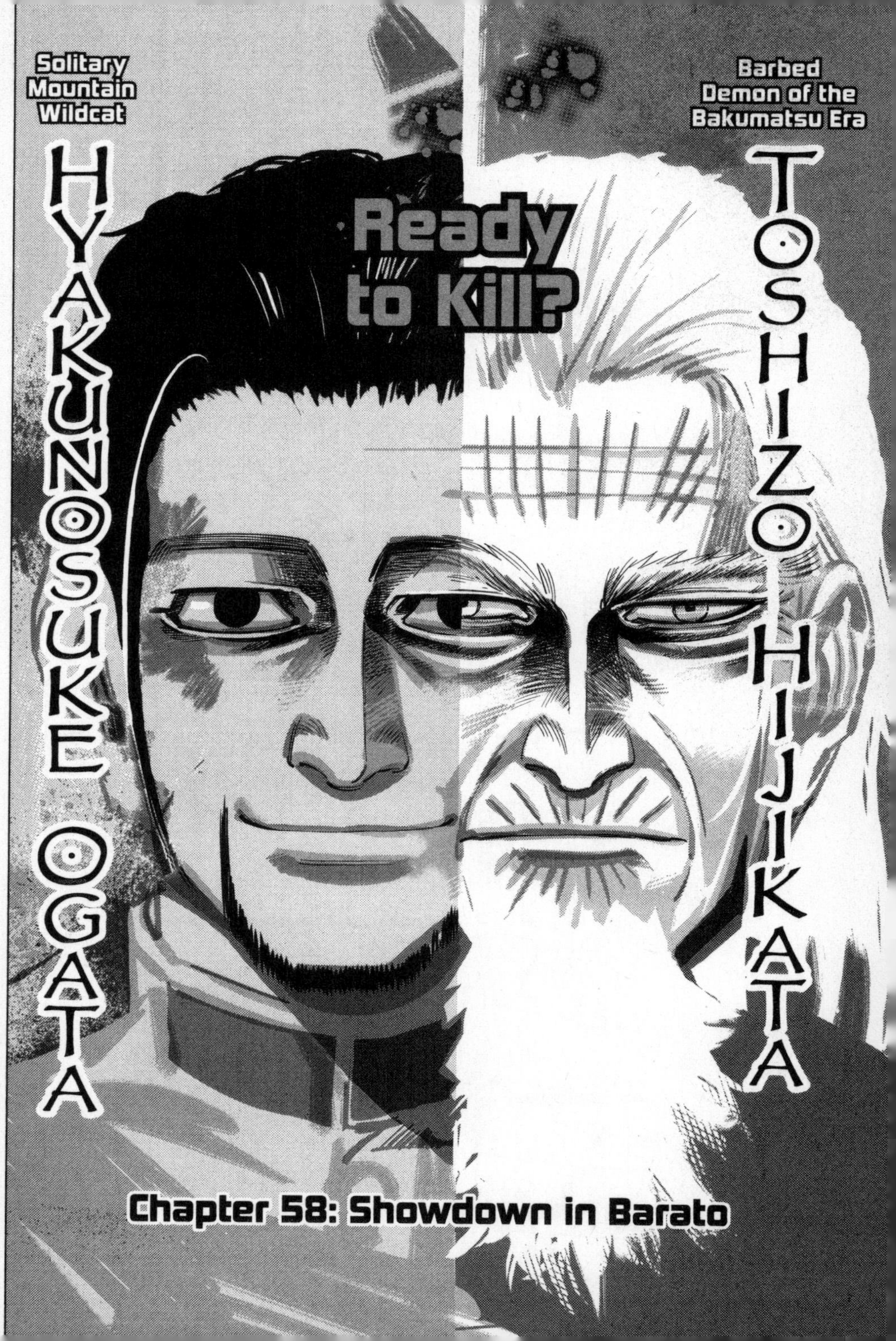

Solitary Mountain Wildcat
HYAKUNOSUKE OGATA
Ready to Kill?
Barbed Demon of the Bakumatsu Era
TOSHIZO HIJIKATA
Chapter 58: Showdown in Barato

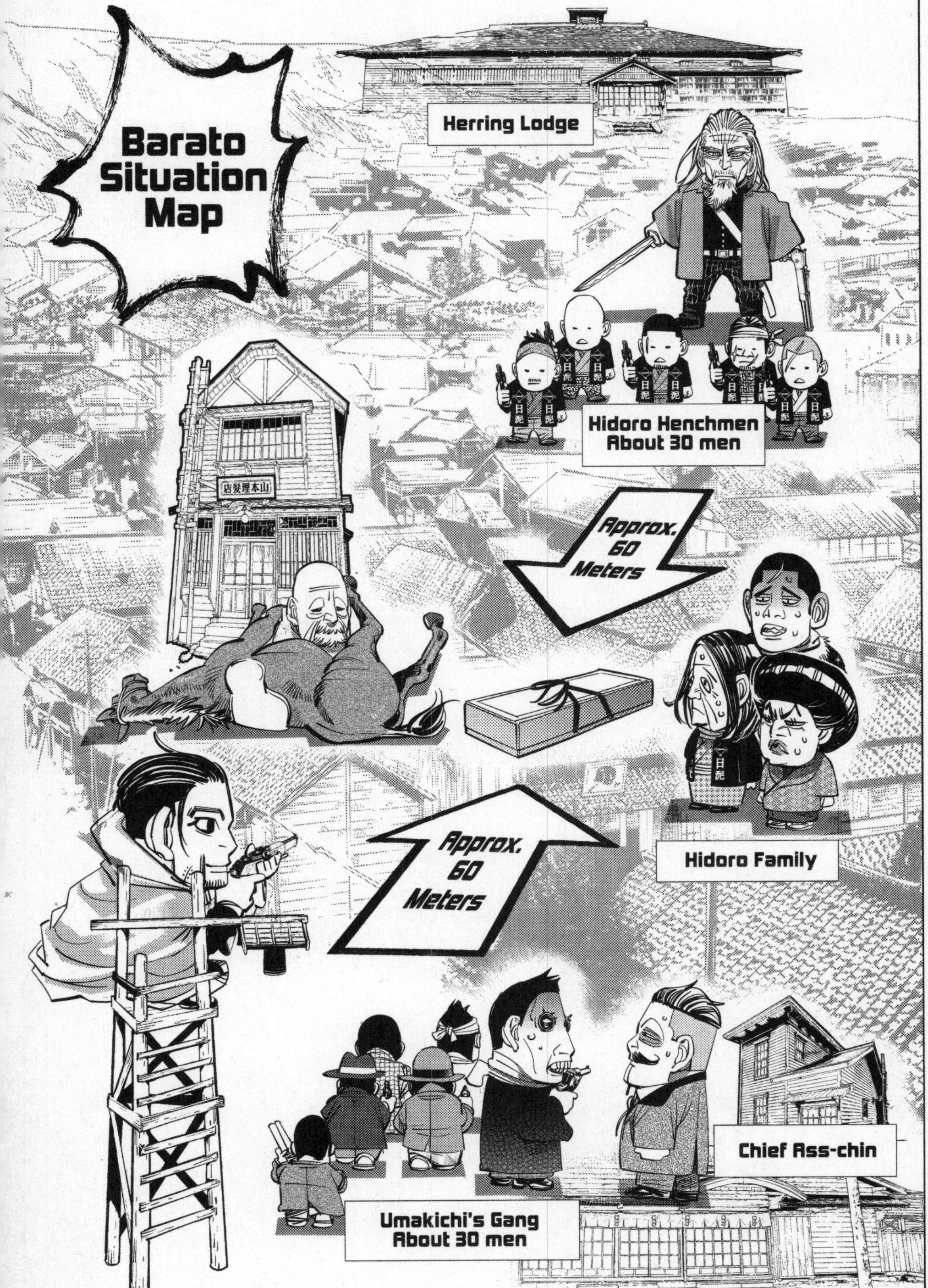
Barato Situation Map
Herring Lodge
Hidoro Henchmen
About 30 men
山本理髪店
Approx. 60 Meters
Hidoro Family
Approx. 60 Meters
Chief Ass-chin
Umakichi's Gang
About 30 men

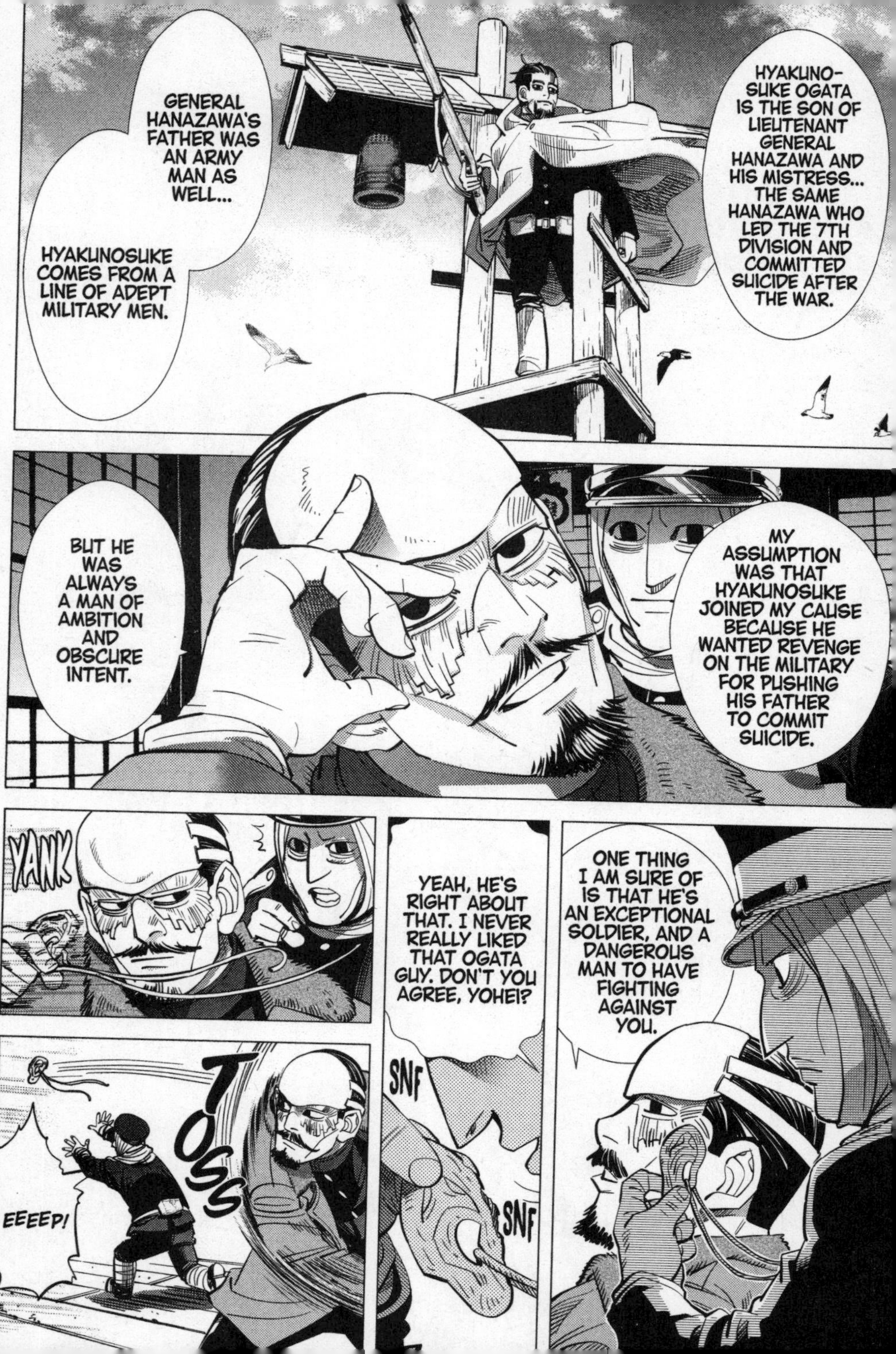
HYAKUNOSUKE OGATA IS THE SON OF LIEUTENANT GENERAL HANAZAWA AND HIS MISTRESS... THE SAME HANAZAWA WHO LED THE 7TH DIVISION AND COMMITTED SUICIDE AFTER THE WAR.
GENERAL HANAZAWA'S FATHER WAS AN ARMY MAN AS WELL...
HYAKUNOSUKE COMES FROM A LINE OF ADEPT MILITARY MEN.
MY ASSUMPTION WAS THAT HYAKUNOSUKE JOINED MY CAUSE BECAUSE HE WANTED REVENGE ON THE MILITARY FOR PUSHING HIS FATHER TO COMMIT SUICIDE.
BUT HE WAS ALWAYS A MAN OF AMBITION AND OBSCURE INTENT.
ONE THING I AM SURE OF IS THAT HE'S AN EXCEPTIONAL SOLDIER, AND A DANGEROUS MAN TO HAVE FIGHTING AGAINST YOU.
YEAH, HE'S RIGHT ABOUT THAT. I NEVER REALLY LIKED THAT OGATA GUY. DON'T YOU AGREE, YOHEI?
SNF
SNF
YANK
TOSS
EEEEP!

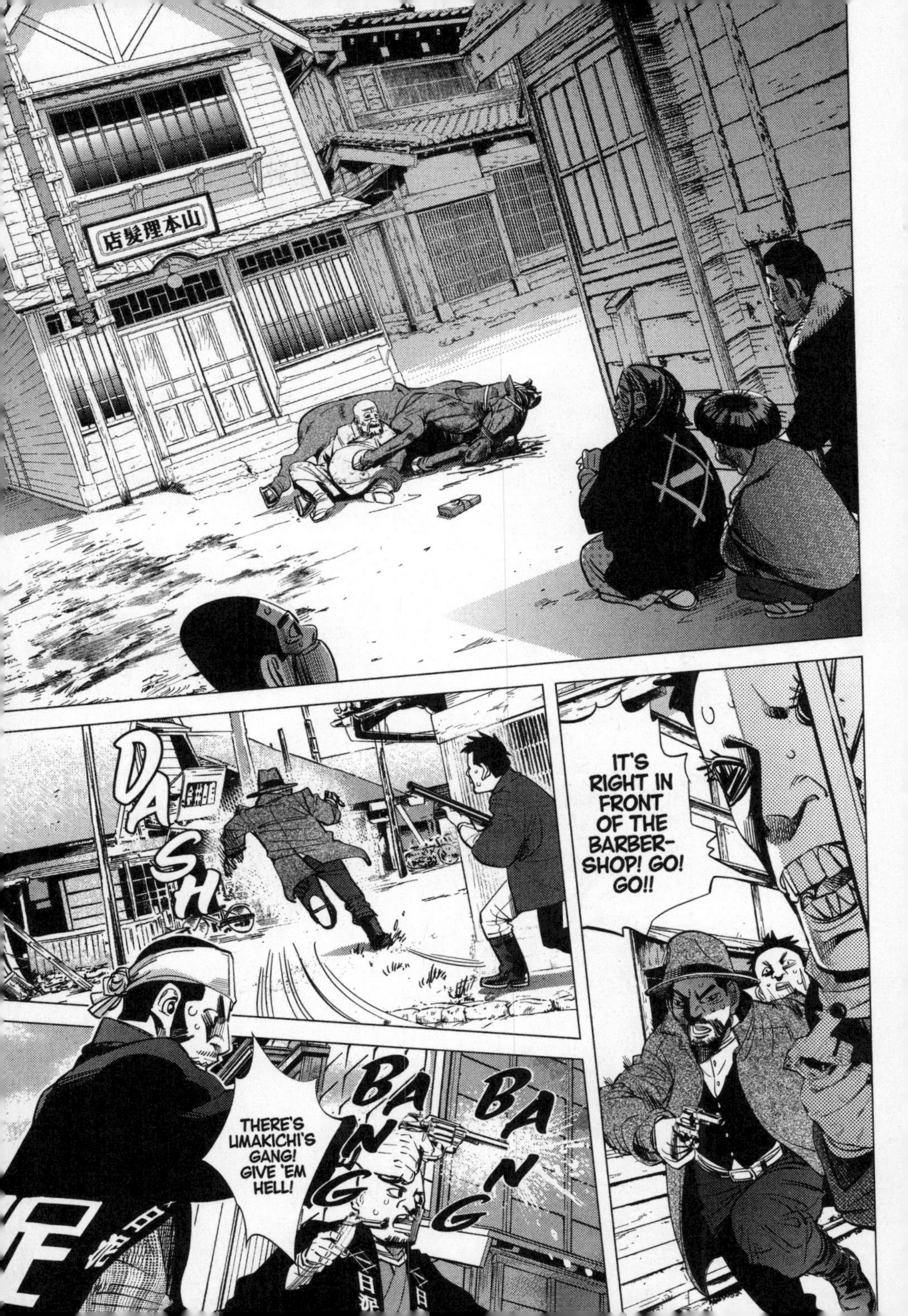
山本理髪店
IT'S RIGHT IN FRONT OF THE BARBER-SHOP! GO! GO!!
DASH
BANG
BANG
THERE'S UMAKICHI'S GANG! GIVE 'EM HELL!

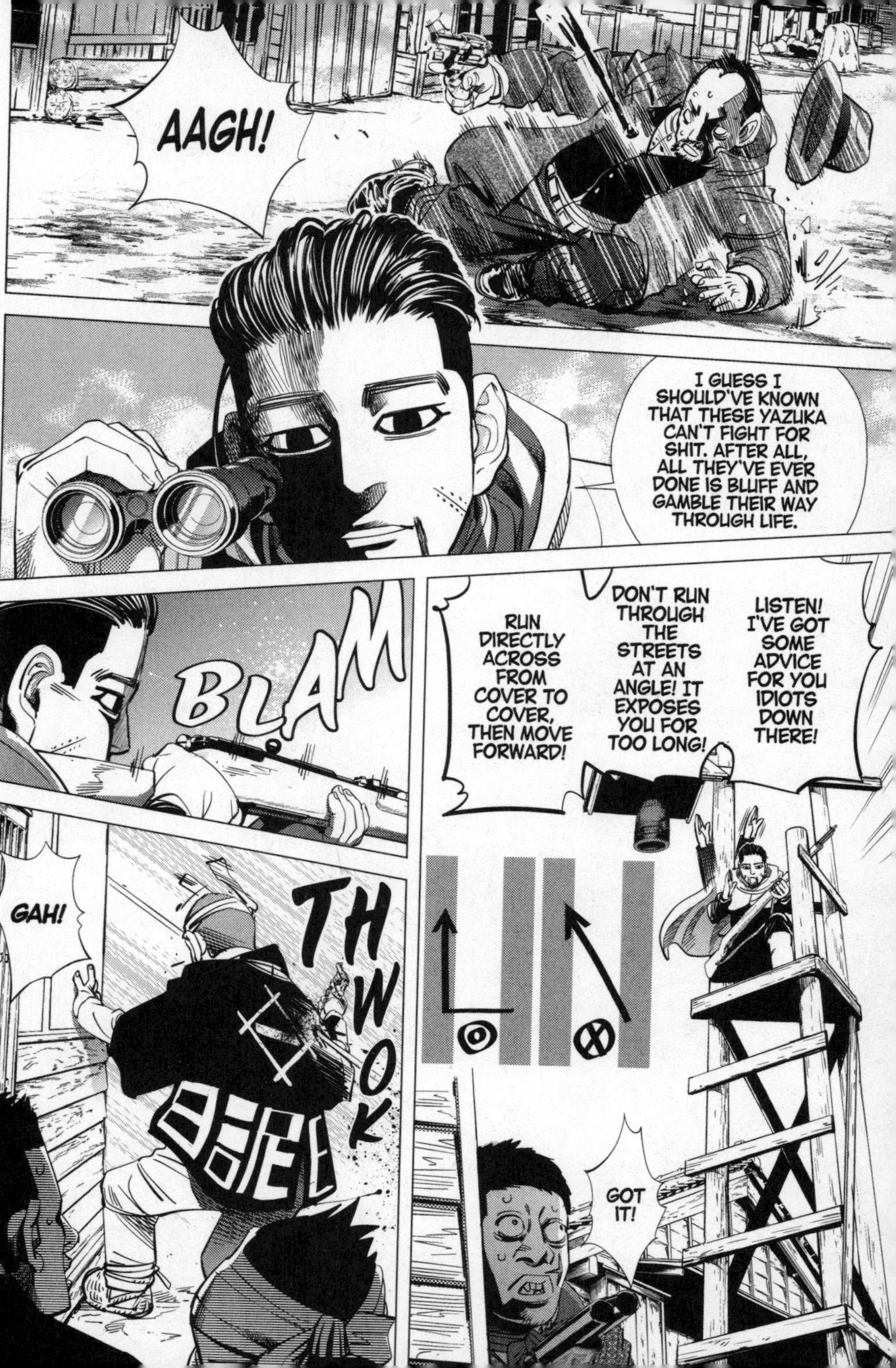
AAGH!
I GUESS I SHOULD'VE KNOWN THAT THESE YAZUKA CAN'T FIGHT FOR SHIT. AFTER ALL, ALL THEY'VE EVER DONE IS BLUFF AND GAMBLE THEIR WAY THROUGH LIFE.
LISTEN! I'VE GOT SOME ADVICE FOR YOU IDIOTS DOWN THERE!
DON'T RUN THROUGH THE STREETS AT AN ANGLE! IT EXPOSES YOU FOR TOO LONG!
RUN DIRECTLY ACROSS FROM COVER TO COVER, THEN MOVE FORWARD!
GOT IT!
BLAM
GAH!
THWOK

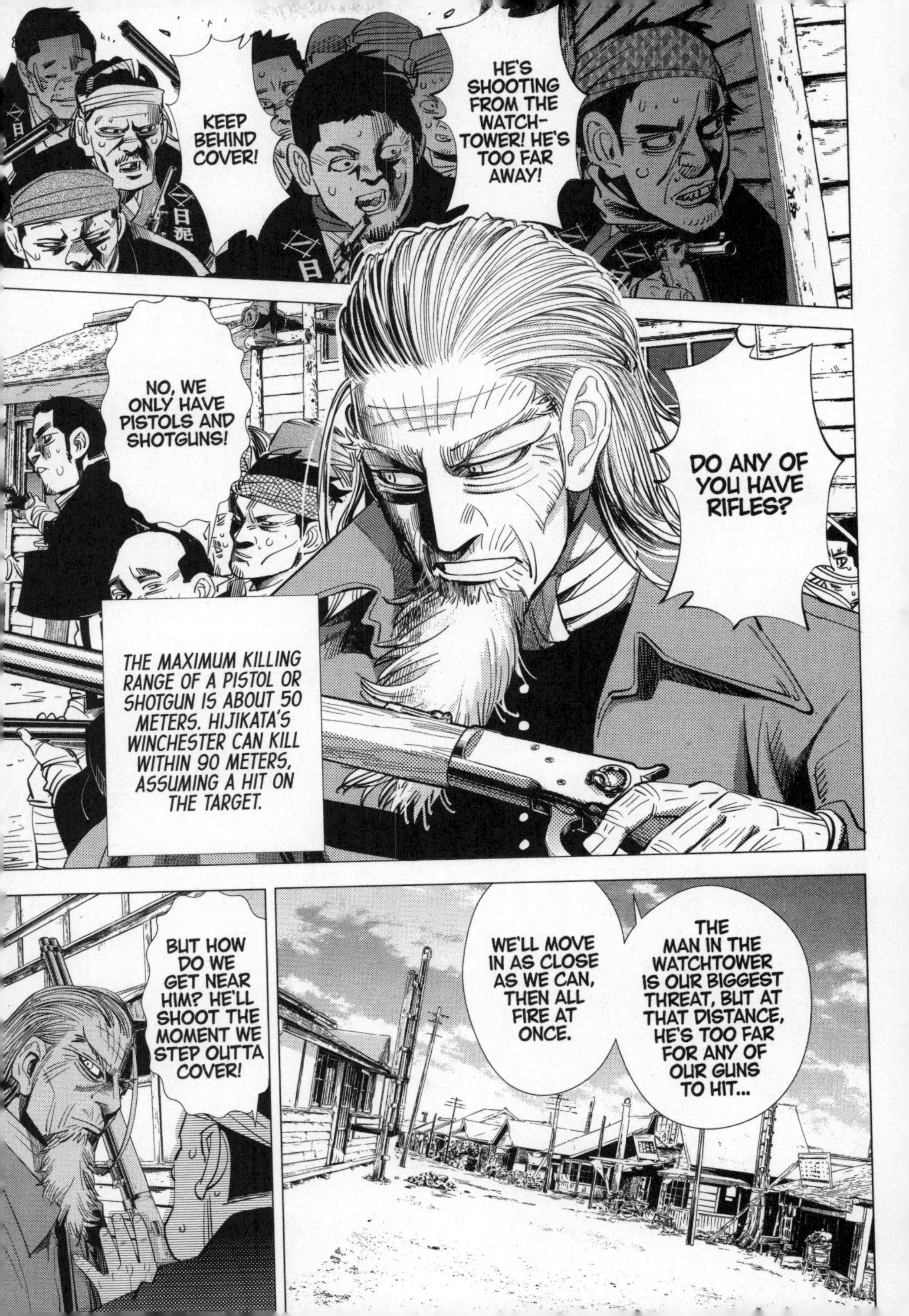
HE'S SHOOTING FROM THE WATCH-TOWER! HE'S TOO FAR AWAY!
KEEP BEHIND COVER!
DO ANY OF YOU HAVE RIFLES?
NO, WE ONLY HAVE PISTOLS AND SHOTGUNS!
THE MAXIMUM KILLING RANGE OF A PISTOL OR SHOTGUN IS ABOUT 50 METERS. HIJIKATA'S WINCHESTER CAN KILL WITHIN 90 METERS, ASSUMING A HIT ON THE TARGET.
THE MAN IN THE WATCHTOWER IS OUR BIGGEST THREAT, BUT AT THAT DISTANCE, HE'S TOO FAR FOR ANY OF OUR GUNS TO HIT...
WE'LL MOVE IN AS CLOSE AS WE CAN, THEN ALL FIRE AT ONCE.
BUT HOW DO WE GET NEAR HIM? HE'LL SHOOT THE MOMENT WE STEP OUTTA COVER!

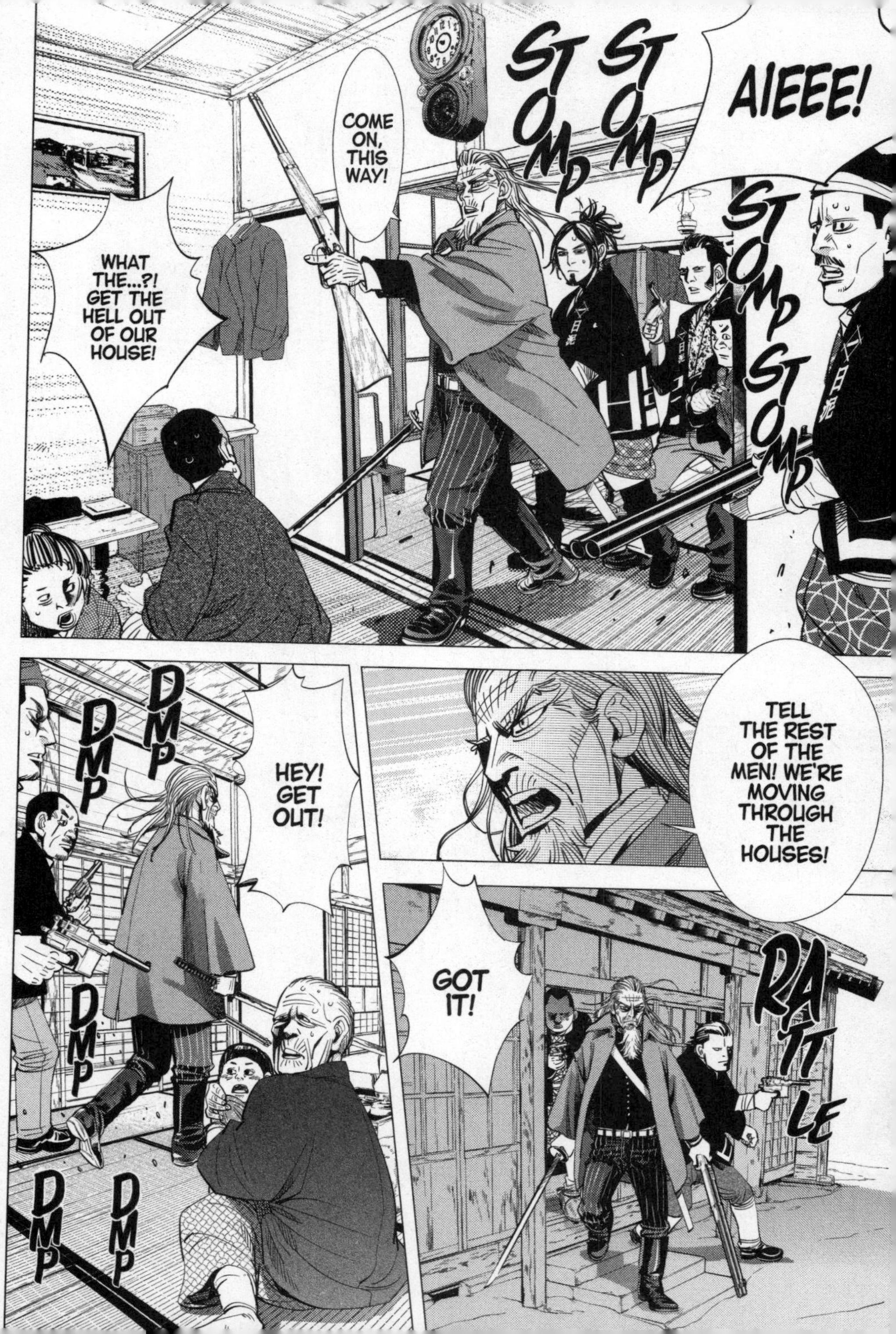
AIEEE!
STOMP STOMP
STOMP STOMP STOMP
COME ON, THIS WAY!
WHAT THE...?! GET THE HELL OUT OF OUR HOUSE!
TELL THE REST OF THE MEN! WE'RE MOVING THROUGH THE HOUSES!
DMP DMP
HEY! GET OUT!
DMP DMP DMP
RATTLE
GOT IT!

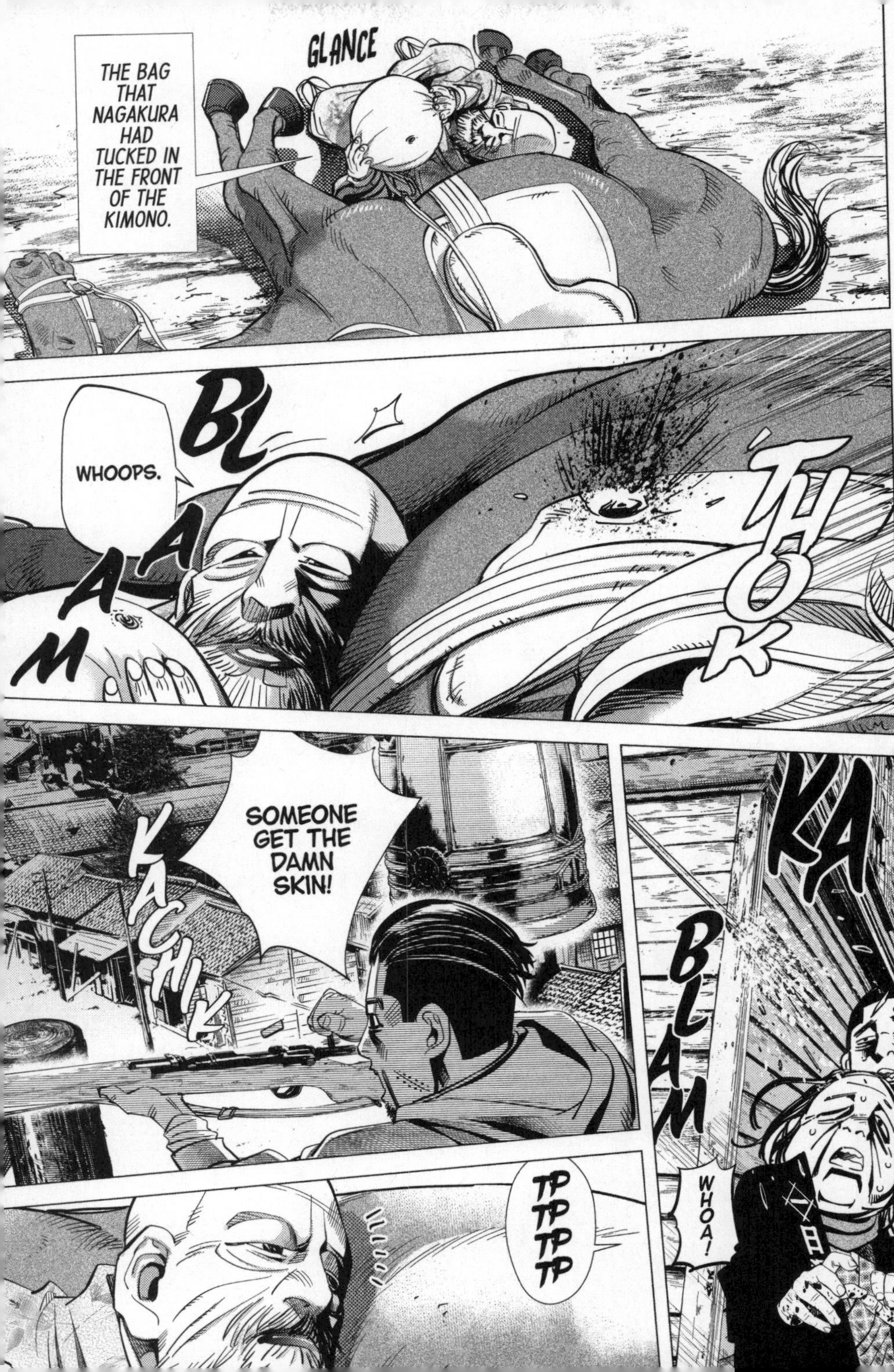
GLANCE
THE BAG THAT NAGAKURA HAD TUCKED IN THE FRONT OF THE KIMONO.
THOK
BLAAAM
WHOOPS.
KA
BLAM
WHOA!
SOMEONE GET THE DAMN SKIN!
KACHIK
TPTPTPTP

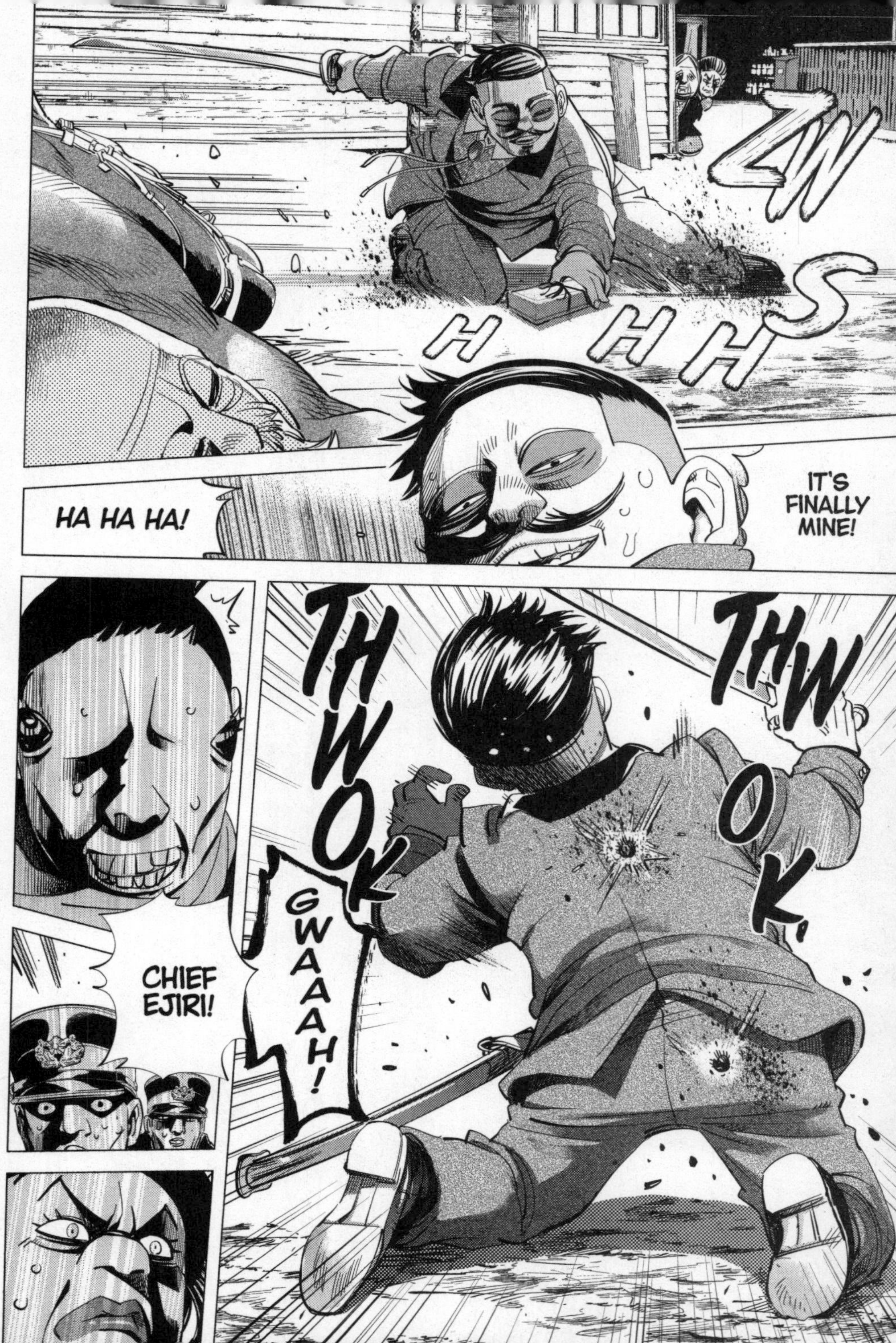
ZAN
HHHS
IT'S FINALLY MINE!
HA HA HA!
THWOK
THWOK
GWAAAH!
CHIEF EJIRI!

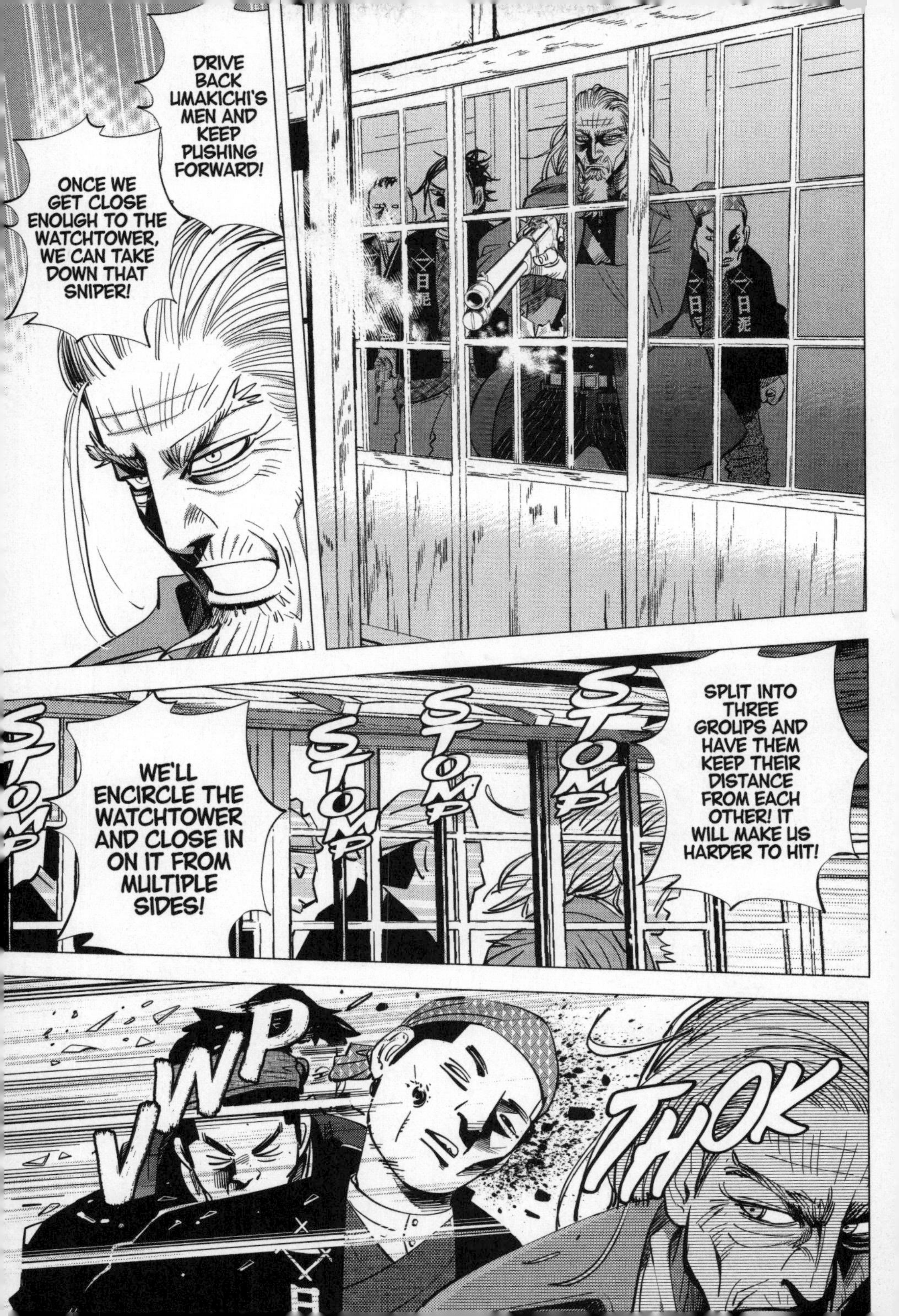
DRIVE BACK UMAKICHI'S MEN AND KEEP PUSHING FORWARD!
ONCE WE GET CLOSE ENOUGH TO THE WATCHTOWER, WE CAN TAKE DOWN THAT SNIPER!
SPLIT INTO THREE GROUPS AND HAVE THEM KEEP THEIR DISTANCE FROM EACH OTHER! IT WILL MAKE US HARDER TO HIT!
STOMP
STOMP
STOMP
STOMP
WE'LL ENCIRCLE THE WATCHTOWER AND CLOSE IN ON IT FROM MULTIPLE SIDES!
THOK
VWP

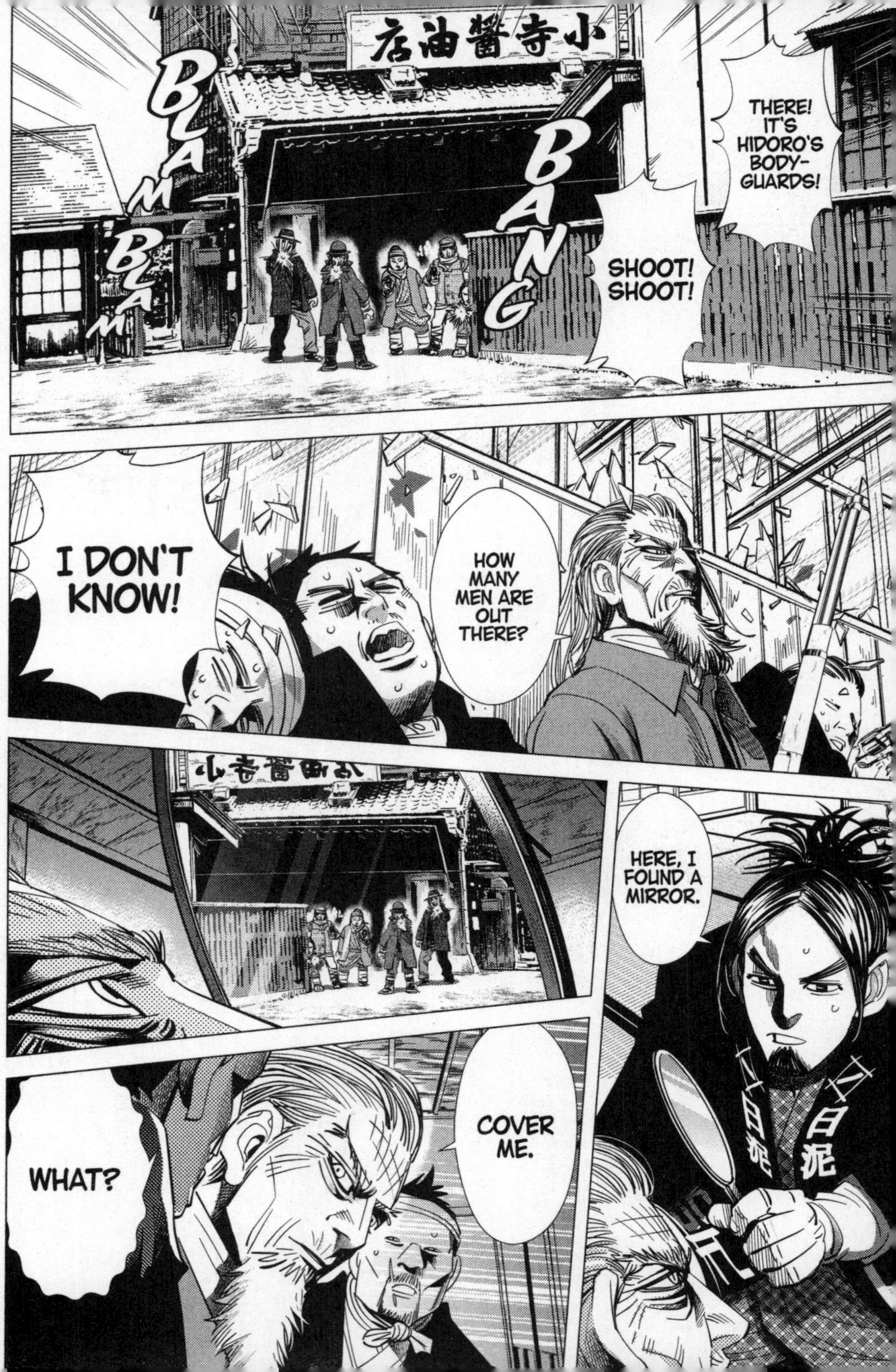
小寺醤油店
THERE! IT'S HIDORO'S BODY-GUARDS!
BANG
SHOOT! SHOOT!
BLAM
BLAM
HOW MANY MEN ARE OUT THERE?
I DON'T KNOW!
HERE, I FOUND A MIRROR.
COVER ME.
WHAT?

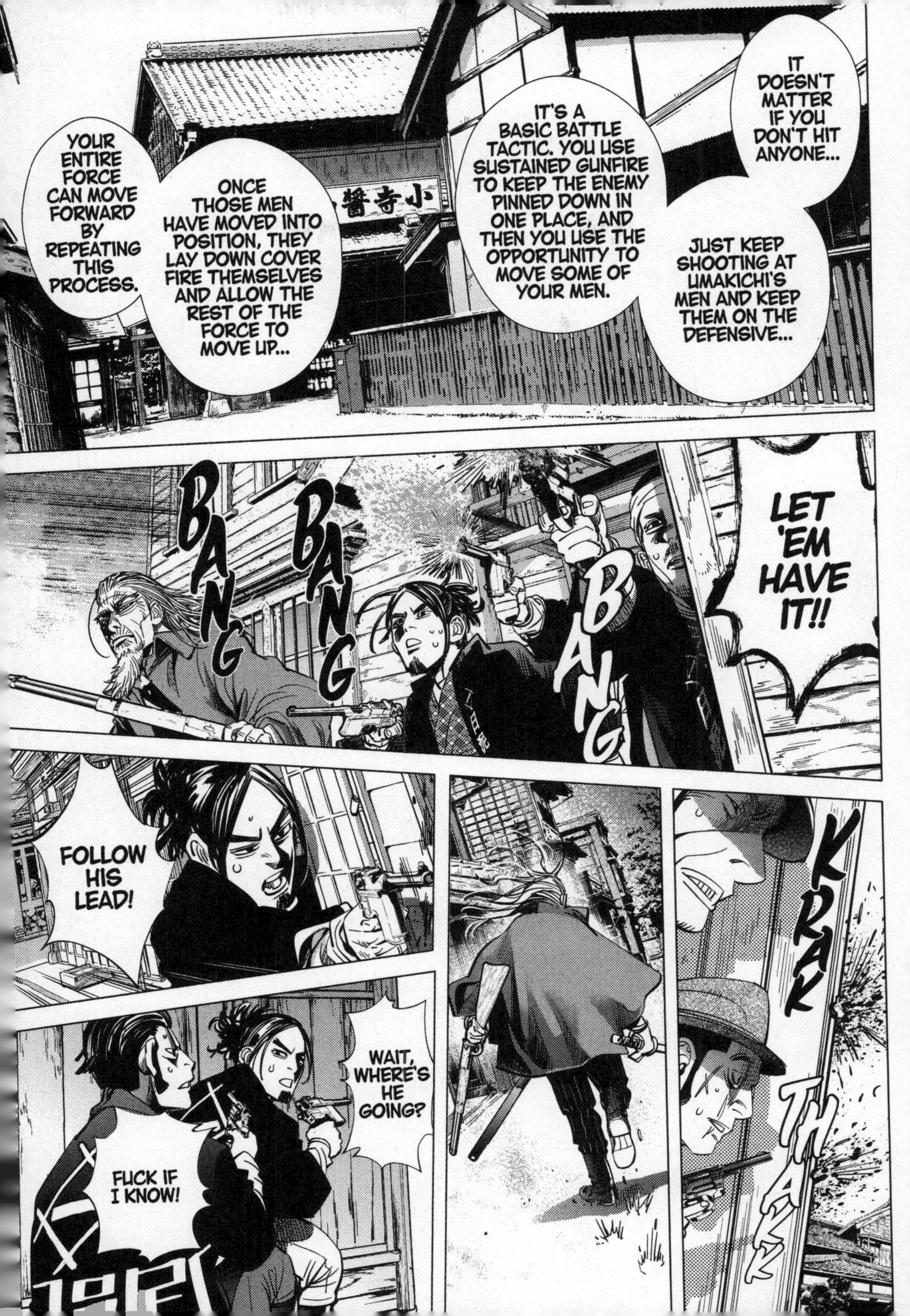
IT DOESN'T MATTER IF YOU DON'T HIT ANYONE...
JUST KEEP SHOOTING AT UMAKICHI'S MEN AND KEEP THEM ON THE DEFENSIVE...
IT'S A BASIC BATTLE TACTIC. YOU USE SUSTAINED GUNFIRE TO KEEP THE ENEMY PINNED DOWN IN ONE PLACE, AND THEN YOU USE THE OPPORTUNITY TO MOVE SOME OF YOUR MEN.
ONCE THOSE MEN HAVE MOVED INTO POSITION, THEY LAY DOWN COVER FIRE THEMSELVES AND ALLOW THE REST OF THE FORCE TO MOVE UP...
YOUR ENTIRE FORCE CAN MOVE FORWARD BY REPEATING THIS PROCESS.
LET 'EM HAVE IT!!
BANG
BANG
BANG
KRAK
THAK
FOLLOW HIS LEAD!
WAIT, WHERE'S HE GOING?
FUCK IF I KNOW!

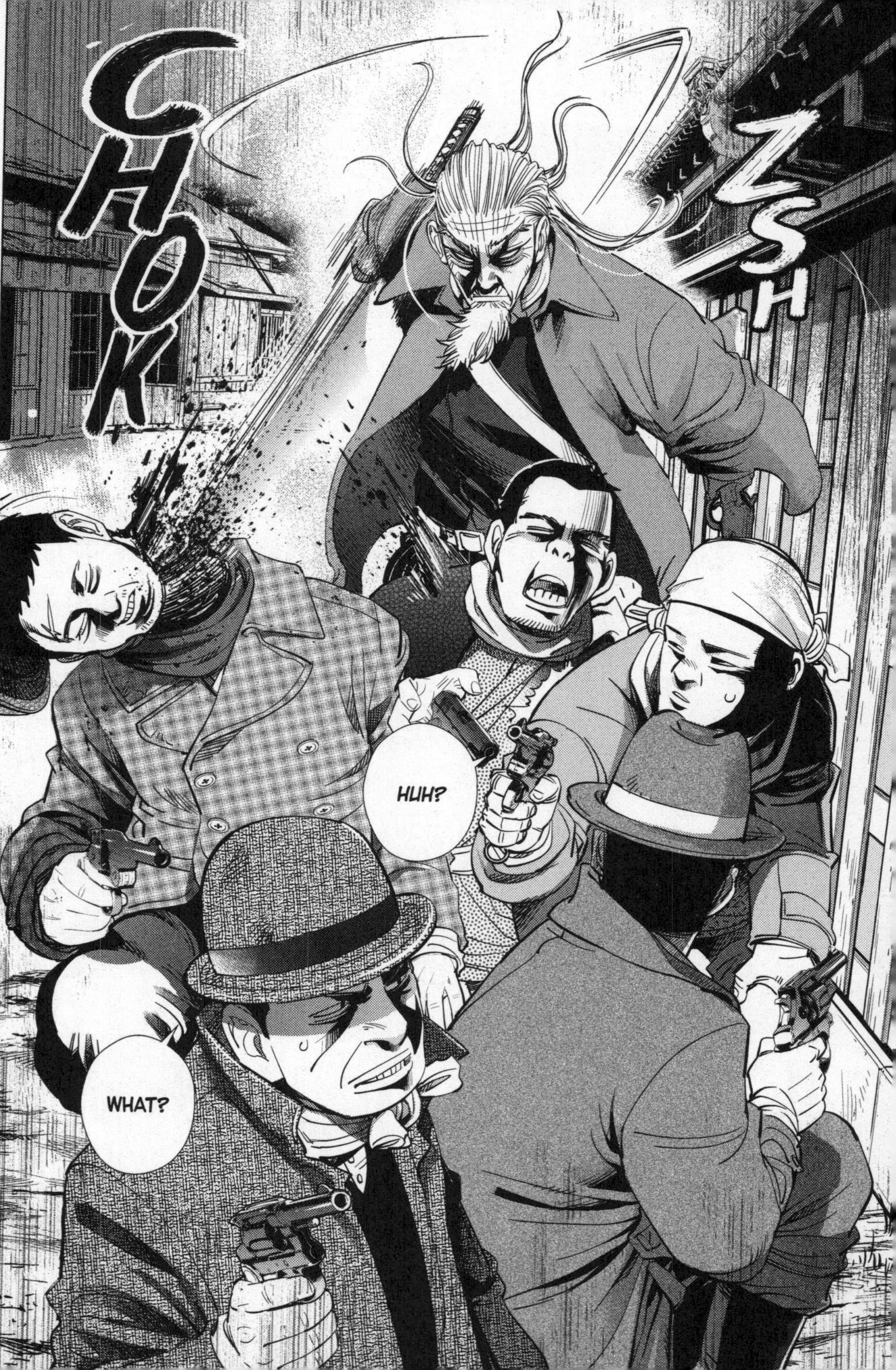
ZSHH
CHOK
HUH?
WHAT?

USING SUPPRESSIVE FIRE TO MOVE SWORDSMEN BEHIND THE ENEMY FORCES AND CUT THEM DOWN WAS ONE OF THE SHINSENGUMI'S FAVORED TACTICS.

ZLASH

SHHK

WHOAA!

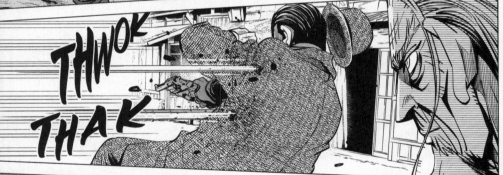

THWOK

THAK

HE'S INCREDIBLE...

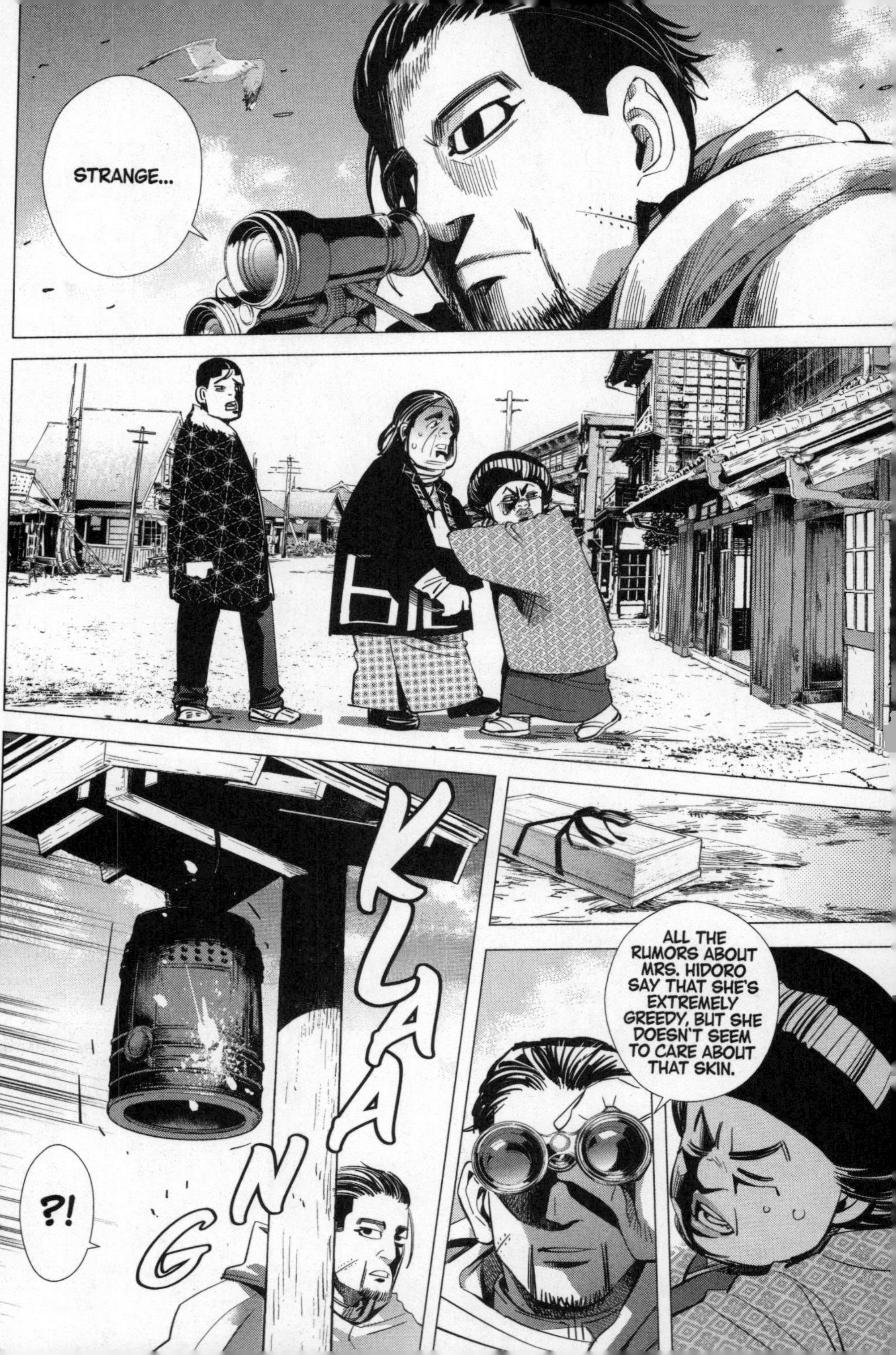
STRANGE...
ALL THE RUMORS ABOUT MRS. HIDORO SAY THAT SHE'S EXTREMELY GREEDY, BUT SHE DOESN'T SEEM TO CARE ABOUT THAT SKIN.
KLAANG
...
?!

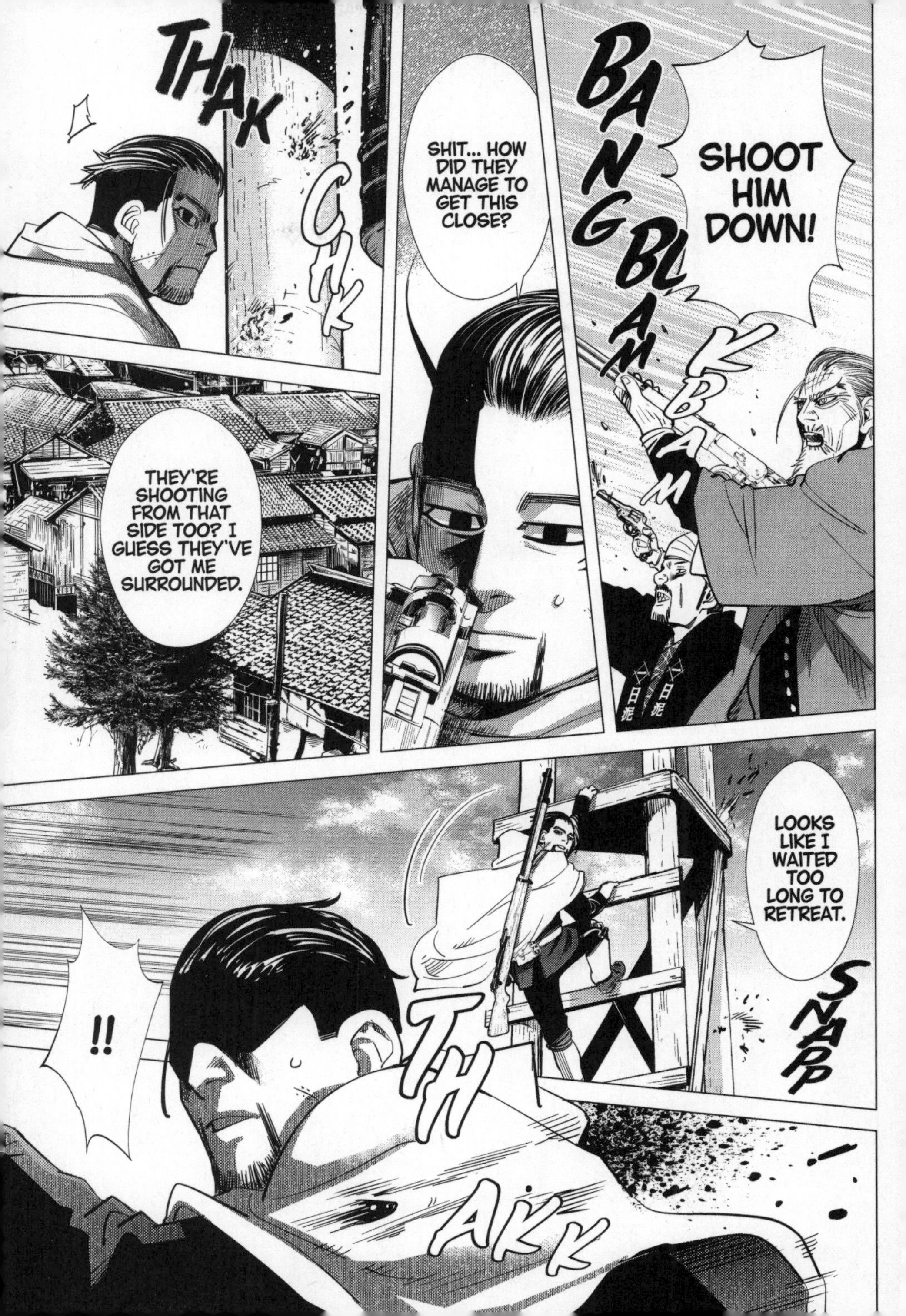
SHOOT HIM DOWN!
BANG
BLAM
KBLAM
SHIT... HOW DID THEY MANAGE TO GET THIS CLOSE?
THAK
CHK
THEY'RE SHOOTING FROM THAT SIDE TOO? I GUESS THEY'VE GOT ME SURROUNDED.
LOOKS LIKE I WAITED TOO LONG TO RETREAT.
SNAPP
!!
THAKK

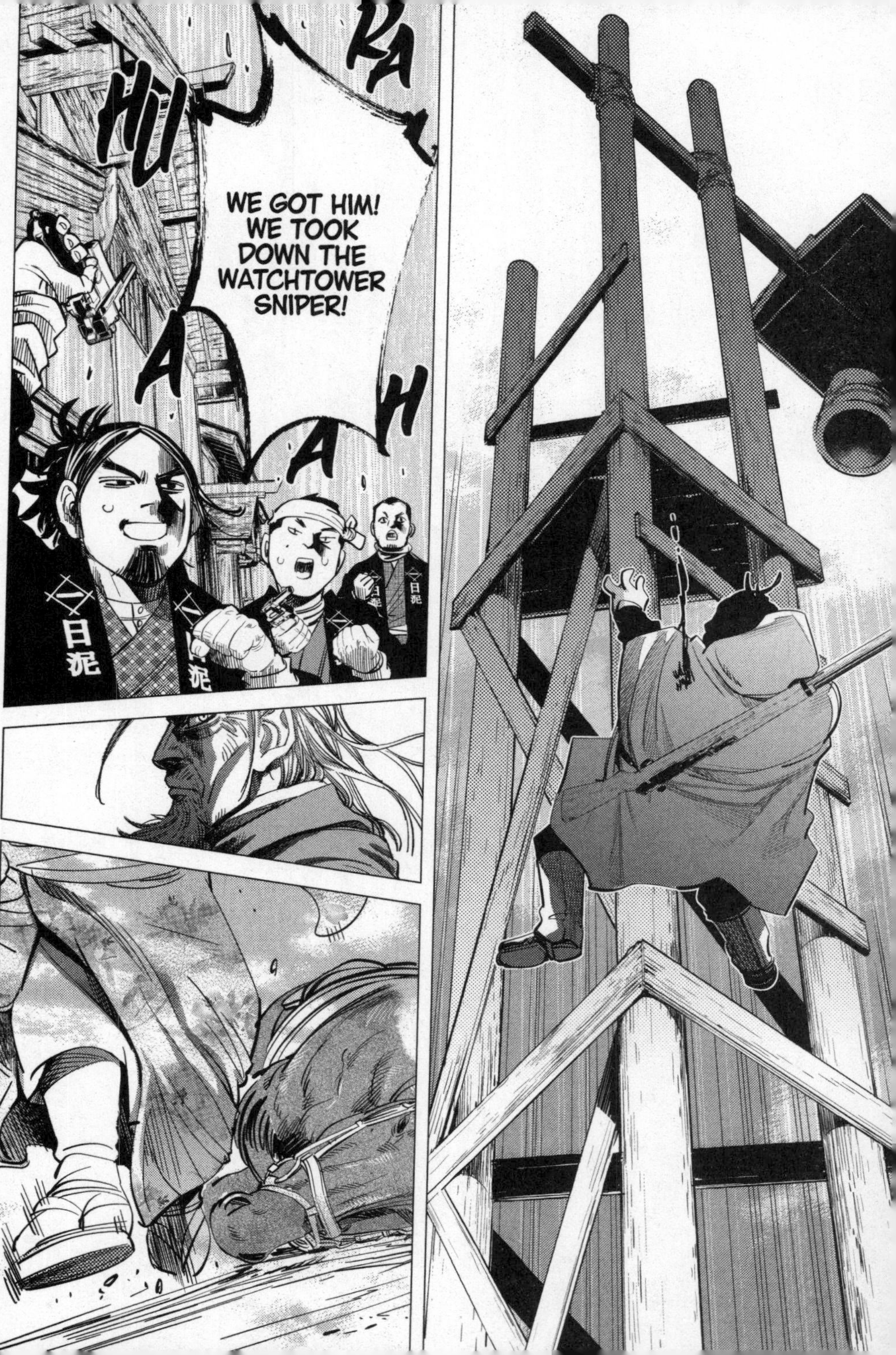
KA
HU
WE GOT HIM! WE TOOK DOWN THE WATCHTOWER SNIPER!
A
H
A
日泥

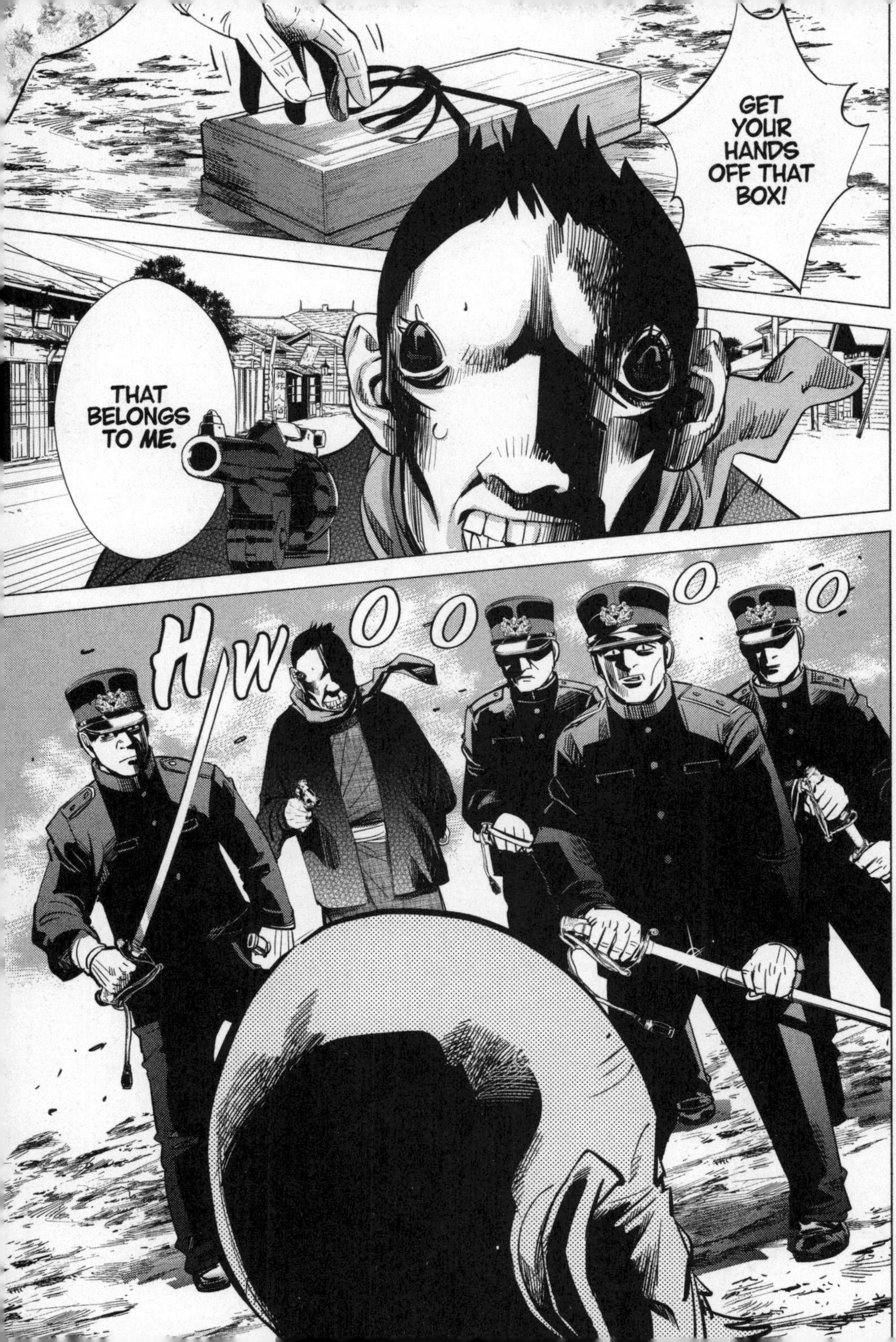
GET YOUR HANDS OFF THAT BOX!
THAT BELONGS TO ME.
HWOOOOOO

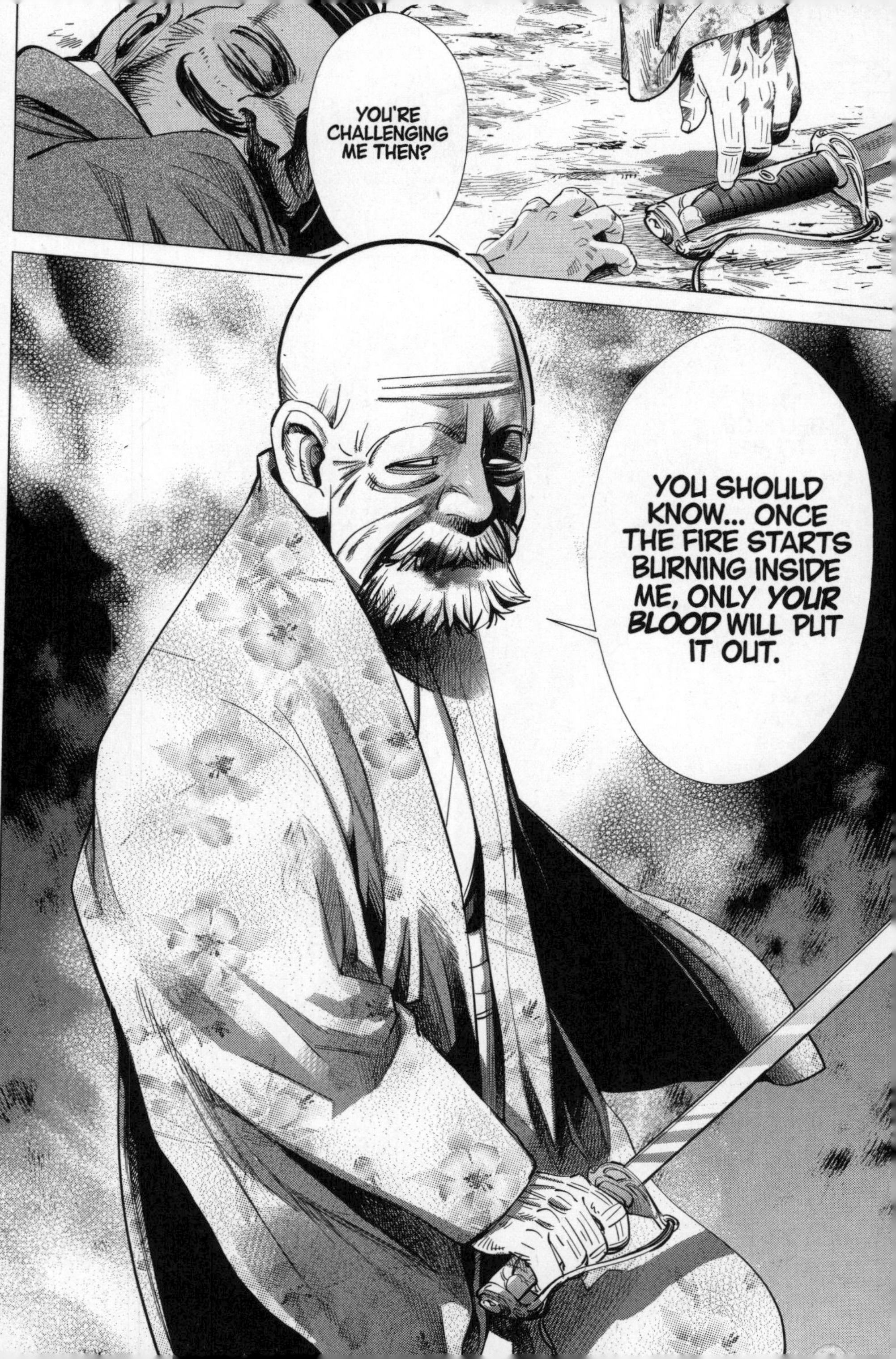
YOU'RE CHALLENGING ME THEN?
YOU SHOULD KNOW... ONCE THE FIRE STARTS BURNING INSIDE ME, ONLY *YOUR BLOOD* WILL PUT IT OUT.

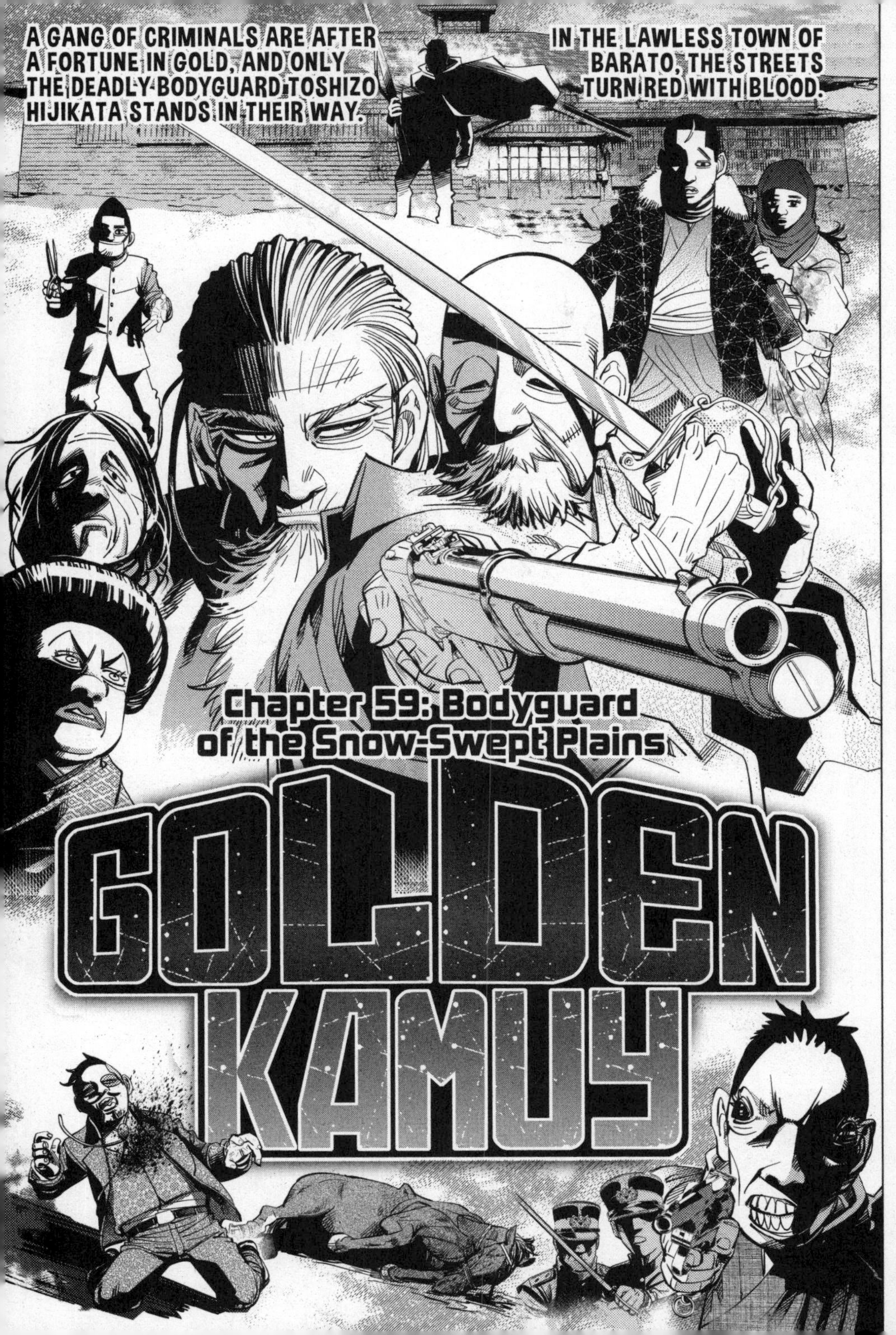

IN THE LAWLESS TOWN OF BARATO, THE STREETS TURN RED WITH BLOOD.
A GANG OF CRIMINALS ARE AFTER A FORTUNE IN GOLD, AND ONLY THE DEADLY BODYGUARD TOSHIZO HIJIKATA STANDS IN THEIR WAY.
Chapter 59: Bodyguard of the Snow-Swept Plains
GOLDEN KAMUY

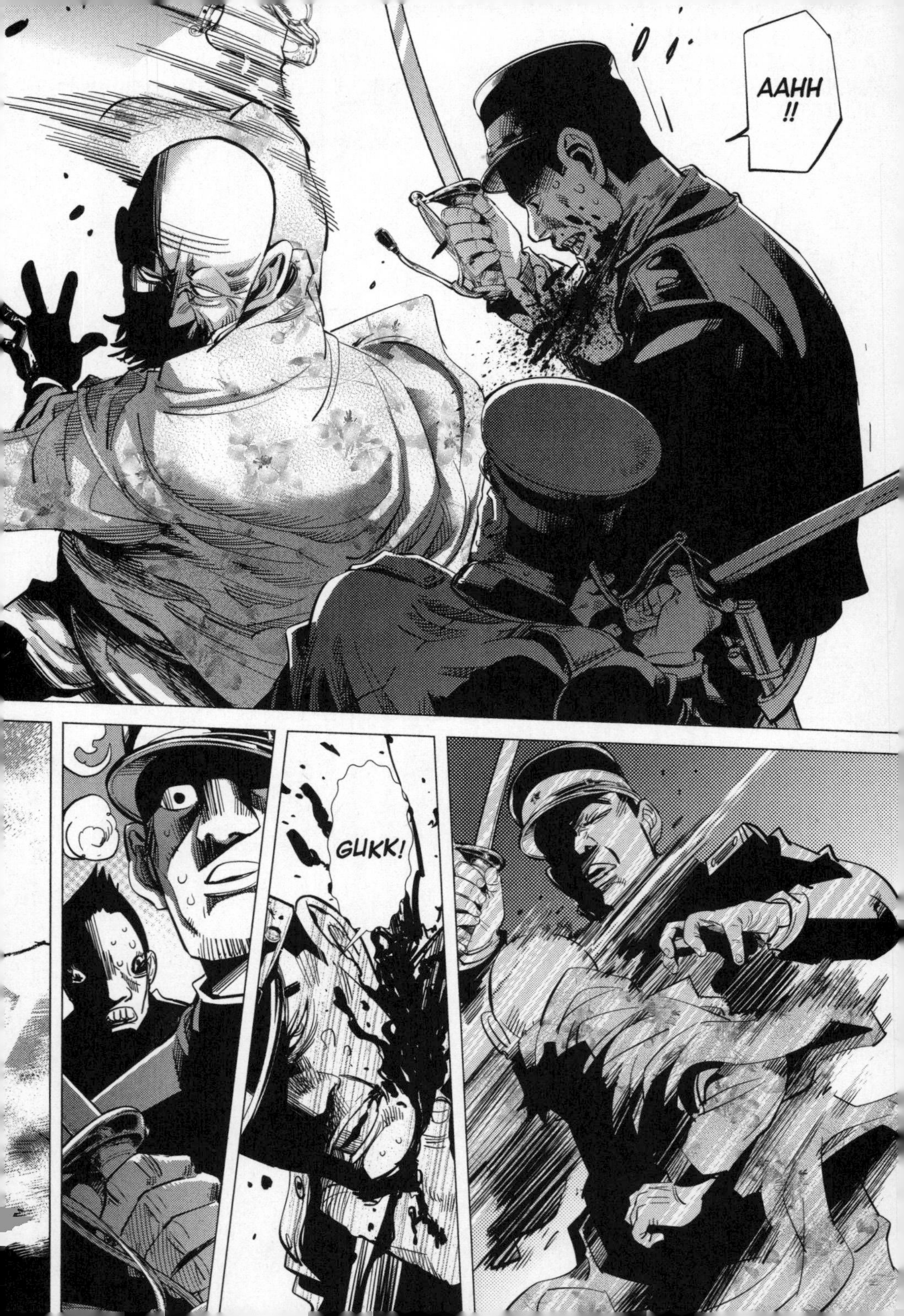
AAHH !!
GUKK!

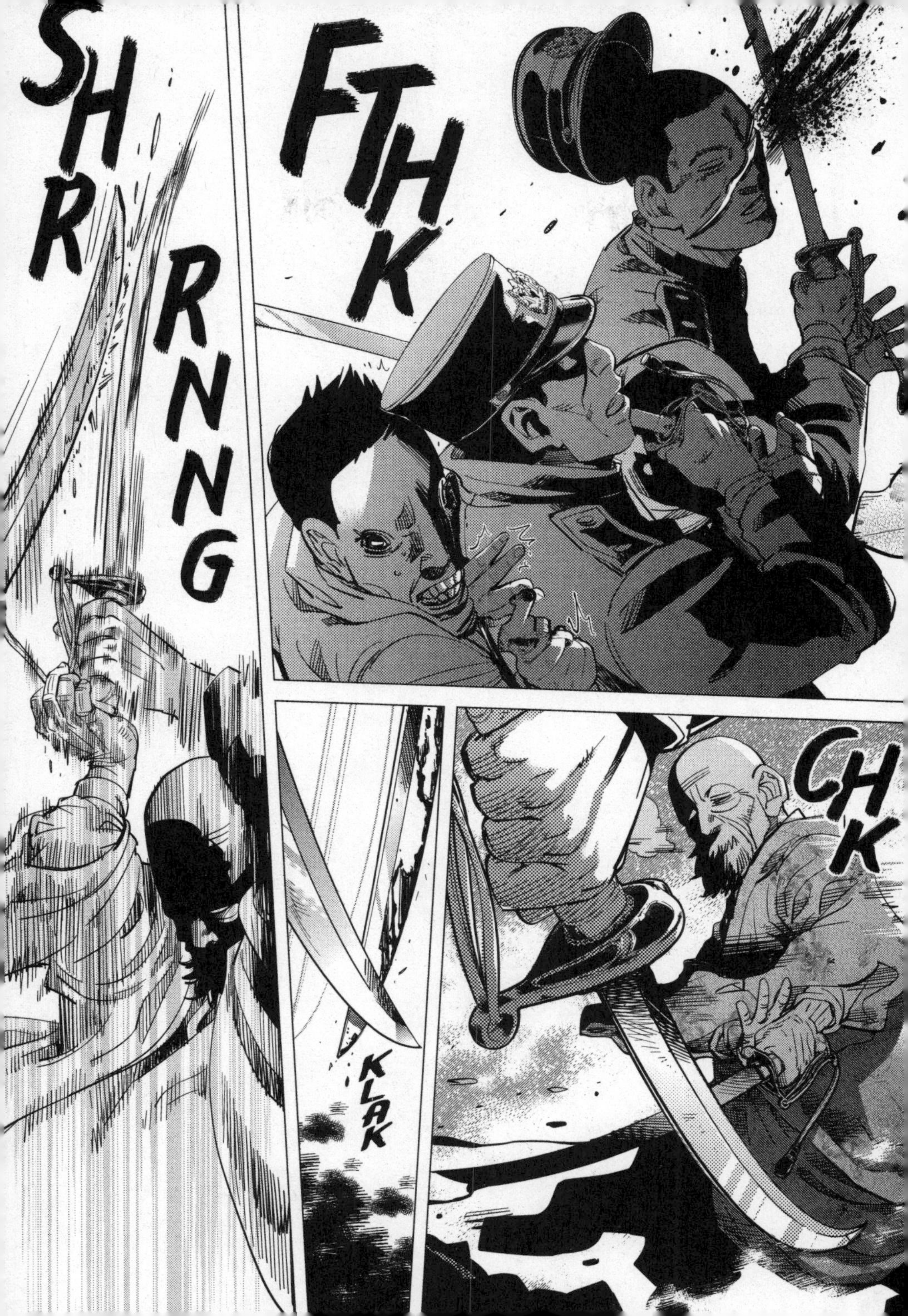
FTHK
CHK
KLAK
SHRRNNG

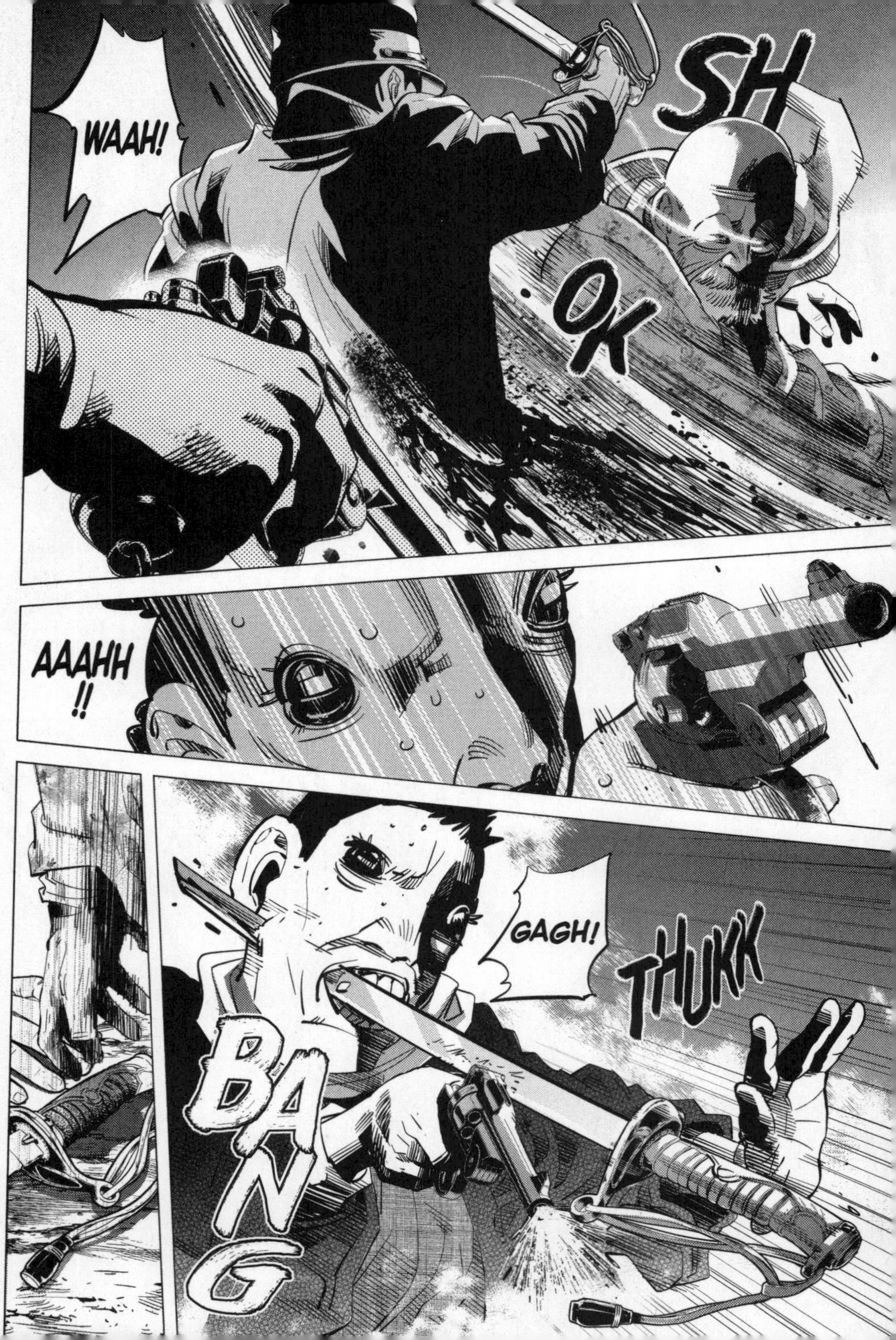
SHOK
WAAH!
AAAHH!!
THUKK
GAGH!
BANG

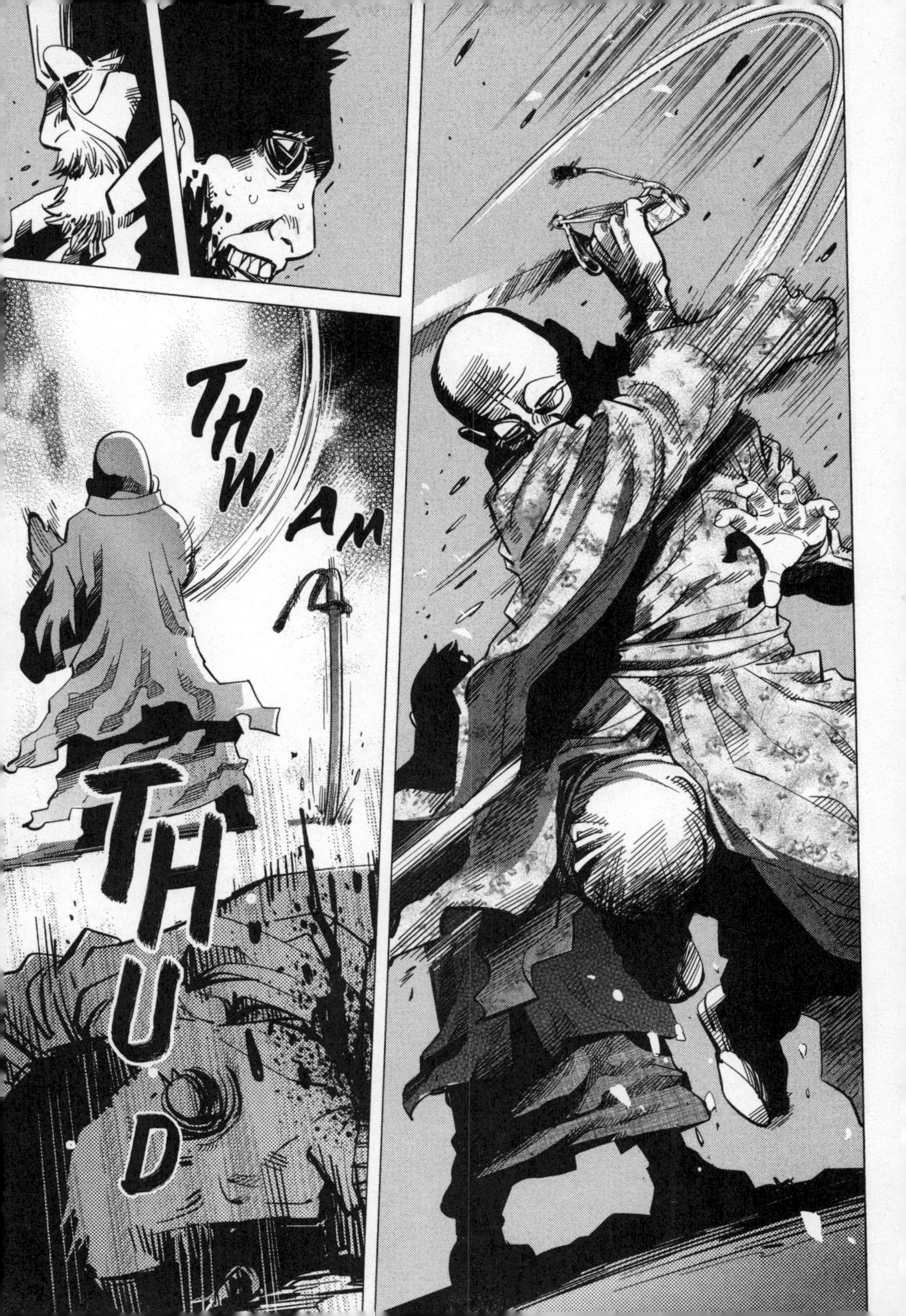
THWAM
THUD

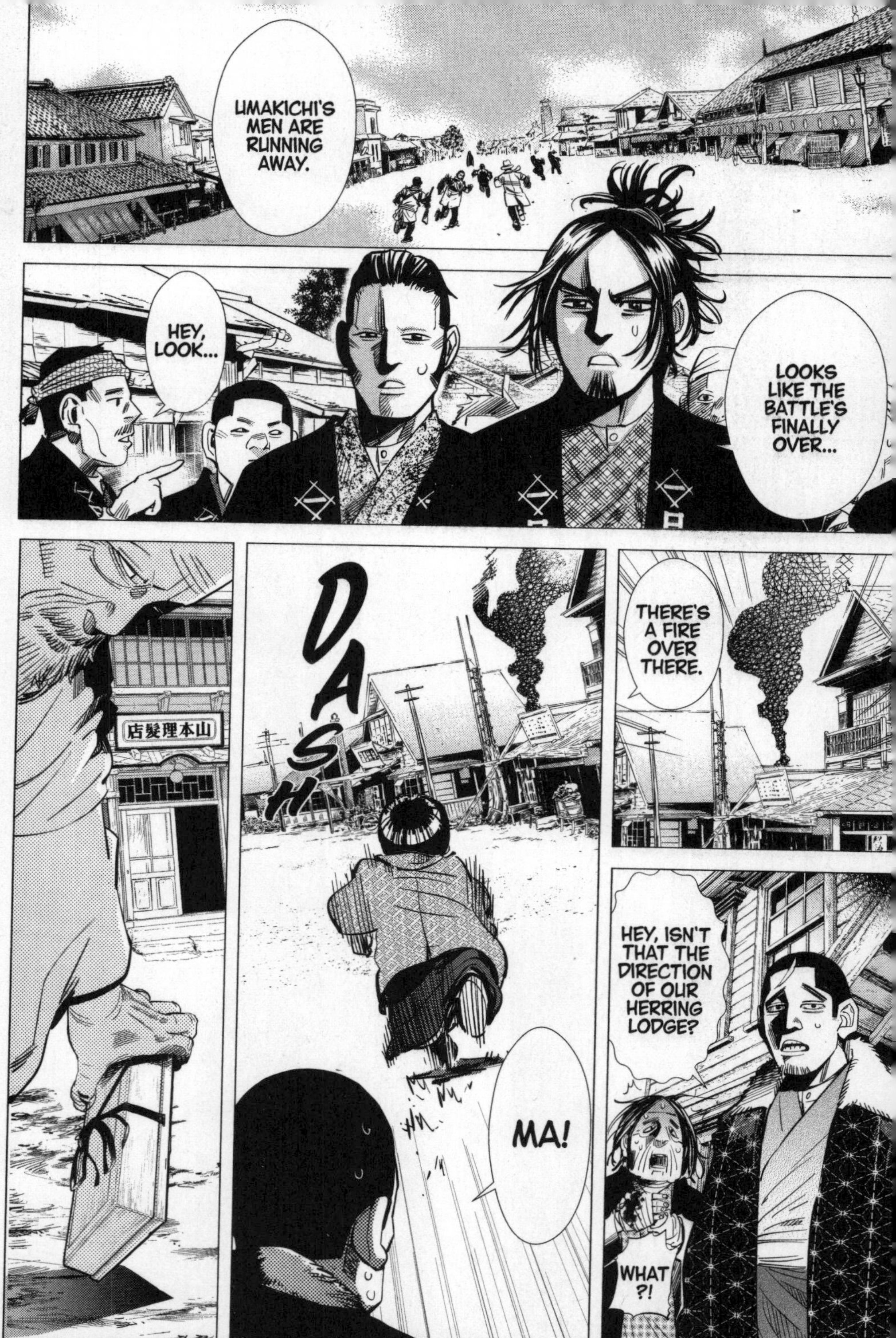
UMAKICHI'S MEN ARE RUNNING AWAY.
LOOKS LIKE THE BATTLE'S FINALLY OVER...
HEY, LOOK...
THERE'S A FIRE OVER THERE.
HEY, ISN'T THAT THE DIRECTION OF OUR HERRING LODGE?
WHAT?!
DASH
MA!
山本理髪店

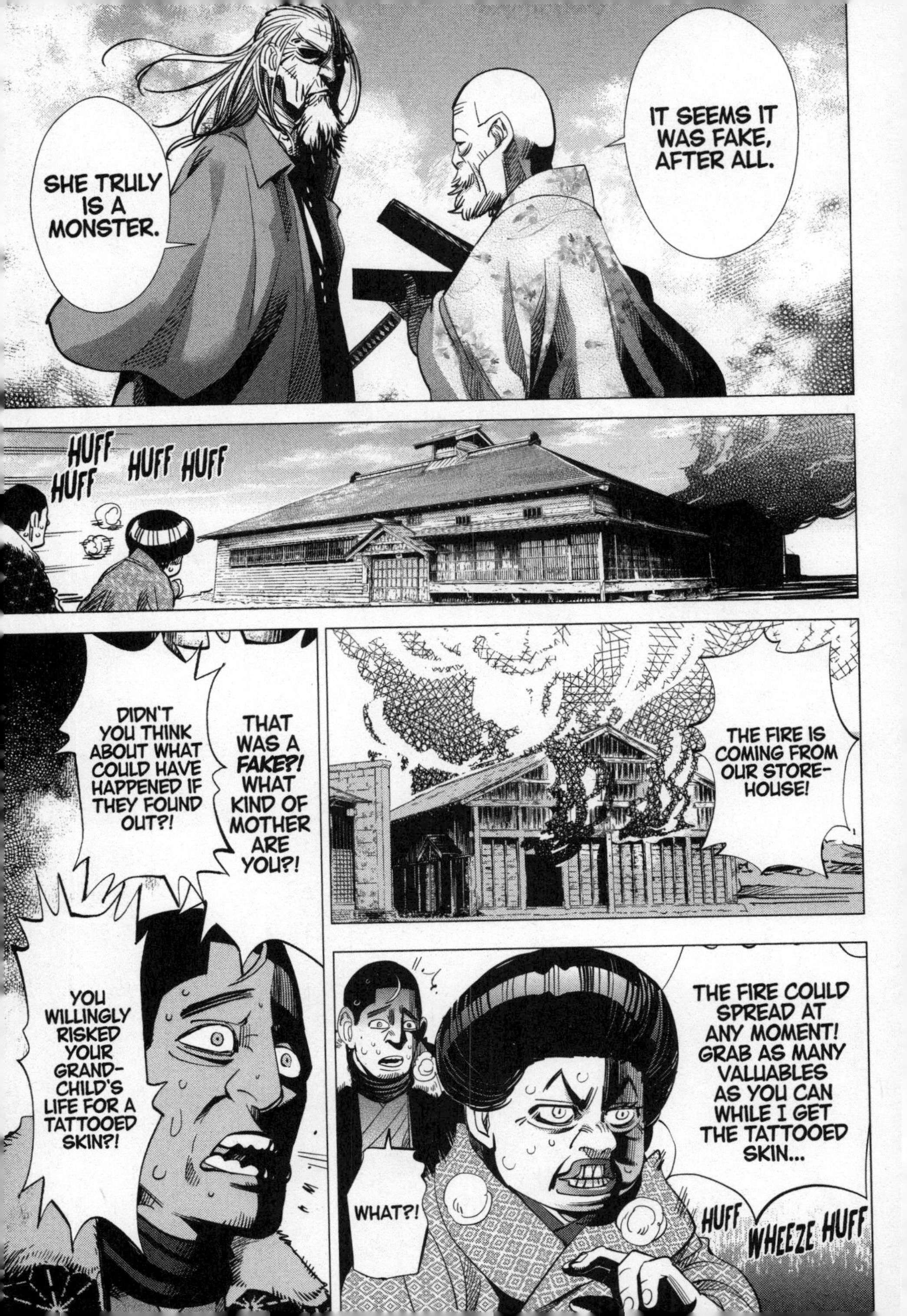
IT SEEMS IT WAS FAKE, AFTER ALL.
SHE TRULY IS A MONSTER.
HUFF HUFF HUFF
HUFF HUFF
THE FIRE IS COMING FROM OUR STORE-HOUSE!
THE FIRE COULD SPREAD AT ANY MOMENT! GRAB AS MANY VALUABLES AS YOU CAN WHILE I GET THE TATTOOED SKIN...
HUFF WHEEZE HUFF
WHAT?!
THAT WAS A FAKE?! WHAT KIND OF MOTHER ARE YOU?!
DIDN'T YOU THINK ABOUT WHAT COULD HAVE HAPPENED IF THEY FOUND OUT?!
YOU WILLINGLY RISKED YOUR GRAND-CHILD'S LIFE FOR A TATTOOED SKIN?!

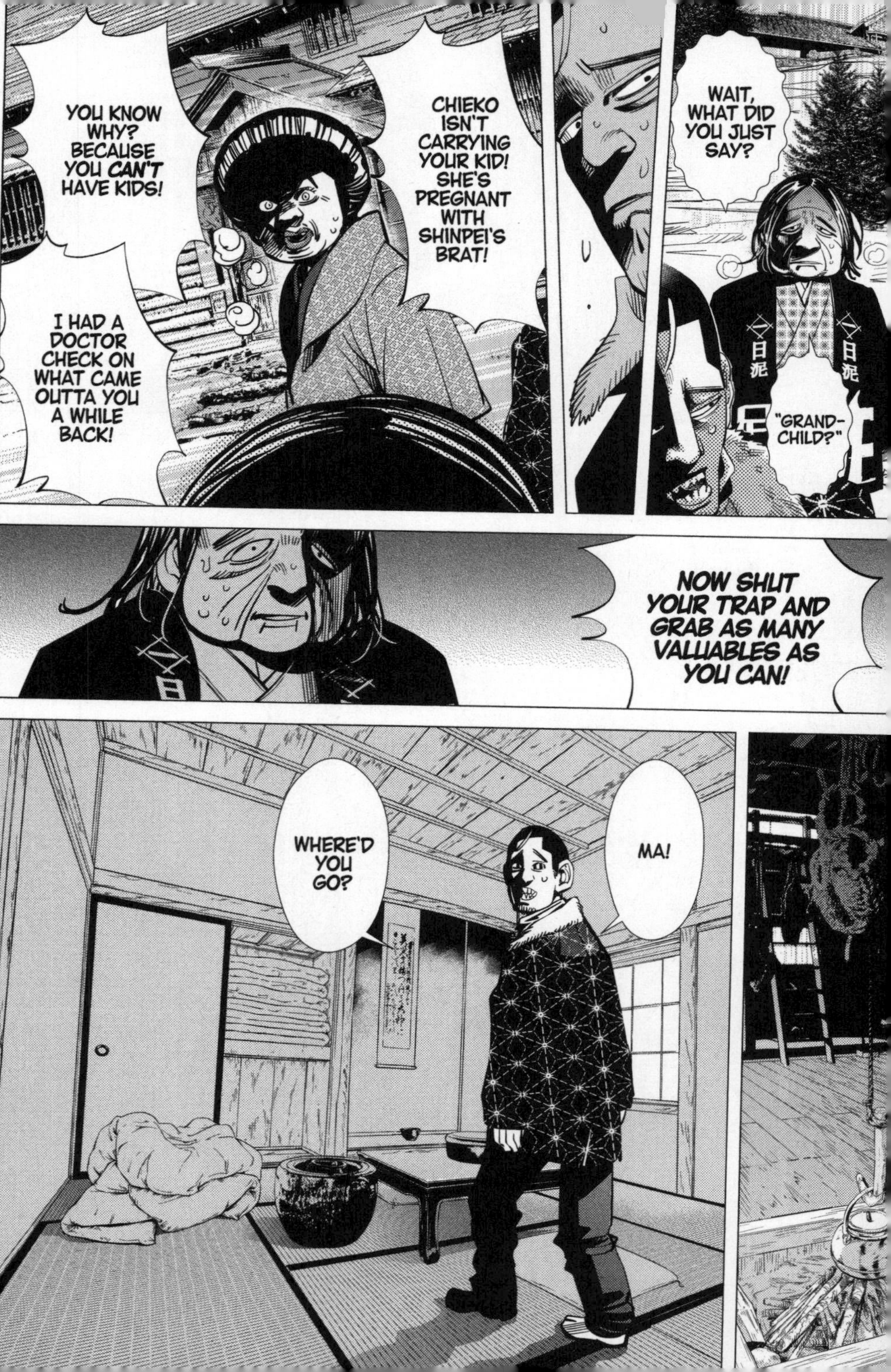
WAIT, WHAT DID YOU JUST SAY?
"GRAND-CHILD?"
CHIEKO ISN'T CARRYING YOUR KID! SHE'S PREGNANT WITH SHINPEI'S BRAT!
YOU KNOW WHY? BECAUSE YOU CAN'T HAVE KIDS!
I HAD A DOCTOR CHECK ON WHAT CAME OUTTA YOU A WHILE BACK!
NOW SHUT YOUR TRAP AND GRAB AS MANY VALUABLES AS YOU CAN!
MA!
WHERE'D YOU GO?

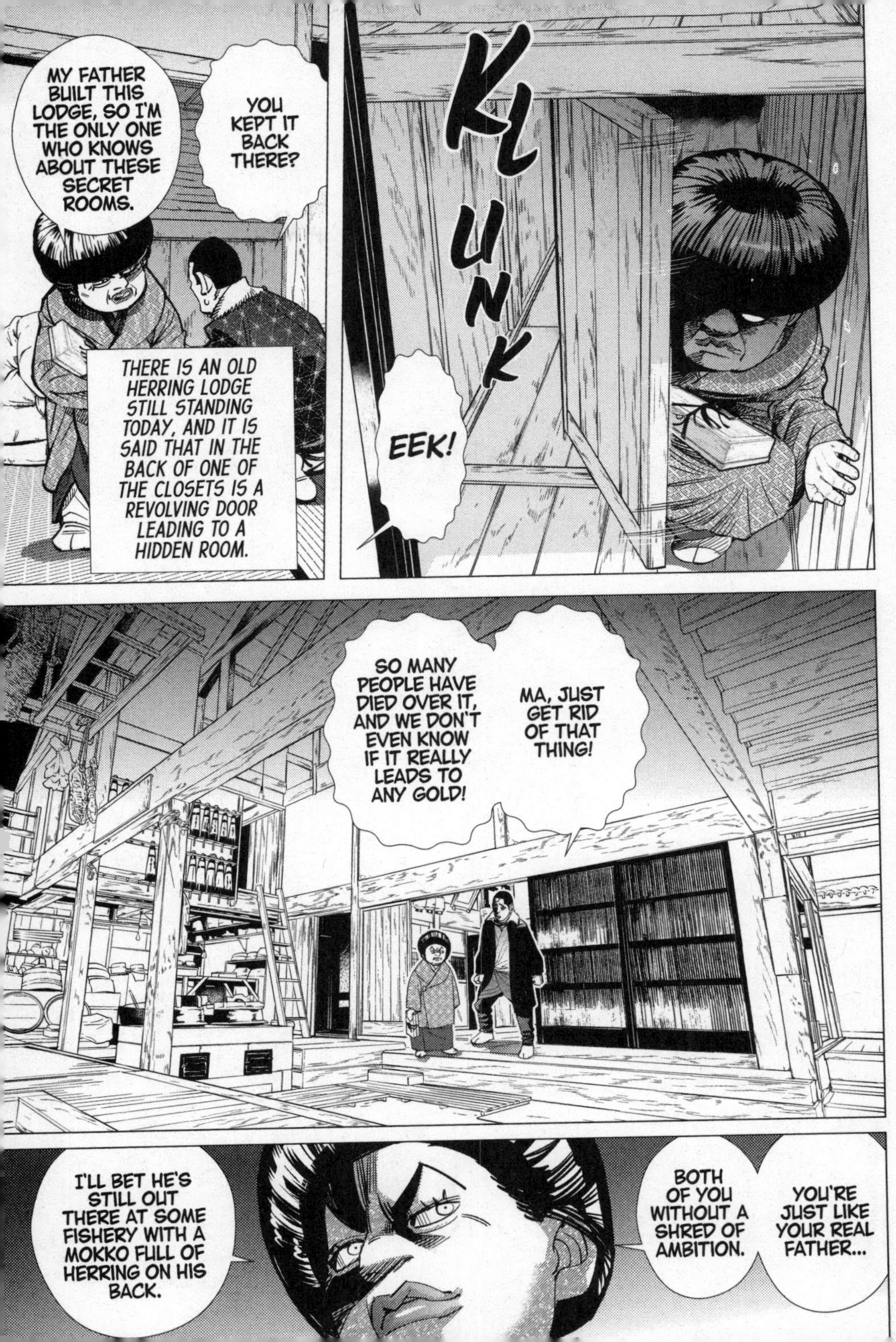
KLUNK
EEK!
YOU KEPT IT BACK THERE?
MY FATHER BUILT THIS LODGE, SO I'M THE ONLY ONE WHO KNOWS ABOUT THESE SECRET ROOMS.
THERE IS AN OLD HERRING LODGE STILL STANDING TODAY, AND IT IS SAID THAT IN THE BACK OF ONE OF THE CLOSETS IS A REVOLVING DOOR LEADING TO A HIDDEN ROOM.
MA, JUST GET RID OF THAT THING!
SO MANY PEOPLE HAVE DIED OVER IT, AND WE DON'T EVEN KNOW IF IT REALLY LEADS TO ANY GOLD!
YOU'RE JUST LIKE YOUR REAL FATHER...
BOTH OF YOU WITHOUT A SHRED OF AMBITION.
I'LL BET HE'S STILL OUT THERE AT SOME FISHERY WITH A MOKKO FULL OF HERRING ON HIS BACK.

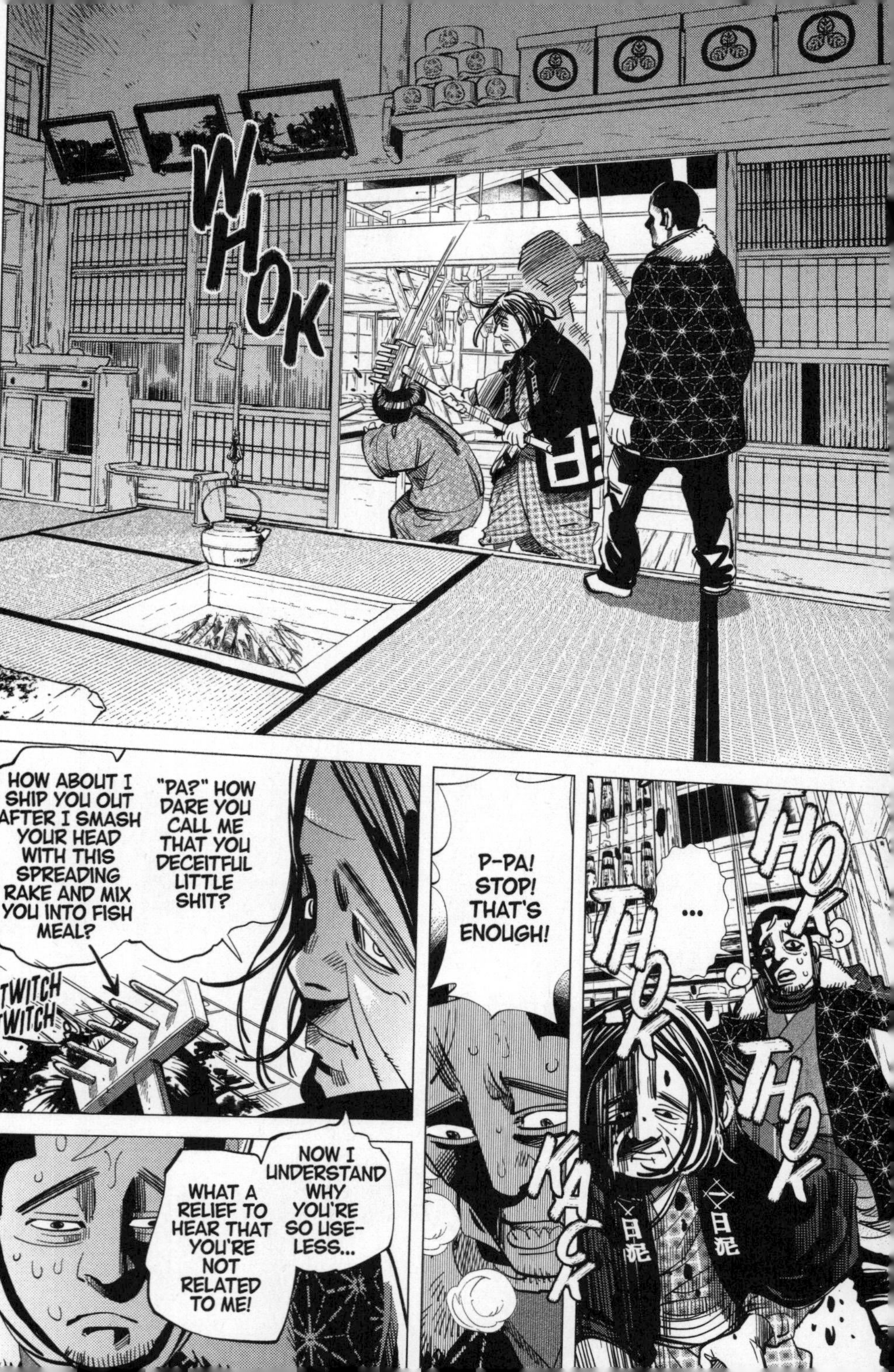
WHOK
THOK
THOK
THOK
THOK
...
KACK
日泥
日泥
P-PA! STOP! THAT'S ENOUGH!
"PA?" HOW DARE YOU CALL ME THAT YOU DECEITFUL LITTLE SHIT?
HOW ABOUT I SHIP YOU OUT AFTER I SMASH YOUR HEAD WITH THIS SPREADING RAKE AND MIX YOU INTO FISH MEAL?
TWITCH TWITCH
NOW I UNDERSTAND WHY YOU'RE SO USE-LESS...
WHAT A RELIEF TO HEAR THAT YOU'RE NOT RELATED TO ME!

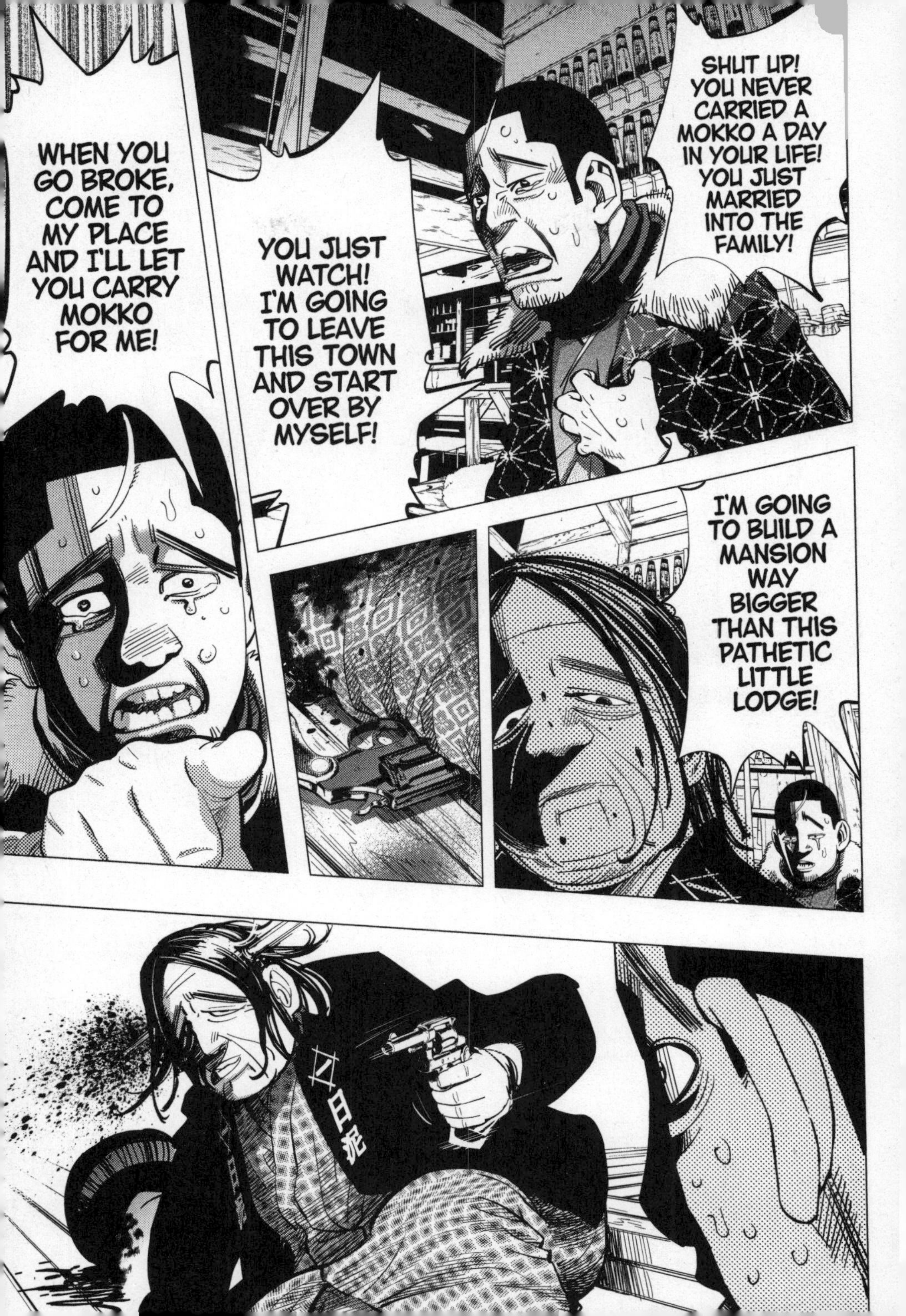
SHUT UP! YOU NEVER CARRIED A MOKKO A DAY IN YOUR LIFE! YOU JUST MARRIED INTO THE FAMILY!
YOU JUST WATCH! I'M GOING TO LEAVE THIS TOWN AND START OVER BY MYSELF!
WHEN YOU GO BROKE, COME TO MY PLACE AND I'LL LET YOU CARRY MOKKO FOR ME!
I'M GOING TO BUILD A MANSION WAY BIGGER THAN THIS PATHETIC LITTLE LODGE!

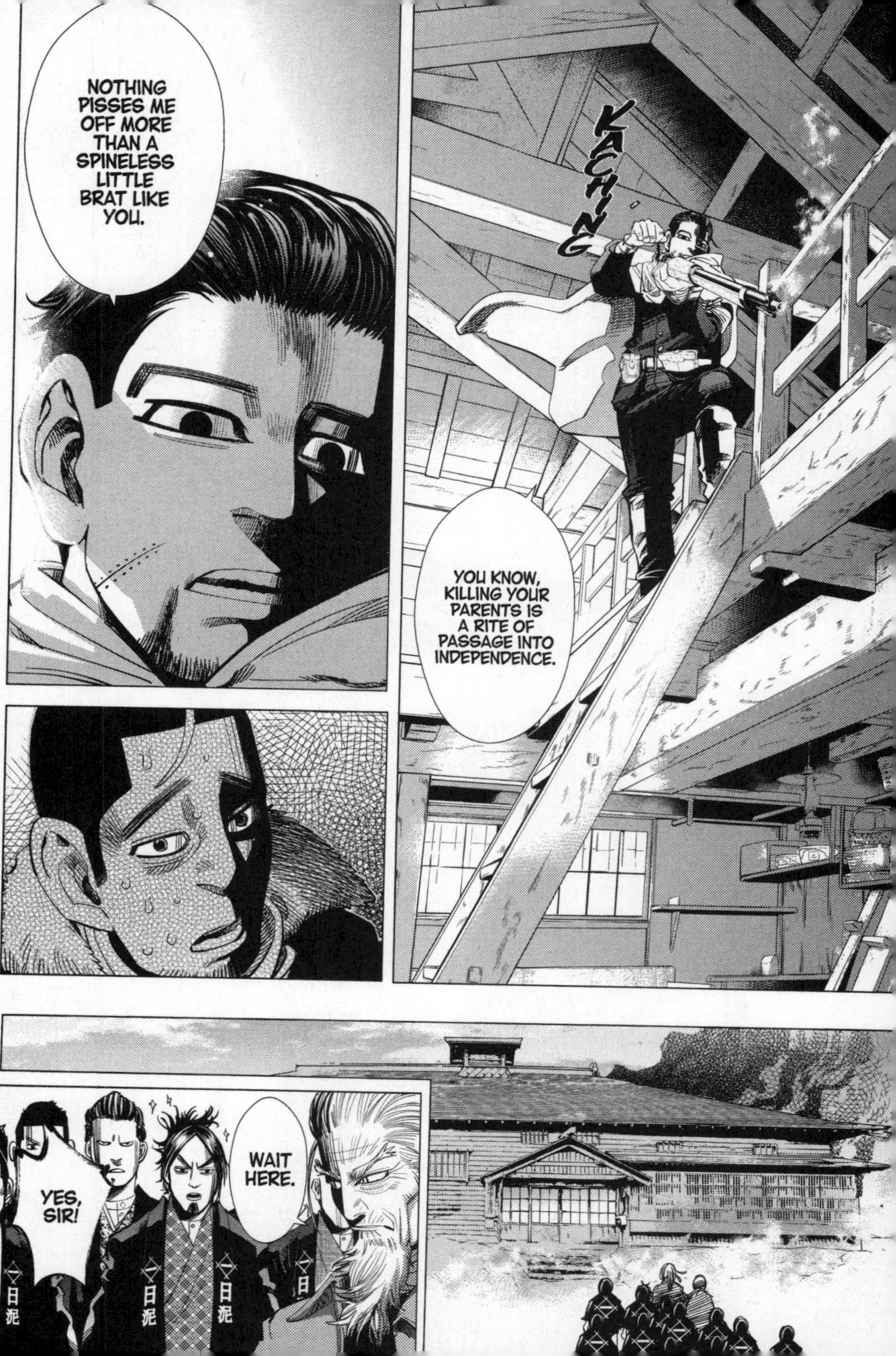
KACHING
YOU KNOW, KILLING YOUR PARENTS IS A RITE OF PASSAGE INTO INDEPENDENCE.
NOTHING PISSES ME OFF MORE THAN A SPINELESS LITTLE BRAT LIKE YOU.
WAIT HERE.
YES, SIR!

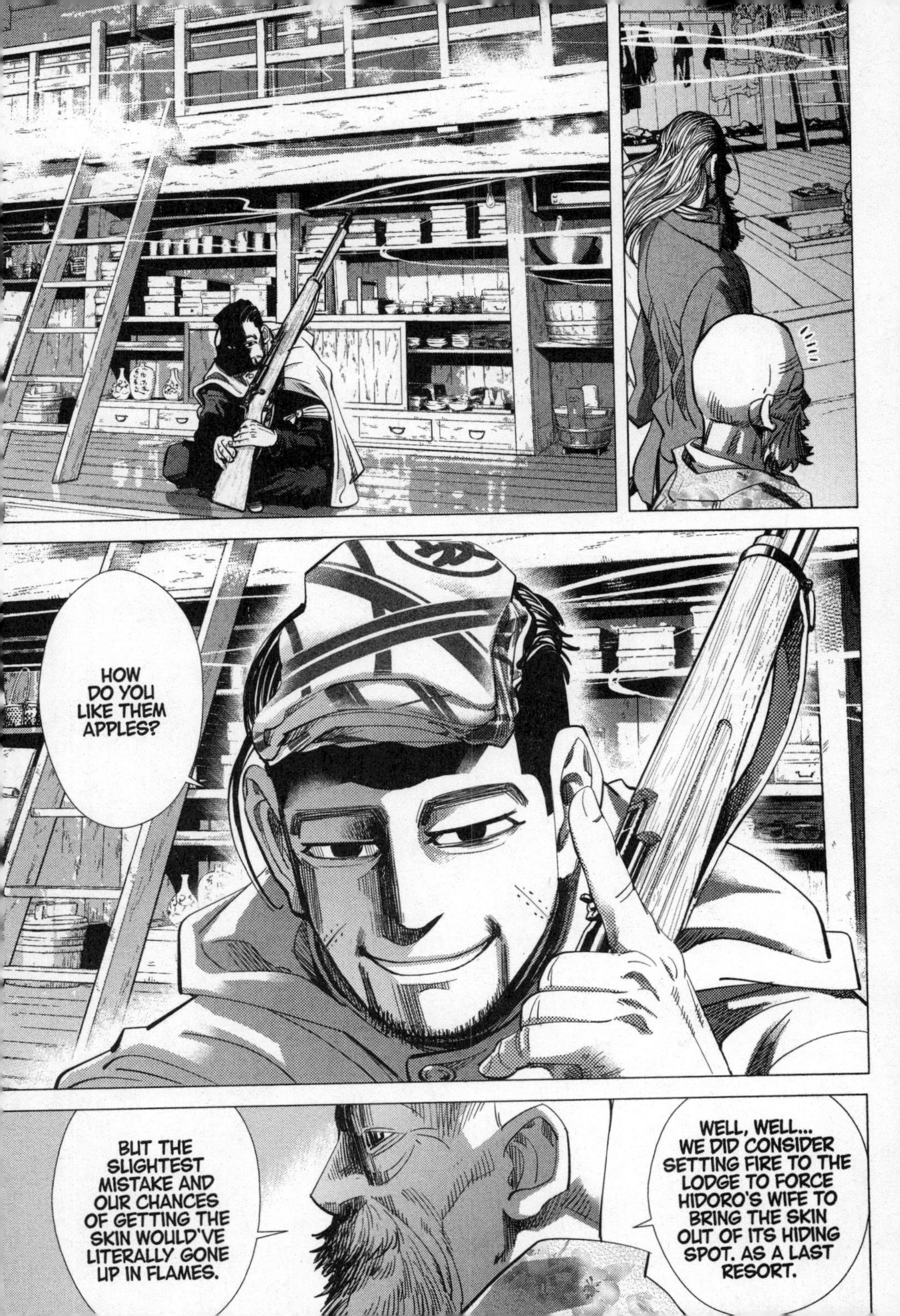
HOW DO YOU LIKE THEM APPLES?
WELL, WELL... WE DID CONSIDER SETTING FIRE TO THE LODGE TO FORCE HIDORO'S WIFE TO BRING THE SKIN OUT OF ITS HIDING SPOT. AS A LAST RESORT.
BUT THE SLIGHTEST MISTAKE AND OUR CHANCES OF GETTING THE SKIN WOULD'VE LITERALLY GONE UP IN FLAMES.

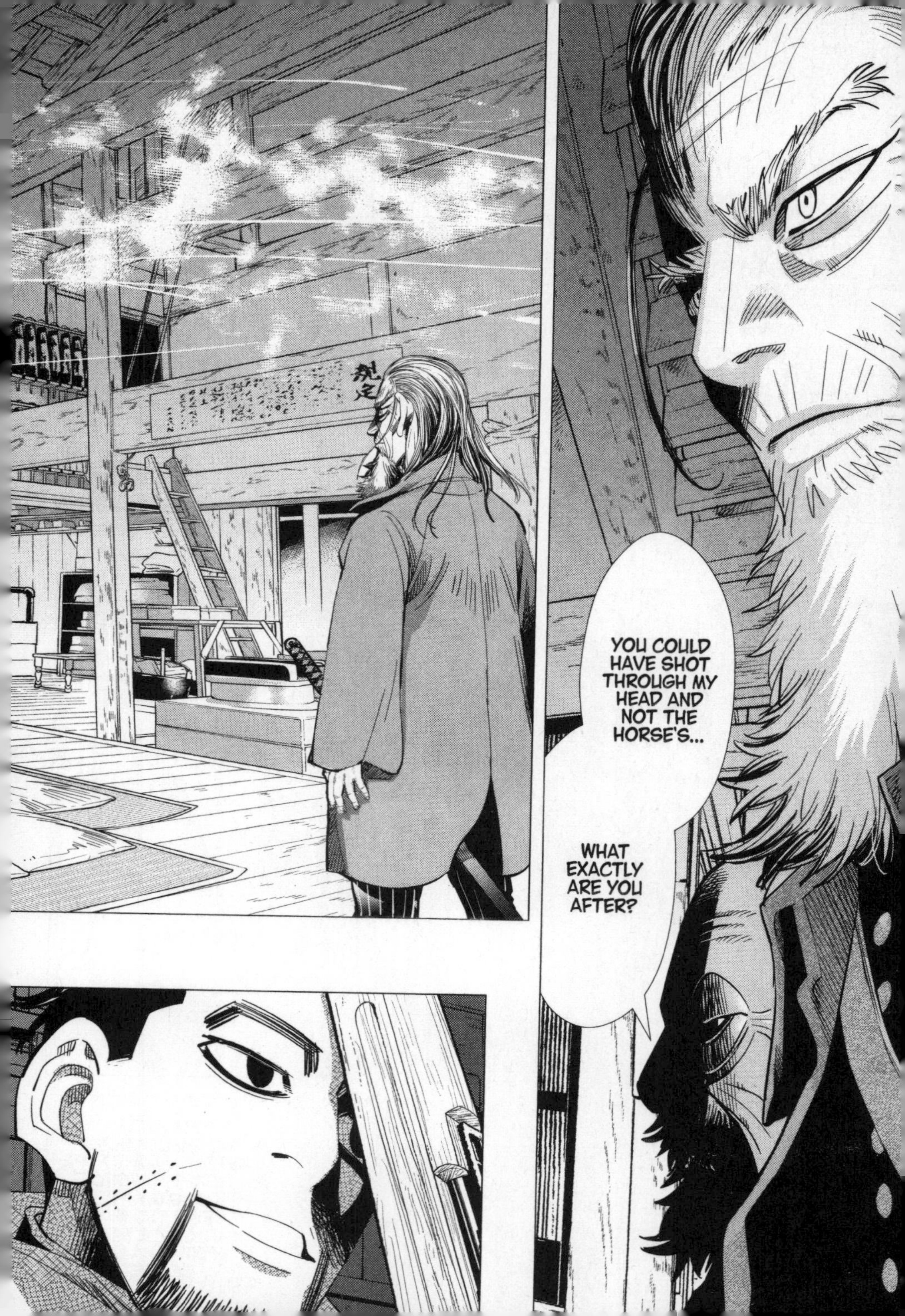
YOU COULD HAVE SHOT THROUGH MY HEAD AND NOT THE HORSE'S...
WHAT EXACTLY ARE YOU AFTER?

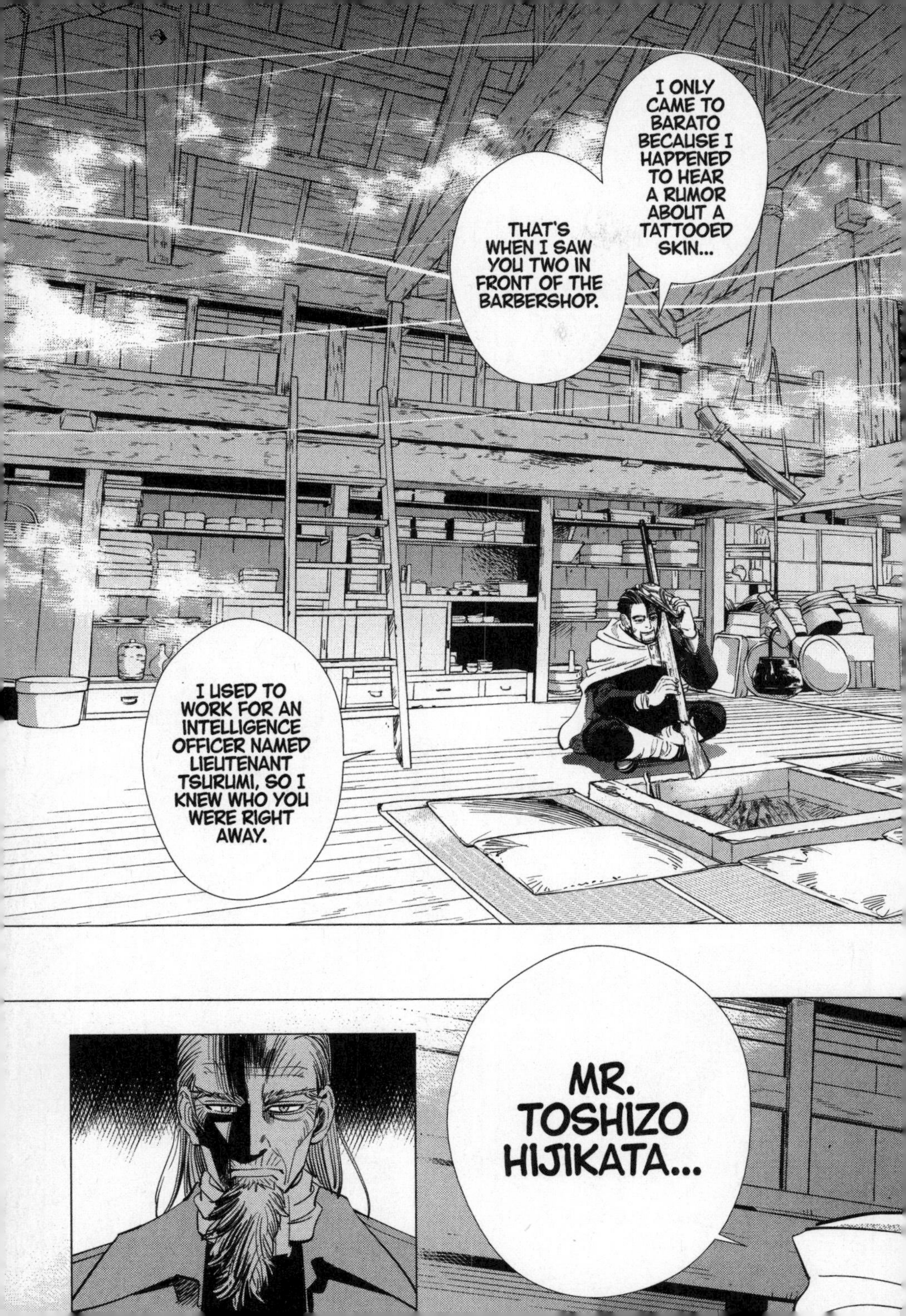
I ONLY CAME TO BARATO BECAUSE I HAPPENED TO HEAR A RUMOR ABOUT A TATTOOED SKIN...
THAT'S WHEN I SAW YOU TWO IN FRONT OF THE BARBERSHOP.
I USED TO WORK FOR AN INTELLIGENCE OFFICER NAMED LIEUTENANT TSURUMI, SO I KNEW WHO YOU WERE RIGHT AWAY.
MR. TOSHIZO HIJIKATA...

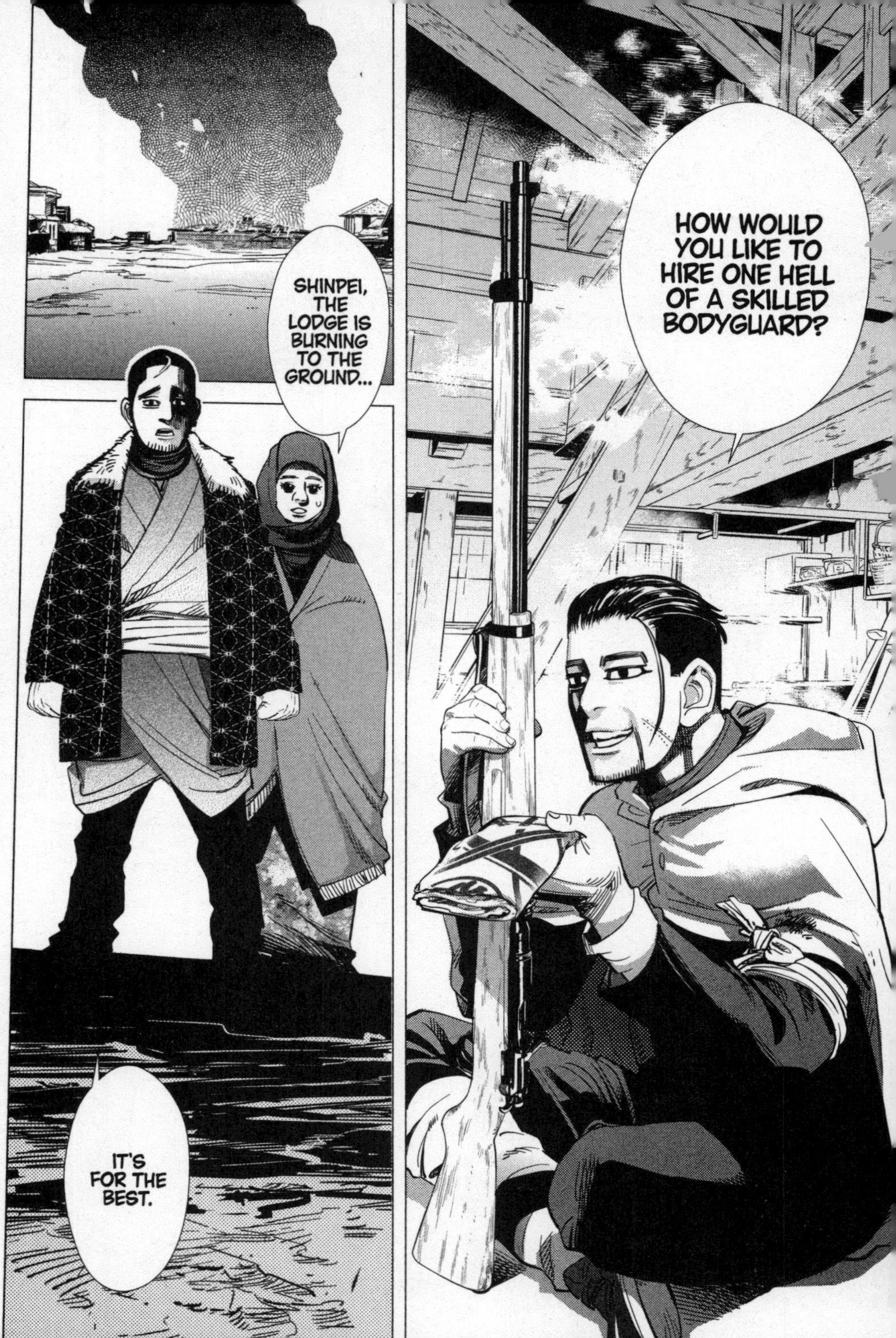
HOW WOULD YOU LIKE TO HIRE ONE HELL OF A SKILLED BODYGUARD?
SHINPEI, THE LODGE IS BURNING TO THE GROUND...
IT'S FOR THE BEST.

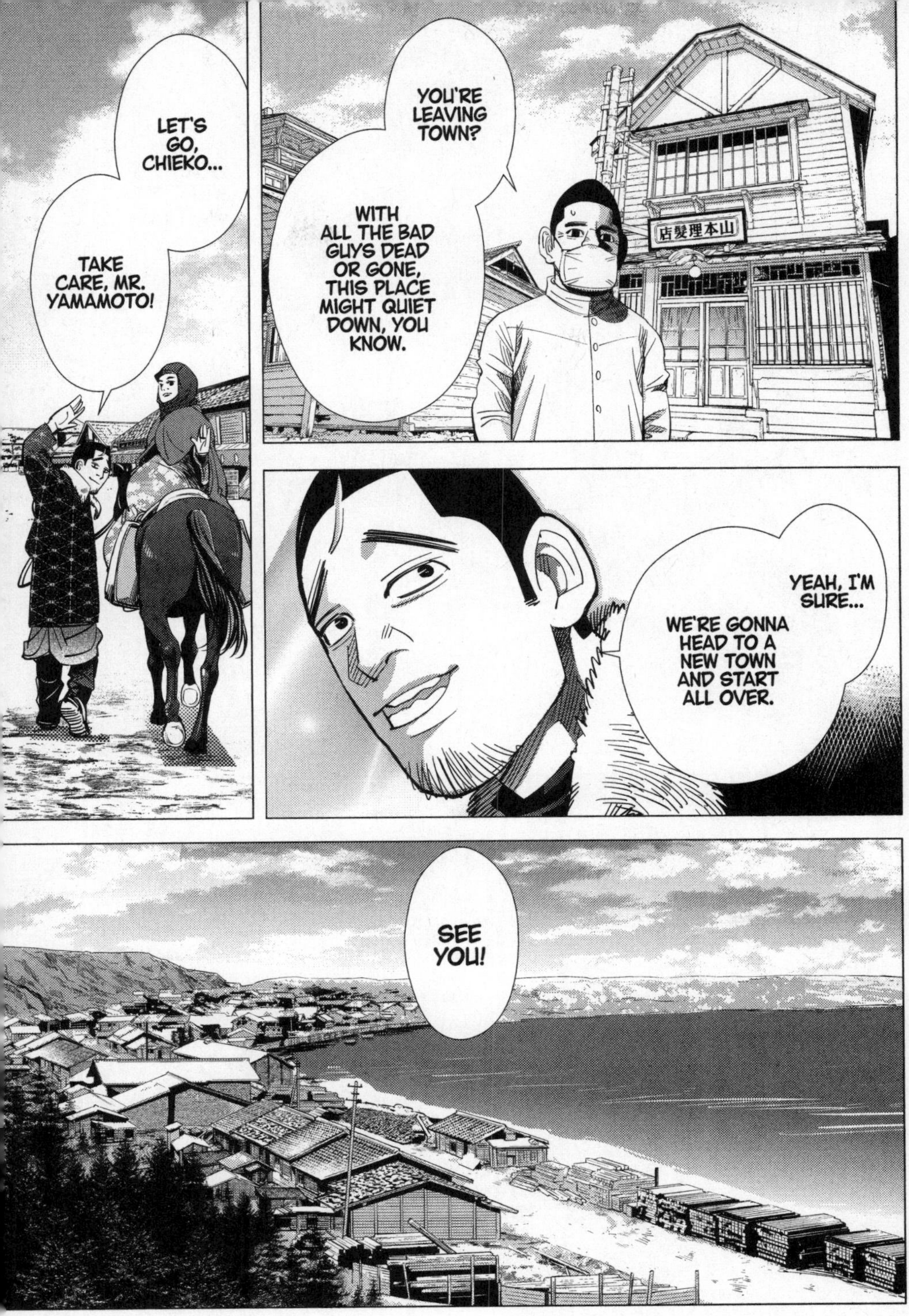
YOU'RE LEAVING TOWN?
WITH ALL THE BAD GUYS DEAD OR GONE, THIS PLACE MIGHT QUIET DOWN, YOU KNOW.
山本理髪店
YEAH, I'M SURE...
WE'RE GONNA HEAD TO A NEW TOWN AND START ALL OVER.
LET'S GO, CHIEKO...
TAKE CARE, MR. YAMAMOTO!
SEE YOU!

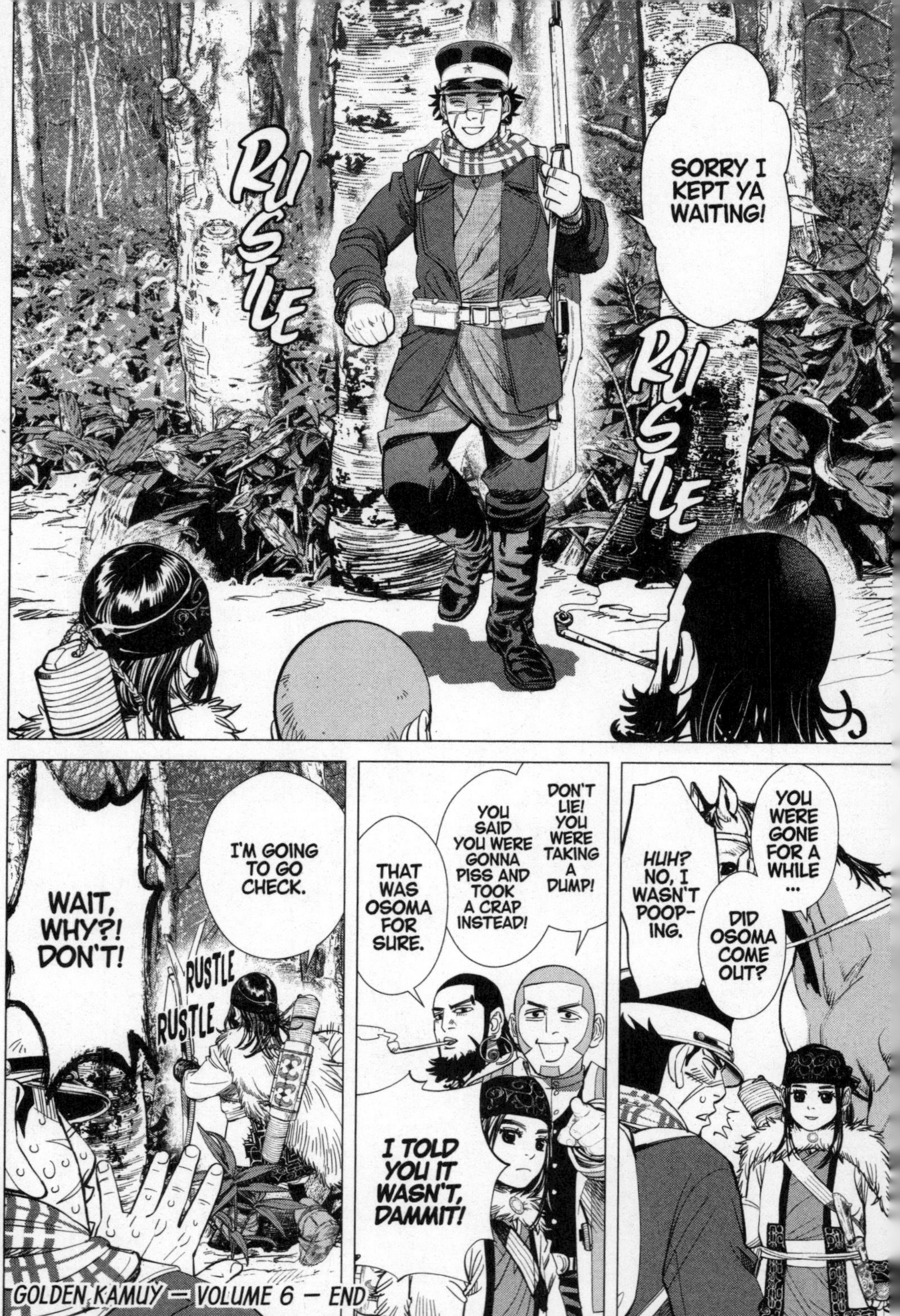
RUSTLE
RUSTLE
SORRY I KEPT YA WAITING!
YOU WERE GONE FOR A WHILE ...
DID OSOMA COME OUT?
HUH? NO, I WASN'T POOP-ING.
DON'T LIE! YOU WERE TAKING A DUMP!
YOU SAID YOU WERE GONNA PISS AND TOOK A CRAP INSTEAD!
THAT WAS OSOMA FOR SURE.
I TOLD YOU IT WASN'T, DAMMIT!
I'M GOING TO GO CHECK.
WAIT, WHY?! DON'T!
RUSTLE
RUSTLE
GOLDEN KAMUY — VOLUME 6 — END

Ainu Language Supervision • Hiroshi Nakagawa

Cooperation from • Hokkaido Ainu Association and the Abashiri Prison Museum

Jirota Kitahara • Kazunobu Goto • Otaru City General Museum

Photo Credits • Takayuki Monma Takanori Matsuda

Ainu Culture References

Chiri, Takanaka and Yokoyama, Takao. *Ainugo Eiri Jiten* (Ainu Language Illustrated Dictionary). Tokyo: Kagyusha, 1994

Kayano, Shigeru. *Ainu no Mingu* (Ainu Folkcrafts). Kawagoe: Suzusawa Book Store, 1978

Kayano, Shigeru. *Kayano Shigeru no Ainugo Jiten* (Kayano Shigeru's Ainu Language Dictionary). Tokyo: Sanseido, 1996

Musashino Art University – The Research Institute for Culture and Cultural History. *Ainu no Mingu Jissoku Zushu* (Ainu Folkcrafts – Collection of Drawing and Figures). Biratori: Biratori-cho Council for Promoting Ainu Culture, 2014

Satouchi, Ai. *Ainu-shiki ekoroji-seikatsu: Haruzo Ekashi ni manabu shizen no chie* (Ainu Style Ecological Living: Haruzo Ekashi Teaches the Wisdom of Nature). Tokyo: Kabushiki gaisha Shogakukan, 2008

Chiri, Yukie. *Ainu Shin'yoshu* (Chiri Yukie's Ainu Epic Tales). Tokyo: Iwanami Shoten, 1978

Namikawa, Kenji. *Ainu Minzoku no Kiseki* (The Path of the Ainu People). Tokyo: Yamakawa Publishing, 2004

Mook. *Senjuumin Ainu Minzoku* (Bessatsu Taiyo) (The Ainu People (Extra Issue Taiyo).Tokyo: Heibonsha, 2004

Kinoshita, Seizo. *Shiraoikotan Kinoshita Seizo Isaku Shashin Shu* (Shiraoikotan: Kinoshita Seizo's Posthumous Photography Collection). Hokkaido Shiraoi-gun Shiraoi-cho: Shiraoi Heritage Conservation Foundation, 1988

The Ainu Museum. *Ainu no Ifuku Bunka* (The Culture of Ainu Clothing). Hokkaido Shiraoi-gun Shiraoi-cho: Shiraoi Ainu Museum, 1991.

Keira, Tomoko and Kaji, Sayaka. *Ainu no Shiki* (Ainu's Four Seasons). Tokyo: Akashi Shoten, 1995

Fukuoka, Itoko and Sato, Kazuko. *Ainu Shokubutsushi* (Ainu Botanical Journal). Chiba Urayasu-Shi: Sofukan, 1995

Hayakawa, Noboru. *Ainu no Minzoku* (Ainu Folklore). Iwasaki Bijutsusha, 1983

Sunazawa, Kura. *Ku Sukuppu Orushibe* (The Memories of My Generation). Hokkaido, Sapporo-shi: Miyama Shobo, 1983

Haginaka, Miki et al., *Kikigaki Ainu no Shokuji* (Oral History of Ainu Diet). Tokyo: Rural Culture Association Japan, 1992

Nakagawa, Hiroshi. *New Express Ainu Go*. Tokyo: Hakusuisha, 2013

Nakagawa, Hiroshi. *Ainugo Chitose Hogen Jiten* (The Ainu-Japanese dictionary). Chiba Urayasu-Shi: Sofukan, 1995

Nakagawa, Hiroshi and Nakamoto, Mutsuko. *Kamuy Yukara de Ainu Go wo Manabu* Learning Ainu with Kamuy Yukar). Tokyo: Hakusuisha, 2007

Nakagawa, Hiroshi. *Katari au Kotoba no Chikara – Kamuy tachi to Ikiru Sekai* (The Power of Spoken Words – Living in a World with Kamuy). Tokyo: Iwanami Shoten, 2010

Sarashina, Genzo and Sarashina, Hikari. *Kotan Seibutsu Ki <1 Juki / Zassou hen>* (Kotan Wildlife Vol. 1 – Trees and Weeds). Hosei University Publishing, 1992/2007

Sarashina, Genzo and Sarashina, Hikari. *Kotan Seibutsu Ki <2 Yacho / Kaijuu / Gyozoku hen>* (Kotan Wildlife Vol. 2 – Birds, Sea Creatures, and Fish). Hosei University Publishing, 1992/2007

Sarashina, Genzo and Sarashina, Hikari. *Kotan Seibutsu Ki <3 Yachou / Mizudori / Konchu hen>* (Kotan Wildlife Vol. 3 – Shorebirds, Seabirds, and Insects). Hosei University Publishing, 1992/2007

Kawakami Yuji. *Sarunkur Ainu Monogatari* (The Tale of Sarunkur Ainu). Kawagoe: Suzusawa Book Store, 2003/2005

Kawakami, Yuji. *Ekashi to Fuchi wo Tazunete* (Visiting Ekashi and Fuchi). Kawagoe: Suzusawa Book Store, 1991

Council for the Conservation of Ainu Culture, Ainu Minzokushi (Ainu People Magazine). Dai-ichi Hoki, 1970

Hokkaido Cultural Property Protection Association. *Ainu Ifuku Chousa Houkokusho <1 Ainu Josei ga Denshou Suru Ibunka>* (The Ainu Clothing Research Report Vol. 1 – Traditional Clothing Passed Down Through Generations of Ainu Women). 1986

Okamura, Kichiemon and Clancy, Judith A. *Ainu no Ishou* (The Clothes of the Ainu People). Kyoto Shoin, 1993

Yotsuji, Ichiro. Photos by Mizutani, Morio. *Ainu no Monyo* (Decorative Arts of the Ainu). Kasakura Publishing, 1981

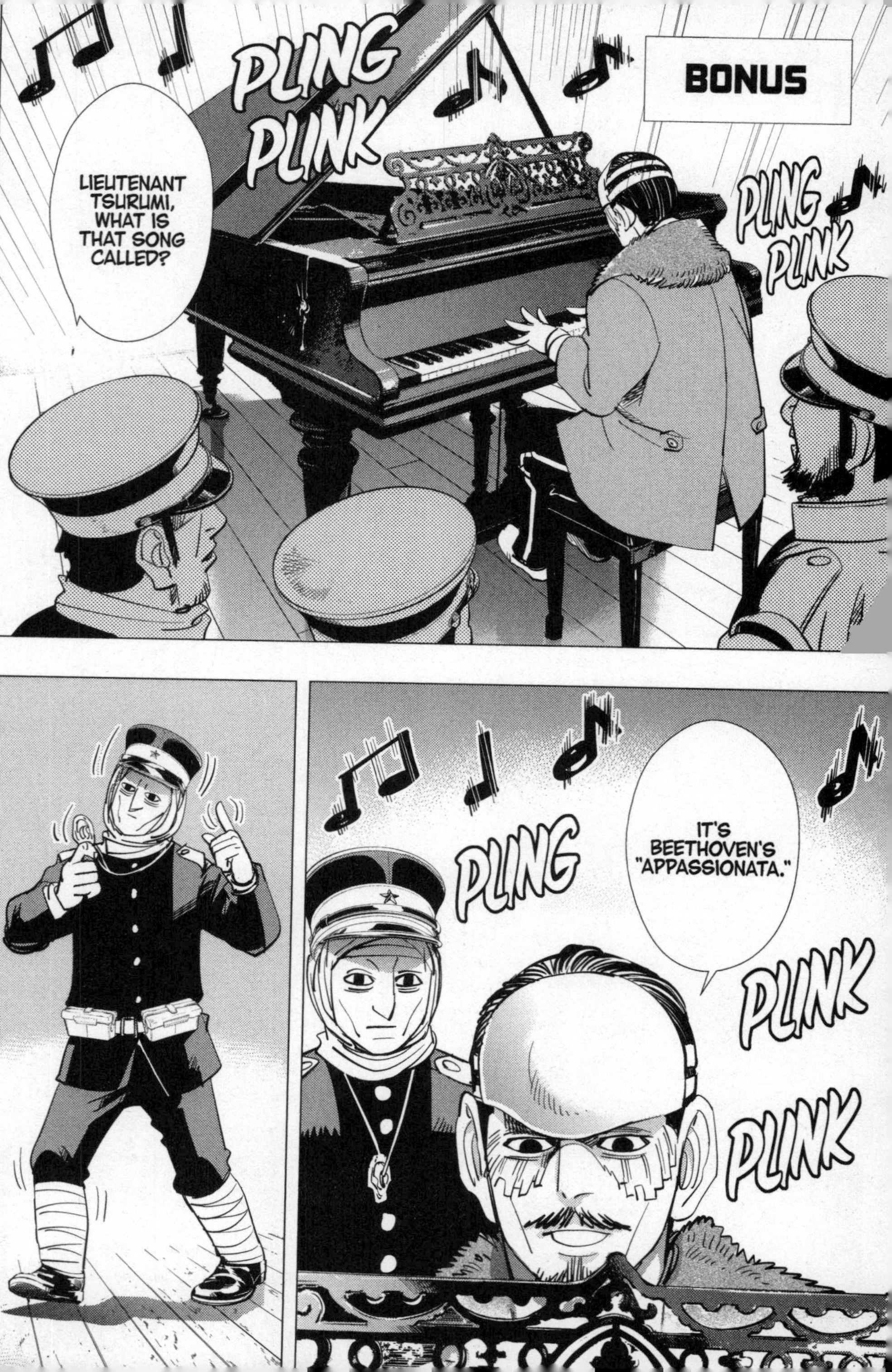
BONUS
PLING PLINK
PLING PLINK
LIEUTENANT TSURUMI, WHAT IS THAT SONG CALLED?
PLING
IT'S BEETHOVEN'S "APPASSIONATA."
PLINK
PLINK

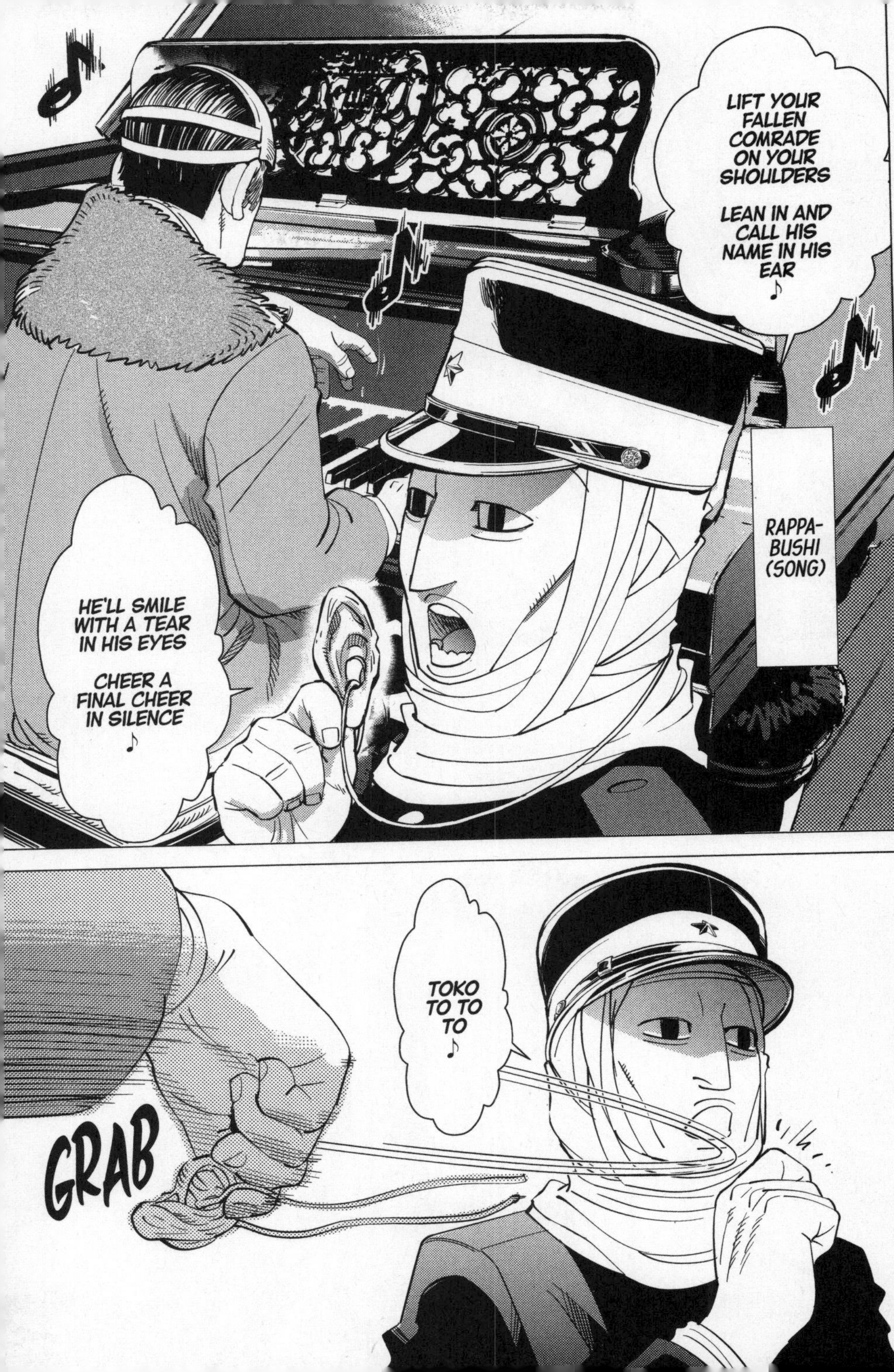
LIFT YOUR FALLEN COMRADE ON YOUR SHOULDERS
LEAN IN AND CALL HIS NAME IN HIS EAR ♪
RAPPA-BUSHI (SONG)
HE'LL SMILE WITH A TEAR IN HIS EYES
CHEER A FINAL CHEER IN SILENCE ♪
TOKO TO TO TO ♪
GRAB

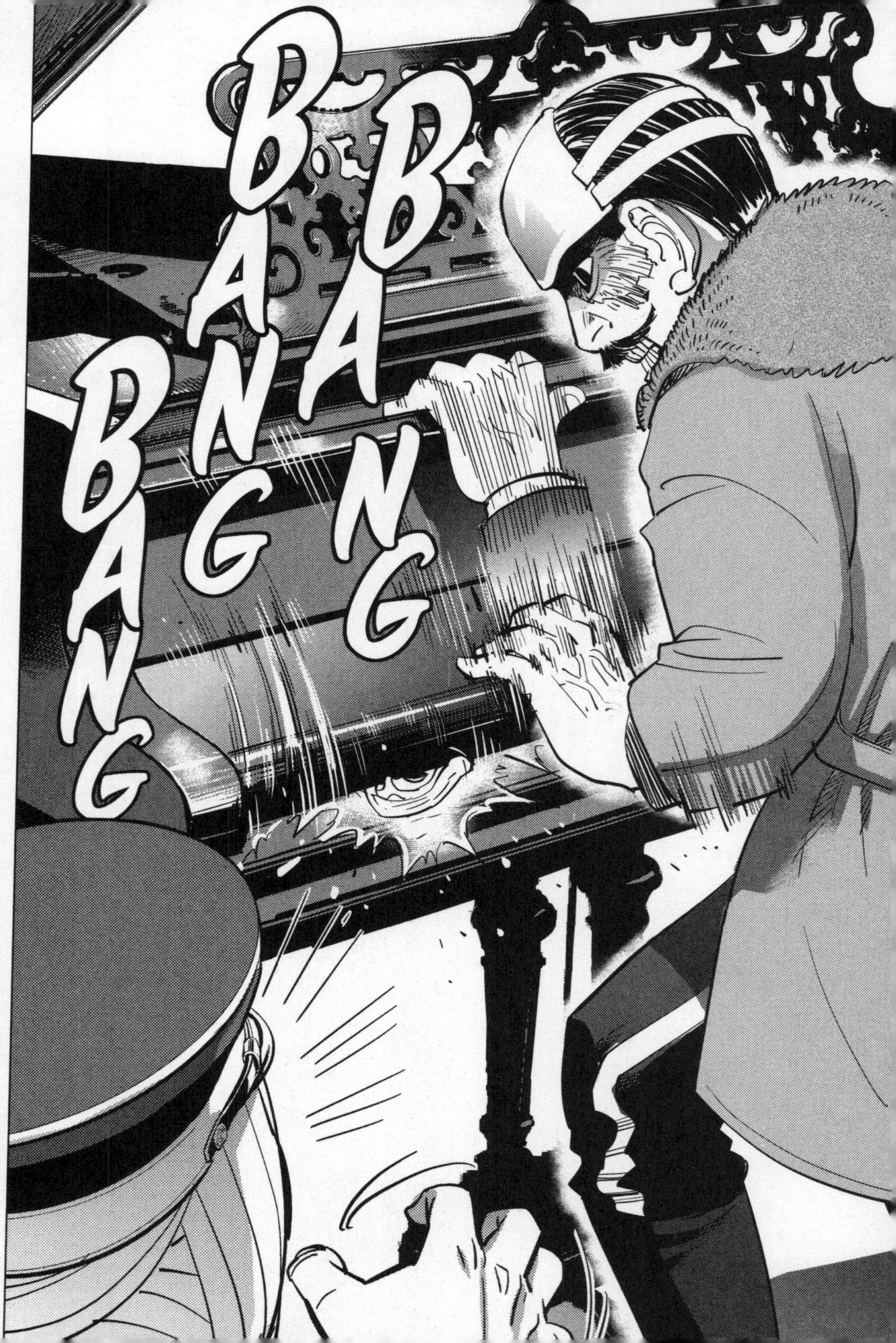
BANG
BANG
BANG

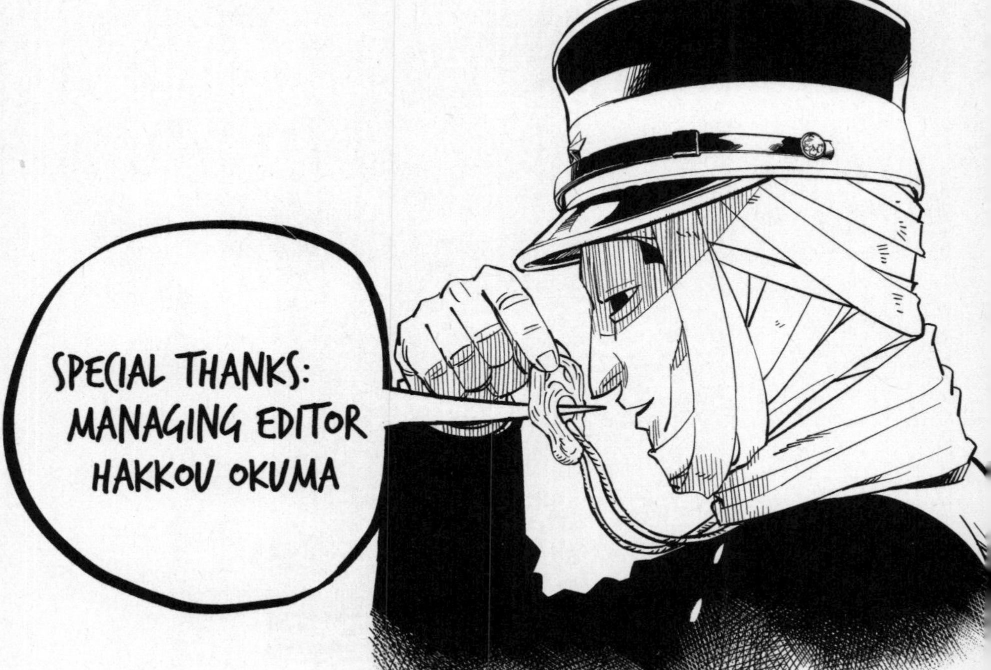
SPECIAL THANKS: MANAGING EDITOR HAKKOU OKUMA

CIKARAKARAPE

CLOTHING MADE BY WEAVING BLACK AND NAVY CLOTH INTO STRIPED COTTON. PATTERNS ARE WOVEN IN ON TOP. UNLIKE OTHER CLOTHING, WHITE COTTON IS NEVER USED.

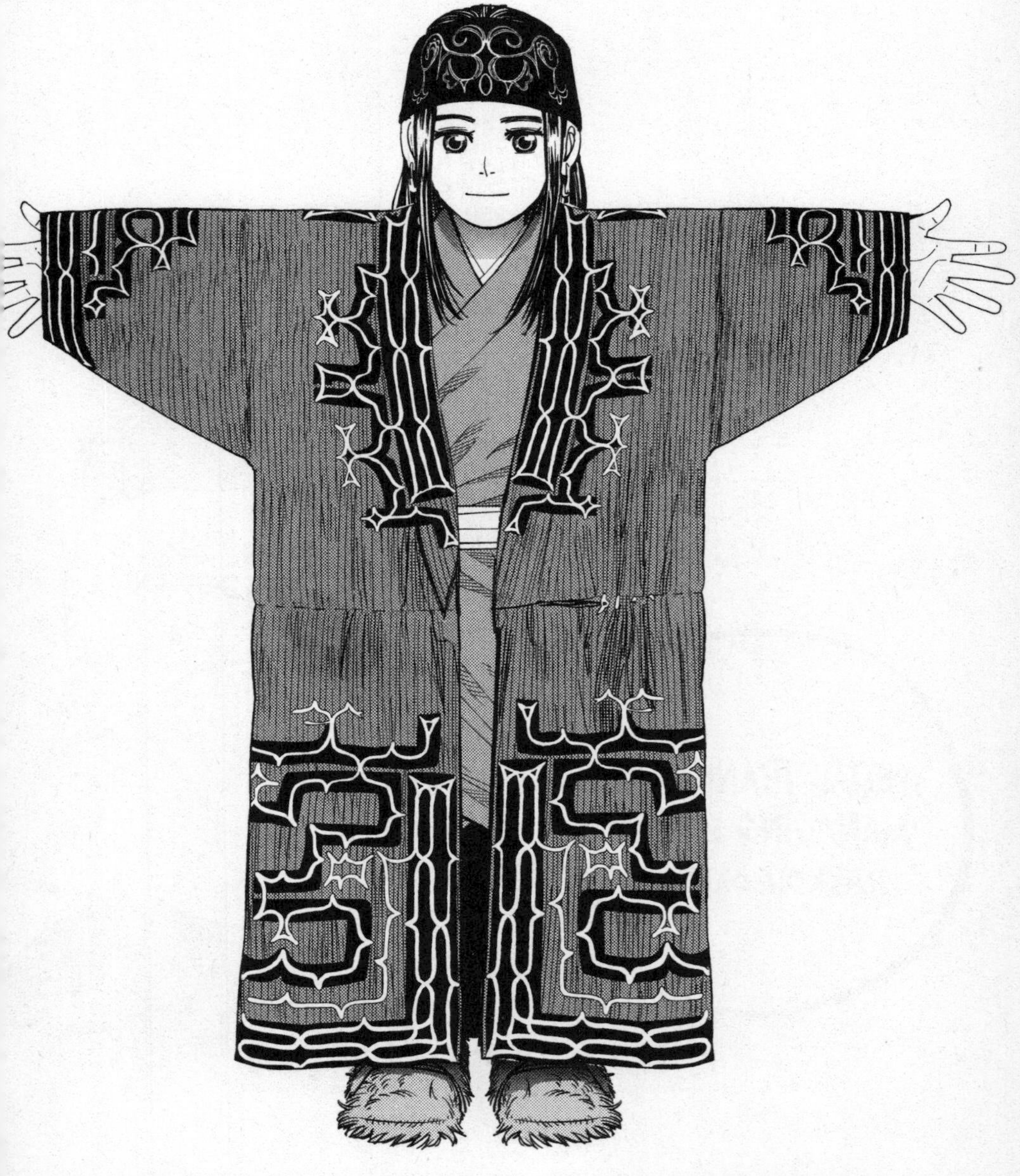

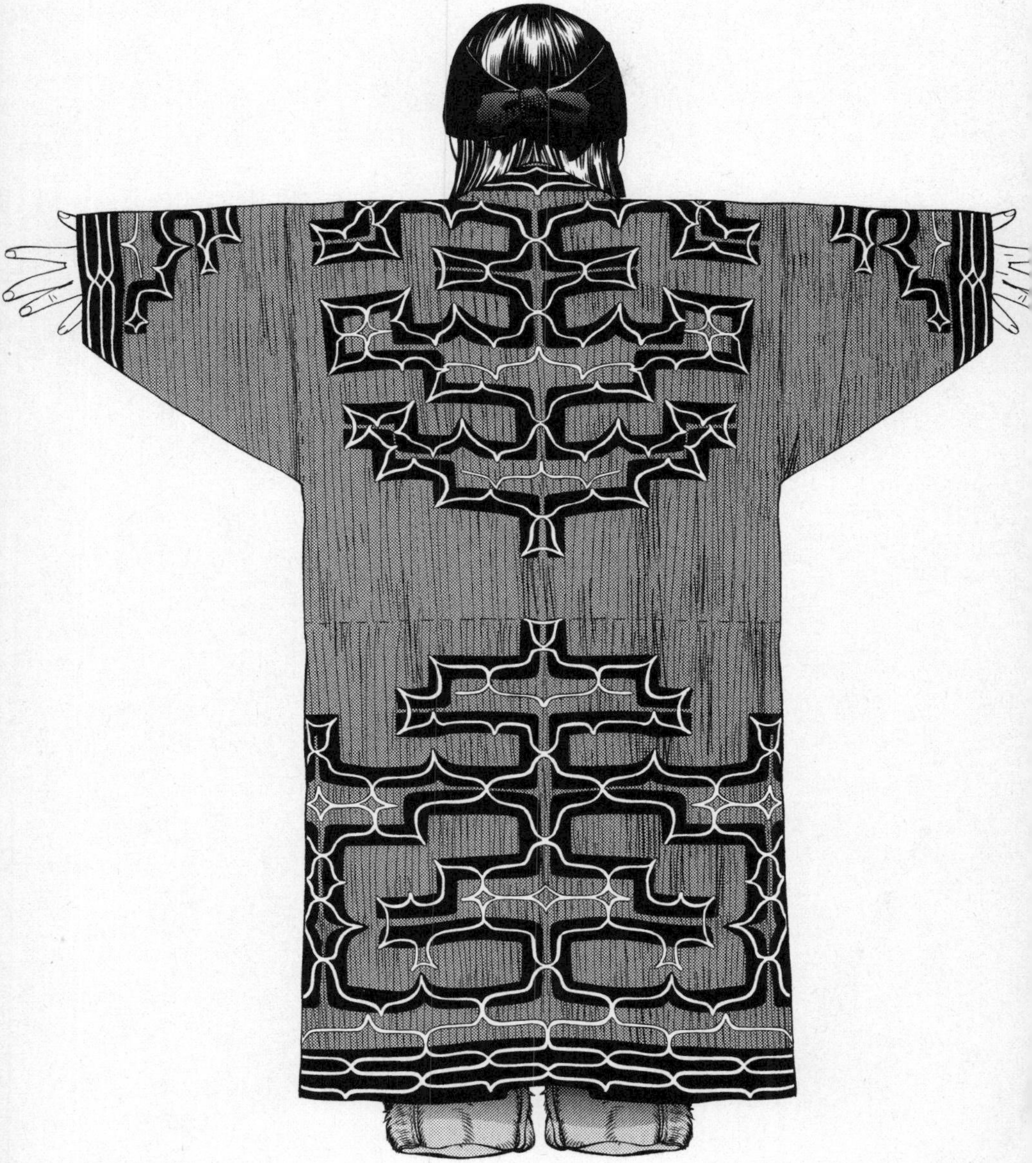

Kanto or wa yaku sak no arankep sinep ka isam.
Nothing comes from heaven without purpose. —Ainu proverb

GOLDEN KAMUY

Volume 6
VIZ Signature Edition

Story/Art by Satoru Noda

GOLDEN KAMUY © 2014 by Satoru Noda
All rights reserved.
First published in Japan in 2014 by SHUEISHA Inc., Tokyo.
English translation rights arranged by SHUEISHA Inc.

Translation/Eiji Yasuda
Touch-Up Art & Lettering/Steve Dutro
Design/Izumi Evers
Editor/Mike Montesa

Printed in the U.S.A

Published by VIZ Media, LLC
P.O. Box 77010
San Francisco, CA 94107

10 9 8 7 6 5 4 3 2 1
First printing, September 2018

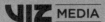

VIZ SIGNATURE

VIZ MEDIA
viz.com